KING ARTHUR CONSPIRACY

Proudly produced and published by

Cymroglyphics Ltd

April 2022

1st edition - 2005

with the kind permissassistance of
Alan Wilson & Baram Blackett

ISBN - 978-1-9162875-7-0

Copyright Cymroglyphics Ltd

All rights reserved. No part of this publication may be reprinted, reproduced, stored or transmitted in any form or by any means electronic, mechanical, photocopying, recording or otherwise, without the prior written permission of Cymroglyphics Ltd.

Inquiries concerning the reproduction or use of any of the elements should be sent by post to Cymroglyphics Ltd or by email to

info@cymroglyphics.com

10 Lansdale Drive, Tonteg, Pontypridd, Glamorgan

Wales CF38 1PG

KING ARTHUR CONSPIRACY
Volume 2

Wilson & Blackett

Acknowledgements

Reproducing *King Arthur Conspiracy* was a bigger challenge than was first expected. Sad to say, many of the original text files and images had degraded over the intervening seventeen years since the initial publication in 2005. The first edition had also been produced in an unusual shape and size which created its own production problems and would need resizing to sit well with the other books in the Wilson and Blackett range being republished by Cymroglyphics Ltd.

So a decision was made to bite on the bullet and to create entirely new print files with the original as a base. This required a huge amount of typing and checking against the original and would not have been possible without the volunteers from the *BritainsHiddenHistory* group that stepped forward to help with this huge task. For which sincere thanks go to Adrian and Andrea Maratty, Anne Bromley, Patricia Gilcash, Mark Austin, Margaret Taylor-Hill, Janet McArthur, Bob Morgan, Michael Tomboline, Chris Wood, James Clark, David Hooper, Darren Cole, David Moseley, Monika Escobar, Stephen Pole, Peter Smith, Angela Zhang and Sally Alden.

Peter Smith and Michael Tomboline then stepped in to help with reproducing the graphics and pages of transcriptions. Michael has also created digital fonts for Coelbren and Cymroglyphics which will be available soon and will create some exciting opportunities to bring these almost-lost writing systems into the twenty-first century.

Special mention must also be given to Marchell Abrahams for the countless hours of dedicated proof-reading that were required to bring the work to the professional standard that a book of this magnitude warrants.

If errors have crept through, they will undoubtedly be owing to any last-minute changes and additions made by me rather than any mistakes by the conscientious volunteers who have been diligent and painstaking in their efforts throughout.

And last, but by my no means least, our ongoing thanks to Alan Wilson and Baram Blackett for their decades of commitment and brilliance in revealing our hidden history before it was lost for ever – as very nearly happened. The whole project has been done with joyous hearts and with so much more of their work still to be published the next project is never far away!

Diolch pawb (thank you all)

Heddwch (peace)

K Ross Broadstock, April 2022

Foreword

This is a stand-alone book and there is no need to worry if you haven't already read volume 1 – it is quite fine to start here! Numbering the pages of the book in this way makes life a lot easier when giving page references and creating the master-index that will cover all books written by Wilson and Blackett.

Volume 1 concentrated on showing how the trail of the British migrations can be traced and followed through, amongst other things, its written language. The same ancient British cipher that is used to translate the inscriptions shown in this book also works with Etruscan, Phrygian and all the way back to the near and middle-east. The trail is then followed back to Britain itself where copious amounts of written and physical evidence still survive to show the ancient *Coelbren* writing system in action, how to read it and what lessons have been left to us by our ancestors.

Sadly, this rich and well-recorded history has been replaced with the eighteenth-century invention of Britain and Ireland being populated by barbaric "Celts" – which it never was – and the massively overblown idea of a "Roman Britain" which has been used to fill the void created when authentic British history was removed.

This is the background to where this volume picks up - with the sixth century migrations to America along with a deeper look into the skulduggery and misdirection that has taken place over the last two-hundred plus years to keep this information from ever reaching the general public.

The problem is that none of the authorities want this history to be known – politically it doesn't suit anyone.

Quite the opposite.

North America was claimed on the principle of *terra nullius* – "nobody's land" – that no one was there before the arrival of Columbus. There were "natives" there of course - but they didn't count. To claim territory only Christians mattered and this is why the idea of a Christian colonisation taking place nine-hundred years earlier is such a threat to the very legal basis of the United States of America and Canada.

It also gives possible credence to the claims of Joseph Smith and the founding of the "Mormon" religion – which doesn't go down very well with the Catholic and Episcopal (Anglican) churches either.

The ongoing tragedy is that this obfuscation of our past has been dressed up and disguised as an attempt to promote a "native American" past that was overwritten to promote a European agenda. This is a thin veil that is easily seen through and is quite the opposite of reality. Native history has many records of the arrival of the "white men" and the interactions and struggles between the two peoples are as much a part of their history as the Europeans – yet somehow it has been made *politically correct* to dismiss the native American historical claims as well. The patronising approach

Foreword

being that it is to protect their indigenous rights whereas in reality their past is being shoved down the memory hole too.

In this volume you will also read about "Welsh-speaking Indians", tribes of "white Indians" and how the ancient migration of the Welsh was well known until the suppression that has taken place over the last few hundred years.

The false trail of a twelfth century migration from north Wales has also been used with great effect since Elizabethan times to hide the true story of Arthur and the migration from south Wales in the sixth century – the true story not suiting the politics and claims of the Tudors either.

This story cuts to the very heart of American and British history – it could even be the reason for the continent being called America!

The official explanation is that the country is named after the rather obscure third son of a minor family called Amerigo Vespucci. If he is indeed the source of the name then why is the country not called after his surname as happens with all other namings after their "discoverers"? If the country is really named after him then why not Vespuccia?

There is huge controversy over whether he even went to America – and its extremely unlikely that he ever went north of Panama. The later English arrivals named their land "Virginia" after their Queen Elizabeth. Indeed, there don't seem to be any other countries, rivers, islands, counties or states named after the first name of an explorer anywhere in the world.

Was the Vespuccia plucked out of obscurity because he had a convenient name?

The famous Arthur of the sixth century was the son of King Meurig / Merrick. The Welsh word for "son" or "successor to" is ap. There being no surnames in old Welsh and Arthur's name Arthur ap Meurig or Arthur *ap Merrick*. Phonetically the same as *"America"*.

The idea of the country being names after the royal Arthur or even named in honour of his, still living, father Meurig/Merick certainly makes a lot of sense.

Who knows?

Maybe the biggest clue of all to Arthur having "discovered" and colonised America has been staring us all in the face the whole time.

Enjoy this brilliant piece of work by Wilson and Blackett

Heddwch (peace)

K. Ross Broadstock, April 2022

Pictures and Photographs

Coed y Mwstyr Cave inscriptions	404
Dying Arthur	420
Arthur's body on boat	426
Pig-pen inscriptions	472-6
Yarmouth Stone inscription	484
Burchall Hemsley Stone	488-90
Burchall Hemsley Stone	493
Grave Creek Tablet	502
Franks Casket	510
Brandenburg Stone	518
Brandenburg Stone examined	519
Dighton Rock	521
Metcalf Stone	526
Davenport Stone	534
Wiggins Point stone	540
Wiggins Point pictograph	543
He struck a violent blow...'	557
Grave Creek Madoc stone	561
Copper bracelets	561
Christian amulets	562
Indian head	567
Bearded head	567
Chunkee stones	574
Inscribed cave walls	578-9
Angel Stone	596
L'ankou statue	602
Qumran copper scroll section	609
Rochester Creek artwork	627
Stoke Dry	660
Arthur's northern routes	689

Acknowledgements		iv
Foreword		v
Pictures and photographs		vii
Contents		viii

Chapters

12	The Prince Madoc Who Sailed to America	351
13	Evicting Roman Squatters	399
14	The Coming of the Dragon	432
15	British Coelbren Inscriptions in America	446
16	American Inscriptions	468
17	Other American Inscriptions	516
18	Snakes, Forts, Pottery and Symbols	553
19	Possible Dark Age Christian Relics in Arizona	582
20	The Dead Sea Scrolls	603
21	Conclusions	628
22	The Reaction in Wales	649
	Appendix 1 – Arthur's northern journeys	686

Sources	692
Index	694

Chapter Twelve

The Prince Madoc who sailed to America

Several hundred books, learned papers, and monographs have been written on the subject of Prince Madoc and his voyages to America. None yet prove anything, and indeed their failure tends to cast doubt upon the very existence of Madoc and the truth of his voyages. During the nineteenth century, as the United States expanded ever westwards, the name and the story of Madoc was known to everyone, and evidence was sought which might prove the story of Madoc and his American voyages.

The basic problem of seeking out evidence for Madoc lies in the total failure correctly to identify him, and we are back to the old adage: "If I were seeking Madoc, then I would not start from here." The credit for the complete misidentification of Madoc probably belongs to Richard Hakluyt, writing around 1582, and the subsequent acceptance of Hakluyt's misinformation by Dr Powell and others who blindly followed this mistaken path. It seems that Humphrey Lluyd provided Richard Hakluyt with the history alleged to be that of Caradoc of Llancarfan, and he added to these papers the folk tale version of the story of Prince Madoc and the ancient discovery of the Americas. Richard Hakluyt failed to realise that these were two separate bodies of information, and he apparently did not know that Caradoc of Llancarfan is thought to have died in 1156, when his history terminates. It is therefore not possible for Caradoc of Llancarfan to write posthumously about voyages which were alleged to have taken place around 1170–1171. Dr Powell then took Hakluyt's version of matters, and published it, and from then on the fiction of a north-west Wales Madoc of around 1170 became set in stone in the academic mind.

Richard Hakluyt simply placed Madoc in the wrong era by six hundred years, misdating his voyage from 562 to 1170, and then transferring him from south-east Wales to north-west Wales, thereby disinheriting him from the family of King Meurig ap Tewdrig and his Queen Onbrawst, by falsely adopting him into the progeny of Owen Gwynedd as a son. The immediate result was that Prince Madoc became totally untraceable in his native Wales.

There was perhaps the propaganda benefit, whereby Madoc and his discovery of America was now attached to the ancestry of the Tudor Kings and Queens of England, whose ancestors were from north-west Wales, Gwynedd, and prominently included Owen Gwynedd. The much-quoted but rarely-printed poetic entry which is used to allege Madoc to be a son of Owen Gwynedd actually states that Owen Gwynedd is a descendant of Madoc. There is something rotten somewhere.

Even the most cursory examination of the historical references to Madoc reveals that there is something very much amiss. The celebrated Walter Map, son of Blondel de Mapes and Tryfil, daughter of the Lord Gweirydd of Llancarfan, wrote mentioning Madoc, and he derided the earlier poetry written by William Fleming concerning Madoc. The problem here is that Walter Map appears to have written around 1135, and if so, he cannot be writing about a Madoc son of Owen Gwynedd sailing in 1171. William Fleming was the grandson of Sir John Fleming who entered the Glamorgan coastal plains with Robert Fitzhammon, the first cousin of William the Conqueror in 1091, as allies of King Iestyn ap Gwrgan against Rhys ap Tewdwr of Dyfed. William Fleming, who must have written before Walter Map, also clearly seems to be writing well before 1171.

Llancarfan, the home of Walter Map, is nine miles west of Cardiff, and William Fleming was his near-neighbour at Flemingston. The Fleming family also had a house in Ely, now a Cardiff suburb some three miles from Cardiff Castle. The third local writer of note of this period was Gruffydd ap Arthur, *alias* Geoffrey of Monmouth, who was a cleric and a nephew of the Bishop Uchtryd of Llandaff in Cardiff. The king, Iestyn ap Gwrgan, would have lived in Cardiff Castle-Iestyn's Tower, and at Caer Melyn or Cu-Bwrd, (or Ca'Melot-Mutual Together Table) four miles to the north-east. His queen, Denise of Powys, daughter of Bleddyn ap Cynfyn, resided at the Castle of Denise of Powys just west of Cardiff.

Much fuss has been made in modern times of a port list from the time of Henry II of England, which lists three ships registered at a harbour named as Porth Kerrick. One of these ships was owned by a man named Madoc, and there are dozens of Madocs named in Khumric History. There is zero evidence to associate this entry in a twelfth-century port list with any son of Owen Gwynedd, and the ancient genealogies do not in fact confirm any Madoc son of Owen Gwynedd. This, however, has not deterred writers anxious to persevere with Richard Hakluyt's catastrophe, and the port list is much discussed as if it were irrefutable evidence of the sailor Madoc as a son of Owen Gwynedd. In the high nobility of kings and princes in Wales,

Chapter 12 - The Madoc who Sailed to America

all children born were faithfully recorded, even if they lived only a few weeks, as with Llywarch son of Iestyn ap Gwrgan, who drowned in the church baptismal font. The usual excuse is that Madoc became forgotten because he sailed away and never returned.

The Port Kerrick list almost certainly refers to Porth Ceri in Glamorgan, now bent into Porthkerry. There was an important harbour here until late mediaeval times when the cliffs collapsed massively into the sea. The Norman fleet of Robert Fitzhammon anchored here when they sailed in to join King Iestyn ap Gwrgan in 1090. Porth Ceri, which was almost certainly named for King Ceri 'Longsword', is just west of Walter Map's Llancarfan, and immediately west of Porth Ceri is Ruthin, which territories were held by the Prince Madoc son of Iestyn ap Gwrgan in the reign of Henry II. So, we have a Prince Madoc right alongside Porth Ceri.

The next ship listed belonged to Rhirid, and at this time there was a Rhirid who was a son of Bleddyn ap Cynfyn, and so Rhirid ap Bleddyn and Madoc ap Iestyn were related as in-laws, apparently second cousins. Rhirid actually lived at the ancient fortress Caer Melyn in north-east Cardiff, where a wedding celebration was recorded as late as 1453. Rhirid, his sister Denis(e), Iestyn ap Gwrgan, and Madoc son of Iestyn ap Gwrgan were neighbours. The third ship was owned by an Owen and appears to have been called Gwennyt, and this is almost certainly Owen Wan of Caerleon in Gwent, the next-door neighbouring lord to Rhirid. Gwennyt is very clearly Gwent, with Gwen meaning 'fair', and Nyth is a 'safe place' or a 'nesting place'. No one can trace a Porth Kerrick or Porth Ceri anywhere in Gwynedd.

With all early reference to Madoc the voyager coming out of South Wales, and highly likely before 1171, it would appear logical to look in south-east Wales. Not so: one American author writing in 1987 claimed that William Fleming, the bad poet, was 'untraceable', and his manor at Ely is 'not known'. Yet the River Ely still runs through western Cardiff, and some twenty thousand people live in the general Ely area. Most writers casually transfer Walter Map out of his Llancarfan home and the Cardiff area, and dump him down in the Hereford area, safely in modern England. This is strange as the preserved lists of Cardiff soldiers who went on the joint Norman expedition to attack Ireland includes this same untraceable William Fleming, and it also dates him. The untraceable Flemingston is still where it always was, marked on Government O.S. maps, and the Fleming family manor at Ely is well recorded.

The current posture of most would-be Madoc researchers is not to attempt to 'buck the system' and to avoid making any politically incorrect waves. They simply fold the matter away and declare Madoc the voyager to be an interesting fiction, a non-existent mythical personage, and a figure of old wives' tales.

This is not a particularly sensible approach to the question, for there is a massive array of surviving evidence pointing directly to a Prince Madoc who sailed the oceans long centuries before 1171. If these records hang together and are correct (and they are), then this must be a very different Madoc. In this respect Wilson and Blackett were given a motivating impetus by extraordinary information coming out of America. Don Weber of Illinois had sent them a copy of a book on Madoc entitled *The Legend of Prince Madoc and the White Indians*, by Dana Olsen, of Indiana, which was, in their opinion, so badly muddled by an elementary lack of knowledge of Wales and its history that they took a look at the Madoc puzzle. As a matter of policy, they normally brought their researches to a halt at 1091 when King Iestyn was deposed. They had known for a long time that they would have to confront the Madoc problem one day, as a stream of information had made this an inevitability, but they did not want to alarm yet another herd of academics.

They had little interest in the Norman histories after 1091, when Robert Fitzhammon seized around a quarter of Glamorgan along the coast after treacherously betraying his ally Iestyn ap Gwrgan. Their interest lay in the British dynasty from *c.* 504 BC to 1091, so matters terminated there. This meant that Madoc's alleged voyages of 1171 were outside their self-determined period of study and research. They knew that 'Prince Madoc' was something of a 'very hot potato', and they already had more than enough trouble with the problems caused by intransigent academics.

Jim Michael of Kentucky is a hard man to deter, however, and he kept on feeding over information to Blackett and Wilson, sending them data which revealed that radiocarbon-14 dating of wooden artefacts found in a Khumric type grave mound in the U.S.A. gave a probable sixth-century AD dating. The remarkable fact was that an inscribed stone was found in this grave mound. This, and other information flowing over from Don Weber and Jim Michael, was nothing short of a revelation, and many artefacts were very clearly of a Christian nature. Suddenly, what Blackett and Wilson had been avoiding made perfect sense. The many sixth-century references to a very important Madoc, who was known as Madoc Morfran-the Cormorant, and as Madoc Morfrwyn-of the Seaweeds (Sargasso Sea?), and the great voyage of Arthur II to

Chapter 12 - The Madoc who Sailed to America

Annwn, 'the other world', all made sense.

There are several detailed descriptions of Prince Madoc's voyages in sixth-century epic Khumric poetry. The voyage of Brendan was said to have been made after he heard of the 'Voyage of the Teyrn' or 'Monarch', and the monarch at Brendan's time was King Arthur II son of Meurig. A St Brendan is in fact easily traceable in the discarded Khumric noble genealogies. Everything pointed to there being a massive array of evidence of a sixth-century voyage of discovery to North America. This seemed to offer a route out of British stagnation and obstinacy. George Abbott, Archbishop of Canterbury, wrote a *History of the World* in 1625, and in this he stated that a Welsh prince discovered America, and King Arthur (Arthur II ap Meurig) knew about it. This account post-dated the muddle caused by Richard Hakluyt, and the old Archbishop had got it right by placing the discovery in the Arthurian era of the sixth century AD.

The sixth-century AD date was published by Rueben T. Durrett of Kentucky in 1908, in his book on ancient voyages to the Americas.

So, in 1991 Baram Blackett and Alan Wilson put away most of their files, and switched the direction of their research away from ancient Egypt, ancient Etruria, ancient Asia Minor and Britain, and began to concentrate on America and the sixth-century British records. The result was an embarrassment of information. The enigmatic Madoc was found everywhere, his very name deriving from 'mad' and 'oc' meaning 'a good man who went aside'. Jim Michael kept feeding the project with American data and photographs of sites and inscribed rocks, stones, cave walls, and cliff faces, all found in the U.S.A., and Alan and Baram deciphered and translated them using the ancient British Coelbren alphabet and the Llewellyn Sion ciphers. They had photographs of the famous Bourne Stone years earlier and had recognised it as being inscribed in Coelbren, but had never before had the necessary American contacts.

Jim Michael sent over copies of the Leni Lenape and the Wallam Olam, the inscribed traditional histories of the Delaware Nation, and data on the remembrances of the Cherokee Nation. These detailed the arrival in antiquity of a powerful nation of white men who seized the territory of Kentucky and areas in the surrounding Mid-West region. The great British-style earth-banked hill forts of the Mid-West now made sense, as did some of the typically Khumric tumulus grave mounds. The Christian emblems found on ancient artefacts, and the Christian statements written in rock inscriptions, also made sense. The radiocarbon-14 dating results gave confidence as they fitted into the consistent pattern that was emerging.

It became unavoidable that the Prince Madoc who sailed the oceans and reached the American continent was Madoc Morfran son of King Meurig Uthyrpendragon, and a brother of King Arthur II. Even the reason for the voyages and the manner in which they were made is clearly stated in the records. It is perfectly obvious that there would be problems in tracing the expeditions ascribed to Madoc if he were misdated by over six hundred years, then disinherited from his family and therefore from the Cathedral Charters, the Triads, the Marwnads (Grave Elegies), the epic poetry, and the histories; and then finally deported from his south-east Wales home and settled into another, north-west area, dominated by another family dynasty.

When searching for Madoc in the correct century it becomes much harder to avoid him and to miss him, than it does to find him. Madoc is recorded everywhere, and once again the major problem and difficulty lies in exhibiting a crystal-clear situation where the university employees have apparently failed to see the very obvious. Once Madoc Morfran of the sixth century is targeted as the Madoc of the discovery of America, a simple search can be made. He can be sought in the Llandaff Cathedral Charters, and those of Llancarfan Abbey. He can be sought in the historical Triads, in the Songs of the Graves and the Marwnads, in the Lives of the Saints, and in the ancient sixth-century epic poetry.

In searching out Madoc, the ancestry of St Brendan can be checked to see if he fits the chronological pattern emerging from the sixth century. What emerged are accounts of four voyages, all of which appear to be indisputably destined for North America. First, when the tauric object, or comet, or asteroid débris struck Britain in 562, causing immense widespread devastation, there are some indications that Madoc was at sea. He was blown out far into the Atlantic by the titanic storms and waves caused by the huge cataclysm and to everyone's amazement he finally returned home after an absence of ten years in *c.* 572. When Madoc returned, the destroyed lands - known to mediaeval romance writers as 'the great waste-lands' - were slowly recovering. Madoc's accounts of the vast new land of huge rivers, mountains, and plains were disbelieved, and the king sent out Admiral Gwenon to check Madoc's star reckonings and discoveries. Admiral Gwenon made the voyage, and returned to verify Madoc's account and the discovery; this around 573. Then a major expedition was organised, and in 574, a fleet of seven hundred ships set sail from Deu Cleddyf-Milford Haven under the command of King Arthur ap Meurig, his brother Madoc Morfran, and his brother-in-law Amwn Ddu son of Emhyr Lydaw.

Chapter 12 - The Madoc who Sailed to America

This is the clear and precise account that is written in the records, which for centuries the Normans and their successors were unable to read and have refused to believe. In our modern times a more enlightened view should have prevailed, but all university employees were convinced of the serenity of the precise clockwork model of the solar system, the galaxy, and the universe, as postulated by Isaac Newton. They therefore could not conceive of vast devastations of Planet Earth, or even thought of such an event, and any such records were safely consigned to the imagined millions of years ago of the distant ages of the dinosaurs by the timid gradualist mentality. The actual catastrophe happening in Britain in 562, and what appears to have happened in Egypt around 1350 BC, was disturbing, and uncomfortable accounts which did not fit with the serenity of favoured theories were ignored or dismissed.

Wilson and Blackett quietly published a notation of the comet strike on Britain in the mid-sixth century AD in June 1986 in *Artorius Rex Discovered.* Also in 1986, and quite independently of Alan Wilson and Baram Blackett, Dr Victor Clube, Head of the Oxford University Astrophysics Department, came to the conclusion that débris from a comet, or less likely from a giant meteor, or even asteroids, had totally devastated Britain in the mid-sixth century AD. He estimated that the destruction caused was the equivalent of that caused by a hundred Hiroshima atomic bombs. In 1997 an eminent dendrochronologist, Professor Michael Baillie, of Queens College, Belfast, published that plant growth in Britain and Ireland had been stunted for several years in the mid-sixth century, and he at first attributed this devastation to the eruption of the volcano of Krakatoa in the Pacific in 535. Wilson and Blackett corresponded with Baillie and pointed out that a Krakatoa eruption would not selectively affect plant life in Britain and Ireland and leave all other countries untouched. They informed him of the comet catastrophe, and Baillie then changed his view and attributed the disaster to the comet. He was stuck with the date of 535, however, which he selected as an anchor-date, falsely believing that the Battle of Camlann took place then and not in 562, and that Camlann was somehow associated with the plant catastrophe. So while he agrees to the comet being the cause he has the dates wrong. In 2003, Dr Derek Ward-Thompson, of Cardiff University Astronomy Department, published that a comet disaster had disastrously affected Britain in the mid-sixth century AD. So, we have a leading astrophysicist, a leading dendrochronologist, and a prominent astronomer all agreeing with the multitudinous ancient records that a comet disaster caused catastrophe in the Arthurian kingdom of Britain in the mid-sixth century. All this authenticates the researches of Wilson and Blackett, who are still derided and abused for their results.

Further researches by others involved ancient Chinese records, and many other scientists around the world became involved as the scientific community of physicists, astronomers, astrophysicists, and others were roused to the danger to Planet Earth when a near-miss asteroid sailed past an American military space satellite.

The Arthurian saga had now taken another extraordinary twist and turn. In April of 1993, scientists from all over the world gathered to discuss the space object, which they named as the tauric object, and the dangers posed to Earth. The conference was widely reported in the Press as scientists from many countries speculated on the best course method of defending Earth. Investigations into the number and range of size of potentially dangerous asteroids and comets were hastily set up. A tauric object might pass by well away from the Earth, or by coming close it could cause damage, or it might even strike with catastrophic results. Much would depend on the size of the tauric object in such an encounter, and ideas were put forward on sending up a rocket to collide with and divert the tauric object, or even to launch a rocket armed with an atomic weapon to intercept and destroy it.

Whilst all this was going on Alan Wilson and Baram Blackett possessed the first-hand, ancient sixth-century accounts of just such a tauric disaster, and were patiently dredging through the records to see if any indication of the direction of approach of this object was recorded. Sadly, they were still under attack from archaeologists, who were not historians, and who possessed little knowledge of ancient Khumric-'Welsh' history. Some of the stones that fell were said to be still identifiable according to the records. It may be important to know the exact nature and size of this shower of boulders, which fell from the comet of *c.* 562. The *status quo* of carefully planned inertia and studied stagnation prevailed amongst British university employees however, and all the taboos about inadmissible Khumric records which had been discarded as politically incorrect remained in force.

The ludicrous situation which now exists is that leading world-scientists accept the reality of the 562 tauric object or comet, but the somewhat lazy and intransigent historians, and the determinedly aggressive and belligerent archaeologists, seem to be deliberately ignoring the evidence. To quote from a leading British national newspaper, *The Sunday Telegraph*, of 25 April 1993, in an extensive article on the International Conference held in Sicily:

Chapter 12 - The Madoc who Sailed to America

'Dr Victor Clube of Oxford University said the danger is that the comet, known as the tauric object, appears to be shedding débris at random, wrecking attempts to predict the next shower of asteroid strikes ... Dr Clube and his colleagues have found that Earth has run into débris from tauric objects several times in the past 2000 years.'

'The threat is bringing Cold War adversaries together in the search for answers. Dr Greg Canavan, senior advisor to the Los Alamos National Laboratory in New Mexico, said American weapons experts favour the use of neutron bombs, while their counterparts in the former Soviet Union prefer the intense X-Rays generated by a nuclear explosion.' Etc, etc. 'Some believe that governments need to be shocked into action. Dr Brian Marsden, a comet expert at Harvard University, said, "The best thing that could happen may be another Tunguska".'

On 30th June 1908, a piece of space débris, thought to measure about a hundred and fifty feet across, exploded in the air over Tunguska, in Siberia. The blast caused immense devastation and totally levelled four hundred square miles of forest at its centre. This explosion is estimated at the equivalent of a fifteen-megaton hydrogen bomb.

Wilson and Blackett believe that the very clear records in British historical sources demonstrating the near-total destruction of the powerful British state in 562 might have a salutary effect in awakening politicians. Dr Marsden is not thinking too clearly when he offers the opinion that another Tunguska would be the best thing. In 1908 a totally uninhabited area of Siberia was struck, but in 562 the densely populated British nation was blasted. Another Tunguska might obliterate France, Germany, or Britain, or very large sections of the U.S.A., and would kill many millions of people. The persistent refusal to acknowledge the existence of the Arthurian dynasty and its proven records, which include the Coelbren alphabet and the records of the 562 comet strike, denies serious scientists information which could assist in dealing with a major threat to Planet Earth. It becomes ever more important to exhibit that Prince Madoc discovered America in 562 as a direct result, and that following Admiral Gwenon's verifications, King Arthur II ap Meurig began transferring his people out of the diseased and devastated British Isles.

In relatively modern times, Edmund Halley, mentor of Isaac Newton, first began researching the records of antiquity to discover as closely as possible the information which the Khumric records exhibit. He looked at Babylonian, Assyrian,

Greek, Roman and other records to try to establish a chronology of comet dangers. He did not look at the British Khumric records.

Newspaper headlines such as *'Comet Disaster Throws New Light on Dark Age'* (*The Daily Telegraph* 04/02/2004), and, *'900 Years Before Columbus Madoc Discovered America'* (*The Western Mail* 09/03/2004) are published and forgotten; and academia slumbers on.

For the purposes of this volume, it is sufficient to note and prove that the British state was virtually destroyed and severely depopulated, and for seven to eleven years in the mid-sixth century much of the land was uninhabitable, and that Prince Madoc discovered America as a direct result of the comet strike of 562. Why else would an entry in the *Songs of the Graves* list Madoc's grave as one of a group of three in a Hazy Hills region, in a hollow near water, exactly matching the three graves at Bat Creek in the Tennessee mountain area? The largest tomb mound contained wood that carbon dated to the sixth century, and a stone was found inscribed in Coelbren, which states 'Madoc the ruler he is'.

However embarrassing the obvious reality of Madoc's being of the sixth century may be, some six hundred years distant from his speculated era, there is little point in concealing the matter further. Prince Madoc, as will be shown, appears peppered all over the sixth-century records, and so also does the comet.

The written evidence for Madoc

'Genius' is said to be the perception of the obvious that no one else can see, and so it is. There is also a great deal of hard work required, and Alan Wilson and Baram Blackett set out on the monotonous task of dredging through the records looking for sixth-century records of Madoc. They also looked for mentions of Eryr, as distinct from Eryri = Snowdon area of Gwynedd. Soon they added mentions of the fleet of seven hundred ships to their search pattern. The importance of the written evidence for Madoc has not previously been recognised simply because researchers were pursuing the wrong Madoc in the wrong age. There are in fact a number of significant entries in the ancient records.

The *Life of St Teilo* contains an important notice of the visit of Prince Madoc to St Teilo at his Abbey Church, and the fact that this visit was considered to be an event of such significance that it was recorded in St Teilo's *Life* makes it more than interesting. So also is the indisputable fact that St Teilo was vigorously active in South Wales in the mid-sixth century AD, and not in the twelfth century in north-west Wales. The entry in the St Teilo's *Life*, as set down in the Llandaff Charters, should be regarded as conclusive evidence. As is common in ancient texts the spelling of names is routinely inconsistent, and Madoc also appears as Maidoc, Madog, Madawg, and so on, and the name has been thought by some to be a derivative of Matthew.

The reference to Madoc in the *Life of St Teilo* in the *Liber Landavensis* is in Section VIII:

> 'for when the blessed Teilo and Maidoc read in the courtyard of the monastery not the fictions of the poets, or the histories of the ancients, but the lamentations of the prophet Jeremiah...'

It is highly significant that Teilo and Madoc were reading from the *Book of Lamentations*, (traditionally said to be written by Jeremiah) for this would indicate that they were comparing the vast and overwhelming destruction of ancient Judaea with the comet disaster which had overwhelmed Britain. Jeremiah actually prophesies destructions from the heavens in this Book of Jeremiah, and he attributes the destructions in Judea to heavenly causes. Jeremiah 4:27-30:

> 'For thus hath the LORD said, The whole land shall be desolate; yet will I not make a full end. For this shall the earth mourn, and the heavens above be black: because I have spoken it, I have purposed it, and will not repent, neither will I turn back from it. The whole city shall flee for the noise of the horsemen and bowmen; they shall go into thickets, and climb up upon the rocks: every city shall be forsaken, and not a man dwell therein. And when thou art spoiled, what wilt thou do? Though thou clothest thyself with crimson, though thou deckest thee with ornaments of gold, though thou rentest thy face with painting, in vain shalt thou make thyself fair; thy lovers will despise thee, they will seek thy life.'

The destruction of Judaea and Jerusalem by the Chaldeans of Nebuchadnezzar is seen by Jeremiah as an action set in motion by the Lord; and the virtual destruction of the country and its citizens is seen as a heavenly punishment for apostasy. This thought and the situation is further described in *Lamentations*.

Lamentations 2:1-4:

How hath the Lord covered the daughter of Zion with a cloud in his anger, and cast down from heaven unto the earth the beauty of Israel, and remembered not his footstool in the day of his anger! The Lord hath swallowed up all the habitations of Jacob, and hath not pitied: he hath thrown down in his wrath the strong holds of the daughter of Judah; he hath brought them down to the ground: he hath polluted the kingdom and the princes thereof. He hath cut off in his fierce anger all the horn of Israel: he hath drawn back his right hand from before the enemy, and he burned against Jacob like a flaming fire, which devoureth round about. He hath bent his bow like an enemy: he stood with his right hand as an adversary, and slew all that were pleasant to the eye in the tabernacle of the daughter of Zion: he poured out his fury like fire.'

It goes on and on in this vein. What is apparent is that St Teilo and Madoc are seeing and interpreting as an act of God the vast destructions of Britain by a heavenly body. The desperate plight of the British survivors matched and mirrored the horrors experienced by the survivors of ancient Israel and Judaea. In Britain, as in ancient Israel and Judaea, almost all the cities, villas, and major buildings toppled and collapsed; many thousands or even millions of the people were killed, and, as in ancient Judaea, there was no place even to bury them. The crops and even the entire lands were ruined and useless; there was little drinking water; the great forests were aflame; the leaders were mostly dead; and fires raged across the land. The parallels, if not the causes, as set out in Lamentations are unmistakable. In yet another parallel, enemies poured in to ravage and steal from the stricken lands; and as the British survivors fled from the poisoned lands to kinsmen in Brittany and Lydaw (Normandy), so also the ancient Judaean remnant had fled to Egypt.

It seems obvious that St Teilo and the Prince Madoc were seeing some form of heavenly wrath in the colossal destruction that had overtaken the powerful British nation. The alleged account of the destructions given in the St Gildas manuscript reads remarkably like an echo from the books and both Lamentations and Jeremiah. St Gildas, although a fourteenth-century copy of an alleged early British manuscript, which is obviously not sixth-century British in its religious sentiments, also attributes the dread catastrophe of Britain to some form of divine punishment upon the people because they were not sufficiently religious. So, the notation of St Teilo and Madoc sitting in the courtyard and reading from Lamentations and Jeremiah appears to have direct relevance to the devastated condition of Britain after 562. As the destructions occurred in 562, and Gildas returned from Ireland in 570, as in the Annals, it becomes certain that Gildas wrote his *Dei Excidio* sometime after the accession of Maelgwn Gwynedd in 580.

Prince Madoc in the Charters

The surviving charters of Llandaff Cathedral and Llancarfan Abbey record the grants of land made to the church by successive Glamorgan-Gwent kings and princes from around 450 onwards. The signing ceremonies were normally attended by the king, with his brothers, his sons and nephews, and other near relatives, cousins and uncles, and so on, and representatives of the major nobility. The bishop and the abbots, and other leading clergy also attended as witnesses, and invariably these senior clerics were close relatives of the kings and princes.

In this way the charters form a cascade of inter-linked genealogical evidence down the centuries, and assist in the construction of a *Who was Who* by linking this evidence to that of the many royal genealogies, the triads, the histories, the epic poetry, the *Lives of Saints*, the inscribed stones, and so on. Princes named alongside their kingly fathers become kings in their turn, and are accompanied by their sons down the generations. The bishops overlap the kings and *vice versa*, and the senior clergy of one king become the bishops of his successors. In this way a continuous dual thread of royal and noble genealogical descents emerges, and direct comparisons can be made with the royal genealogies, the evidence on inscribed stones, evidence in the *Lives of the Saints*, in the epic poetry, the Triads, and everywhere else. A solid matrix of evidence on *Who was Who* in ancient south-east Wales results.

One important Llandaff Charter was granted to Bishop Oudoceus-Docco, the youngest son of Budic of Amorica by his second wife. This charter concerns lands named as Llan Cyngualon, Llan Arthbodu, Llan Conuur, and Llan Pencreig, which are generally identified as being in the Gower peninsula. The witnesses from the laity are recorded as follows; -

> 'Of the laity King Meurig on behalf of his son Arthrwys (King Arthur II), Cyfonog, Gwallonir, Morgeneu, Eithin, Cynfedw, Gweithgen son of Brochwael, (Brochwael-Brocagnus, a brother of King Meurig) Gwynddog, Madoc Artheuman, Ogwyr, Gwrdillig … etc., etc.'

There is a standing stone in Cornwall for Brocagnus son of Natanleod (King Tewdrig).

With the now aged King Meurig affirming this grant on behalf of his son, it is clear that Arthur II is co-regent, and, as in the histories, the executive viceroy. He was probably absent with the army. Significantly, the name of Madoc Artheuman appears, and in Welsh rather than Latin terms this may mean Madoc Attychwel-Madoc, 'who returned again'. Bishop Oudoceus was of course a post-comet catastrophe prelate.

Madoc's listed presence at this official ceremony denotes that he is a royal prince. He is identifiable as the Madoc visiting the Prince Bishop St Teilo, and certainly the Madoc whose Marwnad-grave elegy was written by Taliesin the Chief Court Bard. As a senior prince he is included in the select twenty-five to thirty personages listed in the *Songs of the Graves*. He is also named as the father of Lliwlod who held a conference with the powerful King Arthur, his uncle. It begins to look inescapable that this is the Madoc who crossed and re-crossed the North Atlantic.

The only way to deny this Madoc is to deny or discredit the Llandaff and Llancarfan Charters, and also the *Black Book of Carmarthen*, the *Lives of the Saints*, the poetry ascribed to Taliesin, and all the whole mass of south-east Wales historical evidence.

There is also the awkward fact that King Arthmael-Iron Bear-Arthur II is named on four stones in south-east Wales, along with a host of other kings, princes, and other relatives, and also their grave mounds and sometimes stone coffins. Now there are also the American Coelbren stones and grave mounds to consider. This has proved to be no obstacle to demolition experts in the past, but this time there may be a defence as well as a prosecution.

Prince Madoc in the Triads

The evidence for Madoc, his period, his family identity, and status, is so overwhelmingly stated that it is quite difficult to understand how there could ever have been any mystery in the first place.

Madoc actually appears in all three Series of the Triads, in I, in II, and in III. He is identified as (a) a son of Uthyr, (b) as a sailor, and (c) as the father of named sons. He is, in fact, firmly placed in the sixth century AD. In the *Lives of the Saints*, Anna the

Chapter 12 - The Madoc who Sailed to America

wife of Amwn Ddu and mother of St Samson of Dol is sometimes listed as a daughter of King Meurig and at other times listed as a daughter of Uthyrpendragon. This and other evidence identify King Meurig and his father King Tewdrig as two of six identified Uthyrpendragons.

In Triad No. 82 of Series I:

'Three golden-tongued knights there were in the court of Arthur - Gwalchmai (the Hawk of May), son of Gwyar (Arthur's sister married to Llew son of Cynfarch Oer), Drudwas son of Tryphun (Triphun of Dyfed), and Eliwlod son of Madoc son of Uthyr. Wise men they were, and how much gentle, and how much good-natured in their compulsion to sail about and to the army supervision (supply corps) and no-one fished more subtly to the limits (horizons) to seek messages (information)'.

With Madoc the sailor named as a son of Uthyr, this inevitably links back to King Meurig, Uthyrpendragon. It confirms Arthur II and Madoc as brothers, with Gwalchmai (Hawk of May) as their nephew.

Madoc is sometimes referred to as Madoc Morfran or Madoc the Cormorant. This might refer to the use of captive cormorants to catch fish. He is also once called Madoc Morfrwyn or Madoc of the Seaweeds-sea rushes.

In Triad No. 37 of Series II we find the following:

'Three jewels separated their slaughter from the Isle of Britain, Morfran (Madoc), another Tegid, and Gwron Redsword.'

So, Madoc as Morfran is said to have died in a battle outside Britain. Then in Triad No. 115, of Series III, we have a repetition of the Triad statement of Series I, which concerns Gwalchmai, Drudwas, and Madoc ap Uthyr. This is supplemented by Triad No 125:

'Three chief Bards baptised in the Isle of Britain, Merddin Em-rhys, Taliesin Ben Bard, ac Merddin ap Madoc Morfryn.'

Em-Rhys is 'jewelled/crown prince', Ben Bard or Ben Beird is 'chief/ head bard'.

Merddin Em-rhys is the celebrated Martin associated with Carmarthen, but who lived at St Peter's Church at Caer Caradoc with his mother. Here they had a celebrated meeting with the ambassadors of Gwrtheyrn-Vortigern. Merddin ap Madoc Morfrwyn is of course 'Martin the Wild', associated with the Celydon Forest in southern Scotland, a tragic figure whose twin sister Gwenddyd married Rhydderch Hael or Richard 'the Generous', of the Edinburgh area. The ill-fated Merddin Wylt killed his own nephew, the son of Rhydderch, when he had the misfortune to come against him at the fabled battle of Camlann, some ten miles south of Dollgelly. This Triad gives yet another identification of Madoc.

The third person of the Triad is Taliesin, son of St Henwg, and otherwise known as Merlyn – 'Little Horse', and a central figure in mediaeval and modern Arthurian fables and romances.

'For I am Merlyn and men shall call me Taliesin,' (sixth-century poem).

St Henwg, whose church is in Gwent, is recorded as a very aged man who supplied the information to allow the writing of the *Life of St Samson of Dol*, around 600. The fact of St Henwg's being alive around 600 gives a clue to the era of his son Taliesin, and as Taliesin was Chief Bard at the Court of Arthur, this in turn gives powerful information pointing to the correct era of Arthur II. The chronology, which emerges from detailed genealogical studies, supports the identification of Taliesin and Merddyn Wylt as living in the second half of the sixth century.

The Meeting between Arthur ap Meurig and the Brown-Skinned Man

Baram Blackett and Alan Wilson had long before noted the ancient poem in the *Myvyrnian Archaiology* titled '*Englynion Ymddiddan*' the '*Conversational Metres*', which details a conference between King Arthur II and a man identified as Lliwlod. The attention of any researcher should be drawn to this long poem immediately as it has an introduction.

'Rhwng Arthur ab Uthyr a'i nai Liwlod ab Madoc ab Uthyr oed Farw'- ac wedi ymrithio yn rhith Eryr. Allan o'r Llyfyr Gyrdd.

'Between Arthur son of Uthyr, and his nephew Lliwlod son of Madoc son of Uthyr in the time of his farewell - and after the assumed form (discovery) of the guise (nature) of Eryr.'

Chapter 12 - The Madoc who Sailed to America

'Er' – 'Yr' means 'towards that which is opposite', and should not be confused with 'Eryri', which indicates 'a land of eagles' and is normally the identification of Snowdonia in north-west Wales. Wilson and Blackett consistently found that Eryr, or Er-Yr, is the identification of the great new lands far away – 'towards that which is opposite'. 'Lliwlod' is a word that means a 'coloured person,' and specifically a brown- or red-skinned person and not a black person. This identification immediately directs attention towards lands where such people dwell. It should hardly be necessary to note that brown-skinned men do not inhabit Eryri or Snowdonia in Gwynedd.

The most cursory studies show that the powerful ancient British knew all about North Africa and the lands of the Eastern Mediterranean, and so they knew all about the Arab peoples. The many recorded journeys of the British into these territories proves this. So, when a poem was written in fifty-two verses, in twenty-six of which King Arthur poses questions about a strange land to Lliwlod, and Lliwlod responds in the other twenty-six, then these two are very definitely not discussing North Africa or anywhere else around the Mediterranean. The questions and answers demonstrate this clearly. The place to find huge lands and brown-skinned people is America, and only North America can be described as 'opposite' the British Isles and Ireland.

It is a matter of deep regret to Alan Wilson and Baram Blackett that significant numbers of all those intelligent English people who love crossword puzzles do not throw away and abandon their fear of the Khumric language, and get involved in these really important and solvable puzzles.

Poetry is not a universally popular mode of communication and reading in our modern times, but here we have the earliest written records of a discussion and description of the North American continent. Even the opening verses are dramatic as they describe the destruction of Britain by the comet, and elicit the information that Er-Yr is not damaged by the comet and remains intact as before.

Verse 1. Arthur speaks.
'The surprising star which is produced stretches out.
The noise/din to the top, towering to the summit
Continuously, behold Eryr (towards that which is opposite), is continuously a deliverance.'

Verse 2. Lliwlod speaks.
> 'Arthur be not glad of havoc from without,
> Towards the army be joyful, the passing away of the burning,
> The Er-yr of yore, towards it behold.'

King Arthur son of Meurig is not at first fully convinced of the true nature, the reality and the existence of Er-Yr-America, and this is clear in his questioning and from the answers given by Lliwlod. King Arthur is surprised that America exists and is not a fable, and also surprised that America is undamaged by the comet.

Verse 3. Arthur.
> 'Surprising/wonderful (that) it exists over the black wall.
> The passing away of chaos, to make haste,
> Continuously to restore (and) continuously to renew Er-Yr.'

Verse 4. Lliwlod.
> 'Arthur, tumult/havoc is not in the journey.
> The passing (transporting) of an observant army is joyful,
> Behold the Er-Yr is all along as before.'

Verse 5. Arthur.
> 'The Er-Yr still rests at the top of the tumult/noise,
> If it exists over the freezing (ice),
> Not to be endured by you, neither any water nor tamed.'

Verse 6. Lliwlod.
> 'Arthur, swordsman keen and terrible,
> Do not cast off anything in your haste.
> I am what exists, the son of Madoc, the son of Uthyr.'

So Lliwlod simply tells Arthur that he is the living proof of the existence of Er-Yr and that by reasonable inference Er-Yr is habitable. The dialogue continues and Arthur seeks assurance that Er-Yr is not a land of the Devil, but instead is a place where Christians may flourish. Again, Lliwlod reassures him, whereupon Arthur probes the nature of Er-Yr asking if there is good land to plough and cultivate, and

Chapter 12 - The Madoc who Sailed to America

again Lliwlod assures him that there are vast good lands available for husbandry.

The dialogue goes on and on, with Arthur stating that although Er-Yr exists, as seen from Cerniw the distance is so great that it might as well not exist. Cerniw is of course the area where the city of Cardiff stands and it stretches over to Newport in Gwent. So, it is fairly obvious that the conference is taking place at the Caer Melyn or Cu-Bwrd castle in north Cardiff, or perhaps in Cardiff Castle, which was first built in AD 74. Several times Lliwlod urges Arthur to take the army over to Er-Yr, and assures Arthur that his brother is holding an advanced position. This seems to be Madoc, who is Arthur's brother, but alternatively it may be Lliwlod's brother.

Lliwlod assures Arthur that Er-Yr offers hope, and urges Arthur to break away from those who are sinful. This seems to indicate the old idea that Britain was devastated by comet débris because the people were sinful.

Verse 25. Arthur.
    'The Er-Yr spoken of is smiling?
    And without apparent furrowing/ploughing.
    To make towards it causes that which is mischief?'

Verse 26. Lliwlod.
    'Take possession break off from the faithless,
    And rest with thoughts on high,
    Away from the whole sinful wicked liars.'

Verse 27. Arthur,
    'The Er-Yr spoken of as calm/still/quiet,
    And you say without cultivation,
    What causes you towards age?' (How do you deal with the approach of death?)

Verse 28. Lliwlod.
    'To pray to God every dawn,
    For to have desirable good property (or pardoning),
    And to ask for succour of the Saints.'

Slowly Arthur is won around as the discussion of question-and-answer proceeds.

Verse 29. Arthur.
    'The Ey-Yr spoken of is not poor,
    The hope of a treatise for grain/ploughlands,
    A smart blow which made worse the ploughlands.'
(the comet smashed Britain's lands)

Verse 30. Lliwlod.
    'Arthur, excellent, exalted, wise of speech,
    After taking possession, every process of law,
    Makes things worse and unprofitably challenges the Judge (God).'

Lliwlod tells Arthur to just go over and seize the land and not to bother getting entangled over legalities and ownerships. It is God's will that he take the place. That Er-Yr is not in Britain and can only be reached by sailing, is made very clear.

Verse 31. Arthur (who is making up his mind).
    'The Er-Yr spoken of from existence,
    And is prosperous, in sailing the waters,
    From unprofitable challenges, what is its faith?'

The poem goes on and on, until in Verse 47 and onwards, King Arthur ap Uthyr makes up his mind to take the army and to sail to Er-Yr.

Verse 39. Arthur.
    'The Er-Yr spoken of is distant (out of the way).
    Towards it with hope without unconcerned about retreating,
    What God wills the army will execute.'

Verse 40. Lliwlod.
    'The army (military retinues) if true to delude,
    If complete with God upon them to direct the way,
    Thy one self hold, thy brother is an eyewitness to it.'

Verse 41. Arthur.
> 'The Er-Yr spoken of is weighty,
> Towards it is a mighty hope.
> My brother holds it in an advanced position the entry/course.'

Verse 42. Lliwlod.
> 'Arthur exalted one, a ship,
> Use one's own, conquer truly,
> Gods oneself extends out not.'

Verse 43. Arthur.
> 'The Er-Yr is a heavenly gift,
> To grasp ploughland, (than to see?) limitless,
> Christ to the few, in belief is what to do.'

Verse 44. Lliwlod.
> 'Arthur, monumental joy,
> An army towards it, to attempt to cross quite cleanly in a short while,
> Thy one self, thy brother he cometh as an eyewitness.'

That Lliwlod believes that Er-Yr offers a solution to the immense problems created by the comet destructions of Britain is clear. That the king is slowly making his mind upon whether to sail with the British army to try to seize Er-Yr is evident. That the prospect appears to be almost too good to be true is evident.

Verse 45. Arthur.
> 'The Er-Yr spoken of and observed,
> Towards it pleasant hope to collect an army (host),
> My brother awaits what to carry out, to make populous.'

Verse 46. Lliwlod.
> 'Arthur exalted one stride quickly,
> Towards truth verifying nevertheless,
> To know in that place everybody has room/space.'

Verse 47. Arthur.
>'The Er-Yr spoken of is not profitable,
>To hope towards without strength,
>It is good to get service on a Sunday.'

Verse 48. Lliwlod.
>'Service which envelopes what proceeds,
>With grace in connection with God to pray,
>Happy you are Him to proclaim.'

Verse 49. Arthur.
>'The Er-Yr spoken of it is ignoble/undignified.
>Towards it with hope across to sail,
>Where you go, to transmigrate yourself into a trap.'

Verse 50. Lliwlod.
>'The world proceeds without explaining its splendour,
>To be able to see what extends around, to go is necessary,
>Unto the sight of the other place, laugh not at beauty.'

So, put simply by Lliwlod, the only way to find out about a distant place is to go there and see it for yourself. The proposal that an army be transported over three-thousand miles straight across the Atlantic is being seriously discussed, and Arthur states that the only way to go to Er-Yr is with the strength of an army. In his final statement he says that he will sail to Er-Yr.

Verse 51. Arthur.
>'The Er-Yr spoken of is remarkable,
>I desire (to go) towards there most anciently,
>What is the limit/boundary of the soul?'

The whole poem is resonant with the sentiments which might be expected from a European monarch accustomed to the constant threats of warfare and the aggressive population movements of long-settled and over-crowded Britain and Europe. Arthur clearly has difficulty in understanding or believing that a vast and fertile country can exist without development, and without a strong organised ruler defending it against incomers. A huge undeveloped, uncultivated land with sparse diverse populations is clearly difficult for Arthur to believe. In Alan Wilson's and Baram Blackett's view, only a pedantic or bigoted outlook will deny that this ancient poem tells of the discovery of America by Madoc ap Uthyr around 562.

The full poem can be found on the internet.

So it was that the great adventure was set in motion, and a fleet of seven hundred ships assembled in Deu Gleddyf-Milford Haven, to sail west to America. The majority of the force was Khumric, but there is solid evidence of the presence of Lloegres-English people taking part in the great expedition. The poem *Preiddiau Annwn*, which means *The Voyage to the Other World*, also gives stark clear detail of this adventure in America. What the Spanish nine hundred and twenty years later called 'the New World', the old British under Arthur II called 'the Other World'. Later when 'St Brendan heard of the voyage of the Teyrn,' and Teyrn means 'the Monarch', he wanted to see these great new lands and so he crossed over the Atlantic as well.

The Grave Elegy of Madoc

The Chief Bard Taliesin who was also known as Merlyn was at the Court of Arthur ap Meurig. After the death of Arthur in 579 he was briefly with Prince Gwallog and then attached himself to the Court of the northern regent Urien Rheged. Taliesin means 'high intellect', while Merlyn means 'Little Horse', and would appear to be a Gnostic Christian appellation. The Gnostics believed that God placed the care of the Earth in the hands of a power named Ialdabaoth-The Great Horse, but Ialdabaoth, like Satan, thought he was God himself, and so he was cast down as 'unenlightened'. Then God placed Sabaoth, or Little Horse, who was 'enlightened,' to care for the world.

So, the line in the sixth century poem which reads
>'For I am Merlyn and men shall call me Taliesin.'

has the meaning
>'For I am enlightened and men shall call me high intellect.'

The interest of Wilson and Blackett in Taliesin-Merlyn in respect of Madoc is that Court Bards wrote Marwnads or grave elegies for the families of their patrons. As Taliesin-Merlyn was the Court Bard of Arthur ap Meurig, the point here is that Taliesin wrote surviving grave elegies for Arthur ap Meurig, and for Madoc. This almost irrefutably reinforces the dialogue notation that Madoc was a brother of King Arthur ap Meurig. Taliesin later wrote twelve poems about battles fought by Urien Rheged and also the Marwnad-Grave Elegy, for his later patron Urien Rheged.

Urien Rheged ('Sir Uriens') was a son of Cynfarch Oer and brother to Anarawd ('Sir Agravaine') and Llew ('Sir Leoline') who married Gwyar the sister of Arthur II ap Meurig. Urien Rheged was one of three regents appointed whilst Arthur II was out of Britain, and it was natural for Taliesin the Chief Bard of Arthur to attach himself to the regent Urien Rheged after the death of Arthur II.

Again, the title of the Marwnad of Madoc should have aroused some curiosity amongst readers searching out the Madoc voyages, but somehow it has been passed over. The statement is 'Marwnad Madoc Ddrud Ag Erof', which is translated as 'the Grave Elegy of Madoc the Opening of Erof'. So, the question is 'where or what is Erof?', and, as Alan Wilson knew from experience as an industrial consultant, it is not necessary to know answers, but it is vital to know what questions to ask.

First, 'erud' means 'brave', and so Madoc was thought to have acted bravely. Then just as 'Eryr' is actually 'Er' + 'Yr', and means 'towards that which is opposite', they now had 'erof' or more accurately 'Er' + 'Of'. First there is 'ag', which means 'an opening' or 'a cleft', indicating 'a way through' or 'a way across'. Again, 'er' means 'towards', and 'of' means that which is in an 'elementary state, raw, or crude'. So 'of' means an undeveloped land or a virginal wilderness territory. It emerges from this simple analysis that 'ag er-of' means 'the way through towards wilderness territory' is intended. All this means that the title of the Marwnad of Madoc provides a very distinctive pointer indicating that this Prince Madoc, brother of Arthur II, and also a son of King Meurig Uthyrpendragon, is the European discoverer of mainland America nine hundred and twenty years before Columbus found the Caribbean islands, and in fact never actually reached America.

When Alan Wilson gave a lecture in Louisville, Kentucky, in company with Professor Lee Pennington and Jim Michael, a man approached them after the lecture and told them that he knew that the Madoc maps were in the sailing school at Genoa. He left almost immediately after imparting this strange information, which if true indicates where Columbus might have obtained his navigational information.

The fact that Taliesin wrote the Marwnad of Madoc makes it inescapably a sixth-century record. It also makes Madoc a very high-ranking prince, and brother of

Chapter 12 - The Madoc who Sailed to America

Arthur II ap Meurig. This all matches with the *Life of St Samson* and historical traditions that King Meurig placed Amwn Ddu, the father of St Samson, to rule over part of 'a wilderness', and that Amwn Ddu son of Emhyr Lydaw made a mess of things. Samson's *Life*' records that Amwn Ddu retired to a wilderness or desert land by the seas. This turned out to be important when American stones inscribed in Coelbren were being read. As will be shown Taliesin accompanied Arthur's fleet of seven hundred ships and his army to America in *c.* AD 574.

The American stones bear mute and undeniable testimony to the Madoc arrival, and to the following invasion by his brother King Arthur II ap Meurig around AD 574. For reasons unknown, Edward Llwyd added the word 'greullawn' to the title, which indicates 'greu', or 'daring', and 'llawn', which means 'full', 'complete'. So Edward Llwyd was perhaps signposting that this was the Madoc who made the epic voyages. He would have needed to be discreet in placing this pointer, given the politics in Britain around 1700.

The Grave Elegy of Madoc Bravely Towards the Opening of Virgin Territory.

'Madoc firm of intellect,
Madoc foremost chief it came to pass, the grave,
It came to pass at the fortress of abundance.
From and in connection with a feat,
Son of Uthyr, foremost chief to slaughter,
Well done thine hand set forward,
He came to Er-Of in a vessel full and complete,
A verging point of disagreement
Sadness at discord,
To the limit of what exists, to the aggregate complete of Er-Of,
The wounds of Iesu (Jesus)
With him in belief,
The Earth in trembling (shuddering from comet impacts)
With resembling closely to blackness (vast clouds from comet impacts)
And sweating upon the world (fall-out drops from the clouds killed multitudes)
And baptism upon conflict,
A leap to disagreement,
He came to Er-Of in a vessel full complete,

Mountain ground in good order,
Amongst cold devils,
To that place in the bottom of the Other World.' (= New World = the Americas)

The Prince Madoc son of Uthyr is recorded as having been killed violently outside Britain, and this fits with the discovery of a male skeleton in a large grave mound accompanied by a stone inscribed in Coelbren writing 'Madoc the ruler he is'. This grave mound is at a place where Native American traditional history holds that a battle was fought in antiquity against a nation of white men.

In order to finally lay the ghost of the bogus Madoc, who misleads researchers into the year 1170 some six hundred years after Madoc lived, we have to deal with yet another of the appalling mistranslations which litter the British historical arena. If we look at Ruben Durrett's 1908 publication in Kentucky we can see the source of the problem. On page 141 Ruben Durrett quotes from Lady Frazer's paper in *The Gentleman's Magazine*, in which she refers to a book written in French that she saw some twenty-five years earlier. Earlier than when is uncertain, but the use of the long 's' (which looks so like an 'f') makes it appear to be eighteenth century.

Lady Frazer quotes several sources on Madoc's voyages to America, and begins with James Howells' letters, Vol. ii, page 71, which concerns an epitaph said to be Madoc's. The text is given as written by Sir Meredith ap Rees, who died in 1477.

'Madoc wifmio ydie wedd.	'Madoc wyf mi o ydyw wed/wedi
Jawn ycnan Owen Gwynedd	Iawn yc/ych nan ow-en gwyn(t) edd,
Ni fennum dvi enriddoedd	Ni fenn(um) dyfu en rhidd oedd
Ni dv mawr ondy mervedd.'	Ni dy mawr on dy mer fedd.'

Lady Frazer offers a translation:

'Madoc ap Owen I was called,
Strong, tall, and comely, not enthralled
With homebred pleasures, but for fame,
Through land and sea, I sought the same.'

What the verse actually says is:

Chapter 12 - The Madoc who Sailed to America

> 'I am with Madoc afterwards identified,
> Lawfully/rightly behold what is the breath essential wind (for) sailing,
> Without the airs (winds) to move on an obstacle there existing.
> No great house in continuity thy parting off outwards.'

If we have 'ow' and 'en', not Owen, and 'gwynt' and 'edd' rather than 'Gwynedd', as is probably correct, then Owen Gwynedd as the putative father of Madoc vanishes from the scene. At best Owen Gwynedd is a distant descendant of Madoc. Either way this 'translation', published in good faith by Ruben Durrett, is appalling nonsense. It typifies the cavalier and careless romantic approach which is routinely found in translations of important texts into English from the seventeenth and on through to the twentieth century. Tragically nothing is done to eliminate these dinosaurs in print.

The fact that Madoc was not a son of Owen Gwynedd is obvious, and at best he was an ancestor or otherwise no relation at all. Lady Frazer actually gave the game away when immediately after this she quoted from the work of George Abbot, the Lord Archbishop of Canterbury in 1625, referring to pp 255-257 of his *History of the World*. Here the Archbishop informs us that: 'King Arthur had some knowledge of the Americas, and that a Prince of Wales first found it out.' If Arthur II knew of the Americas, then Madoc had to have sailed in the sixth century and not late in the twelfth.

With Arthur and Madoc Morfran as brothers, sons of King Meurig, then the learned Archbishop was striking right at the very core of the Arthurian problem. Clearly George Abbot was aware of the sixth-century records, and was far more accurate than Dr Powell, or Richard Hakluyt, who invented the idea that Madoc was a son of Owen Gwynedd, and that Madoc sailed around 1170.

To conclude on a lighter note, we might mention Robertson's *History of North and South America*. This worthy quoted from a Mr Pennant, and he sought to prove that the ancient British-Welsh had no navigational skills and could never have discovered America. This because when the Welsh saw large flocks of white-headed birds on the coasts at the Strait of Magellan, they called them 'pen-gwyn', meaning 'Head White'. This is perfectly correct, as there still are large flocks of white-headed 'pen-gwyn' birds living there. However, Robertson insisted that all the genus of penguin in the ENGLISH language have black heads, and none are white. He failed to see that the pen-gwyn – 'white heads' of the Welsh - are white-headed birds that fly, and not the swimming penguins of the English tongue. So much for critics.

Madoc in the *Songs of the Graves*, and genealogy

Alan Wilson and Baram Blackett spent perhaps too much time labouring to seek out and identify the graves of the various long dead royalty listed in the *Songs of the Graves*. The fact is that almost all are traceable which supports the authenticity and reliability of this ancient record. Where the geographical details of the grave locations can still be accurately traced the *Songs* prove to be impeccably precise and accurate. Verses No. 20 and 21 deal with the Grave of Madoc. If the highly imaginative 'translations' of the nineteenth century are set aside and ignored, sense emerges.

> Verse 20.
> 'Three graves, three drownings, in the hazy hills,
> in the hollow (in) fair blessed state,
> Mer and Meilir and Madauc.'

> Verse 21.
> 'The grave of Madauc fixed in the gulf of countrymen,
> The branching out chief,
> The overcast senator, to create, itching desire, for the pale blue.'

Whether the Hazy Hills fits with Bat Creek in the Tennessee mountain area is matter for the reader to decide. The stone reading 'Madoc the ruler he is' came from the largest of the three grave mounds at Bat Creek. The text of the *Songs of the Graves* informs us of a 'branching out chief' and a 'senator' with a desire for 'pale blue', which indicates water and sailing. There is then the support from the dialogue between Arthur ap Meurig and Lliwlod – brown-skinned man son of Madoc ap Meurig.

What results finally is a Madoc who: 1. existed, 2. lived in the mid to late sixth century, 3. sailed to America, 4. died in America and lies in a recorded grave, 5. was buried in an identifiable grave mound, 6. had a Native American wife, 7. had a son Lliwlod who spoke with Arthur II, 8. was a son of King Meurig, Uthyrpendragon, 9. visited his cousin the Archbishop St Teilo, 10. had a grave elegy written by King

Chapter 12 - The Madoc who Sailed to America

Arthur II's chief bard Taliesin, 11. was recorded in the *Songs of the Graves*, 12. was present at Cathedral Charter Grants with his father King Meurig.

The Genealogies of the Madoc muddles

We can leave aside the marriages of three other sisters of Arthur II and Madoc to sons of Emhyr Lydaw. One sister, Gwyar, married Llew son of Cynfarch Oer, and had sons in Modred and Gwalchmai. Madoc was father of 'Lliwlod' which is titular and means emphatically 'coloured man', and he was also the father of Merddyn Wylt - Martin the Wild, whose twin sister Gwendydd married Rhydderch Hael. Merddyn Wylt had the huge misfortune to come up against his own nephew, the son of Gwendydd and Rhydderch Hael at the battle of Camlann, and to kill him.

These four marriages of King Meurig's daugthers to sons of Emhyr Lydaw in Northern Gaul, and the other marriage of Gwyar to Llew in Northern Britain, and Madoc's daughter marrying Rhydderch Hael in the North give good indications of the politics of the disturbed era.

Correctly-

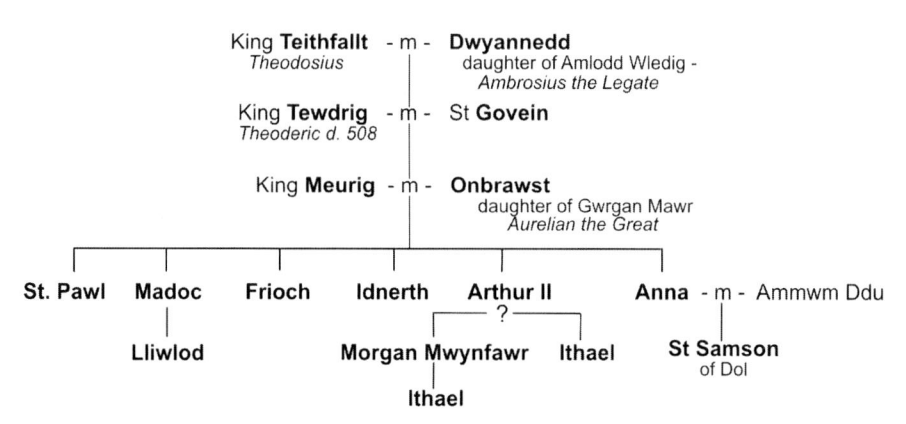

```
              King Teithfallt  - m -  Dwyannedd
                   Theodosius          daughter of Amlodd Wledig -
                                             Ambrosius the Legate
                                │
              King Tewdrig  - m -  St Govein
                Theoderic d. 508
                                │
              King Meurig  - m -  Onbrawst
                                       daughter of Gwrgan Mawr
                                             Aurelian the Great
  ┌────────┬────────┬────────┬────────┬────────┐
St. Pawl  Madoc   Frioch   Idnerth  Arthur II          Anna - m - Ammwm Ddu
            │                         ┌──?──┐                │
          Lliwlod              Morgan Mwynfawr   Ithael   St Samson
                                       │                    of Dol
                                     Ithael
```

379

Ammwn - Ammon, Eammon, becomes Aloth in the English *Bruts* and then Loth of Londenesia (Lesieux in Lydaw) in *Brut Gruffydd ap Arthur*. His father Emhyr became Eleyn or Eleyne.

There is doubt over the parentage of Morgan Mwynfawr and Ithael who succeeded Arthur II, and the likelihood is that they were Arthur's nephews and Madoc Morfran was their father.

The later Madoc Scenario of the Three Shipowners around 1120

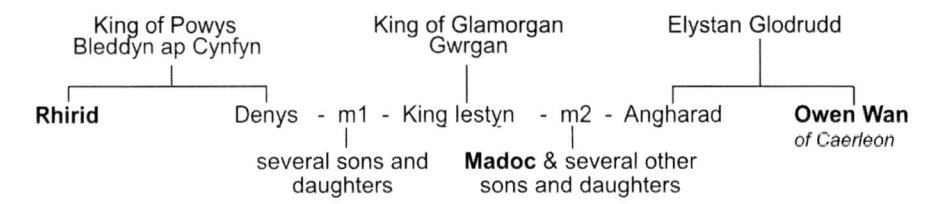

```
    King of Powys           King of Glamorgan         Elystan Glodrudd
   Bleddyn ap Cynfyn              Gwrgan
   ┌───────┴───────┐                │                 ┌───────┴───────┐
Rhirid        Denys  - m1 -   King Iestyn   - m2 -  Angharad      Owen Wan
                │                             │                   of Caerleon
         several sons and            Madoc & several other
            daughters                  sons and daughters
```

The three probable shipowners are Rhirid, Madoc, and Owen Wan.

Frequent attempts are made to confuse the histories by replacing the Glamorgan Prince, and later King, Owen the son of King Morgan Mawr and Queen Leuci with Owen the son of Howell Dda of Dyfed. This allows the deliberate obliteration of all the correct ancestors of large numbers of Glamorgan and Gwent kings and princes and creates a childish fiction of these Arthurian Dynasty Kings being vassals of the lesser Princes of Dyfed. Owen Wan, of Caerleon in Gwent, is also frequently and deliberately replaced by Owen, son of Howell Dda of Dyfed, in attempts to obliterate and confuse the histories. This despite the fact that Howell Dda is a hundred years earlier, and that he lost a war to the Glamorgan King Owen when King Edgar of England arranged the peace. Also, his son Owen ap Howell Dda sent his son Einion against Glamorgan and his army was defeated at Coed Cad Einion - Woods of Battle of Einion at Pencoed where Einion was killed 972. The phony idea that the king of Glamorgan and Gwent was a vassal of Dyfed princes is vigorously promoted and fabricated in desperate attempts to obliterate the Arthurian Dynasty.

Pre-Columbian fifteenth-century sources of the voyages of Madoc

Whilst it would seem obvious to place the Welsh Triads amongst the oldest of

Chapter 12 - The Madoc who Sailed to America

Welsh records, the majority of system-trained academics refuse to acknowledge their antiquity. The events listed in the *Triads* are also written without any form of dating, and this presents a problem for any researcher delving into the matter of the voyages of Madoc. What is beyond dispute is that the *Triads* containing entries concerning Madoc Morfran were written long centuries before Christopher Columbus was born.

The most widely publicised source containing references to the legend of Madoc sailing to America is the work of Guttyn Owain. This was made widespread knowledge in the nineteenth century by Southey. As might be expected there are the usual objections, which are pedantic to say the least. Guttyn Owain lived for much of his later life at Strata Florida Abbey in West Wales, the lodging place of the Nant yr Eos wooden cup, thought by some to be the Holy Greal, and died there as a very old man at an uncertain date around 1485. It was here that he continued to write his later poetry.

If Guttyn Owain died around 1485, then he was writing about Madoc's voyages some seven years at the very least, before Christopher Columbus sailed. There is no way of saying exactly when Guttyn Owain wrote about Madoc at this time, and he may well have written as early as 1440-1450 when he was young. This would have been several decades before Columbus set sail to discover the West Indies, and long before Europe awoke to the reality of America after 1492. Allegations that Guttyn Owain wrote about Madoc after hearing news of Columbus' feat are pedantic and appear to be ill-founded.

Guttyn Owain wrote of Madoc and he could have done so at any time during his life, when he was thirty, forty or fifty years old, and long before he died in old age. The matter does not rest here, however, for Guttyn Owain is not the only pre-Columbus fifteenth-century writer who is presented as recording the Madoc voyages. There are in fact two other Welsh manuscript records that are known to have stated the fact of Madoc's voyages years before Guttyn Owain did so.

An entry in the *Musical and Poetical Relicks of the Welsh Bards* published by Edward Jones inp1794 has a strange notation listed on Page 16 where the following illuminating entry is to be found:

'Cynvrig ap Grono a Poet and a Genealogist who flourished about 1450. This Bard and Sir Meredudd ap Rhys who flourished in 1440, mention the discovery of America by Madoc son of Owain Gwynedd.'

Suddenly there is a wholly different situation, with two other well-known writers both being identified as writing about Madoc sailing over to America. Not only this, but both are known to have been active around 1440-1450, some fifty years before Columbus sailed. This radically changes the picture, for there is no way that Cynfrig ap Grono and Sir Meredudd ap Rhys can also be cited as writing after the time of Columbus. There is yet another entry on this same page 16:

> 'Guttyn Owen a Herald Bard and historian resided chiefly at Ystrad Flur Monastery in Cardiganshire ….1480.'

So, Edward Jones, the Herald Bard to the then Prince of Wales, worked out that Guttyn Owain died in 1480, some twelve years before Columbus's voyage in 1492.

Other quick checks revealed similar notations. In Robert Owen's book *The Khumry* of 1891, there is the following entry:

> '..the legend related in the Triads of Madoc having sailed westward in the quest of a new land, whence he never returned. It is traced to Cyneuric ap Grono and Guttyn Owain in Edward IV's time, who yet have left no proofs to establish it.'

The only date here in the book of the typically negative Robert Owen is that of sometime during the reign of Edward IV of England, which is 1461-1483, and which is again a decade before the Columbus voyage of 1492. It is in line with Robert Owen's Oxford University miseducation that he states that neither Bard has left 'proofs to establish it'. Just how any writer could possibly prove that a fleet set sail in antiquity and never returned is difficult to imagine. In fact, Madoc is generally credited with making two voyages.

The point remains that there are at least two other mid-fifteenth-century sources written decades before the voyage of Christopher Columbus in 1492, both of which mention the tale of Prince Madoc, and these accounts of Cynfrig ap Grono and Sir Meredudd ap Rhys cannot be simply set aside. Sir Meredudd ap Rhys does not detail the voyages directly but he does list Madoc's activities. There are, therefore, at least three fifteenth-century Welsh sources that can be seen to deal with Madoc's voyages long before 1492, and there may be others.

Chapter 12 - The Madoc who Sailed to America

The Prophecies of Eryr

One of the most detailed and telling accounts of the mid-sixth century destruction of Britain by the comet débris, and the subsequent attempt to colonise North America lies preserved in the *Prophecies of Eryr*:

'The bellowing of what exists, a being, the distant red lightening subtlety hot darkening over what exists as a living principle.'

'The Dragon amazing (the Comet) the worst bad pungency with chafing wrathful irritations the maw of the particles conveying as beneath hell the whole island with the spread of contagion.'

'From out of oration of the elders, it is good to make calm this place to have faith to begin to move about on the oceans.'

'Excellent the good that is devoured the far-off awful bat flashing with regeneration of lightening, the government the corrupt spoiler, has a drought of truth.'

'The cancer (crab = comet) is to the limit of the horizon of the wretched seas that devours with lightening, the place outward to explore, the vanishing away of freedom from liberty to speak to move onward the hoe (turned) into a spear.'

'To make dirty, the toothed one without deliverance, far off the cancer with fluid provoking disease in the brambles with the hatred of aliens in the reproach to go to travel the Kingdom.'

'Woe the mark of the dirt of the increase/growth, a messenger (sent) towards this and to cross abroad the opening of the sunshine the discovery so as there is around the destitute state a holdfast.'

'In blood a little while ago the father the sons upon the first what is superior vowed to unite (under) the foremost chief, (Arthur) the borders of the Kingdom superior in matter. Nevertheless like a flower in a lamb's meadow before naked strength it is a withered scar.'

'From the little doings of the old, the state of inertia, the sons hard by their father over crime, the first with faith to put things on the ravishing seizing the hindmost.'

'The mighty sons on both sides about in accepting their father and with vengeance uncalled for in sin the crown/diadem separated from and postponed, and with twining together in opposition to the gravel particles.'

'Worse a wild savage wilderness to receive their worst courage finished is the upper part (Alban-Scotland ?), wailing in punishment that which pervades to hurry and without hope what (which ?) may be essential (to) the very bottom in that place what is in being flowing (= the ocean) in powerful commotion moaning in the east amazing, with the west with progeny having roots (for) everyone it is beneficial Ireland to wrest from the breast, to humble the princes, and after the agreement/covenant of the tangle (destroyed lands?) to covet the corn hard by.'

'Disease a second excess in the verging point whence an apparition/to make apparent the father in the heart of the mother.'

'He impotent the ruler of the progeny a little while ago from renewal that which devours going with severity the fluxion and no pubic hair.'

'The iron primeval light in an open state the gift of them of Normandy what is produced of him the island with great falling snow a flight to move him unconfined to pour out the sword in touch with the crown. From this cause/reason in weakness they see the cultivated land to prosper to build another track.'

'The chariot swelling out to subdivide streaming/gleaming the four parts and afterwards to make apparent the shape/form of viticuls the insulting rage with devilish trampling of the kingdom. In extremity to implore at last the Dragon the fair one, to bring tranquility to the agitation and gall, with tears that portion, the portion wretched the discretion of the ruler of lances a treasure of the standing corn ready to cut, to drive (out) from the western regions over the black sea, the ignoble serious/sedate the thrifty portion, a second reckoning in the vile/base country, the opening to turn back spreading continuous havoc descending over the east from Lydaw in the region with a contagious proceeding he will have.'

'With the army strong what is large, the eagle of the island above gleaming,

Chapter 12 - The Madoc who Sailed to America

increasing from them afterwards what is burning hatred, their flags torn apart and without ceasing in seizing them unconfined. The coasts/borders fires the holding of sparkles of fire to proceed with, the agitation the fear of the island motionless, in overgrown wildness, above the gleaming increasing the wounds of the slanderers upon the second declaration with faith worse than the first.'

''After the scarecrow/bugbear of death (the comet) that ravages the innocent, the comfort of the fair king of blessed lineage in the island of Britain (Arthur). The first time in flight excellent in horsemanship, excellent in the descent (on the enemy) and in the pursuit, here the prisoners he put in the bird lime. Excellent to carry away (to migrate) and to show a country vast/huge and that is spoken of, it is the blessed king of correct lineage.'

'Thereupon the assembling together of the faithful he, and pledging to cross over with himself. Towards that which is beyond, vast/huge, and in that place the world to obtain, the men like so for oxen or because of this gift, the thought that this place (Britain) full of clefts, and with no life, the one out of them has vertigo/staggers, and in this place the increase of rage (destructions), and the good of this (other) place, the fellowship, the sunshine, over the place an accident, the sun is another in that place spoken of in the island of a heated quality the king is not king.'

'Speaking of that aspect, he the head, and of the barbarousness/inhumanity that exists in the kingdom over a great many activities, it is sad what is impending upon each profitable activity. Speaking of the rupture of a great many without (in) the world, to (lead to) correctness in that place it forever, the impulse to cast off the contract with groans and sighs everyone of the oppressed of faith vigorously towards this place into the sea seven hundred (ships).'

'And in that place in the world to force upon to impel with blood and gore above a solid body heavenly over and against the church above thus much rejoicing (with) each other, it is what is good, and above the lofty soaring hero without the one who has overcome mortality, and in the ejection out (emigration) joining together of men the world loves as it happened. Over thus much with the foremost chief swearing by the relics over the distinctions of the morning of the depravity. Excellent the coasts of the south (South Wales) above the timber war-horse (ships) upon the foam of the sea to carry to Erir (towards that which is beyond) with the sea as wings with the virtue/grace of the island of Britain the land, and in the place of him and the ejected (migrants) and you the Erir and with the conquest, and in that place the world to foresee in the island of a heated quality (hot) a year and a half, and in that place a languishing and reward of nothing to carry away to exchange, except everybody who is transmigrating is firm/strong, the combat the enlivening he oneself with the seeking of good for everybody.'

'Excellent the good of the king of blessed lineage (Arthur), the region upon the west, who believed in the circumference (of the world) he along with the ancients, a place ahead at hand, the currents/waters and in that place the good, the judges in the right/towards, and the ordaining of everybody in the place in the circumference along with him.'

'The chief of waters and with the judges he put into a method above the remainder of those he stayed/tarried. In this place to expand oneself profitably will be their payment and the barren dried-up place to depart from, and in this place (Eryr) they to glide (to sail) with the king of blessed lineage, the gale/blast of the winds. Excellent the nestling place of the chick of Eryr, in greatness/loftiness rocky than the whole island of Britain, waiting without lapse in youth (virgin land) in the boon he also above old age in this place glorious prosperity without him excellent, against the law neither disgrace to himself and afterwards the barbarous nephews inherited the monarchy this without lapse.'

The content of the Prophecies of Eryr

That this record tells of the vast destructions of Britain by some heavenly agency, a comet, or débris from a comet, or asteroids or meteorites, is indisputable. That the country was in ruin and subject to lawlessness in the chaos, is clear. Irish incursions to steal the surviving standing corn crops are described. The flight or removal of the large British army to Brittany is mentioned, as is its return to restore order and destroy invaders. The shattered and lifeless condition of the devastated Isle of Britain is plainly stated.

The discovery of vast new distant lands across the oceans to the west is made very clear, as is the gathering of the fleet of seven hundred ships. The 'king of blessed lineage', who is undoubtedly Arthur II ap Meurig, sets the land in order under legates

Chapter 12 - The Madoc who Sailed to America

and judges before leaving to lead the emigration across the oceans to the Americas. The story of the planned voyage to vast new uncultivated virgin territories westwards across the ocean is told with stark clarity.

Interesting details are included, indicating that Arthur II was impotent and also that his nephews succeeded to the throne after he died. This accords with Glamorgan historical traditions that Arthur II ap Meurig left no heirs and that Morgan Mwynfawr and his brother Ithael who succeeded Arthur II were in fact his nephews. It appears that Morgan and Ithael were sons of Madoc Morfran a brother of Arthur II.

The fact that these prophecies were widely published makes it all the more difficult to comprehend how this vital evidence could have been overlooked.

The prophecy of the eagle of Caer Septon

This document is yet another astronomical and astrological record which appears to link to British historical events. Alan Wilson and Baram Blackett make no claim to understand it all fully, but it does clearly indicate a disaster in Britain caused by an object from the skies. It begins:

> 'As the red dragon often drove off the white, thus is the white driven away. The worst and terrible dragon flees, and with a blast from its mouth burns up the whole island with fiery flames.'

This much is clear enough, and it is a statement that the British Khumry, identified with the Red Dragon, often drove off the Gewissae, identified with the White Dragon, and also perhaps the Saxons. Then, however, the most terrible Dragon, the comet, strikes the island setting it on fire and 'flees' by zooming off into outer space, or plunging into the oceans.

The Hermetic principle of 'as above, so below' may be applied here and it is possible that this most terrible Dragon is William I the Bastard from Normandy. Next there follows a series of identifications of constellations:

> 'And from its behaviour comes the ram (Aries) with the splendid fleece, that frequents and strikes with his hurricane horns in the East. That one is the king with the poisonous appearance, and in his sight faith and religion tremble. The lion (Leo) is next to him the lightening king, he that defends the strength of truth under the

government. The sea crab (Cancer) comes next to the lion (Leo), with this freedom vanishes from freedom by returning to the harrowing/hoeing state of affairs of the painful lance. Next to the crab (Cancer) is the toothed wood-boar, that sharpens his teeth among the oaks of the kingdom, setting by that his throne in the thick bushes.'

The ram - Aries - is probably William II Rufus, and the lion - Leo - is Henry I the second son of William I. Then comes Stephen of Blois - the sea crab - Cancer, who married Matilda the daughter of Henry I, and their subsequent destructive wars. Then comes the 'toothed wood-boar', the dangerous Henry II Plantagenet. As Henry I the youngest son of William I fought for the English crown against his eldest brother Robert, Duke of Normandy, this would account for Gemini, the contending twins.

To continue with Henry II:

'From the adultery of that Boar are born those of the vixens that return to their father from seeking scraps. Shame on the father who slays his sons. The first of them ascends suddenly to the summit of the kingdom, but already like a spring flower is vanishing.'

Henry II forced Louis King of France to surrender his wife Eleanor of Aquitaine to him, the Pope granted this enforced divorce, and Henry II married Eleanor. Then Henry II had four legitimate sons in Henry, Richard Lionheart, Geoffrey, and John. The eldest son Henry was crowned king of England whilst his father Henry II was content to rule most of France. This 'unnumbered' Henry ruled England as King for twenty-two years and died before his father Henry II, vanishing like a spring flower.

'From the sin of the father the sons sin against their father and the most hateful sins are those after him. The sons rise up against their father and avenge the sin of the bowels that they commanded in the womb. He rises up a cruel man, a source of their despair, until he weeps his penance as a pilgrim.'

All four of Henry II's sons joined with Philip, the youthful King of France, in a war against their own father Henry II. The sin is that of seizing the Queen of King Louis.

The 'weeping of penance as a pilgrim' refers to the act of contrition enforced on the youthful Henry by the church after the murder of Thomas à Becket, Archbishop of

Canterbury.

> 'A whirling scorching storm comes with daybreak, rushing towards the west, and uprooting all the oaks of Ireland. Before his breast the princes kneel and they are bound to one another by the everlasting love of a sword-stroke of agreement. Grief turns to happiness when they kill the father in the womb of the mother. A lynx comes from the seed of the Lion that whitens the bareness of the marks of iron in the oak trees. In that way everyone (has) cornfields in Normandy, but strangely this change separated the sword from the monarch's staff.'

The prophecies of Merlyn and the comet

Countless thousands of people have read *The Prophecies of Merlyn* by virtue of there being modern hardback and paper-back editions of *The History of the Kings of Britain* by Gruffydd ap Arthur/Geoffrey of Monmouth. Unfortunately, as with the *Mabinogi* tales, these editions are frequently the works of English and American editors and are as such not understood.

Wilson and Blackett recognised *The Prophecies of Merlyn* as being in line with the *Prophecies of Eryr*, and as simple straightforward accounts of actual events. As with the prophecies of the Hebrew records we know as the Bible, these prophecies are not foretellings, but simply later explanations for events which have already taken place. There was the usual problem of established mind-sets; and the difficulty involved in the Merlyn prophecies was again academic incompetence and inertia. The prophecies record disturbances in the heavens and great comet activities, which devastated Britain.

The Bible and Isaac Newton were the major obstacles to understanding these records. The Bible proposed a creation of Earth, the solar system, the galaxy, and the universe by God as one immediate act. It proposed that this act was stable and eternal and that Planet Earth was the major and central part of the system. Newton in his time knew that the Earth was a minor planet in a solar system, and that the galaxy and universe existed, but Newton hypothesised an unreal system of eternal stability. For Newton the whole creation worked like a gigantic clock, with all the wheels and gears controlled by gravity and whirling and turning in perpetual harmony. As Newton was believed, and he knew nothing of the great magnetic fields surrounding planets and stars, and other forces, or of the idea of great comets bouncing off planets and perhaps colliding, and planets appearing to run out of orbit, and the Earth slewing around onto a different polar axis, all this was simply disregarded. It was a serious religious heresy until 1803 to state that any stone could fall from the heavens to Earth, and so all asteroids, meteors, and comets colliding with Earth were an impossibility. Therefore, all ancient British history was a serious heresy as it told of a great comet causing the destruction of the powerful British state. Therefore, the British history had to be rejected.

In 1986, when Alan Wilson and Baram Blackett spoke of a comet affecting the Earth and débris striking Britain in the mid-sixth century, and published a note to this effect in *Artorius Rex Discovered*, they were ridiculed. Yet within a few short years the world's leading astronomers, astrophysicists, and other scientists were holding major international conferences disregarding the barriers of the Cold War, on the subject of how to deal with the threat to Planet Earth posed by comet or asteroid impacts. When their views on the comet were published in *The Holy Kingdom* in 1997 there was silence.

Mathematical astronomers had for years set up planetaria, and they had confidently demonstrated to the unsuspecting public what they said the starry heavens looked like thousands or even millions of years ago, and what the heavens would look like in the equally distant future. This cosy, rosy little scenario of Newtonian mathematics was in no way able to cope with a real recorded situation where planets in the solar system we occupy are newly arrived, or when they were affected by both each other and by great comets, and changed their orbits in historical times. Nor could the safe, stable mental security predicted by Newton cope with the Earth shifting onto a different polar axis, or changing its orbital path slightly, with the view of the heavens from Earth radically changed.

So, the *Prophecies of Merlyn* and other British records were relegated to the status of myths in conformity with unhistorical thinking. The events described in Merlyn's (Little Horse = Sabaoth) Prophecies are those of the fifth and sixth centuries AD, and in order to set the scene it is best to read the last two prophecies, No. 93 and No. 94 first. (Wilson & Blackett numbers.)

93. 'Before the amber glow of Mercury the bright light of the Sun shall grow dim and this will strike horror into those who witness it. The planet Mercury, born in Arcady, shall change its shield; and the Helmet of Mars shall call to Venus. The Helmet of Mars shall cast a shadow and in its rage Mercury shall overrun its

orbit, iron Orion shall bare its sword. The watery Sun shall torment the clouds, Jupiter shall abandon its pre-ordained orbits and Venus shall desert its appointed circuits. The malice of the planet Saturn shall pour down like rain, killing mortal men as though with a curved sickle. The twelve mansions of the stars (the Zodiac constellations) will weep to see their inmates so transgress. The Gemini will cease their wonted embraces and will dispatch Aquarius to the fountains. The scales of Libra will hang awry, until Aries props them up with its curving horns. The tail of Scorpio will generate lightening and Cancer will fight with the Sun. Virgo will climb on the back of Sagittarius and so let droop its maiden blossoms. The chariot of the Moon shall run amok in the Zodiac and the Pleiades will burst into tears. None of these will return to the duty expected of it. Ariadne will shut its door and be hidden in enclosing cloudbanks.'

94. 'In the twinkling of an eye the seas shall rise up and the arena of the winds shall be opened once again. The winds shall do battle together with a blast of ill omen, making their din reverberate from one constellation to another.'

All this is absolutely in common with the records of every other ancient nation where great disturbances in the heavens are closely described as historical events. In the 1950s, the 1960s, and the 1970s, Immanuel Velikovsky wrote a series of erudite and detailed books drawing together the multitudinous records of nations from every continent on our globe, all of which told of great catastrophes in ancient historical times which involved changes and disturbances in the heavens. People of intelligence took note, but academia set out to defend its indefensible positions with their usual tactics of mindless ridicule and blockade by preventing Velikovsky from gaining access to forums where he could present the facts.

It is becoming increasingly accepted that the *Prophecies of Merlyn* encompass the disaster which befell Arthurian Britain around AD 562 and the older records of the similar catastrophes which their direct ancestors saw around 1350 BC. The logic is simple. The Khumry–'Welsh' are easily proved to be the descendants of the Ten Tribes of Israel - as distinct from the Two Tribes of Judea - and their ancestors were therefore with Moses when the Hebrews left Egypt in the midst of these colossal disasters. They had knowledge of what happened around 2167 BC with the great Flood, and they now knew what happened in the Exodus. The appearance of the comet, which threatened Earth and then devastated Britain, brought these records forth as prophecies of what might occur again.

Greek and Roman records, so beloved of academics, record these disturbances of the planets, with the stars appearing to be askew, and the consequent disasters on Earth. The Hebrew, Egyptian, Assyrian, Hittite, Chaldean, and every other associated record, all make the matter clear. The records from nations on the South and North continents of America corroborate this mass of evidence and record. African nations record these solar confusions and disasters, as do Asian and Pacific nations. So also does the British record preserve evidence of these past catastrophes.

Wilson and Blackett at first knew nothing of the avalanches of cash grants of public funds flowing continually out of the puppet Welsh Office in Cardiff, nor did they know of the sordid little cliques and conspiracies of the frightened and incompetent recipients ever-anxious to preserve their comic status as 'experts'. So they became involved in tracing the ancient historical migrations of the British: the history and voyage of Albyne back to Syria around 1650 BC; the history and voyage of Brutus back to Western Asia Minor around 504 BC; and the voyages to North America of Madoc Mofran, Gwenon, and Arthur II in AD 562, 574, and 575 respectively. In this way they sought to move their project out of and away from decadent British academia.

The voyages to America of AD 562, 574, and 575 resulted from the comet disaster of AD 562. The older records involved great ancient histories, which in turn contained earlier records of similar disasters; and it was in this context that they were to examine the *Prophecies of Merlyn* and those of *Eryr*. Their interest lay in the fact that there appeared to be a great comet cycle of around six hundred and seventy-four to six hundred and eighty years in which the AD 562 comet played no part and from which it was quite separate. The next visitation of this great cycle would be early in the twenty-first century, possibly around AD 2015.

The content of the prophecies of Merlyn

The *Prophecies of Merlyn* begin with a general historical statement which recounts the fact that the usurper Gwrtheyrn, *alias* Vortigern, invited Jutes (Saxons) over into Ceint (Kent) as coastguards and a buffer against the enraged Amlodd Wledig-Ambrosius the Legate in Brittany. The licentious, alcoholic, incestuous, aged reprobate Gwrtheyrn had murdered his nephew by marriage, Cystennyn Bendigaid or Constantine the Blessed, a grandson of Magnus Maximus, and a cousin of Amlodd Wledig, in *c.* AD 426 and the whole nation was gathering against Gwrtheyrn. The Jutes, or Saxons, did run amok in Britain, as prophesied, and a great number of the British nobility were massacred at the famous Peace Conference at Caer Caradoc, and large numbers of churches were destroyed.

The invitation of Gwrtheyrn to Hengist and the Saxons, the destruction of the churches and the over-running of Britain, and primitive Saxon savagery, are set out in Prophecies 1, 2, and 3. Then in No 4:

> 'The Boar of Cerniw shall bring relief from these invaders, for it will trample their neck beneath its feet.'

This refers to the Em-Rhys Wledig or Crown (Jewelled) Prince, who destroyed the Saxons and executed Hengist, and became King Teithfallt *alias* Tudfwlch or Theodosius. A great-grandson of King Arthur I, who was known as Andragathius-Arthun the son and General of Magnus Maximus, from Cerniw the Royal or Privileged Cantref of Glamorgan.

Prophecies No. 5, No. 6, and No. 7 revert back to Arthur I describing his domination of the British Isles and surrounding islands. No. 6 expresses his conquest of Rome in AD 383–388:

> 'The House of Romulus shall dread the Boar's savagery,'

which recalls that Arthur I killed the illegitimate Emperor Gratian at Lyons after defeating his armies at Soissons. No. 7 tells how the exploits of Arthur I become fond tradition:

> 'the Boar shall be extolled in the mouths of its peoples, and its deeds shall be as meat and drink to those who tell tales'.

Then No. 8 states that:

> 'six of the Boar's descendants shall hold the sceptre after it, and next after them shall rise up the German Worm. The Sea-Wolf shall exalt this Worm and the forests of Africa shall be committed to its care'.

This is all straightforward as the six descendants of Arthur I son of Mascen Wledig (Magnus) were Tathall, Teithrin the Subtle, Teithfallt, Tewdrig, Meurig, and then Arthur II.

The great German tribal confederation of nations led by the Vandals attacked Gaul in 406, and after being defeated in Gaul by the British armies under Constantine Coronog, they were allowed through the passes of the Pyrenees south into Spain by the British general, Geraint. Under Gaiseric the Vandals crossed over into Africa in 422 and seized Carthage and Hippo, and then proceeded to dominate all North Africa and the Mediterranean with their fleets and armies until 532. In 548 they left North Africa in a massive fleet and invaded Ireland, then, when confronted by the Irish and British armies, they invaded Britain, leaving the British army stranded behind them in Ireland. The British under Arthur II pursued the Germanic Vandals, who fought their way through Wales to cause devastations in Lloegres (now England). All this is detailed in *Artorius Rex Discovered* and in *The Holy Kingdom*. This was in the time of Arthur II son of Meurig the sixth descendant of Arthur I the Boar of Cerniw in Glamorgan.

These first eight statements in the prophecies are clearly identifiable and simple accurate history, and they immediately debunk labels asserting that the Prophecies are mystical, mythical or legendary.

The history of the Prophecies rolls on. No. 9:

'Religion shall be destroyed a second time and the sees of the primates will be moved to other places. London's high dignity shall adorn Durobernia, and the seventh pastor of Caer Effrawg will be visited in the realm of Amorica. Menevia shall be dressed in the pall of the city of the Legions, and a preacher from Ireland shall be struck dumb by a child growing in the womb.'

The most obvious statement is that the Archbishopric of Caer Leon near the Roman fortress of Isca would move to Menevia or St David's, and David is recorded as asking permission from King Arthur II to remove the see from Caer Leon - the Castle of Leon the Mighty - to Western Dyfed. Caer Effrawg means the Castle of the Hebrews and is the capital city of Uriconium-Viroconium or Wroxeter. The seventh Bishop moved to Lydaw-Amorica (later Normandy) when cometary débris struck Britain. The arrival of Austin, a monk from Rome, in 597 saw a move from London to Canterbury-Durobernia, only in the sense that a Roman archbishopric was set up at Canterbury whilst the Apostolic British church at London probably continued.

'Religion will be destroyed a second time' indicates that the first destruction was that of the persecutions launched by Diocletian and Maximinius in 290.

The importance of all this is that everything points to these prophecies being accurate historical accounts of events in early Britain and not mystical accounts of Norman and Plantagenet 'English' kings of the eleventh and twelfth centuries as is usually proposed.

It remains incomprehensible to any thinking person that the national histories of Britain are persistently and deliberately ignored, and are replaced by ludicrous and even childish archaeological theories. Not one single university employee thinks it necessary to even investigate British records. In the matter of 'the Holy Greal', which consumes whole oceans of printers' ink and vast forests of trees to print foolishness, not one single writer has seen the obvious, that the Mabinogi records and the Greal Legends are solar stories of the creation of the solar system we live in and of disturbances in that system in recorded historical times. Ancient knowledge, which the Roman Church feared:

'A shower of blood will fall and a dire famine will afflict mankind.'

This would appear to refer to the devastations of Britain caused by the mysterious 'Yellow Pestilence' which killed a Maelgwn - probably Maelgwn of Llandaff, a brother of King Meurig and an uncle of Arthur II.

'The Red One = Wales will grieve for what has happened but after an immense effort it will regain its strength.'

This would be the British recovery in Wales led by King Meurig the Uthyrpendragon.

'Calamity will next pursue the White One (= Lloegres = 'England') and the buildings in its little garden will be torn down.'

Ancient British sixth-century poetry states that the buildings of Lloegres were shattered, the roofs slid off, the walls tumbled, and the very foundations shaken, by the comet débris impacts of 562. Next:

'Seven who hold the sceptre shall perish, one of them being canonised.'

The historical muddles make it difficult actually to identify these seven kings who perished. Several kings were also 'saints', so their identification is a little difficult.

The possible list is:

1. King Meurig ap Tewdrig, who was alive at the time of the comet disaster,

2. King Arthur II ap Meurig,

3. King Morgan Mwynfawr,

4. King Ithael I, brother of Morgan,

5. possibly Gwaednerth (Mighty in Blood), son of Morgan,

6. King Ithael II son of Morgan,

7. King Ivor, and perhaps King Alan.

If Morgan Mwynfawr is the 'Cadfan', or 'Prominent in battle', and Gwaednerth is 'Caswallon', or 'Viceroy - Ruler of a Separated (part of the) State', and Ithael II is the 'Cadwallader' or Battle Sovereign, it is Ithael II who was canonised as a saint.

Gruffydd ap Arthur and the comet

As Alan Wilson and Baram Blackett drew back the curtains concealing these ancient histories, the fogs and mists surrounding them began to disappear. There emerged a classic case of 'the baby being thrown out instead of the bathwater'. For many years it has been customary for putative scholars to pour scorn and derision on *The History of the Kings of Britain*, written in 1135 by Gruffydd ap Arthur, *alias* Geoffrey of Monmouth. It is doubtful if any of them have realized that there is a parallel history in the *Brut of St Tyssilio c.* 684AD. It is equally doubtful that any of them have ever taken the trouble to investigate the history portrayed by St Tyssilio or Gruffydd.

In the *History of the Kings of Britain* there is a very clear account of a great comet over Britain, in the era of an 'Uthyrpendragon'. As there are two Dragons recorded and four Uthyrpendragons, this is not quite as simple as it appears. The chronology however points to the declining years of King Meurig Uthyrpendragon, who appears

Chapter 12 - The Madoc who Sailed to America

to have lived to a great age, and in the period when his son Arthur II was the Ail-Teyrn, or Alternative/Second Monarch = Viceroy.

By abandoning the histories of St Tyssilio and Gruffydd ap Arthur, the story of the comet over Britain in *c.* 562AD is also rejected and abandoned. This is the account in Gruffydd ap Arthur:

> 'While these things were happening at Winchester there appeared a star of great magnitude and brilliance, with a single beam shining from it. At the end of this beam was a ball of fire, spread out in the shape of a dragon. From the dragon's mouth stretched forth two rays of light, one of which seemed to extend its length beyond the latitude of Gaul, while the second turned towards the Irish Sea and split up into seven smaller shafts of light.'

> 'This star appeared three times, and all who saw it were struck with fear and wonder. Uthyr the King's brother, who was hunting for the enemy, was just as terrified as the others. He summoned his wise men so that they might tell him what the star portended. He ordered Merlyn (Taliesin son of St Henwg) to be fetched with the others, for Merlyn had come with the army so that the campaign might have the benefit of his advice. As he stood in the presence of his leader and was given the order to explain the significance of the star, he burst into tears, summoned up his familiar spirit and prophesied aloud. "Our loss is irreparable," he said; "The people of Britain are orphaned. Our most illustrious King has passed away, Aurelius Ambrosius (Gwrgan Mawr) the famous King of the Britons has died..."'

Uthyr is then urged to attack his enemies quickly and is assured that the star signifies him in person:

> 'The star signifies you in person, and so does the fiery dragon beneath the star. The beam of light which stretches towards the shore of Gaul signifies your son, who will be a most powerful man. His dominions shall extend over all the kingdoms, which the beam covers. The second ray signifies your daughter, whose sons and grandson shall hold one after the other the Kingship of Britain.'

Here Gruffydd is confusing Arthur I son of Magnus Maximus, who conquered Western Europe and North Africa for his father in 383-388, with Arthur II son of King

Meurig. Gruffydd also makes a most significant statement that Arthur II ap Meurig will leave no heirs, and will be succeeded by his nephews Morgan Mwynfawr and Ithael I. This appears to be true from many other sources.

In due course Uthyr makes two golden models of the strange dragon-shaped comet, and places one in Winchester Cathedral - which is not known to exist at the time - and retained the other. Remarkably an ancient Coelbren-inscribed stone found buried deep in St Paul's churchyard in London, in 1852, depicts this strange dragon comet. Gruffydd's description of the strange heavenly body matches that of a comet, and the tails of comets are known to be affected by the gravitational pull of the sun and of planets. So, the splitting of the tail is not unusual, nor is the reversal of the tail to precede the comet as a tongue.

Chapter Thirteen

Evicting Roman Squatters

That British history is in chaos has been clearly stated. Experience has proved, however, that it is hugely difficult actually to fix this thought in the reader's mind. In order to make the point, and to show the consistent jerrymandering which has gone into the fabrication of a politically acceptable bogus ancient history, it is necessary to deal with two great pillars of the establishment's fictions.

First it has become a commonplace for lecturers, teachers, authors, in fact anyone and everyone, to aver that around AD 411 the Romans 'abandoned' Britain. In fact, they were rarely in Britain. The final wars began in AD 310 when King Euddaf-Octavius, the grandson of Gwrtherin-Victorinus Emperor of the West, rose against Constantine the Great. By AD 322, Euddaf had killed Trahaearn the General of Constantine the Great in Britain, and had control of all Britain. So it was that again the Romans were clean out of Britain until around AD 389 when Theodosius the Great sent a brief expedition after he had killed Mascen Wledig-Magnus Maximus in 388. Upheaval again followed and Eugene-Owain brother of Arthur I and son of Magnus Maximus was active in Gaul.

That Britain was independent is very clear when in AD 406 Cystennhyn Coronog - who was Constantine the Crowned, and who appears very clearly in the royal genealogies - led the British armies into Gaul. The objective was to block the western advance of the avalanche of tribal nations led by Godigeisel of the Vandals, with the Alans, and Sueves, which had crossed the Rhine in 406 and was devastating Gaul. The British army did this very successfully, and Constantine became Western Emperor. The British General Geraint-Gerontius held the passes through the Pyrenees, and the Vandal confederation milled around trapped in Southern Gaul. These are facts. Geraint finally became exasperated with Constantine's inactivity and failure to attack Honorius in Rome, and so he allowed the Vandals, Sueves, and Alans through the passes of the Pyrenees and into Spain and North Africa, to weaken Honorius and Rome. This action by Geraint ultimately sealed the fate of Rome. Geraint then set up his own puppet Emperor Constans and the British in Gaul were at odds.

Matters crumbled when with most of the British army in the south under Geraint, the strangely inactive Constantine Coronog, was defeated by a Roman army in 411. At this same time Honorius in Rome had major problems as Alaric the German king was ravaging Italy. As Alaric moved southward towards Sicily, Honorius sent a famous letter to the citizens of Rhegium the local capital of Brittium on the Strait of Messina. He warned the citizens of Rhegium in Brittium in Italy of the approach of Alaric and his army, and told them that he could not assist them. This letter to Brittium, in Italy, has somehow been bent and twisted into an imaginary letter to the powerful British state from their enemy Honorius with whom they were at war in Gaul, to tell them that he could not assist them.

Contrary to the written evidence of powerful British armies controlling Gaul, and at war again with the Romans of the illegitimate line of Theodosius the Great, the pretence is that the pre-Angle and Saxon British were instead weak and dependent on Rome. Anyone is free to read the accounts in Olympiodorus and Zosimus of the letter that was sent to Italian Rhegium in Brittium.

A second farcical piece of nonsense foisted onto the unsuspecting British public again concerns these imaginary wonderful, marvellous, beloved Romans, amazing, superior, clever Romans, so loved and eulogised by the universities. The British sent a letter to Gaul to seek some military assistance in the fifth century. Again, this is a crucial letter because it is used to set the dates of fifth- and sixth-century British history.

Gildas - whose manuscript is admittedly a suspect late mediaeval source, the original of which no longer exists - states that the letter was sent to Agitus, or Aegidius. The Khumric histories of Tyssilio and Gruffydd ap Arthur say it was sent to Aganypus, Acanipys, or Acanypus. To a sane person this would indicate Aegidius. In fact, there was a very powerful British king, a kinsman and ally, ruling in Northern Gaul only separated from Britain by the twenty-one miles of water of the Channel. It is indisputable that Flavius Afranius Sygagrius Aegidius was the ruler of the Seven Cities of Northern Gaul and for eight years also King of all the Franks. It would seem to be a straightforward matter to identify the correct recipient of the letter from Britain, who was apparently married to a British princess.

Obsessive Romanism gets in the way of sanity, however, and instead, English scholars nominate the enemy of the British in Aetius the Roman, as the person to whom the letter was sent. Now Aegidius, or Agitus, or Aganypus, is clearly Aegidius, and never Aetius. Matters have to be stretched to accommodate this peculiar attribution to Aetius to say the least. It also requires a total re-writing of

Chapter 13 - Evicting Roman Squatters

British history to make the ten million-strong, powerful British state somehow weak, and dependent upon the hated Romans.

This is where the confusions begin.

The early Welsh Annals have no dates and like the Anglo-Saxon Chronicles they were written retrospectively. So, the problem and the question is: when was Year 1 of the Annals? for all we have is Year 1, Year 2, Year 3, and so on. If the letter was sent to the unlikely Aetius, Consul of Rome, then Year 1 of the Annals is around AD 440, and all other events in the Welsh Annals are then dated in this sequence. If, however, the letter was sent to the powerful and most likely King Aegidius in Northern Gaul, then Year 1 of the Annals was *c.* AD 474. This means many things, not least that the great Arthurian Battle of Baedan did not take place in AD 517, but in AD 550 or later. The same applies to everything else; and the famous Battle of Camlan, ten miles south of Dollgelly, took place correctly around AD 570, which dating fits precisely with all the very many genealogies and histories associated with it.

The irrational academic obsession with the Romans, which ignores facts, evidence, records, and tangible remains, has disfigured and distorted ancient British history. This re-evaluation and correction of chronology eliminates a mass of chronological mismatches and re-establishes clarity in records. Unless it is understood that this irrational obsession with fake Roman history exists, then all efforts to study the perfectly clearly recorded fifth- and sixth-century Arthurian history will be continually frustrated.

The voyage of King Arthur II and his return home

It is a fact that débris from a great comet devastated Britain, and perhaps parts of Ireland, in the mid-sixth century AD, and that these vast devastations were directly associated with the European discovery of America. Chronological investigation places the date of the great disaster at AD 562.

Whether Prince Madoc, the Admiral, was at sea when the disaster struck Britain, or whether he sailed in a hopeful voyage to seek out a new homeland for the surviving British population, is yet to be finally decided. The phrase 'according to the ancients', which concerns the distant lands across the oceans, occurs in the *Prophecies of Eryr*. What appears to be certain is that King Arthur II son of Meurig was persuaded to summon an army and to assemble a fleet of seven hundred ships for an expedition, and to seize these vast, new, untouched, undeveloped lands. It is provable to the unbiased reader that Khumric scripts and artefacts are found in many areas of the East coasts, and the Mid-West of America. This volume exhibits a selection of these relics.

Alone amongst the nations of Western Europe, the British have preserved a detailed record of these voyages and discoveries. No other European nation has such an early record. From these ancient texts Wilson and Blackett found clear evidence of the assassination of King Arthur II, as described in the Khumric record. They found the story of his body being embalmed and wrapped, stored through the winter under a cliff overhang, and taken to an embarkation point in Yarmouth Bay in Nova Scotia.

In this way all the bits and pieces of the strange end of King Arthur, which appeared in poetic Romance tales in Western Europe some six or eight centuries after his death, now make sense. The notion of an aged, dying king sailing away across an unknown sea, accompanied by three queens in a mysterious boat, has firm roots. Three ladies of the Court washed and embalmed ('dry-withered') the body of the dead king, and they wrapped it in a leather bag made from three deerskins. This we learn from the entries in the repetitive ancient poetry. Possibly being unwilling to accept the stark and clear evidence in several very ancient poems, that King Arthur II left Britain by his own free will to migrate to another land, and was brought back home when dead, writers have dismissed these clear authentic ancient records as being 'mystical'. To admit the real evidence, which exists in abundance everywhere one looks, would also then compel recognition that King Arthur II was a Khumric-British King, and in the twentieth century the truth played very little part in the examination and exposition of ancient British history.

The mother of St Illtyd was Rhainguilda, or Gweryla, a sister of King Meurig-Maurice, the son of King Tewdrig-Theoderic. This makes St Illtyd and Arthur II first cousins. In the *Life of St Illtyd*, and also in Nennius's *Historia Britonorum* in the section of *The Marvels of Britain* (believed to be compiled *c.* 670 to 822), there is the account of a ship bringing the body of the dead king home:

> 'There is another wonderful thing in Guyr (now Ogwyr), an altar is in the place called Loyngarth (Llwyngarth) which is held up by the will of God. The story of that altar it seems to me better to tell than be silent. It happened when St Illtyd was praying in a cave, which is by the sea which washes the land above the said place, the mouth of the cave is towards the sea - that behold, a ship sailed towards the saint from the sea, and two men sailing in it. And the body of a holy man was with them in the ship and an altar above his face, which was

held up by the will of God. And the man of God (St Illtyd) went forth to meet them and the body of the holy man, and the altar was continuing inseparably above the face of the holy body. And they said to St Illtyd: "This man of God entrusted it to us that we should conduct him to thee, and that we should bury him with thee and that thou shouldst not reveal his name to any man, so that men shall not swear by him."'

And they buried him and after that burial the two men returned to the ship and set sail.

But that St Illtyd founded a church about the body of the holy man and about the altar and the altar held up by the will of God remains to this day.

There came a certain regulus (local sub-king) to make a test carrying a rod in his hand. He bent it around the altar and held the rod on either side with his two hands, and drew it towards him. And he tested the truth of the matter, and afterwards he did not live a full month. And another looked under the altar and he lost the sight of his eyes and he finished his course before a full month.

The place Loyngarth is Llyfngarth or Llwyngarth (there are differences in spelling in both Nennius' and St Illtyd's accounts), and it means 'smooth ridges' or 'sand dunes'. *The Life of St Illtyd* calls the area Lingarch, and as modern Llyfngarth this is a perfectly accurate description of the estuary of the Ewenny River in Ogwyr - 'Guyr' in the Manuscripts - where there is a considerable area of very large sand dunes. Other episodes in the *Lives of the Saints* give the location of St Illtyd's cave in the Coed-y-Mwstyr (Woods of Mystery) above the Ewenny river in Ogwyr. One story in the *Life of St Gildas* tells how Gildas cast a bell for St David, who was at Menevia, and the monks from Llancarfan Abbey, who were carrying the bell along the old main road, were heard by Illtyd, who came out of his cave to speak to them. The old road is now the modern M4 Motorway, and still passes close to the edge of the Coed-y-Mwstyr. Another story records Illtyd fleeing for his life from the soldiers of King Meurig and hiding in the cave. St Illtyd and St Cadoc had given absolution to the murderer of Prince Idnerth, a son of King Meurig, and a brother of King Arthur II and Prince Madoc Morfran, and Meurig Uthyrpendragon was infuriated with rage and grief.

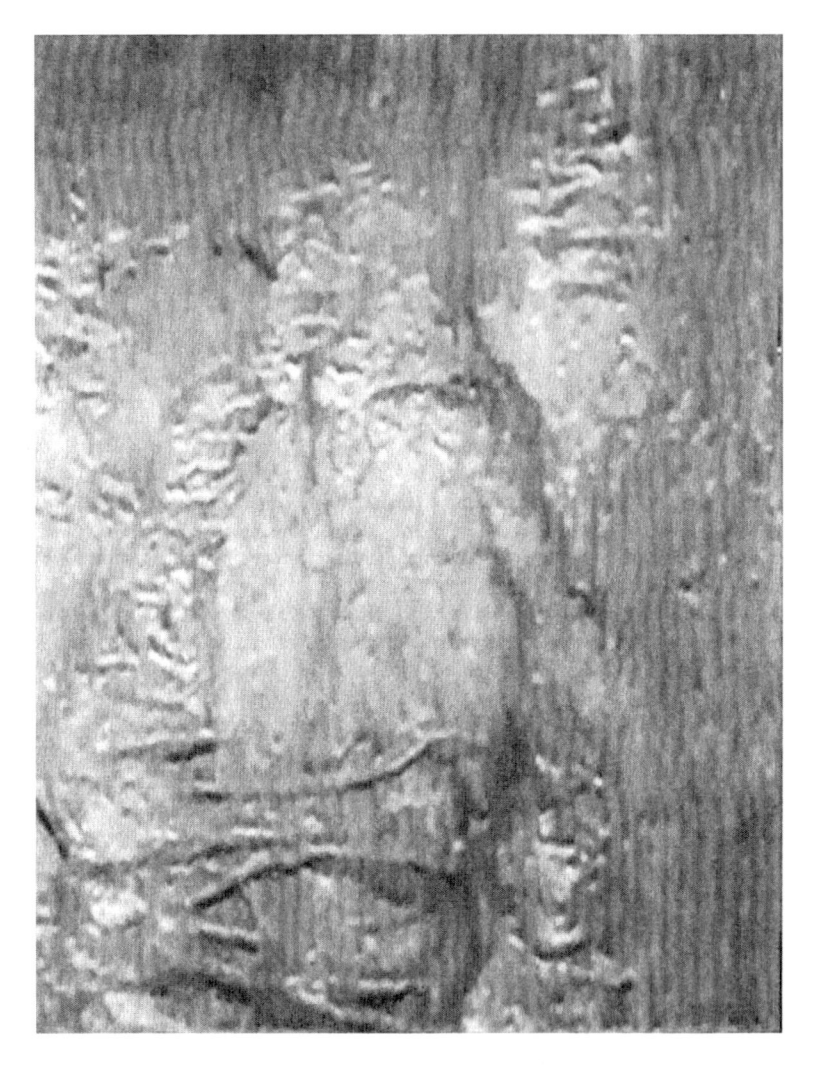

The Coed y Mwstyr Cave Inscriptions

Chapter 13 - Evicting Roman Squatters

The accounts in *The Life of St Illtyd*, and in Nennius, match with the accounts in the ancient and authentic *Gwarchan Maelderw* (*Incantation of the Druids*) and the *Addfwyneu Taliesin* (*The Courtesy of Taliesin*). In addition there is another clear account in the *Preiddeu Annwn - The Migration to the Other World*.

Early in their researches Alan and Baram had consulted books on caves in Wales, and found no mention of the Coed-y-Mwtsyr cave. First, they found two persons who were experts in the practice of caving. Both assured them that there could not be a cave in the Coed-y-Mwstyr area as the rock of the area was too hard for caves to be worn by water. So they drove down to Pencoed, at the north end of the woods, and asked the real experts, a gang of local children aged around ten to twelve years, who were playing football. They gave instant directions and good advice on how to get to the cave.

Old Mr Leyshon who lived in the bungalow near the farm gate was ninety-five years old around 1990, and his son Mr Leyshon was seventy-three, when on a visit to the farm old Mr Leyshon sat on the garden wall and told Alan and Baram that there was a cross cut into the roof of the cave above the grave-pit. He also stated that around 1920 there were no trees obstructing the view of the sea from the cave, and that the trees there were new and subsequent growth. The report of a mark like a cross cut in the rock over the grave-pit was in fact known to several of the older people in the area. Alan and Baram had already established from Ordnance Survey Maps that the estuary of the Ewenny meeting the Severn was visible from the cave if the tree growth of the past seventy years was eliminated.

The cave was actually sealed until modern times, and a Cardiff man made several Saturday visits in 1887, and with the aid of a local workman he drilled holes between the stones that were welded together by stalactite drips, and he carefully dynamited the entry open. He was hopefully seeking ancient fossils of cave bears, mammoths, hyenas, and so on, from huge antiquity, but he came up with nothing. He intended to return the next year, but failing health prevented this. Alan Wilson and Baram Blackett dug out the piled earth at the cave entry, as this was causing water falling from the cliff face above to run into the cave. Under the recent soil accumulation, they found the remains of the stalactite-welded wall that had been blasted open.

Some fifteen yards into the low, narrow entry of the cave, the passage widens out and the roof becomes much higher. Here they found a grave-pit lying across the cave floor west-to-east in Christian fashion. It is very obviously a man-made pit, with squared-off corners and straight edges, cut into the very hard stone of the cave. Just a few feet past the pit, the cave narrows to a passage of around eighteen inches in places for some twenty yards, before reaching a very large, high, round chamber. There is no other place available to cut out a grave-pit other than where it is. The pit is around ten to eleven feet long, some four feet wide and four feet deep. To test the rock, David Bushell set up a portable generator and used a heavy-duty power drill. He was hardly able to scratch the surface. The test was to prove that this pit was cut for someone very important, and that it required huge labour and effort to do it.

Some twenty-eight men worked a weekend to make a safe stairway of logs down the end of the cliff to allow easy access from the farm end, using a generator, and stringing up lighting in the cave. David Bushell erected a very strong steel gate about twelve feet inside the cave entry. Almost immediately vandal attacks began by angry and frustrated rival groups. It would have required sledge hammers and crowbars, and some strength and effort to destroy the steel gate, but it was broken down. The generator inside was smashed, the lighting was torn down, and filthy graffiti was painted all over the walls and on the cliff above the cave. The large letters S.C.F.C were in several places, and this is probably for Swansea City Football Club, an identification for Swansea-based people.

Finally, the vandals had filled the grave-pit with timber from the woods, and set it on fire, probably with inflammable fluids. This cracked and damaged the far (north) side of the grave-pit. This pattern of attacks from the Swansea area was to continue for years.

St Illtyd, as a close kinsman of King Arthur II, would be a natural choice to approach with the body of the dead King. This is as certain as anything can be, and a multiplicity of records all come together, and all point in the same direction. In fact, there is an entry in the Gwarchan Maelderw, which states that Taliesin and others were directed to convey the body of the dead King Arthur to St Illtyd. There was, however, a totally unexpected development which actually produced quite extraordinary tangible physical evidence. The almost immediate vandalisation of the lighting in the cave had made examination difficult, but Colin Games and Blair Urquhart, then at the Caerleon Film College, went to the cave to film the interior. They had the use of high-quality superior portable lighting, expensive cameras and other equipment, and high-quality film, available from the college.

When panning across the wall surfaces of the cave the camera caught what the human eye might have missed. The film definitely showed Coelbren writing on the rock above the grave-pit. The first letter does in fact closely resemble a cross. It was not until a year or two later that Martin Langford brought it to Alan's and Baram's attention that there might be writing revealed by the film, and so it turned out to be. There is an old statement in Khumric Coelbren written on the rock, and it is covered with a film of stalactite, which has run down and glazed over the surface. This means that the inscription is indisputably ancient.

The text reads that this is the place of the Bier or Crib where the 'dry-withered' (embalmed) 'highest ruler who was impotent' was placed. The frantic, and candidly quite ludicrous, counter-claims by anti-British academic that this extraordinary pit in the hardest of rocks was a ludicrous 'animal trap', are disposed of. The statement is as clear and as meaningful as that on any modern tombstone in any graveyard.

After tackling hundreds of inscriptions in Britain, Etruria, Rhaetia, Lemnos, Asia Minor, and America, Wilson and Blackett have the expertise to tackle this vital and even priceless inscription. They offer:

'the ashes the manger/crib the husk Uthyr = wonderful the spirit a groan/sigh to the ruler rightful lawful.'

'the lord high" (the High Lord) furthest/extremity.'

Whether Uthyr is intended as the title as in Uthyr-pen-dragon, or simply as its normal meaning of 'wonderful', is uncertain. Four Uthyrpendragons ('wonderful head of dragons') are known and two 'Dragons', making six in all.

Alan Wilson and Baram Blackett find that it is not possible to describe how they felt when they had photographs of the inscription lifted from the video tape by a company at Llanishen in Cardiff, and they were able to read the message. It was almost as if they felt that the message should have been expected to be there anyway. The immediate necessity was to impose secrecy and security, to try to ensure that this inscription was preserved from persons with sledge-hammers who would inevitably seek to protect their monopoly hold on huge government grants and public funds in Wales, and also vast tourism revenues elsewhere.

The situation was in fact absurdly simple. The many records were simply honest and accurate, straightforward accounts of the events which had occurred in British history.

If Arthur II dwelt in Cerniw, then that meant that he dwelt in Cerniw which is the area of Cardiff across to Newport in Gwent, and Cerniw is not Cornwall and never was. Coed Cerniw and Llangerniw are still marked on today's maps of Wales.

Evidence was littered everywhere. Down near the estuary of the Ewenny River is a church dedicated by St Illtyd. A number of very ancient stones lie there neglected under a rusting corrugated roof, and one (thought to be sixth-century) reads 'Pavli-fili Ma...' and is almost certainly St Pawl son of Meurig, another brother of Arthur II. St Pawl appears in several sixth-century Lives of Saints as 'King Poulentius'. This very ancient church of Merthyr Mawr – 'The Great Martyr' was demolished around 1850 and a new building erected alongside the ancient site. This has left the grave and effigy of a king out in the open and exposed to the elements. Formerly this would have been in the centre of the ancient church and protected by the building.

The migration to Annwfn: 'Preiddau Annwfn'

The chaos and confusions which reign in ancient British historical studies have already been explained, and forgers like the incredible J. Gwenogfran Evans, his disciple Griffith John Williams, and their followers have been allowed to run riot. Inventors including the Rev Robert Williams, and the chemist Thomas Stephens, have obliterated and deformed at will. The long-suffering British have been left with their clear and precise Dark Age history thrown into a complete muddle and confusion.

It is necessary to restate this, or readers may wonder how and why Alan Wilson and Baram Blackett can discover and reveal what they do in the manner in which they do. Wilson and Blackett have an unusual set of rules for dealing with the Dark Age historical records, and their methods differ markedly from those of the demolition experts at the Universities and other institutions.

The rules are these:

1- **Take the texts from the oldest surviving copies of manuscripts available.**

2- **Do not alter anything: no editing, no revisions.**

3- **Do not delete anything, and do not add anything.**

4- **Translate with the oldest known archaic words, and translate literally.**

5- **Make no attempt to produce sweet-sounding poetry in English, or even perfect syntax or sense from ancient Khumric poetry.**

6- **Compare difficult words with the same words in other manuscripts or sources in different contexts to establish meanings.**

Chapter 13 - Evicting Roman Squatters

In short, take the surviving evidence exactly as it is, with no tampering.

Industrial techniques of analysis are then employed. No attempt is made to make anything fit into or to conform to a preconceived scenario. The assumption that alone amongst the nations of Planet Earth our British ancestors conspired together to produce a cleverly written vast series of inventions and interlocking forgeries, and that for a thousand years thousands of them lied, fabricated, distorted, and invented, is in itself the lie. Our British ancestors wrote down the truth as they knew it, and kept records as honourably as they could.

Modern Don Quixotes and their Sanchos, revelling in the limelight of sensationalism and their ability to shock the public by 'exposing' non-existent forgeries and forgers, can be seen to be shallow men of no worth or substance. This simple method, of reading the preserved records, works, and the mysteries alleged to surround King Arthur I, King Arthur II, Prince Madoc, Taliesin-Merlyn, and all the others, causes the former to evaporate and disappear. All that is required is to read the records set down by our forefathers and to follow the trails along which they lead us.

There is no need to 'edit' anything, or to alter or re-write, or to change anything. It is simply important to note **(1) what is said, (2) who said it, (3) when it was said, and (4) in what context was it said.** That is all there is to do.

In the case of the *Preiddeu Annwfn*, one of the best-known of ancient British historical poems, the first thing, as always, is to read the title. It is constructed from 'preiddio', meaning 'to migrate', and 'deu', which means 'to come to, to arrive'. Then Annwfn (often spelled Annwn) means either 'the other world' or 'the great deep', and which are meanings which fit the Americas as 'the other world' and the Atlantic Ocean as 'the great deep'. This title obviously meaning 'The migration to arrive in the Other World' is similar to the Spanish calling the Americas 'The New World'.

By no way or stretch of the imagination does the title 'Preiddeu Annwfn' mean 'the Voyage to Hell', or 'the Return from Hades', as one over-imaginative and hugely inaccurate Oxford professor averred. Naturally he received a knighthood. Nor does 'Preiddeu Annwfn' mean 'King Richard's Voyage to Acre and Joppa' as the fraudulent J. Gwenogfran Evans stated. Evans pretended that this sixth-century record was a thirteenth-century AD poem, and he falsified the text to the extent of including the name of Saladin, the opponent of Richard I of England, in a one of his many monumental displays of academic chicanery and duplicity. The idea that a voyage across the Atlantic by Arthur II, and his bard Taliesin, could ever become a voyage through the Mediterranean six hundred years later by Richard I - who is not named - is stupefying.

The poem was written by Taliesin ap Henwg, who was the Chief Bard to Arthur, and in it, Taliesin clearly states that he made the voyage with Arthur. He recounts that seven persons were sent on a mission of a return trip back to Britain. This is a real-life voyage and not a poetic flight of fancy or imagination. The text reads:

1- I will praise the sovereign, the supreme King of the Land (Arthur),

2- Who has extended his domain over the shore of the world (America).

3- It came to pass with the fouled ploughland of the fortress of the zodiac (the comet disaster, and other detail research shows that Britain is the Fortress of the Zodiac),

4- Through the covering over by the colt (comet) of Saturn and Jupiter (Pryderi),

5- Somebody before, in a restive state, he what is impending, he went into it,

6- Who to stay migrated to arrive in Annwn, hard what stretches out to be born,

7- And his brother (Madoc?) lasted easily as in bardic poetry afterwards.

8- Three full seasons fair the went into it, because of (us),

9- Except seven, we to draw near from the fortress revolving (the Earth spins),

10- To wish for earnestly I am, to carouse, to come together, a desire the art of poetry, alas to be heard true.

11- In the fortress quarters, at the feet towards the dispenser,

12- In it to frequent the horizon immeasurable, whence to talk,

13- From the breath of nine seas rage cold ancestors,

14- To wish for, to cause the Head of Annwn in an advanced position, a

Chapter 13 - Evicting Roman Squatters

                nod/gesture,

15-   Strong valiant with his utterances to become pearls,

16-   We judge food apt to go off, anathema to a she-goat,

17-   The sword flashing, a slaughter pungent, freedom the least that may be.

18-   And in the hand of the leaping one the velocity/speed well done,

19-   And the entrance door portals of Uffern (hell) a beam of light burns,

20-   And when he went, we with Arthur, the business of overlaying and draining.

If we pause at this point, we see that we have arrived at the point where Taliesin informs us that Arthur is dead. His body has been covered over, and 'drained' or dried out of fluids embalmed. This is called 'dry-withered' in other sources. The opening line tells us that the King of Britain has extended his dominion across the very horizons – 'the shore of the world' - and the reason is stated in Line 4 where the Colt (Comet) of Saturn has overlaid the land with mud. A survey of place names in Wales reveals numbers of names associated with such mud. Somebody, presumably Madoc, went into Annwfn previously, and stayed and survived there, and this somebody is described as a brother of the king in Line 7, which confirms that he is Madoc.

Arthur the King was in Annwfn for three years – 'three full seasons fair' - and now just seven persons accompany him back home. The writer longs to be safe in a fortress, sitting at the feet of his lord in his hall, to tell him of the nine seas and their limitless wastes and immeasurable oceans. Nostalgia brings him to long for a gesture of approval from his dead lord (line 14), and he tells of rotten food which had gone off – 'anathema to a she-goat' - and of the 'leaping one', probably a porpoise. King Arthur is dead, and his body is drained and wrapped. And so, the poem continues:

21-   'Except seven we draw near from the outward fortress without denial,

22-   Longing I am for carousal, shelter, desire for the art of poetry, the ruler of musicians,

23- In the fortress of the four quarters of the world, the door of strength encloses,

24- To be still, with rapid motion co-mixtured, again a rupture,

25- To struggle, their spirit was as liquor in the van of his retinue.

26- Three full seasons fair he went around us, upon the open plough land a passage,

27- We beneath heaven, the manslayer disciplined, directing what is essential,

28- Across the fort wall of him, behold they are refused progress by Arthur.'

Much hinges on how 'he' is identified. 'He' appears to be the Native Americans who for three years went across open ploughland in their nomadic peregrinations. They are like liquid before the vanguard of Arthur's soldiers, under Arthur's direction of disciplined warfare. Finally they are refused passage beyond the fortress walls.

29- 'Three twenties of slingers established thou on the wall,

30- It was inopportune; his watch was mutually subdivided,

31- Three seasons fullness fair because of Arthur for fair corn he went.

32- Except seven to draw near from the fortress of wealth,

33- We beneath heaven, to the disciplined manslayer, them circling,

34- We with tenacity, what is involved, all day hold the advanced position,

35- What hour that fine day the hold fell.

36- To batter, to execute upon what is impending, he went to form a ring as is customary.'

Here we have the core of the Arthurian drama, for we are told how sixty slingers were stationed on the fortress walls, and by misfortune or bad luck the watch was somehow divided. The native Americans it seems were after the corn crops, and standing fields of crops cannot be protected from behind fortress walls.

Chapter 13 - Evicting Roman Squatters

We, the British 'beneath heaven', or perhaps 'at heaven's mercy', the native Americans circling around, and the manslayer Arthur is containing the position by disciplined tactics. Then the poem tells how at an unknown hour, on an unknown fine day, the fortress which they had built, fell. Arthur then went to form a defensive ring or perimeter, and so this long-forgotten battle in ancient Kentucky is being laid out before us.

37- Hurtful they to the dun ox, fat his head to excess,

38- Seven twenties of knuckles on his collar.

39- And fur.'

It may be that the Native Americans are following a buffalo herd, for the dun-coloured ox, with the large head and a hundred and forty whorls or knuckles of hair forming its mane or collar of fur, is undoubtedly the North American buffalo.

39- 'And fur, grief because we with Arthur's unsuccessful visit

40- Except seven to draw near from the fortress of covering the Ruler.

41- We beneath heaven, (with) the disciplined manslayer, directing his bier,

42- Hurtful they of what is involved to hold a perilous day to end,

43- At what hour in that fine day the holding of possession,

44- When in grief we with Arthur unsuccessful formerly old,

45- Except seven we draw near to the fortress of the essential spirit's side.'

In grief because of the tragic end to the migration adventure for Arthur. The seven are coming from the fort where the ruler was covered over, or wrapped up embalmed. They are directing the bier of the 'disciplined manslayer', and they are drawing close to the side or edge of the fortress of the Essential Spirit. As the ship may have arrived at the Ewenny river estuary, we have 'ew' for 'what glides', and 'eni' for 'to exert the soul'. This may be a reference to a 'Holy Ghost' concept.

46- 'Monks carried the leader to the closure of the circle (choir).

47- From over against to them dried withered at break of day,

48- Which one journeyed the wind, this one the seas waters,

49- One for whom the humble heaped a fire of medium stature,

50- Monks carried the son of the wolf,

51- From the battle dried withered unto them with difficulty.

52- We twisted in cloth, who cast off foreseeing the break of day,

53- To hope for the wind long-tedious beating his not many (= few followers),

54- What is enveloped/wrapped is blameless, what is involved,

55- Is necessary for against plague.

56- From the grave of the blameless saint, to the grave at the altar.

57- Bound up is the Legate, the great noble gentleman,

58- Not to weigh the sadness of Christ with denial.'

The language is archaic, and some of the words may be open to differing interpretation as a result, but the main bulk of the story remains the same. Suffice it to show how the Rev Robert Williams should have translated Line 46:

'Monks howled like dogs in a kennel', whereas it actually reads 'Monks carried the leader to the closure of the choir/circle.'

The Incantation of the Druids - Gwarchan Maelderw

The extent of the political difficulties confronting Alan and Baram are nothing if not enormous. The academic stance is that there are very few accounts of King Arthur, and whether 'he' is two persons rolled into one is never discussed. That he was Arthur I son of Magnus Maximus, and Arthur II son of Meurig, welded together into one giant figure, is not even suspected, and if it is, then it is never discussed or debated. The few scraps of evidence which are accepted on 'King Arthur' are the scant mentions in the *Annals of Arthur* at the Battle of Baedan, and at the Battle of Camlann, along with the strange assertion of a misread one-line mention in the *Songs of the Graves*. There is also the entry in *Caradoc of Llancarfan*, which laments the neglect of Arthur I's grave in the great graveyard of the illustrious of the British in Glastennen/Glastonbury, near Lichfield.

The idea that there is virtually no evidence of Arthur and his burial is firmly rooted. By stark contrast Alan Wilson and Baram Blackett are exhibiting that both the Arthurs are very well recorded, and copiously described in a multiplicity of authentic ancient texts. In fact, Arthur I and Arthur II had what are easily the best recorded funerals in the Dark Age history of Britain if not all Western Europe. It is simplicity itself to see that the alleged vague one-line entry in the *Songs of the Graves* is nonsense. The great kings and princes get one three-line verse each, or if very important they get two, or even three, three-line verses to describe their grave sites. So immediately we have to ask what happened to the other two lines, or the second, third, and fourth verses?

In fact, Verses 42, 43, 44, and 45 all deal with the burial of Arthur II, who died *c.* AD 579. There are long and detailed accounts of Arthur II's death and funeral, and there is an unavoidable confrontation between the position of the academics ("There is little or no evidence") and Wilson and Blackett's presentation that there is a wealth of evidence in abundance.

The simplest example of misreading is perhaps the Rev. Robert Williams' comic 'bet elchuith', which he claimed meant 'the grave of Elchuith', when in fact it reads as 'An extremely windy grave'. The Rev Robert Williams dictat that there was only one line reading, 'anoeth bit bed y Arthur', meaning 'concealed for ever is the grave of Arthur' is a total nonsense. What we have is:

Verse 44
Bet y March, bet y guythur,
The grave of the Knight (Arthur) the grave of the wrathful one (Arthur),

Bet y Gugawn Cletyfrut,
The grave of the angry red sword (Arthur).

A Noeth bid bet y Arthur,
A bare/exposed place is the grave of Arthur.

Verse 45
Bet Elchuith yn gulich glaw,
A grave extremely windy in a narrow flat place,

Maes Mevetauc y danaw,
The field of the Helpless error the Reproach,

Dyliei Cynon yno y cunaw,
The duty of the chiefs to bear him thither.

The reader will be spared the rest of the Rev Williams' 1869 translations. In this reading 'maes' = 'field'. 'Mevetauc' is a difficult name, which is important, as the field named is the exact place of Arthur II's burial. It seems to be either 'methdigaeth', or 'medd-digaeth', where 'meth' = 'error or failure', or 'medd' = 'drunken' and 'digaeth' = 'helpless or unconfined'.

If we add the description to 'the place of reproach', we undoubtedly have the location at Caer Caradoc where three hundred and sixty-three British leaders were massacred at a Peace Conference *c.* AD 456. The British leaders got very drunk and the Saxons had brought concealed weapons with them, and the event became known as the 'Place of Reproach' elsewhere in epic record. With every other source pointing towards Caer Caradoc on Mynydd-y-Gaer, it was a simple matter of consulting the local tithe maps where every field is listed by a number, its acreage, tithe values, and also by its name in Wales.

The *Gwarchan Maelderw – Incantation of the Druids*, attributed to Taliesin the Chief Court Bard of Arthur II, is but one of several such sources of detailed accounts. This historical poem is of 321 lines, and it is hardly insignificant in both size and content. The poem describes the ancient disasters that struck Britain and ruined the Arthurian Dynasty. In Khumric form it has a typical triad triple structure, which links together

1- the disastrous massacre around AD 456, that took place at the Caer Caradoc Peace Conference, where the Saxons sued for peace and then brought concealed weapons to the conference and murdered some three hundred and eighty-three British leaders,

2- the catastrophe of the near-total destruction of Britain by the comet débris *c.* AD 562 and

3- the disaster of the assassination of Arthur II in AD 579.

The *Gwarchan Maelderw* tells of many things. It describes Arthur's voyage, of his search for new lands, of native peoples attempting to steal the standing corn crops, of battles and defences, and of the assassination of Arthur by a naked savage. The detail is extraordinary and it is specifically stated that Arthur's bones were transported back across the oceans to St Illtyd to whom this mission is directed. There is mention of a temporary grave place, obviously in America, which is traceable. There are statements of 'doing with leather', and the dead king's dried-out remains were made ready for the long journey home by wrapping them in a leather deerskin sack, made by three noble ladies of his court. Madoc's absence

Chapter 13 - Evicting Roman Squatters

for ten years without harm is specified as are his antecedents. The fleet of seven hundred ships assembled at Dau Gleddyf is described; and so the three entwined tragedies are dealt with in detail, down to Hengist's one blue eye, and the drunken stupidity of Trahaearn (Gwrtheyrn-Vortigern).

There are passages that describe the track of the comet, or whatever it was, and the parts played by Mars and Mercury, and then Saturn in this cosmic disaster. The nature of the disaster it caused is also described, and this has to be one of Britain's most important historical records.

Taliesin begins the *Gwarchan Maelderw - Incantation of the Druids* with:

'I have been with a space parted off. In the land of battles coming forward.' Therefore, he has been out of Britain. Then: 'We, a number separated, overgrown what it is, human flesh, whether flesh or fish, I towards it have been without irony. Pure all faith-the-foundation', which may read as 'A number of us were separated in what is an overgrown place. Human flesh or whether it is flesh or fish, I have been towards it without irony. All pure faith is the foundation.'

It is clear that this is a hugely personal statement from a man who has been sorely tried and who has seen wonders. Taliesin had risen to be Chief Bard in the court of Arthur II, King of Britain, and then he had seen the great island country devastated beyond human belief by the shattering impacts of the missiles in the shape of comet débris from the skies. He describes himself: 'For I am Merlyn and men shall call me Taliesin'; and the copious records indicate that this tiny man was regarded as a sage. He was a son of St Henwg, and a younger man than Arthur II. This basic truth of course is contrary to the English children's fables about 'King Arthur' in which Merlyn is portrayed as older and taller than a young Arthur, whereas the reverse is the case.

That Taliesin has been beyond the limits of the known geography of Western Europe and the known view of the heavens at night as seen from Western Europe is clear.

Line 7-   I with reliance continuously (with) the segregated brothers, (emigrants)

    8-   Ploughlands the visage of earth's opportunity, (the vast American expanses) I have been in the chair of the boundary (of Earth = America)

9- I have been in the chair of the boundary (or Earth = America)

10- Above the revolving fortress (the wheeling Zodiac and stars)

11- With those absent in the roll of faith (the emigrant expedition).

There is later a reference to Lliwlod's persuasions which encouraged Arthur II to mount the expedition to North America.

13- When wonderfully fresh the segregation

14- Than not upon to be brought forth in being,

15- The man with pervading quality whence to discourse (Lliwlod).

The beginning of the expedition is described:

20- We (nyth-pure) armed and outwards,

21- Having no mind impulsive (other than) the fat (land) to enclose

Then the reason for leaving is given:

24- Not day land to leave utterly with the request of reward the reason,

25- Upon (it) the red dragon has made mud upon the high places,

26- To go astray an element a blast of wind the flowing together of atoms and particles,

27- With force/rapidity and somebody tenacious his life pure,

28- Upon the plough land the horizon turns the faculties to make fair to display,

29- Carried in a cart he, the retinue great (as) firm ash-trees (= ash spears)

A survey of areas of Wales shows a remarkable preponderance of names with 'mud' associations and contents in several areas, many of which are high mountain areas.

Then the *Gwarchan Maelderw* relates how an opening or pass is sought, 'hunted for', to get through to the ploughland plains, and there is one strange line in the poem. This reads 'Budic o reu eny Annuad Wledig', and appears to cite Prince Budic of Amorica, who certainly was in South Wales and left the famous 'Bodvoc' stone, now at Margam Abbey.

It could mean 'Budic to move vigorously Amlodd Wledig', but the word 'buddig' means 'victorious', and 'annawd' means 'infrequently'. That Amlodd Wledig was an ancestor of the Prince Budic is fairly certain.

There were contentious quarrels as how to proceed and acrimony over the need and objectives of the expedition in Lines 36 to 40:

40-   'And the flowing fair aspect of face the heir apparent,

41-   Upon a course to explore a way partly to spread around good profit.'

There follows a description of the heat and sunshine and uphill movements, and then there is:

45-   'Barleycorn overgrown wild to make drunk with joy/gladness,

46-   Northwards lavishly he supreme lord in excess,

47-   Ears of corn because/for to discourse to return.'

Then there is a strange passage that tells of the elevation of 'the stripling' to the throne, and a telling reference to the attempted election of Maelgwn Gwynedd as king in Britain, arranged by Ugnach. It seems that this passage is being written for an informed audience, and there is mention of 'unnatural lust', which again seems to refer to Maelgwn Gwynedd. Then there is mention of the difficulty in the passage of the seas with the Knight and what appears to the death of the Knight.

69-   The Knight to penetrate with protection from affliction.

70-   Three white wreaths of gold the shirt of command holy,

71-   A native defending a conflict it came to pass to stab to pierce through.

72-   Dusky/swarthy in excess of killing, long tedious they slaughter them.

73-   And journey to the horizon (with) honour in faith (Christianity).

74- Weak wanting what is essential the beat/throb (= pulse) they listened.'

So, it appears that Arthur II had been struck down by a dark-skinned man, possibly after removing his golden armour, and his followers are searching and listening for his heartbeat and pulse. Lines 85 to 102 tell the story of how there is fighting as Native Americans apparently seek to raid the crops being raised on the plough lands. The assassin is described as creeping round to the rear through thickets without causing alarm and with one well-aimed thrust of a lance committing the murder. Then the assassin seeks to hasten away whilst there is uproar in the camp.

In the *Gwarchan Maelderw* the fact that Arthur was killed abroad and brought back home in a boat by seven persons is made very clear, as is the fact that his desiccated corpse was placed in a leather sack made of deerskins. Line 185 summarises this:

185- 'One standing insult to fill up a sack, seven of us, gloom upon the basted stitch.'

Madoc is actually named as making his voyages and Gwenun is cited as sailing to confirm Madoc's findings. The origin, the course, and the direction of the object that shattered Britain, are described in a remarkable passage. The nature of the pieces and particles which struck Britain are also clearly described. Detail upon

Chapter 13 - Evicting Roman Squatters

detail is laid out in this remarkable poem. There is actually a statement that Arthur's body was directed to be brought to Glamorgan, to St Illtyd, a former military commander and a first cousin of Arthur:

102-	'Covering a being essential in the course of,
103-	The bones the holy journey, to go to cast a splendour the servant we pine not shirking our journey.
104-	A present state to render, timely the bracelets of the leader,
105-	Whence to fetch to carry from the ocean the leader in time that may be sent.
106-	He the follower wincing, the man, the gold wreath wearer,
107-	Him to give a bright shape, pure, the hero's protective guard,
108-	To manage to contain on the hero respect,
109-	A mission necessary-essential to Illtyd the Knight.'

Three hundred gold-wearing mayors, or rulers, gather for Arthur's funeral, which soon takes on the guise of one of the best-recorded funerals of the Dark Ages. As stated at length in *Artorivs Rex Discovered* and in *The Holy Kingdom*, there are detailed records in the *Life of St Illtyd*, and in Nennius, of a ship arriving at the mouth of the Ewenny River in Glamorgan at Llwyngarth - Smooth Ridges, an area of giant sand dunes. Two noblemen from the ship convey to St Illtyd at his cave in 'Coed-y-Mwstyr', the 'Woods of Mystery', the embalmed body of a very holy man. This body is then interred in a pit in the cave, and later transferred for burial elsewhere. Here in the *Gwarchan Maelderw* is corroboration of the accounts in St Illtyd's *Life* and in Nennius' *History*.

It is no accident that the St Peter's super Montem church area is called Llanbad Fawr, which means the 'Great Ship's Rowing Boat'. There is even a description of the burial of the King, which is extensive to the point of being exhaustive. For example:

| 130- | Star knowledge (navigation skills) to endure to reach the waves/billows. |
| 131- | Before somebody the face kind pray for what is enveloped (wrapped in the leather sack) |

132-   Debased from one who demands of rulers/mayors is the First Chief enclosed.

And so the entwined story rambles on with passages on the Caer Caradoc massacre c. AD 456, and then switching back to Madoc and the comet of c. AD 562.

172-   Blasting/hurting the antecedents of Madawc, the   Earth/world,

173-   When ten salutations nesting time, a duration of life without harm (Madwac was away for ten years as this states.)

The tale goes on entwining the three disasters of the massacre, the comet, and the death of Arthur II (and presumably much of the army) in America. There is as stated a passage describing the origin and nature of the heavenly object that caused the huge devastations in Britain and parts of Ireland. Then follows a description of the nature of the devastations and plagues that emanated from this unearthly body and what followed this vast catastrophe.

As will be seen there are persistent corroborations in all the ancient records of King Arthur II ap Meurig's death, embalming, transport, and arrival home for burial. The king's body is always dried out, and placed in a leather bag made of the skins of three female deer, and accounts mention bracelets, gold armour, a gold face mask, and so on. The king was assassinated by a young man who is described as a naked savage, and this hardly fits a European or British scenario. The body is kept in an overhang, a 'bargod', during winter and brought home by sea in the summer.

The long poem ends with a statement that it is best to let America lie, partitioned off, waiting for the future:

317-   'To assuage the outcry for the Bear (Arthur) fierce and cruel,

318-   Upon him heaping up greatly flowers in the place of sailing sobbing.

319-   Long the host bowed it came to pass to snatch the son of the fair one on parting

320-   For the sake of not base origin, to bleach the whole well beloved,

321-   Of pure descent, joyful of a partition, let it be profitable to

Chapter 13 - Evicting Roman Squatters

lie in wait without.'

As might have been anticipated a Scottish lecturer at Cardiff University began loudly objecting that Wilson and Baram Blackett were incapable of translation. This man was not Welsh, and had no qualification in history, certainly none in Welsh history. He could not speak, read, or understand Welsh himself, but he also had the massive advantage of being Scots. So, Terry De Lacey, a television producer and director for thirty-one years, set up a trial. After a meal, Baram and Alan sat one side of a long table, and a seventy-one-year-old lecturer in Welsh sat on the other armed with a mass array of large dictionaries. Terry De Lacey sat one end of the table with a typewriter, and Ray Hudson sat at the other end as a witness.

It was agreed to take the last twelve lines of the *Preiddiau Annwn* poem as the trial piece. The old gentleman opened by saying that Wilson and Blackett were 100% incorrect in their translation. Then they all began taking one word at a time and discussing it. This laborious effort went on for three hours, and finally on seeing what had emerged, the lecturer agreed that Wilson and Blackett were 95% correct. Alan Wilson then said: "That makes all these other guys 95% incorrect." The point was that the lecturer had never questioned the supposed accuracy of the translations of ancient texts, which are constantly regurgitated as dinosaurs in print.

What is tragic is that the Welsh Office has set up a committee to construct a vast new Welsh Dictionary. This committee is blithely including all this garbage from the Rev Robert Williams and others into these new authoritative tomes, and perpetuating these nonsenses with a stamp of approval. Alan Wilson often says that he has been in many towns and cities, and in the squares, parks, and museums, but he has never seen a statue of a committee. The best committee is three persons, two of whom are perpetually absent.

Arthur's return from Eryr in Taliesin's Addfwyneu

This poem is Taliesin's account of how he brought King Arthur II's embalmed corpse back across the oceans from Eryr =America. In pairs almost every two lines begin with '1. Brought back...', and '2, Another brought back...', and everything in this poem of fifty-eight lines tells of this bringing back of the desiccated body of Arthur ap Meurig.

The poem opens with:

1- 'Brought back a virtue excess penance to ask earnestly.

2-   Another brought back wherefore robed in God here redeemed,

3-   Brought back of necessity an ardent desire a refusal of equal rank.

4-   Another brought back (who) from the horn drank mutually.

5-   Brought back (through) fog/mist the chief wolf of heaven.'

Lines 11 and 12 are more explicit:

11-   'Brought back the knight who desired to share a wilderness.

12-   Another brought back (across) the great flood it is daring adventurous.

13-   Brought back (from) beyond the horizon and opening wealthy with husbandry.

14-   Another brought back thy fair passage the seas through."

15-   Brought back from Eryr to the churchyard on the shore where is the estuary.'

As Taliesin was the Chief Court Bard of Arthur ap Meurig it is fairly obvious that the knight being brought back across the 'great flood' or the ocean, is Arthur. Eryr, or 'towards that which is beyond', is America, and 'the estuary' is that of the River Ewenny where the account in Nennius and the *Life of St Illtyd* specify that the embalmed corpse was brought to St Illtyd the first cousin of King Arthur ap Meurig.

17-   'Brought back the Knight upon golden armour bearing.'

Line 17 illustrates that the corpse is dressed in the King's golden armour in order to identify the embalmed and withered body beyond all question. Next come a statement of the wait for the best weather to cross the Atlantic from North America:

21-   Brought back in May me very carefully and he the challenge

22-   Another brought back whence reliance to change the weather is more feasible.

Then there comes a statement confirming the wrapping of the corpse in a leather bag:

25-   Brought back in mind with atonement to give extreme unction,

Chapter 13 - Evicting Roman Squatters

26- Another brought back conveying the leather bag.'

This intention is further confirmed:

29- 'Brought back to lay prostrate hymn-singing in the church,

30- Another courteous of his spirit he in the large grave room,

31- Brought back to the community to receive the ruler.'

There follow statements of 'summer with slow/mild long days', and the bringing back of the corpse to 'the projecting ridge'. All this is reinforced:

39- 'Brought back to a solitary spot in deerskin (hind or doe) and salved/embalmed.

40- Another faced foaming spume around apt to overtop conical/towering.

41- Brought back from an encampment whence to prosper turned mouldy the intellect

42- Another brought back fringed in dread doing with (= wrapped) in leather,

43- Brought back to society the King.'

So, the Knight who is brought back salved and embalmed in a leather sack is identified as the King, and Taliesin was Chief Court Bard to King Arthur IL The poem is so explicit that it is impossible for the statements that are being made to be simply misinterpreted.

46- 'Another (= Taliesin) brought back applied with salve perfect, ('cymman' = 'perfect')

47- Brought back (from) the heath where faith is empty,

48- Another brought back to the sea brink (Ewenny estuary) to keep at home,'

That the King is brought back as a corpse is emphasised by

53- 'Brought back as a fish in his proceeding governance,

54-   Another brought back the clamour of the sword stilled/placid.'

In short, the King lies in the bottom of the boat like a dead fish that has been caught, and his sword is stilled and will play no part in any future battles.

So, we have a poem of fifty-eight lines, which tells of the bringing home across the oceans of a dead king who is also styled as 'the Knight'. The person in charge of conveying the salved and embalmed corpse is none other King Arthur II's own Chief Bard, which dates the event and identifies the dead king. The king is dressed in his golden armour and is wrapped in a leather deerskin bag. He is buried besides, or close to, a large and isolated church, the ship arrives at the estuary of the River Ewenny, and the person to receive the corpse is St Illtyd, a first cousin of King Arthur II.

There is no question of the identity of this king who died and was conveyed home to Britain across the foaming oceans. The repetitive allegations which flow from academia that there is little or no information surviving on 'King Arthur' when in fact there is a near superabundance on both Arthur I ap Mascen Wledig and Arthur II ap Meurig, have to be ranked as either the greatest known display of near-total incompetence, or alternatively the most insolent and audacious political and academic falsehood ever perpetrated. It demonstrates the fate of small nations that are swallowed up by less civilised, larger, and more aggressive nations. One lie has to be covered with a larger lie, and in turn that needs concealment by yet another larger falsehood, and so the corruption grows until it is out of control.

The positive point is that with the graves of both King Arthur II and his father King Meurig now known, and with the grave of King Tewdrig definitely identified by excavations in 1609 and 1881, there is the possibility of linked DNA tracing. In addition, the grave mound of Bedd Morgan Mwynfawr, the successor of Arthur II and either a son of Arthur II or of his brother Madoc, is also known in Glamorgan.

Then there is another exciting prospect, for there may be a scrap of deerskin surviving in Arthur II's burial place. It might be possible to DNA-test for a Mid-West American deerskin and not a British or European animal type. As pollen is virtually indestructible in the normal course of events, there is again another possibility that pollen from the Mid-West of America is in Arthur II's grave, having been carried there on the deerskin. This may be a remote possibility, but one worth seeking. It is for these and other reasons that Alan Wilson and Baram Blackett never touch any these hidden sites that they discover.

Duhuddiant Elphin, or *The Consolation of Elphin*

The Consolation of Elphin is yet another clear and detailed account, in a poem of a hundred and twenty-eight lines, of the bringing home of the embalmed corpse of King Arthur ap Meurig across the oceans. The text links together the triple tragedies of the massacre of the leaders at Caer Caradoc, the destructions caused by the comet débris, and the death of King Arthur II in his overseas venture. A parallel is drawn between the treacherous eruption of the Saxons and the shock of the impacts of the asteroids or comet débris on Britain.

The king involved in the bartering with Hengist the Saxon is correctly named in Line 14 as 'Cynan ap Bran II'. This King Cynan ap Bran II was the brother of the deposed Edric ap Bran II and of Trahaearn ap Bran, who is better known as Vortigern or Gwrtheyrn.

11-	'Towards a summons (to) the strong place,
12-	Before the Battle Sovereign,
13-	When to escape ceased full of energy.

14- Upon Cynan ap Bran,'

Tutuwlch, or Kfog Teithfallt, is several times mentioned in his role as the restorer of Britain around AD 456-466. The majority of the poem concerns the massacre at Caer Caradoc; the mentions of the western oceans are drawn in as comparisons.

Locating Caer Caradoc

It was a matter of constant concern and surprise to Alan Wilson and Baram Blackett to be continually confronted with an almost total lack of any previous serious research into the identification of named ancient British sites of importance. Vague guesses and unfounded speculation were normally the order of the day.

The famous Arthurian battlefields of Llongborth, Camlann, and Mynydd Baedan were all the subjects of imaginative, random speculation. Yet all these three sites are easily traceable on modern government Ordnance Survey maps, which must be a cause for academic embarrassment. In the same way, no one seriously thought of properly identifying the often-mentioned Caer Effrawg, which was guessed as being York. Caer Effrawg is named in contexts that make it seem to be the Roman-British capital city. York, however, was the Roman Eboracum, and Caer Effrawg appears to mean 'the castle of the Hebrews', which brings echoes of the Brutus migration of the Ten Tribes into Britain. Caer Effrawg is very likely Uriconium, also known as Viroconium, or Wroxeter, which great city was virtually obliterated by the comet disaster of AD 562.

The most important of all the ancient British sites requiring identification, however, is Caer Caradoc. A number of important events took place at Caer Caradoc, and the lack of traceable efforts in attempting any identification is extraordinary. St Peter's church is said to have stood at Caer Caradoc, and there is a very ancient St Peter's church on Mynydd-y-Gaer, or Fortress Mountain, above Brynna in Glamorgan. At the highest point of this mountain lies the grave mound of Twyn Caradoc, presumably the tumulus grave of King Caradoc I ap Arch, who fought the Romans from AD 42 to 51. After the infamous Peace Conference Massacre c. AD 456, King Teithfallt buried the three hundred and sixty-three murdered British leaders in a circular monument called Mynwent y Milwyr at Caer Caradoc, and on the second highest point of the Mynydd y Gaer are the visible ruins of a circular monument that is still called Mynwent y Milwyr.

'Caer' means there had to be a fortress, and just a hundred and fifty yards north

Chapter 13 - Evicting Roman Squatters

of St Peter's church, there are the remains of very thick ancient walls and circular gate towers. Then there are numbers of ancient records that state that there is a giant circle at Caer Caradoc and that an Uthyrpendragon lies buried in this great circle. Around a hundred yards north-east of St Peter's church is the western end of a great boat-shaped 'circle' mound and ditch. The boat-shaped, mounded 'circle' is some hundred and ninety yards long and some seventy yards wide. In what might be described as the 'helmsman's position', at the starboard stern area of this great earth boat, is a large grave mound. This is around a hundred and thirty feet long and over thirty feet wide. So there is a great 'circle' at Caer Caradoc and there is a grave mound in it. The Uthyrpendragon is almost certainly King Meurig, as all the other five Uthyrpendragons lie elsewhere, and Meurig died around the time indicated in the history. As St Peter's at Caer Caradoc is also named Llanbad Fawr, which means 'the Great Ship's Boat', the huge ditch and mound boat-shaped 'circle' is identified.

The Uthyrpendragon buried in the grave mound is virtually certain to be King Meurig ap Tewdrig, the father of Arthur II. The *Brut Tyssilio* and *Brut Gruffydd ap Arthur* state that Merddyn Emrys and his mother lived at St Peter's at Caer Caradoc, and that it was at this St Peter's church that a celebrated conference was held at some time around AD 450 with the ambassadors of Gwrtheyrn Vortigern. Other records in the Llandaff Charters cite King Lleirwg as building a church at this site around AD 170. The Triads twice name the church at Caer Caradoc as one of the three most important churches in Britain. Caer Caradoc is first named with two other churches, and then it is again named with two other alternative sites. It was clearly Britain's most important church. Services at St Peter's were continued in relays by two thousand, four hundred monks for twenty-four hours a day, seven days a week, fifty-two weeks a year.

The vicinity of St Peter's at Caer Caradoc is almost certainly the final destination of the embalmed corpse of Arthur II son of King Meurig, when it was taken from the cave grave in the Coed y Mwstyr woods, clearly visible just south below the site of St Peter's, and the accounts of the burial make this abundantly clear. The grave has been located.

Into this analysis now comes the ancient poem of *Cyhylyn ai Cant*, roughly the *Song of Cyhylyn*. As Cyhylyn was a Prince Bishop and a brother of King Meurig, he was an uncle of King Arthur II. Therefore, his poem is both important and contemporary. Cyhylyn speaks of the treachery of Hengist the Saxon, and the drunkard Gwrtheyrn-Vortigern, and he makes a specific mention of the 'St Peter's quadrangle'. This 'St Peter's quadrangle' would be still the walled area of an 'etw' (one Welsh acre is roughly two English acres), surrounding the church as it is today. Cyhylyn calls it the 'great cor (choir) of opulence' and the excavations of 1991 showed that it had been a church of unusual decoration and wealth. Cyhylyn describes the negotiations with Hengist, and the subsequent Saxon revolt and the devastations, and he parallels this with the enormous devastations and destructions wrought from the heavens.

Cyhylyn presents no problem to the obliterators, and they simply re-date him to around AD 700, some hundred and fifty to two hundred years out of time, and so chronologically Cyhylyn becomes irrelevant. The enormous boat-shaped circle called Llan-bad-fawr, or 'the holy estate of the great ship's boat', and its burial mound, are said by CADW in the most staggering piece of nonsense, to be a sheep-fold. In 1990, CADW made a seemingly innocuous announcement in the Welsh Press, which simply stated that St Peter's-super-Montem church above Brynna was a twelfth-century Norman structure. This statement puzzled many who contacted them, but Wilson and Blackett saw through it immediately. If the church was a twelfth-century Norman building, then all the entries in the Welsh histories, the Cathedral Charters, the Triads, Lives of Saints, and poetry, were all wrong and forged. In one fell swoop all native British records could be thrown aside and the nineteenth-century trash invented by Edwin Guest and Bishop Stubbs would reign supreme.

The fact that the Normans only seized the coastal plain of Glamorgan, and the very well recorded detail of local struggles showed that they never got up to St Peter's-super-Montem, did not appear to matter. The fact that there was an obvious 'Early English' style window of the era around AD 650-850 seemed not to count. So Wilson and Blackett had no alternative other than to apply for permission to excavate the St Peter's site.

The rules governing this procedure should take a maximum time of seven weeks, but all through a fine spring and a glorious summer Wilson and Blackett waited. It took three angry meetings with the Junior Minister of the Welsh Office and twenty-four weeks of unexplained delays to finally get the necessary permission on 24th August.

The result was a late-autumn excavation in worsening weather nine hundred and fifty feet up on a hill which is notorious for its winds, which sweep straight in from across the Atlantic. The site was finally struck by three storms; one with winds gusting to a hundred miles an hour, and two with winds over seventy miles an hour. The excavation, however, was a stunning success and set the date of the church in the first century AD, buried beneath three later churches. There was evidence of the comet in a terrible destruction by burning which actually melted human bones onto the earliest first-century floor. The drain on finances was shattering, however, and the policy of publishing history rather than expensive digging was in ruins. The project was in effect without funds.

Chapter Fourteen

The Coming of the Dragon

The destruction of most of the great British state by débris from a comet must have been an awesome event and should be burned deep into the national memories and psyche of the people. With an advanced and literate nation like the British there should be written as well as physical evidence surviving. So it is; there are many records of this unparalleled disaster and tremendous natural catastrophe which came upon the British nation in AD 562. There was, however, the dogma of the Church of Rome that held that no stone, meaning meteorites, asteroids, or comets, could fall from the sky. Therefore, any history of a nation with a set of clear records that told of the near destruction of the huge population of the great island of Britain, had to be a nation with a false forged history. Not until 1803, when a great shower of meteorites fell close to a European potentate who was holding a ceremony in public before many thousands of people, did the Church dogma begin to crack. Another similar shower of meteorites then fell close to large numbers of people in France, and it had to be admitted that stones can and do fall from the sky.

Researching the British catastrophe once it is identified is not without problems. There is very sound evidence, as exhibited in a two-part television programme in August of 1999, that a colossal volcanic eruption occurred at the island of Krakatoa off Southeast Asia in AD 535-537. This most massive of volcanic eruptions, well recorded by neighbouring Asian nations, caused clouds of ash to encircle the skies of planet earth for several years, darkening the sun and stunting plant growth. The effect on plant life was to limit growth as a direct result of diminished sunlight, and modern dendrochronological studies have identified diminished tree ring growths for the alleged years around AD 535-537. The study of ice layers in Greenland has also produced evidence of the volcanic ash from Krakatoa and its effect upon the annual layers of ice formation.

So, from a position of no identified sixth-century catastrophe there are suddenly two known catastrophes. There is no direct comparison between the British comet event and the evidence of the Krakatoa volcanic eruption as the two are quite separate and differently described and identified events. A difficulty has arisen, however, in that at least one dendrochronologist, who totally lacks insights into British history of the era, has unfortunately chosen to assert that the several

Chapter 14 - The Coming of the Dragon

years of winter conditions following the Krakatoa eruption of AD 535 mark the collapse of the Arthurian British State. These two quite separate events are thus asserted to be one, and again this has the effect of completely distorting British history. All the most careful reconstructions of British ancient genealogy and historical chronologies arrive at the date of AD 562 for the comet. Gregory of Tours, a contemporary writer in France, confirms the date of the destruction of Britain and Ireland at AD 562 in his book *The History of the Franks*.

There is now a third record emerging that asserts that a bolide passed over Argentina in the mid-sixth century AD.

The gigantic destruction of Britain is detailed in several authentic records, yet no history book written for the schools, or the public, ever mentions a single word of it. It is as if the Hebrews were to have omitted, or had lost, Moses and the story of the Exodus out of Egypt from their national remembrances. It defies imagination that ancient British writers set down the story for all future generations, and that these records still exist, yet there is a vast pretence that what is recorded never happened. The truthful record means that there was no 'Anglo-Saxon conquest,' as claimed, but instead a series of infiltrations into a ruined devastated land where the population had mostly been killed.

In AD 562, a great comet was seen in the skies, and it approached very close to our Planet Earth. Whether this comet struck Earth, or merely passed very close to a collision course, showering the Earth with monstrous masses of débris from its tails many thousands of miles long is not quite clear. What is recorded is that Britain was a point of such impact, and the land was devastated by enormous blasts in this collision. Vast tracts of the island kingdom were laid in total ruin. Mud slithered everywhere, and poisonous clouds enveloped the land. Nothing could live in a wide sweep of stricken areas. Everything died; the animals, both domesticated and wild, the birds, the fish, the reptiles; all died.

Across Britain the Roman-style cities and towns of the British were shattered, and the great country villas and farms, and the basilicas, all tottered into ruin. The walls were shaken to their very foundations, and the roofs slithered down in a rush of débris. The capital of Uriconium-Wroxeter fell into ruin and was forgotten, and was only briefly again inhabited, and never rebuilt. A huge event and a deserted ruined city quite unique in Western Europe.

Amidst this colossal shambles of total ruin, the survivors stumbled around under darkened skies full of poisonous clouds, the droplets from which brought inevitable death to those who were unfortunate enough to be soaked by them. A great powerful state of at least ten million inhabitants had been brought to near-destruction and inevitable ruin in one disastrous moment. This is how the Arthurian mediaeval stories of the great Wastelands, written by romance poets and sung by troubadours centuries later, came into being.

In more ancient times, around 1350 BC, Egypt was struck by a similar disaster at the time of Moses, when in remarkably similar conditions Moses led his followers out from the stricken land. Modern researchers, analysing the tales of the great storms, the huge clouds, and the plagues and pestilences, all of which struck ancient Egypt around this time, have concluded that some form of disaster caused by a heavenly body from outer space was probably responsible for the ruin of Egypt.

In our modem times a similar event occurred in the vast empty wastes of Siberia. On 30th June 1908, an object from outer space struck the remote district of Tunguska, in Siberia. The exact nature of this object is unknown and is still debated. It may have been a vast ball of gas, a small comet, or a meteor, or, less likely, even an asteroid. Modern Russian scientists have even proposed that whatever it was, it may have caused an atomic explosion. The result was that the entire area for hundreds of miles around was entirely devastated, and it took investigators years to reach the centre point of the explosion. The Tunguska event very closely parallels the Dark Age British accounts of what they called 'the terrific blast'.

Siberia was, and still is, sparsely populated, and in 1908 the coalmines of the Tunguska region were undeveloped. In stark contrast, ancient Egypt around 1350 BC, and Britain around AD 562, were by any standards densely populated lands. Julius Caesar, writing some six hundred years before the British disaster, stated that the population was huge. As almost four-fifths of Planet Earth is covered by oceans and ice masses, and many of the land areas were historically both unknown and uninhabited - the Sahara and other deserts, Siberia, vast areas of North and South America and Australia, plus the Antarctic and Arctic regions, and so on - we may only know of those collisions with Planet Earth which fell on densely populated areas and within our limited sphere of historical knowledge and record. It was a sheer fluke that a train on the Trans-Siberian railroad just happened to be passing through the wilderness at the time that the object from outer space struck Tunguska. Few people bother to read the very clear statements of Ovid the Roman poet and others of his kind.

The matter of comets or asteroids in possible collision, or near collision, with Planet Earth has been researched, the principal early exponents being Ignatius Donnelly, and the remarkable genius Immanuel Velikovsky, whose generally accurate research fell victim to assassination by intellectual pygmies. There is no need to rewrite what these researchers, particularly the remarkable Velikovsky, have already stated in detail, and the matter of possible asteroid collisions with Earth became a major scientific study in the late twentieth century. It is sufficient to state that ancient British records give accounts which very closely match the analysis of events which could occur in a near-collision with a great comet as proposed by Velikovsky and Donnelly. A huge blast accompanied by vast

Chapter 14 - The Coming of the Dragon

screeching or squealing noises; earthquakes; vast dark clouds like mushrooms; poisonous fumes and inflammable liquids or gases - probably naphtha - that burnt freely; fires raging over the devastated lands; and the creation of vast areas of temporarily uninhabitable lands.

The British records tell of a vast, red fireball, and in 1908 at seventeen minutes past seven on the morning of 30th June, people travelling on the Trans-Siberian railway saw a glowing mass like a fireball shoot across the sky, and out across the empty wastes of Siberia. Then a thunderous shock shook the train, and the din of vast explosions followed. The shock, like that of an earthquake, is recorded as causing the Irkutsk seismograph to quiver for almost an hour, and seismographic stations all over Planet Earth recorded the quake of this explosion. Later, investigators found whole forests where the trees had been sheared off at the stumps, even as far as forty miles from the explosion centre-point. For many miles further around the trees stood bare without branches. There were also unmistakeable traces of a vast conflagration in the centre of the blast.

No traces of meteoric iron or any other metal have ever been found at Tunguska, even though a considerable number of impact craters of all sizes were found in the marshes of the area. The 1963 expedition, led by Solotov, concluded that it was highly likely that there had been an atomic explosion at Tunguska.

There is one strange feature of this Tunguska happening which parallels British records, and needs to be detailed. For nine days and nights after the Tunguska explosion the whole of Northern Europe was lit up for twenty-four hours a day as if it were bright noon. People did all the frivolous human things that they always do in strange circumstances. They played tennis all night, and sat in their gardens reading books, and they went fishing and played golf. They photographed and filmed each other during these nine nights of noon-like daylight. No one ever thought however of looking at the much-derided British records as preserved from old manuscripts by Edward Williams and published by his son Taliesin. The followers of the nineteenth-century know-it-alls from Cambridge and Oxford said nothing.

One such manuscript states-

'In the year 269 the sky appeared as if on fire, so that the light at night became vivid as that of day for nine days, after which an intense heat came on, and a general want of water in rivers and wells.'

The 'year 269' is the year listed in the manuscript, and this is not AD 269, and so 'year 1' must be calculated. Nine days of extreme brightness for twenty-four hours a day is however a strange reoccurrence. All this was then followed by severe famines and great pestilences that caused many deaths. This we know.

If the comet débris, or meteorites, or fireballs, or whatever they were, which struck Britain in AD 562, were comparable to the Tunguska disaster of 1908, then it is worth noting that trees standing eleven miles from the epicentre of the impact were set on fire in the moment of impact, and that secondary shadows were cast a hundred and twenty-four miles from the epicentre. These details have been published by the investigating scientists, who have concluded that the explosive power at Tunguska matched that of a ten-megaton atomic bomb. Everything in fact pointed to an atomic explosion. As Gregory of Tours wrote contemporaneously in AD 562, 'the two islands in the ocean were set on fire from end to end' - meaning that the forests of Britain and Ireland were ablaze.

What exactly hit Britain in AD 562 is not the sphere of interest of Alan Wilson and Baram Blackett, whose only concern is to point to the identicality of the events in Britain in 562 and in Siberia in 1908. All the contemporary records refer to the cause as being a comet, and until some better evidence or scientific confirmation is forthcoming, they continue to identify the cause of the disaster with a comet. One record tells of the origin and direction of the comet, but how accurate this is may be uncertain. The primary historical interest is to demonstrate that Arthurian Britain, under the rule of the Ail-Teyrn ('second monarch' or 'alternative monarch' = the Regent, King Arthur II son of King Meurig), almost collapsed in the wake of this monstrous disaster. The devastated great wastelands of the mediaeval Arthurian Romances came into being as deathly areas that were uninhabitable for seven to eleven years, and government of the great kingdom under the Ail-Teyrn and the regional sub-kings was thrown into chaos. Histories written later by clerics for the immigrant Angles and Saxons, and the later Normans, were unable to fully comprehend the accounts of the destructions, and they refused on religious grounds to believe the British records of the disaster. Finally, in the nineteenth century, a story of unrecorded conquest was introduced. Mediaeval church historians were keen to distort and to avoid the subject. So it was that the most awesome event in all British history - all copiously recorded in detail - was obliterated and written out of the history books.

The most obvious sources are the *Brut Tyssilio* and the *Brut Gruffydd ap Arthur*, alias 'Geoffrey of Monmouth'. It must be admitted that these are confused histories, which blend the career of Arthur I, son of Magnus Maximus and Ceindrech, with that of Arthur II, son of King Meurig and Queen Onbrawst, making one great king out of two. Also, there is no indication that six warrior-kings used the title 'uthyr-pendragon'. It is a relatively simple task to disentangle these two very well-recorded kings named Arthur. The major reason for disregarding these otherwise accurate records is that a great comet was seen to take on the shape of a dragon in the skies in the time of the sixth-century AD Uthyr-pendragon.

The earlier uthyr-pendragons and dragons can easily be eliminated. King Carawn, or Carausius, the Emperor and uthyr-pendragon, died in AD 293. So

Chapter 14 - The Coming of the Dragon

Casnar Wledig (Chrysanthus the Legate of Roman records) the dragon, who immediately followed Carawn, and Gwyrthelin Uthyr-pendragon, who died around 460, are all too early. King Tewdrig-Theoderic Uthyr-pendragon was mortally wounded at Tintern in 509, which leaves only his son King Meurig-Maurice Uthyr-pendragon, and his grandson Arthur II Uthyr-pendragon, who were both alive in AD 562. Logically it appears that Taliesin-Merlyn is prophesying to King Meurig or to his son King Arthur II in the historical Bruts. This is how the comet is described:

> 'There appeared a star of great magnitude and brilliance, with a single beam shining out from it. At the end of this beam was a ball of fire, spread out in the shape of a dragon. From this dragon's mouth stretched forth two rays of light, one of which seemed to extend its length beyond the latitude of Gaul, while the second turned towards the Irish sea and split up into seven smaller shafts of light. This star appeared three times, and all who saw it were struck with fear and wonder.'

Both Tyssilio and Gruffydd ap Arthur set this scene at the time of the death of the leader known as Aurelian Ambrosius, who can be shown to be Gwrgan Mawr - Aurelian the Great, the father of Queen Onbrawst, the mother of Arthur II. The Uthyr-pendragon is identified as his successor son or brother which neatly fits with King Meurig as the son-in-law of Gwrgan Mawr.

Later in these narratives the Uthyr-pendragon has two golden dragons made, placing one in a cathedral, and carrying the other with him in his wars. It is typical of these records that when St Dyfrig called the British to arms, he is said to state that:

> '...Arthur himself put on a leather jerkin worthy of so great a king. On his head he placed a golden helmet with a crest carved in the shape of a dragon.'

This would obviously be St Dyfrig the son of Brychan Brecheiniog, and not the much earlier St Dyfrig the grandson of King Pebiau 'the Dribbler'.

The lives of the British saints of this mid-sixth century period are filled with dragon references, and amazingly not one single historian has previously seen the obvious, and linked the dragon comet of the British histories, and the epic poems and prophecies, with these references. Instead, they have chosen to regard these references as those of children's fairy tale dragons, and they have then been able to abandon these valuable British and Breton historical sources altogether and to ridicule British-Khumric history.

Wilson and Blackett have previously illustrated the definitive evidence of the great catastrophe that toppled Arthurian Britain from the Manuscript Book the *Cottonian Titus D. XXII. I*, held in the British Museum. This contains a notice of the

History of Llandaff Cathedral and of St Dyfrig-Dubricius. The text contains a notice of the founding of the church by King Meurig ap Tewdrig, and then it immediately proceeds to the crowning of King Arthur by St Dyfrig, said to be dated at 506 (more likely AD 539) when he was allegedly fifteen. This early date is presumably because the writer was attempting to reconcile facts with the earlier St Dyfrig grandson of Pebiau and mistaking him for St Dyfrig son of Brychan. The coronation is however said to have been in the 'civitas circestrie' which actually means 'the state of government surrounded by missiles' and not Cirencester. There is obviously a clear descent from Tewdrig to Meurig to Arthur, and an indication of the heavenly bombardment.

The *Life of St Teilo*, which follows in the *Book of Llandaff*, is also illuminating, and Teilo is specifically stated to have succeeded Dyfrig as Bishop. We find that:

> '.... St Teilo received the pastoral care of the Church of Llandaff to which he had been consecrated, with all the adjacent diocese, that had belonged to his predecessor Dubricius, in which he could not long remain, however, on account of the pestilence, which nearly destroyed the whole nation. It was called the Yellow Pestilence, because it occasioned all persons who were seized by it to be yellow without blood, and it appeared to men as a watery column of cloud having one end trailing along the ground and the other above, proceeding in the air and passing through the entire country like a shower going through the bottom of the valleys. Whatever living creature it touched with its pestiferous blast, either immediately died or sickened for death. If anyone endeavoured to apply a remedy to the sick person, not only had the medicines no effect but the dreadful disorder brought the physician, together with the sick person, to death.'

We are then told that the dread sickness killed the king named Maelgwn in North Wales, and here, given the general chronology of the *Life of St Teilo*, we have Maelgwn of Llandaff, a brother of King Meurig, and not Maelgwn Gwynedd the son of the Caswallon Lawhir who became king in AD 580.

It became clear that the possibility of pestilences and diseases arriving from outer space had been noted by other researchers. *Diseases from Space* had been published in 1979, by the notable astronomer Sir Fred Hoyle, and Professor Wickramasinghe, Head of the Department of Applied Mathematics and Astronomy at Cardiff. Later, Channel 4 TV broadcast a ninety-minute programme on research into the possible actual causes (other than the popularly guessed spread of bubonic plague) of the great plague of 1348. So, the matter of a cosmic catastrophe causing pestilence on Earth, as set down in the ancient British records, was not perhaps incorrect. Alan Wilson had an appointment to talk with Dr Wickramasinghe but decided not to do so when the professor publicly stated that a fossil of a small, feathered dinosaur in the British Museum was a fake. It was

Chapter 14 - The Coming of the Dragon

immediately pointed out to the startled professor that there were four other specimens of the same species in the Berlin Museum.

Both Alan and Baram had long thought that the mention of *The Coming of the Dragon* in Triad Number eleven, Series Three, dealing with Gormes, or historical oppressions and tyrannies of an extra-terrestrial nature, was associated with the comet impact of AD 562. These Gormes are listed as:

1. 'Gormes March Maelen the Malignant Horse,
2. Gormes Galanmai the May Murders,
3. The Gormes Draig Prydain, the Dragon of Britain, and the Gormes Gwr Lledrithawg, the Man of Illusions, Haunting, Apparition.'

The last is said to have occurred at the time of the Treacherous Meeting, and at the time of Beli ap Mynogan or Tumult son of 'Tumult Within the Country' (mynogi), or 'He with the Lord'. Some early Welsh writers, including Robert Owen, have identified the March Maelen which occurred 'tramor' or 'overseas' with a feared heavenly body.

The Great Horse was Ialdabaoth who was cast down by God and indicates the remote antiquity before Brutus arrived in Britain, and the factual nature of the Historical Triads rules out the possibility of the Draig Prydain, that is the Dragon of Britain being some children's fairy tale.

The obvious course of action for Wilson and Blackett was to trawl through the various records to see what could be found to corroborate with the accounts already available.

The life of St Oudoceus-St Docco tells the same story as that in the *Life of St Teilo*. The ancestry of Oudoceus is given, and this, with other related genealogies, firmly places the saint i`nto the second half of the sixth century, and to his being active as a mature person in south-east Wales around AD 570-590. His father, Prince Budic, took ship from Cornouaille in Brittany and fled to the court of Aircol Lawhir-Agricola Longhand in Dyfed. The site of this court ruin has been located, and the genealogies of Aircol Lawhir are impeccable. In Dyfed, Budic was married to a second wife, Anauued-Arianrhod the daughter of Ensic, son of Hydwn Dwn, a grandson of the Cuneda Wledig. Budic, who is certainly the Bodvoc named with his father and great-grandfather Eternus Vedomavus on the sixth-century stone now at Margam Abbey, in Glamorgan, was given military assistance, and he regained his lands in Brittany. The entry in St Oudoceus' *Life* is virtually identical with that in St Teilo:

> 'And after a very long time the Yellow Pestilence came to Greater Britain, which was called yellow because it occasioned all persons who were seized by it to be yellow and very pallid and it appeared to men as a watery cloud, having

one end trailing along the ground and the other above proceeding through the air, and passing through the whole country like a shower going through the bottom of valleys.'

The text proceeds with the same statements as in St Teilo, with inevitable death caused to anyone who got wet from the cloud and those who endeavoured to treat them.

The story then relates how St Teilo and his clergy were forced to flee overseas to Brittany for several years. Here they educated Oudoceus, the youngest son of Prince Budic by his second marriage, as a priest. Finally, around AD 570, when the diseases subsided in Britain, and the land was again habitable, Oudoceus sailed to south-east Wales to become the new Bishop of Llandaff. Oudoceus was welcomed, and elected Bishop by King Meurig, Queen Onbrawst, and their sons Arthrwys (Arthur II) and ldnerth, and other close relatives of the royal clan. The detail of the chronology, tied in with family genealogies of other noble families and saints, is discussed fully elsewhere, and the arrival of St Oudoccus is certainly in the era around AD 570. Suffice it to say that the South Wales records state that the Cuneda Wledig, who was not a king, succeeded Owain Ffindu in the military command in AD 434. Yet, favoured North Wales guesswork, based on zero evidence, places Cuneda as appointed by Magnus Maximus in AD 383, causing a time-slip of fifty-one years and chronological chaos. The idea that Oudoceus, or Docco, arrived in Wales as the new Bishop of Llandaff around AD 537 (itself a consequence of the dendrochronological notion that the Krakatoa volcanic eruption caused the total devastation of sixth-century Britain) would cause a complete dislocation in all genealogies, and all dating of Cathedral Charters, and chronological chaos in sixthhcentury British History.

Nennius, writing *c.* AD 822, places Maelgwn Gwynedd as ascending his throne a hundred and forty-six years after Cuneda. Cuneda took over military command from Owain Ffindu in 434, so 434 + 146 = 580. As Arthur II can be proved - repeatedly proved - to have died in AD 579, then Maelgwn Gwynedd ascended in Gwynedd in 580. The records constantly make sense. *The Llandaff Charters* record a grant of lands at Cilcinhinn, Conuoy, and Llangennei, made at this time by King Meurig to St Oudoceus, in the presence of Queen Onbrawst, and Princes Arthrwys (Arthur II) and Idnerth.

The events in the lives of St Teilo and St Oudoceus relate directly to the titanic disaster that fell upon the British people. These narratives, and others in the lives of several other contemporary saints, fit precisely with the well-known Breton tradition of King Arthur being compelled to spend several years in Brittany and Llydaw. In fact, everyone who could get out of the affected areas of Britain did so, and much of the great island lay uninhabited for between seven and eleven years.

Chapter 14 - The Coming of the Dragon

Almost all the high-ranking British saints who fled to Brittany to escape the dread calamity are credited with the feat of 'dragon-slaying,' and most are claimed to have accomplished this by persuading or leading the dragon away by the power of prayer. The Life of St Tugdual preserves a typical example of these holy exploits. This St Tugdual was educated by St Illtyd, who was a first cousin of Arthur II, at the Llan-Illtyd-Fawr college in Glamorgan. The *De Excidio Conquestu Britanniae,* or *Of the Destruction and Conquest of Britain,* claimed to have been written by St Gildas, gives graphic descriptions of the enormous catastrophe. St Gildas, the father of St Cennyd of Glamorgan, and grandfather of Fili the Bishop, or Ufelwyn a suffragan bishop of Llandaff, also fled from South Wales to Roche-sur-Blavet in Brittany and traditionally he lies buried in the Rhuys Monastery. There was of course the famous meeting of reconciliation between St Gildas and Arthur in AD 570 at Llancarfan Abbey, nine miles west of Cardiff, after Arthur executed Huail, a brother of Gildas ap Caw, at Ruthin. See *Artorivs Rex Discovered*.

The Life of St Efflam, written by one Dubricius, tells how Efflam met King Arthur on a beach in Brittany. Arthur was unable to subdue a mighty dragon, not surprising as it was a comet, so Efflam took over and defeated the dragon with his holiness and his prayers.

> 'And the beast obeyed, rolling his dreadful eye, uttering such an awful hissing noise, that the shore resounded for miles. Vomiting blood as he went, he mounted the black rock of Hyrglas, and with a terrible roar he flung himself into the sea, where he perished miserably in the waters.'

It sounds like a comet splashing down in the Atlantic. St Paul Aurelian, St Samson son of Anna, the daughter of King Meurig, and therefore a nephew of King Arthur II the brother of Anna, also fled to Brittany and Cornwall with dozens of others. St Padarn son of Pedrwn, son of Emyr Lydaw, famous for losing a confrontation with Arthur II at Llan-Badarn-Fawr also fled. Both this St Samson and St Padarn had signed the papers of the Second Council of Paris in 557, and they help to confirm the dating of Arthur II. Four sons of Emyr Lydaw (later to become Normandy in AD 911) married daughters of King Meurig and this provides another clue to the politics arising from the great disaster.

Whilst no other historians in Britain were willing to hazard their careers by entering the forbidden territory and writing about the politically unmentionable, the physicists, the astrophysicists, the astronomers, the senior military officers of other countries, and other professional scientists around the world were unaware of this prohibition. A large, potentially immensely destructive asteroid, which passed too close to Planet Earth for comfort, was recorded by an American military space satellite. Previously the leading astronomers had been persuading governments to pour vast sums into a pointless, futile, and wasteful pursuit of the 'Big Bang' origin of the universe. Now, however, the real danger posed to mankind from comets and asteroids, clearly recognised and recorded in ancient historical times, was finally understood by twentieth-century politicians. So well-funded research began, and international conferences were held around the world, to examine the real danger from comets and asteroids, even bypassing the politics of the Cold War.

Vital to these studies are historical records of comet disasters and of the near passage of comets and asteroids close to Earth. One brave researcher was Dr Victor Clube, of the Astrophysics Department at Oxford University, who was prepared openly to recognize the mid-sixth-century British disaster described in Gildas' *De Excidio* as being the result of a scatter of comet débris striking Britain. The main body of the comet, or whatever it was, may not have struck Britain, but part of the huge shower of boulders and débris, whistling along in the comet train, certainly showered the island. The wreckage was massive, and Dr Clube estimated that it would have been the equivalent to a strike of a hundred Hiroshima atomic bombs.

This should have opened the study of British historical records, but vested interests protecting bubble reputations, grants, funds, publications, and so on, were deemed to be more important. So Alan Wilson and Baram Blackett, who had already published a notice of the comet strike in 1986, before Dr Victor Clube's announcement, and well before the asteroid frightened the American military, were left isolated. The clear explanations of how and why the British Arthurian kingdom began its decline and collapse, exactly as stated in detail in the much abused truthful and accurate records, remains a no-go area. Anything that does not conform to the past three hundred years of political policy is still classified as allegedly forged records. It raises the question of why Ministers of State, who have never read any of Wilson and Blackett's books, write letters declaring them to be idiots. Paradoxically, the university-employed astronomers and astrophysicists are declared to be reputable and respected men (which undoubtedly many of them are); whilst using at least some of the same data, and producing the same conclusions in far greater detail, Alan Wilson and Baram Blackett are labelled as misguided fools and far worse.

Would any alleged forger, fabricating away two hundred years ago, have dared to invent a record stating that many centuries ago, for a period of nine days and nights, the whole land was lit up as bright daylight for twenty-four hours a day? No forger would dare invent it, yet this is precisely what happened in 1908 after the Tunguska event. Learning of Dr Clube's initiatives, Wilson and Blackett were further motivated in attempting to date the British disaster, and to seek for records of sightings, of stones which fell, and of directions from which the comet arrived. They were already on the historical trail of another potentially dangerous comet with a periodicity of around six hundred and seventy-eight years, the record of which had again passed unnoticed.

Modern archaeology has proved conclusively that around the mid-sixth century AD the coastal settlements of Angles and Saxons on the east of Britain were suddenly and inexplicably abandoned. These farmer settlers packed up and returned to their homelands in Holland, Heligoland, and Germany, where they remained for a relatively short period, estimated ten years, before beginning to return to British east coastal areas again. This extraordinary behaviour matches with British accounts of the deathly uninhabitable wastelands for seven to eleven years, as a direct result of the titanic destructions and conflagrations in Britain and parts of Ireland, caused by the near impact of the comet.

This awesome event was mentioned by Gregory of Tours in his *History of the Franks* at precisely the same time when these immigrants were returning to Holland and Germany. In Book IV, Chapter Thirty-one, Gregory describes the strange events. Violent earthquakes shook parts of France causing huge destruction. Four extra bright lights are seen around the sun, 'making five suns,' and a great comet with a vast tail like a sword appears to set the whole sky on fire. Plagues that seem to be very similar to the Black Death plagues accompanying the comet of 1360 swept through France. That these plagues were highly unlikely to have been bubonic plague and were not spread by fleas in the fur of black rats was a theory demonstrated by one bold researcher in our own times. He met with the same fate as befalls all who question the unfounded dogmas of establishment theorising.

In Chapter Twenty-four of Book VIII, Gregory of Tours gives the following account of the strange disaster:

> 'This same year two islands in the sea were consumed by fire, which fell from the sky. They burned for seven whole days, so that they were completely destroyed, together with the inhabitants and their flocks. Those who sought refuge in the sea and hurled themselves headlong into the deep died an even worse death in the water into which they had thrown themselves, whilst those on land who did not die immediately were consumed by fire. All were reduced to ash and the sea covered everything. Many maintained that the portents which I have said earlier that I saw in the month of October, when the sky seemed to be on fire, were really the reflection of this conflagration.'

Gregory then goes on to describe how a pool of blood a yard deep fell onto an offshore island close to Vannes, which is in Brittany. The two islands which were devastated are not named, and it is reasonable to identify them as Britain and Ireland. It is evident that this account by Gregory of Tours is a clear parallel with the account attributed to St Gildas in *De Excidio*.

When Wilson and Blackett published a notice of the comet in 1986 the silent treatment emerged. They expected some form of outcry, but no one took the slightest interest. No one takes the slightest notice of the recorded and evident facts that areas of land in Wales at Conway, Cardigan Bay, and Glamorgan, in

Heligoland off the Dutch coast, and the Scilly Isles, are known to have subsided beneath the seas at the same time. A television programme was made of an underwater exploration of these otherwise unexplained sixth-century subsided areas in Heligoland, but no link was made to any other areas. The *Life of St Genovesius* tells how Genovesius worked with two thousand, four hundred other monks under the direction of St Illtyd 'in the land of Arthur' to construct defensive sea dykes. These dykes ran from the River Taff to the Rumney in Cardiff, and they were recently destroyed by the civic authority, and the dykes still stand from the River Rumney in Cardiff to the River Ebbw at Newport, and further east of the River Usk on up to near Chepstow, a colossal feat of civil engineering by any standards.

St Illtyd directed the contemporary College of Llan-Illtyd-Fawr in Glamorgan, and was undoubtedly in Glamorgan, and therefore Genovesius' *Land of Arthur* is also south-east Wales. At this same time, the Orchard-Aballach Ledges off south Cardiff slipped beneath the waves and the Porth-maen-mawr, or Great Stone Port, the massive ancient harbour of the British kings, lies in the mud flats that were created. Parts of this huge sunken harbour were encountered when the Roath and Alexandra docks were being constructed at Cardiff a hundred years ago. This is unmistakeable evidence of the comet disaster on a huge scale.

There was until recently a long straight road in south Cardiff, which ran south across the old Griffith Moors, directly towards the great sunken harbour. It is spelled as Portmanmoor Road, yet Porth-Maen-Mawr means Port of Stone Great, or the Great Stone Port, and Porth-Maen-Mor means Port of Stone in the Sea. The name has been misunderstood for centuries and was recorded some eight hundred years ago. Accurate maps drawn in 1858 show the great horseshoe-shape of the harbour sitting on the edge of the sunken Aballach-Orchard Ledges, and with twice-daily tides of thirty-nine feet this is the only location where such a massive harbour could be constructed.

So, what happened to this Great Stone Port? The very ancient Brecon manuscripts tell how the then Duke Tewdrig sent his daughter Marchell over to Ireland to safety at the time of the Saxon revolt around AD 456. Three hundred horsemen fought the Saxons on three occasions as they tried to get Marchell to a port at Kidwelli, and then to Porth Ceri, before finally getting the Princess aboard a ship at the Great Port. In Ireland she married Enllech Coronog son of Hydwn Dwn the son of Ceredig (a prince criticised by St Patrick for mistreating the Irish) the son of Cuneda Wledig. Mediaeval manuscripts tell of Arthur and L'Ancelot sailing in fleets carrying armies out of Cardiff, and unless this now sunken harbour existed and was in use in the sixth century AD, this would not have been possible. Everything points to there being a massive landslip and flooding at the time of the comet. How else did the great port vanish? Here we have the answer to why King Arthur ap Meurig sailed out of Deu Gleddyf (Milford Haven) with a fleet of seven

Chapter 14 - The Coming of the Dragon

hundred ships around AD 574, because Porth Maen Mawr was lying sunken and in ruins.

The late twentieth century has witnessed major scholastic interest in underwater archaeology in the ancient sunken harbours of the vanished civilisations around the Mediterranean. No one ever attempts to disturb the massive ancient harbour of the British. If there are sunken wrecks, then this is where they will be. Gregory of Tours records massive landslides of whole cliffs into great rivers. St David asked King Arthur's permission to move the archbishopric from Caerleon to Menevia at Valle Rosina - the Valley of Roses. Land subsided beneath the waves in the Scilly Isles, at Conway, and Cardigan Bay, the capital at Viroconium-Wroxeter was destroyed, the city of London was burned, and the great harbour at Cardiff was submerged. The pattern is there for all to see.

Other physical evidence exists in the pre-562 church foundations. Ancient Welsh churches frequently take the form of several buildings tacked onto each other in a row and all of course facing east. What happened was that when a church needed to be enlarged, an additional building was constructed, and it was built onto the west end (sometimes onto the east end) of the existing structure. This resulted in three or four joined buildings of various eras and various lengths and heights, all in a row. In the case of St Illtyd's at Llan-Illtyd-Fawr (Lantwit Major) there are six buildings in a row like a train. The interesting feature of many of these churches is that whilst the ancient British were master astronomers and mathematicians, the earliest sections of the pre-562 churches do not align precisely due-east as do the other later sections. All are noticeably around one and a half degrees skewed to the south, and the Nevern church is a good example of this. Astronomers and others might do well to note this. Something caused north Africa to turn from an area dotted with great Roman cities and the grain basket of Rome, into an infertile desert area in the late sixth century AD. Ancient cities lie stranded in ruins, like the bones of schools of giant whales high and dry on a sand beach.

Chapter Fifteen

British Coelbren Inscriptions in America

In putting forward coherent accounts of some of the extant written evidence available for ancient British history, and in linking that evidence to a multitude of inscribed stones and ancient sites, Wilson and Blackett do not ask that anything that has been scientifically proved should be abandoned. However, they do ask that a great deal which has been assumed and presumed and conjectured should be set aside.

There is a famous seventeenth-century woodcut picture that is sometimes reprinted in our modern times. It shows two teams of four strong dray horses striving to attempt to pull apart two copper hemispheres which were simply placed together without any fastenings of any kind. In 1654 thousands of people crowded into the town square of Magdeburg, where the mayor, Otto von Guericke, placed together two perfectly fitting copper hemispheres and pumped out all the air inside the sphere he had created. The mayor was creating a vacuum inside the copper sphere, and this was impossible, as it was impossible for a vacuum to exist according to academic dogmas and religious beliefs. The eight huge sweating horses could not separate the two hemispheres, and finally Otto von Guericke opened the valve and let the air re-enter the sphere. Then he called forward a ten-year-old boy who easily pulled the two hemispheres apart.

The point is that earlier experiments by Von Guericke had shown that sound could not travel, nor light be diffused, in a vacuum; and even after this most public of demonstrations that a vacuum could exist, von Guericke was for decades the target of academic attacks and spleen. The university employees were totally wrong, as always; and they always have to be wrong or otherwise there can be no progress. For over twenty years after the Magdeburg public demonstration, academics still maintained that a vacuum could not exist, and they explained Von Guericke's triumph as a fluke.

When Georg Freidrich Grotefend made what is by far the most monumental of all feats of decipherment ever by successfully decoding and reading cuneiform, in

Chapter 15 - British Coelbren Inscriptions in America

1801, this humble village schoolteacher sent his thesis to the university of Göttingen. This institution refused to publish his thesis, and it lay unpublished until 1892. During these ninety-one years others used Grotefend's work as a quarry to enhance their own reputations.

In 1845 Dr Robert Mayer proved absolutely the universally known and accepted 'law of the conservation of energy', which is the first law of thermodynamics. Immediately, Dr Mayer, who was a humble ship's doctor, became the target of a massive hate campaign by academia. What he had done was to notice the difference in colour of venous and arterial blood of Europeans, which was lighter in hot tropical areas than when they were in the colder European climates. In the tropics the body is required to produce less heat, so less oxygen is produced; and it is oxygen which maintains the bright red colour of the blood. So, if work produces heat, and this work can therefore be convertible into heat, then the reverse must also be true. Following these observations Dr Mayer carried out an organised series of experiments scientifically to evaluate and prove his discovery.

The subsequent assaults made upon Dr Mayer were so vicious and persistent that he became ill, and developed encephalitis. This illness was seized upon as a pretext, and through a disgraceful intrigue, his enemies were actually able to get Mayer incarcerated in a lunatic asylum as a megalomanic. This disgusting academic triumph endured for ten years, until the determined efforts of an English scientist forced the release of Robert Mayer from his diabolically unjust imprisonment. Attempts were then made to deny Mayer's priority of discovery, and prominent academics actually ruined Dr Mayer's medical practice with on-going assaults against his character and person.

The list of academic criminality is almost endless, and includes such a ridiculous farce as the French Academy deciding that Thomas Edison's phonograph, the forerunner of all record players, was simply a trick of ventriloquism by the assistant whom Edison sent to demonstrate the phonograph to the Academy. Other antics include the more effective and more common misrepresentation. The world's first steam locomotive was designed and built by Thomas Trevethick in 1797 to run from Merthyr Tydfil down to Cardiff, in Wales, some seventeen years before the Englishman George Stephenson built his later locomotive in 1814. A full-scale replica of Trevethick's locomotive, the first in the world, stands in a Cardiff Museum.

Whole books can be, and indeed have been, written about the myriad of spasms of irrational behaviour and the uncivilised outrages constantly committed by academics against more able and capable researchers when any threat of change to the stagnant, moribund, and always wrong *status quo* is forced upon them by progress. In the 1950s a most horrific campaign was waged against the character and work of Dr Immanuel Velikovsky. At the time the Great Panjandrum figure protecting American astronomical theories was one Professor Harlow Shapley, Director of Astronomy at Harvard University. He and a motley crew of frightened academics attacked the findings of Dr Immanuel Velikovsky in a devious and vicious conspiracy. Shapley made only one accurate correct statement in this farrago: "If this Dr Velikovsky is right, the rest of us are idiots." Over the years Velikovsky is being proved right, and right, and right again and again.

Once it had become clear that the ancient British inscriptions were readable, and that the correct decipherment of Etruscan and 'Pelasgian' was well beyond dispute, serious attempts were made by Wilson and Blackett to make contact with and involve British and other academics. The majority of progress made on Planet Earth is made by mentally free people who are not shackled by institutional dogmas. It soon became clear that the iron curtains protecting the ivory towers of parrot-learning were impregnable. The denizens of these sheltered monastic retreats would only talk to each other, and, quite incredibly, they actually believed that they have more ability than anyone else. The years were flying past and it was unavoidable that a person who was not a member of the academic mafia, holding the correct 'membership cards' and 'union cards' was going to be allowed to publish anything serious in Britain.

All publishers and media outlets approached - TV, Radio, and Press - automatically consulted their academic contacts. This relieves the publishing and media person of any decision-making responsibility. It also guarantees the inevitable ruthless blocking of any and all discoveries. The mind of the academic contact will (a) never ever admit to being unaware of research, (b) will never ever say "I don't know", (c) will never admit that another person knows more, (d) never ever allow his/her own papers, books, pamphlets, diatribes, or lectures to be shown to be ill-founded and plain wrong, or even inadequate. Protected, planned inertia, and stagnation are the order of the day.

It was inevitable that an attempt to make contact with progressive intelligent minds outside Britain had to be made. Sources were scoured and approaches were made to twenty-two magazine publications, which specialise in language and decipherment studies around the world. Most failed to respond and those that did were aggressively dismissive and, in some cases, derisively rude. The propaganda war of obliteration waged against British and Khumric history and Culture is so

Chapter 15 - British Coelbren Inscriptions in America

universally successful that even the most cursory of hearings is denied.

It was clear that the British inscriptions were indisputably readable, and that the correct method of decipherment of Etruscan, Rhaetian, and Asia Minor's 'Pelasgian' had been discovered. The Rhaetians were described as Etruscan migrants by Pliny the Elder, and this made this particular effort automatic. The ivory towers of academia remained firmly locked, bolted and barred, and the inmates were deaf and blind to all approaches. By 1987 Alan Wilson and Baram Blackett were reluctant to do anything more on the ever-expanding opportunities opening up in ancient British history, other than on the most casual basis.

The project, as it progressed over the years, had thrown up a series of linked opportunities in other areas. First it had been a quest for Arthur II, which rapidly transformed into a search for Arthur I as well as Arthur II. This had then had expanded to involve the early British histories of Albyne and Brutus, and this had brought in the project on the British alphabets. This had then led to ancient alphabet decipherments in Italy, Switzerland, and Asia Minor, and on to Assyria and Palestine. Along the way another project was developing, with information that Coelbren alphabet inscriptions existed in North America and elsewhere. More important than all this, the examination of ancient British records had pointed directly to a massive project dated *c.* 2150 to 306 BC. This began to claim Alan Wilson's interest and attention since the first experimental probes in 1984 proved astonishingly successful.

Along with the wish to avoid fruitless 'spitting matches' with those who had made no study whatsoever of the British histories there was a serious difficulty developing. In 1986 Alan Wilson was diagnosed as having cataract problems in both eyes. Before long he was unable to read properly, and whilst he could still type reasonably well on the same antiquated typewriter, he soon became unable to do any progressive work. By 1988 the weight of the many linked projects had fallen onto the shoulders of Baram Blackett.

It was not until 1989 that any worthwhile contacts were made in the U.S.A. This followed a conscious effort to transfer all interest away from Britain, and to abandon all attempts to publish the remainder of the Arthurian research, which, even after this volume, remains some 70% unpublished. Limited resources, limited finances, and Alan's incapacity, made it necessary to try to concentrate on one area that just might get a reasonable reception. Early American contacts had made the same routine mistakes of contacting British universities, who had universally neglected the study of the entire area of history and culture being dealt with by Alan and Baram, and it was not until 1989 that a contact was made with a person with common sense - James B. Michael.

The chain of contacts went from Orange County in California to Sun City, where interested and willing persons were simply not capable of assisting, and on to Maryland. In Maryland, Mark Slater, a Cardiff man, had set up a shop attempting to sell Welsh products. He sold a few of the books which Alan and Baram had published. This led to Don Weber up in Illinois, who sent a copy of a book written on Prince Madoc by Dana Olsen, from Indiana. This then led to a message being passed to and contact made with Jim Michael, President of the Ancient Kentucke Historical Association.

In common with other writers Dana Olsen had played 'follow-my-leader', unwittingly misidentifying Prince Madoc, the phantom son of Owen Gwynedd, who is said to have sailed to America around 1170. As we have seen, the real Prince Madoc was Madoc Morfran son of King Meurig, who would have reached America around 562. Jim Michael was on a different track, however, and he was well aware of a large number of inscriptions cut into rocks, on stele, on cliff faces, and onto artefacts. Strenuous efforts were being made by other researchers to mangle these inscriptions into Ogham, and to label them as Irish. A child can see that these texts are emphatically not either Welsh or Irish Ogham. Other enthusiasts were claiming that they were an unknown undecipherable form of Viking runes, and others even saw them as equally undecipherable Hebrew. All manner of theorising was going on, one modern author declaring a stone to be trilingual in Egyptian, Iberian-Punic, and Carthaginian.

Whilst he had no knowledge of the existence of the British Coelbren alphabet, Jim Michael reasoned that it was only the Welsh who had a traditional and generally unexplored history of early voyages to America, and that these strange stroke inscriptions just might be Welsh. So, when Jim Michael first wrote to Alan and Baram, he had no knowledge whatsoever that there was a Coelbren alphabet.

Like most people he had assumed that the establishment propaganda on Ogham, which exhibits Ogham musical scores as alphabets, was correct. So, there was considerable surprise on both sides of the Atlantic when first Baram Blackett opened Jim Michael's package and found himself staring at photographs of stones showing very clearly inscribed Coelbren texts. He got a large magnifying glass for Alan to see the photographs through the green-brown mists of his cataracts, and he began to organise the decipherment of the texts, with Alan advising as best he could. Then, in January of 1990, he sent the decipherments and translations of these first texts back to Kentucky.

Chapter 15 - British Coelbren Inscriptions in America

Seven years earlier Wilson and Blackett had attempted to contact Barry Fell, the author of *America BC*, which exhibited a number of Coelbren inscriptions, yet made rather strange claims that these were written in the totally dissimilar Ogham. These inscriptions were mainly in New England and Massachusetts, and they appeared to read correctly as Coelbren using the Khumric language. No reply was ever received from Barry Fell. The twentieth-century curse of unquestioning conformity under authority was everywhere.

Alan Wilson and Baram Blackett were suddenly presented with a vast array of ancient Coelbren inscriptions, all made available by Jim Michael and his organisation. Dana Olsen had mentioned the histories of Native American nations, but Jim Michael was able to provide the entire texts of these preserved histories. These told of a Great White Nation that had invaded America in antiquity. Jim also knew where the sites of major battles, fought between this ancient White Nation and the Native Americans, were located, where there were earth-banked religious 'cors', as in Wales and England, huge stone snake mounds as in ancient Wales, England, and Scotland, great earth-banked hill forts, and other ruins.

Jim Michael was also into the matter of medical evidence, and he had recruited a professor of dentistry, Tom Watson, into his group. European Aryan skulls differ from Native American skulls, and the bicuspid teeth are very different. Skeletal remains also provide evidence of diseases, which can be shown to be non-Native American. Radio Carbon 14 dating of wood found in, and associated with, tombs also reveals dates that match with the six-century AD timescale of British histories. One tomb in particular contained an inscribed stone, and Radio Carbon 14 dates placed this at around the mid-sixth century AD. Even Aryan mummies of greater antiquity, and which were wrapped in woven cloth, had been found in caves and tombs in the Mid-West. As the universal opinion is that Native Americans did not weave on the scale found with these mummies it is assumed that these are not of Native American origin.

All manner of unexplained single finds came to notice. When the bridge across the Ohio River at Louisville was being built as a major link between Kentucky and Indiana, a cluster of ancient coins was found deep in the mud. These coins were stuck fast together in the shape indicating that the purse or pouch they had been in had long since rotted away. They turned out to be late-period silver Roman coins, which a person on an expedition of *c.* AD 562 might well have carried with him. On one excavation the skeletal remains of two domesticated cows were found in a stratum, which again indicated the sixth century AD. Cows are not supposed to have existed in America before Columbus found the islands of the West Indies.

An inscription in Coelbren was found at Yarmouth Bay in Nova Scotia. Another very large Coelbren-inscribed stone known as the Dighton Rock lies preserved in a specially constructed building in a bay in Massachusetts, and there are several others including the Bourne Stone. There appeared to be a stretch of evidence from the Cumberland Gap through the Appalachian Mountains down along the Warriors Trail. There was a possible route roughly identifiable up from Tennessee, past and into West Virginia, on into Kentucky, and through Indiana to Ohio and Iowa. There is even a cache of inscribed lead crosses in Arizona, and other relics in many other areas.

The revelation that there was an ancient British Coelbren alphabet, matching the lettering on stones found in North America, fired Jim Michael into a spate of quite ferocious activity. Books, papers, photographs, video films, newspaper and magazine cuttings, copies of early paintings of pioneering America; all flooded through Alan and Baram's letterbox. In truth they found it almost impossible to cope with this barrage of new information.

A major problem was that Baram and Alan were working from an historically correct scenario that no one else knew about or recognised as even existing. They had liberated Madoc Morfran the Cormorant, son of King Meurig ap Tewdrig, from his centuries'-long exile in Gwynedd, in north-west Wales, and brought him home to his native south-east Wales. They had removed him from the adoptive family of his descendant Owen Gwynedd and returned him to his kinsfolk, who included his brother King Arthur II ap Meurig. They had put him back aboard his ship of AD 562 and sunk the phantom *Flying Dutchman* of 1170, which had never reached any port. This was of course a series of major heresies against the assumptions, presumptions, and unfounded theories of academia.

As if this was not enough, Alan and Baram were following the massed array of British evidence, which clearly exhibited the virtual destruction of Arthurian Britain by a comet or its débris, or some other body from outer space. This was an even greater heresy in a climate where evidence and facts are considered to be irrelevant.

The Route to America

The opinion of Jim Michael is that the AD 574 expedition of Arthur II and Madoc Morfran entered the Mid-Western region of North America by sailing south around Florida and entering the Bay of Mexico before sailing up the Mississippi river and then branching off on up the Ohio to arrive finally at the Falls of the Ohio near Louisville. This makes sense of the voyage of Admiral Gwenon, who was sent out

Chapter 15 - British Coelbren Inscriptions in America

after the return of Madoc Morfran to Britain. Gwenon would have had the task of checking Madoc's star references for sailing directions and also finding the route for the fleets.

Madoc himself may well have first arrived somewhere between Nova Scotia and Massachusetts, and moved inland through the Cumberland Gap in the Appalachian Mountains. When looking at maps, at first sight the route west across the Atlantic and down southwards along the Eastern seaboard of the North American continent to round the cape of Florida, and passing through the Florida Strait, skirting the Keys, before finally turning northwards up the Mississippi, appears to be a long and twisted route. The view of this route is somewhat distorted, however, by the projection of parts of a sphere onto a flat surface in the map-makers' unavoidable construction, and it makes much more sense when examined on a globe. On a globe the route becomes almost a straight line. Once the Atlantic Ocean crossing had been accomplished the fleet could stop at any point, wherever necessary, for water and for hunting and fishing, or to make repairs.

Madoc Morfran may well have made his first landfall in Canada, or on the northern seaboard of the U.S.A. Certainly the later voyage of St Brendan appears to have arrived somewhere near New York, and Brendan may have gone inland towards the Great Lakes, through a gap in the Appalachian Mountains.

In ancient times journeys by sea were much preferred to travelling overland even in the developed countries around the Mediterranean and in western Europe. Sea travel was faster and actually safer, and the only way to transport a veritable multitude in seven hundred ships into the fertile heartlands of the Mid-West was to sail up the great rivers. Much negative argument has been raised against ancient British sea-going capabilities, and this generally ignores the recorded facts. If we pause to reflect for a moment and set aside the emotional jingoistic approach to history we can perhaps see how this voyage was possible. Julius Caesar was surprised at the size and strength of British ocean-going ships and this was as early as 55 BC.

In the era of early warfare with Rome King Ceri Longsword is recorded as building fleets to harass and deny the Romans easy access to western Britain. This is generally ignored, as are records in the Triads of three princes commanding fleets of a hundred ships, each carrying a hundred and twenty men. Not so easily ignored is the fact that the British King Carawn, known in Latin texts as Carausius the Emperor and the Admiral, ruled Britain and most of Gaul as co-Emperor with Diocletian and Maximinius from AD 270 to 293. The power of this British King-

Emperor lay in his powerful fleets that operated from British and Gaulish ports as far south as Bordeaux. Carausius left a memorial stone at Penmachno in Wales, now in a Welsh museum, despite the claims made in a BBC 2 TV programme by 'experts' that King Carawn-Carausius left no memorial stone.

Next, Wilson and Blackett point to Mascen Wledig (Magnus Maximus) transporting his armies of sixty-two thousand men, along with their horses and baggage, out of Britain and across the Channel to invade Gaul in AD 383. As only one person is credited with being able to walk on water, it has to be accepted that the D-Day invasion of 383 involved a massive fleet. This feat of military logistics and sea-power was repeated in AD 406 when King Constantine III Coronog, the Crowned, also crossed the Channel with his armies to confront the hordes of Vandals, Sueves, and Alans, which had crossed the Rhine, were devastating Gaul, and clearly posing a threat to Britain. The defeated Romans were powerless to defend Gaul, yet the British armies under Constantine III and his general Geraint had no trouble in defeating the Vandal confederation and penning them down against the Pyrenees in southern Gaul.

Even the Breton prince titularly known as Rhiotafwys (Rhiothamus in Latin), who was almost certainly Rhun Dremrud - Red-Eyed Warrior, son of Rhun, son of Brychan I of Britanny, had sufficient sea-power to sail to the Loire River in AD 467, transporting a force of twelve thousand marines. Rhun Dremrud hired out with these marines to assist the Roman Emperor Anthemius against the Visigoths. Rhun Dremrud most likely saw the possibility of acquiring large fertile territories for himself in mid- to southern Gaul. In the event he was defeated in battle with the Visigoths, and he finished up moving eastwards into Germany where tradition has it that he set up a kingdom.

The point of all this is that the ancient British rulers, and their migrant relatives in Brittany, always had very large numbers of large ships at their disposal. These vessels were used for trading, for coastal defence, and for offensive military actions. Large fleets were the order of the day and not the exception. Welsh shipwrights built and navigated Alfred's first English navy around AD 870, and Alfred did not found the first British navy as the propaganda asserts. The size of fleet operations can be gauged by the fact that Harold of Norway attacked Athelstane of England with a fleet of twelve hundred ships, and the redoubtable Athelstane destroyed him. The Dark Age records of the warfare between the kings of Wessex and the Welsh, the Danes, and the Scots are peppered with accounts of large fleets supporting the armies.

So the record, and the idea of Arthur II ap Meurig assembling a fleet of seven

Chapter 15 - British Coelbren Inscriptions in America

hundred ships in Deu Gleddyf, or Milford Haven, to sail for America in AD 574, are perfectly sensible and reasonable. The author's view is that the entire situation should have been used to benefit the whole nation, right from the start if British history had been approached objectively in the past in a properly professional manner instead of as a political and religious propaganda exercise, these illustrations would not be necessary, and the record of the paramount British king organising a fleet of seven hundred ships to sail to America should cause no surprise whatsoever. Haste, greed, and jealousy have overshadowed any productive way to deal with Wilson and Blackett and their researches.

How many individuals sailed on the expedition is not known. If Prince Geraint's warships were manned by a hundred and twenty men, as recorded, then it is probable that trading vessels were larger. If an average of a hundred and twenty men sailed in every ship then the figure could be eighty-four thousand. The fact is that at the present time the numbers in the expeditionary force of 574 AD are simply not known, and may never be known. Even an average of only fifty persons per ship gives a total of thirty-five thousand. Figures of this order of magnitude are in fact reflected in the Native American histories relating to the invasion by a powerful nation of White Men in antiquity. If the numbers, the size, and the geographical spread of the ancient hill-fortresses of the Mid-West are of ancient British origin, then these figures are reasonable. Much earlier Roman vessels are known to have carried up to seven hundred passengers, and so the question of numbers has to remain a mystery for the present.

During their wars of the late fifth and early sixth centuries AD both the Vandals and the Romans several times assembled battle fleets of in excess of five hundred ships. If British histories are correct, when the German Vandal-Mercian king assembled his entire nation and evacuated it from North Africa in AD 548, he transported a hundred and sixty thousand people first to Ireland, and then over to Britain. That the entire Vandal nation was evacuated from North Africa in 548 is an incontrovertible historical fact. Extraordinary as it may seem, historians have been content to record the fact that the entire Vandal nation took to their ships and left North Africa in 548, and none of them ever bothered to seek them out in their new homeland. Procopius three times refers to the Vandal king as the King of Africa, and both St Tyssilio and Gruffydd ap Arthur name the King of Africa as the Germanic invading king of *c.* AD 548.

In 1991 Alan Wilson wrote to Jim Michael enclosing some handwritten pages and a few photostats from various publications. These notes dealt with the Yarmouth Bay Stone found in Nova Scotia, which carries an important British

Coelbren inscription. The confusions caused by Establishment manipulation of history are apparent from what Alan Wilson wrote to Jim Michael in 1995:

> 'Dear Jim,
>
> I have to confess that I found these handwritten pages and the interspersed photostats a little disturbing. We were into the alphabet study in 1980 and we published an eighteen-page monograph paper in 1984. My mother, who was very old at the time, was still going to evening classes learning Welsh. She died aged eighty-two in July 1987. These are in her handwriting, and she would spend time in the libraries looking through old records for us. I must have sent this to you when we were looking at the account of the Indian record of the White Men sailing up-stream in a large 'house'. Strange that this message should come back, as we had no idea of Coelbren being extensive in the U.S.A., as we were not in touch with you until after my mother died.
>
> It is odd to be helped by one's mother even five years after she died. Strange that this last piece of the puzzle was with us for years, but not understood, as we were not interested in Madoc, who was thought to be around 1170. So we know where they sailed from in 579, and we know that they arrived at the Ewenny River in August, on a bright sunny day three months later.'

Blackett and Wilson had long suspected that King Arthur II's Voyage to Annwn – 'the Other World' was a journey to America, but they had no way of proving this without corroborative evidence from America. To them the mediaeval romance stories of the dying, or newly dead 'King Arthur' being carried away across the seas in a ship carrying three queens, appeared to be some inaccurate folk remembrance of this event. The interesting fact was that amongst the information collected by Mrs Elizabeth Wilson was the record that a stone, clearly inscribed with Coelbren, had been found just above the high-water mark in Yarmouth Bay in Nova Scotia. This stone was so clearly inscribed that it could not be ignored. Discovered in 1812, the Yarmouth Stone remained generally unpublished until 1948 and 1949, when a Dr William Evans wrote of it in the magazine *Y Drych*.

The text of the Yarmouth Stone reads into Welsh, and concerns the placing of a bag or pouch into a ship for transportation, and includes a statement about a shrouded or distinctive well-beloved ruler. At the time they first read the text Blackett and Wilson did not realise the significance of the bag or pouch. They also lacked the evidence to establish that the bag or pouch contained the body of the ruler, or that it could be associated with King Arthur II ap Meurig. It was much

Chapter 15 - British Coelbren Inscriptions in America

later that evidence emerged that the bag was in all probability the leather sack made of three deerskins in which the dried corpse of the king was wrapped for transporting home. It also later became inevitable that the Yarmouth Bay Stone marks the embarkation point where the dead king's body was placed into the ship which then sailed to the Ewenny River estuary in Glamorgan in south-east Wales.

Sixth-century Khumric poetry records the bringing home of the body of Arthur in a leather bag made of deer skins, but the Yarmouth Bay Stone simply states a record of such a bag, and nominates a beloved ruler. That King Arthur II is identified several times in records as a beloved ruler is significant, and will for most people place the matter beyond reasonable doubt. No other British-Khumric king can be associated with North America; and no other is described as being 'dried-withered' and placed in a leather bag. The further corroborative information did not emerge until after 1991.

The fact that university employees were prepared to recognise this inscription on the Yarmouth Stone as being an ancient Coelbren inscription runs counter to the on-going propaganda campaign which alleges that the British Coelbren alphabets were invented or forged around 1800. Even though some University of Wales employees attempted to decipher the inscription, this lunatic allegation still remains generally unchallenged.

When, in more modern times, around 1800, white settlers were moving westwards in North America, in the wake of Daniel Boone and other pioneers, chiefs of the Cherokee Nation expressed their open astonishment that anyone would want to settle and live in Kentucky. This was a land that had been drenched in blood and slaughter in ancient times, and the Native Americans chose not to live there.

General Rodgers Clark and others were told how long centuries before a powerful nation of White people had arrived and settled in the Kentucky region. These White people were very strong and the surrounding Native American nations were unable to prevail against them. Not for a long time were the Native Americans able to force a passage through the area fortified and controlled by the White men, until finally the Native American peoples combined in an alliance which included many nations, and fought an all-out war against the White Nation which dwelt in Kentucky.

This is how the Kentucky region became a blood-soaked land, a place where there had been so much slaughter that the whole area was avoided as a place of residence. A final great and decisive battle had been fought on Sand Island, close to the Falls of the Ohio, where the Whites involved had been defeated and slaughtered. It seems strangely perverse that having fought vicious and bloody wars to drive the White Nation out of Kentucky, the Native Americans then considered that the land was too spirit-ridden and defiled with blood, and so they henceforth avoided it.

In Kentucky the sites of the ancient battlefields of this long war, remembered by the Native Americans down the centuries, yield up skeletons of both Native Americans and of Aryan 'White' men. The White skulls do not have the same bicuspid teeth as those of Native Americans, and they also lack the Inca-bones.

This would seem to offer proof of the Native American traditional histories of the ancient immigrant White people. However, nothing is simple or straightforward when the non-historian archaeologists become involved. Instead of acknowledging the probable truth of an ancient migration of a White nation in considerable force and numbers into the Mid-Western region of North America surrounding Kentucky, the growing presence of an increasing number of discoveries of skeletons with Aryan skulls and bicuspid teeth is now interpreted as 'proof' that some North American Native peoples were racially different to the others. The race differences being shown by the European-type skeletons, skulls, and teeth. Even when these very ancient European type skeletons exhibit signs of diseases not otherwise known to have existed on the North American continent, the irrational dogma of 'No Discovery Before Columbus', no matter what the evidence, is adhered to. This, in despite of the fact that Christopher Columbus never actually reached or discovered either the North or the South American continent.

What has become self-evident in the course of this research and the investigations involved, is that there are several remarkable bodies of evidence which demonstrate that currently accepted views are in need of revision.

1. There were large, well-constructed hill fortresses set out in an organised, militarily defensive pattern along the Ohio River, and encompassing other areas of Kentucky and neighbouring states. Both the style of these fortresses and their pattern of placement mirror the systems of ancient Britain as analysed by Blackett and Wilson. See *Artorivs Rex Discovered*, published in 1986.

2. There are clear Native American traditions of a powerful White Nation occupying the Kentucky area in antiquity.

3. There are a number of clear ancient stroke alphabet inscriptions in

Chapter 15 - British Coelbren Inscriptions in America

Kentucky and in the general Mid-West area, which are clearly identifiable as inscribed in the ancient British Coelbren. These inscriptions then be deciphered and translated into Khumric, and several bear Christian statements and emblems.

4. A number of ancient artefacts have been found which also bear Christian emblems, and at least one such artefact with an emblem is accompanied by Coelbren letters.

5. Skeletons found on ancient battlefields, which were pointed out by Cherokee leaders, have been found to have skulls which lack Inca bones common to Native Americans, and they also have Aryan bicuspid teeth.

6. British Khumric sixth-century records in Epic Poetry, Lives of Saints, and Histories, all very clearly match with a growing mass of evidence accumulating in the U.S.A.

7. Snake mounds - large, long, winding, serpentine mounds of stones and earth shaped like giant snakes, each with an egg-shaped ovoid at the mouth, common to ancient Britain and Ireland, are also found in the Mid-West. The Wallum Olam and Leni Lenape histories of the Native Americans tell of the Snake People, and this would indicate early Israelite and Judaic practise. This can be discussed a little further.

8. Several cloth-wrapped mummies have been found in the U.S.A., usually in caves where nitrates and other natural preservatives in the caves have preserved these burials.

9. As the Native Americans are believed not to have woven cloth, other than small items, these pose yet another problem of identification.

10. There are also mounded ritual circles in the Mid-West which very closely mirror those still found in England and Wales, and which are called 'cors' in Khumric. These ritual circles are arguably in the British style, and probably are of British origin.

These major areas of interest are exhibited and supported by a wide range of other items that do not fit with the favoured academic theories. Sixth-century epic poetry - very carefully avoided in Victorian Britain - tells of endemic venereal disease, and this may have resulted from the comet impacts. At least two skeletons exist -of teenagers, without Inca bones and with Aryan bicuspids - which arc scientifically dated to the AD 600-800 era, and both exhibit syphilis. This line of enquiry needs to be pursued as one Native American tribal nation later suffered from endemic syphilis.

If the fleets got up the Ohio as far as the Falls, and the construction of major fortresses there indicates that they did, then these ships would have had to be kept up in the creeks along the Ohio below the Falls, to avoid damage from river floods. One ship was recently found in the gravel beds along one creek, but it turned out to be an identifiable vessel only two hundred years old. Whether any ancient ship lies somewhere buried in the mud is conjecture. As the fleet of seven hundred ships sailed from Dau Gleddyf-Milford Haven, there is an unparallelled opportunity to investigate the places of both sailing and arrival of one of the most important ancient ocean migrations in history.

Professor Henry Schoolcraft had the vital key in his hands back in 1840 when he was appointed to examine the Grave Creek Tablet. He stated that the stone bore twenty-four letters and one hieroglyph, the hieroglyph being a Christian cross. European experts who themselves had restricted knowledge of the British Coelbren alphabets were of the opinion that at least ten to fourteen of the letters were British, and linked other letters to Etruscan and Iberian, which matches with the ancient historical migration routes from Asia Minor to Etruria, Iberia, and Britain. In fact, all twenty-four of the letters on the Grave Creek Tablet are recognisably British Coelbren, and are so arranged that the text on the stone can be deciphered and translated into a meaningful statement in Khumric with no difficulty.

Accounts of Welsh-speaking Indians

There are a number of records and stories concerning contacts with White or Welsh-speaking 'Indians' which are too extraordinary to be easily dismissed. In almost every case clergymen, army officers, and other professional men of good standing were involved. So these are not the wild tales of illiterate hunters and wanderers.

One case concerns the Reverend Mr Jones, a parson in West Virginia, when an expedition was sent by Major-General Bennet and Sir William Berkley to establish a base at Port Royal, later to become South Carolina. The Rev. Morgan Jones was sent along as Chaplain to the men in the two ships which set out from Virginia on 8th April 1660, and in eleven days they arrived off Harbour Mouth at Port Royal, where they were joined by the main fleet sailing in from Bermuda and Barbados. The new Deputy Governor of this territory was a Mr West, and the Rev. Morgan Jones found himself sent with the smaller vessels on up a river to a place named as Oyster Point.

Chapter 15 - British Coelbren Inscriptions in America

After some eight months of near-starvation in this wilderness outpost, the Rev. Jones and five others decided to make for home. They went inland until they reached the territories of the Tuscarora people, who promptly took them as prisoners when they declared their destination to be Roanoke. The Tuscaroras took Mr Jones and his five companions to their town and held them overnight, and on the next day they decided after a meeting, that these six intruders were to die. That evening the Tuscaroras told their captives to prepare for death the next morning, and this caused the Rev. Morgan Jones to break out into the British-Welsh tongue, bemoaning this miserable state of affairs. "Have I escaped so many dangers and must I now be knocked on the head like a dog?" Well, it was Morgan Jones' lucky day, for a War Captain of the Sachem of the Doegs heard him, and came over to him and raised him up. This Tuscarora then spoke to Morgan Jones in the Khumric-'Welsh' tongue and assured him that he would not die.

So, this War Chief of the Tuscarora went to his Emperor and arranged to ransom all six men. This caused a complete change of heart on the part of the Tuscaroras and the former prisoners were made welcome and treated with every civility. Morgan Jones then stayed for four months amongst the Tuscaroras, and spoke with them in the British-'Welsh' tongue, apparently without any difficulty. Finally, when it came time for Morgan Jones and his companions to leave, their hosts provided them with everything they needed for their journey home.

The location of this nation of the Tuscaroras was identified by Jones as being on the Pontiago River, not far from Cape Atros. Pontiago is of course 'pont Iago', or James' Bridge. Later Morgan Jones returned to Bassaleg near Newport, some ten miles east of Cardiff. The names of the locations given by Jones in his account were garbled, with Monsoman County in Virginia being probably Nansemond, Cape Fair would be Cape Fear, Pontiago river would be Pamlico river, and Cape Atros would be Cape Hatteras. The origin of these names is an unasked question, for Cape Fair in Khumric is the Eminent Cape, as Pontiago is James' Bridge, Cape Hatteras is probably Cape Athrais for 'violent, fierce', and Mansoman, if it were originally Mansyman, would be 'fair/pretty place which exists'. Perhaps the native people named these places, and the Rev. Morgan Jones was correct and not wrong as was assumed.

Ruben Durrett noted that the Doeg element of the Tuscarora nation was located in Maryland, where they entered into a treaty with Lord Baltimore in 1666. What is regrettable is that the Rev. Morgan Jones seems to have made no effort to write anything of the Tuscarora-Doeg history or traditions, and he makes no mention of Madoc whose legend he must have known. Perhaps he took it for granted that these people were of Khumric descent and from the Madoc expeditions, and saw no reason to enlarge on this. Maybe he wrote home to Bassaleg about these people with whom he lived for four months, for he named his father as John Jones of Bassaleg.

The Rev. Morgan Jones' letter was written on 10th March 1685, and published in London in 1740 on page 103 of *The Gentleman's Magazine*. So the trail had by that time gone cold. The publication of another letter was exhibited by Morgan Edwards in a book published in Philadelphia in 1770. Here, six men, five of whom had distinctly Khumric names, wrote to the British Missionary Society in London, volunteering to go to try to find ancient Khumric-descended migrants of the Madoc expedition. Their letter was dated 1st March 1733. They actually proposed carrying the Christian Gospel to these people if they found them. The absurdity of all this passes comprehension, but the letter states: 'Some relics of the Welsh tongue being found in old and deserted settlements about the Mississippi make it probable that they sailed up river'. So they were quoting from reports of traces or contacts.

Absurd, because the ancient Khumry were the original Christians, who accepted some form of this faith in AD 37. Absurd, because the 'Christian' religion they sought to spread was quite different, having been developed by councils and committees, and recreated in Rome following the official establishment of the Christian Church there by the British Emperor Constantine the Great in AD 324. Absurd to imagine that any London-based organisation would have the slightest interest in the Khumric-Welsh language whatsoever. The ancient British were the original Christians; and the letter actually expressed the sentiment that proof of 's expedition would somehow give 'proof and prior right to the whole continent' to the English. Muddled thinking by any standards.

In modern Britain there is a Welsh Grand Committee made up of all the Khumric Members of Parliament. When a new Welsh Language Bill was being discussed in June-July of 1993, it was clear that the Committee intended to propose that Khumric-Welsh, the original language of Britain, should be declared an official language of Britain. The London Government reacted predictably, and eleven English Members of Parliament, who had no interest in, no knowledge of, and no connection with Wales, and who were all extreme right-wing politicians, were appointed to vote on the Committee. This then enabled the vote on the recognition of the British Khumric Language to be defeated on a tied vote, with the English imported Chairman of the Welsh Committee having the negative casting vote. Nothing changes.

Chapter 15 - British Coelbren Inscriptions in America

In America the strange adventures of Welsh contacts continued. In 1782, Captain Isaac Stewart, of the Provincial Cavalry of South Carolina, made a statement that was published in July of 1787 on page 82 of the second volume of *The American Museum*. In this account Stewart tells how he and a number of other white men were captured by Indians about fifty miles west of Fort Pitt, about eighteen years earlier (1769-1770), and taken to the Wabash. The others were killed in what he described as 'circumstances of horrid barbarity', but he was lucky to be ransomed by a good woman at the price of a horse. After two years Stewart and another captive named John Davey, who was from Wales, were redeemed from their captors by an exploring Spaniard. They travelled west with him, crossing the Mississippi near Red River, and went up the Red River for about seven hundred miles. Here they met and spoke with 'Indians' who were white people and who spoke in Welsh with John Davey, who was Welsh Stewart related how the chiefs of these 'Indians' told Davey that their ancestors came from a foreign country and had landed in what is now Florida. When the Spanish seized Mexico their people had abandoned Florida and moved north. As proof these chiefs showed Davey and Stewart an old rolled parchment, which was wrapped in otter skins for preservation. On this parchment were writings in black ink, but neither Davey nor Stewart could identify any of the letters. Ruben Durrett identified the region as that of the Padoucah tribe of reputed 'white Indians' on the Ria del Norte, and quotes General Bowles, the Cherokee-Irishman, who claimed that these people spoke Welsh. As Durrett comments, the geography of all early explorers was not very accurate, and with no maps and a totally unknown geography of the vast territories, this is hardly surprising.

Around 1790 interest grew in the traditional history of Madoc amongst groups of Welshmen living in London, and principally amongst those known as the Golden Grove Group. In 1796 the Rev, John Williams LLD. published *An Enquiry into the Truth of the Tradition concerning the Discovery of America by Madog*. Amongst other facts the volume related the story of one Benjamin Sutton, as reported by Mr Chas. Beatty, who was a missionary from New York. It tells how in 1766 Mr Beatty, accompanied by a Mr Duffield, went inland for some four hundred miles south-east of New York. Here they met with Benjamin Sutton, who had visited a number of Native American nations, and had dwelt for some time with the Choctaw nation on the Mississippi, where the people were whiter than the other Native Americans. These people, according to Sutton, spoke in Welsh.

Benjamin Sutton also stated that these people had a book which he thought might be a Bible, and they kept it carefully wrapped in a skin. He also claimed that in a place that he called the Lower Shawanaugh Town he had heard a prisoner named Lewis speaking in Welsh with some of these people. The recorded account of President Thomas Jefferson sending an army officer to get an ancient book kept by a Native American woman is well known and documented. By some strange mischance the woman's house burned down and the book was apparently destroyed.

Another man, Levi Hicks, also claimed to have been amongst 'Indians' in a town on the west side of the Mississippi, where Welsh was spoken. The interpreter with Chas Beatty and Duffield was named Joseph, and he also claimed that he saw 'Indians' who spoke Welsh. He could identify Welsh as he had acquaintance with Welsh-speaking people himself, and knew some of the language. Benjamin Sutton saw as evidence the fact that the women of the Delaware nation observed the same Mosaic laws as would the Jews.

All attempts to make use of the information flowing back from a succession of claims by explorers and pioneers in the west who met with Welsh-speaking Native Americans were constantly bedevilled by the problems of trying to relate the British discovery of America to a putative Madoc son of Owen Gwynedd around 1170. No one seemed to care that Caradoc of Llancarfan finished his *History* in 1157, and almost certainly died that year. So he could not have recorded a voyage made in 1170 some thirteen years after he died. Most were blissfully unaware of Walter de Map the son of Blondel de Mapes and Nefydd of Llancarfan, daughter of the Lord Gweirydd, writing sarcastically of the poetry written about Madoc by his neighbour William Fleming some thirty-five years before 1170.

Either way, the Kentucky pioneers were firm believers in the story of Madoc and it was very firmly established as the folklore of the territory. One remarkable account appeared in *The Public Advertiser* of Louisville, which reported how a Lieutenant Joseph Roberts met with a Welsh-speaking 'Indian' at Washington. This is probably the village of Washington, Kentucky, identified as such by Jim Michael. On 15th May 1819, this report detailed how Lieutenant Roberts, who was a Welsh speaker from North Wales, jokingly rebuked a Welsh youth who was a waiter at the saloon-hotel in Washington, using their native language. An 'Indian' chief, who was there present in the room, immediately approached Roberts and asked him if that was his native language offering his hand in friendship. When Roberts confirmed that Khumric was his native language, the chief informed him that it was also the language of his parents and of his nation.

It transpired that the chief had heard of England but not of Wales, and had no idea of it. What he did know was that his ancestors had come from a country far away to the east across the great waters, which of course could be Britain across the Atlantic. The custom was to teach their children in Khumric and to prohibit any other language with them until they were twelve years old. After that they were free to learn any other language they wished. Roberts was reportedly amazed to speak the language with a man who painted his face and wore feathers in his hair; and this is important as he reported that the man had shaved his hair on both sides of his head, leaving only the crown as a form of cockscomb. This matches with Julius Caesar's account in *De Bello Gallico* of British warriors, where he described them plastering their hair upright in the centre like a cockscomb, or the hogged mane of a horse.

This nation which spoke Khumric were reported as dwelling about eight hundred miles west of Philadelphia, and according to Roberts, they possessed considerable knowledge of herbal medicines, which again would accord with British traditions.

Another story of an encounter with Khumric-speaking 'Indians' was reported at second hand by the Hon. Harry Toulmin in 1804. Whilst Toulmin was a man of repute, whose integrity and veracity could not be questioned, he got the story from a John Chiles of Woodford County, who in turn had been told the story by Maurice Griffiths who had emigrated from Virginia as a boy. This would never stand up in a court, but if Griffiths spoke the truth and the account is accurate (for Toulmin was the Secretary of State for Kentucky, President of Transylvania University, and a Judge of the United States District Court, as well as the distinguished author of law books and histories), there is something to consider. Toulmin was also a Unitarian minister of the gospels.

The story is thiat Maurice Griffiths was captured by Shawnees in 1764, and after two to three years he went with a hunting-party of five braves to explore up the Missouri river. After a long and difficult journey up-river, the group came upon a nation who were light of complexion and who spoke Khumric. 'After passing the mountains they entered a fine, fertile tract of land, which having travelled through for several days, they accidentally met with three white men in Indian dress. Griffiths immediately understood that their language as it was pure Welsh, though they occasionally made use of a few words with which he was not acquainted.'

The parties now went forward for four or five days before arriving at a village where everyone was white skinned, 'having all the European colour'. Fifteen miles further on was a second township where the king and chiefs met at the council house in immediate session for three days. Griffiths apparently said nothing in Khumric all this time, for well over a week. The decision of the council was to put the five Shawnees and Griffiths to death, the reasoning being that if they were spies for their nation, then their return and report would bring an invasion into this good land, whereas if they were killed then no one would know of the existence of this nation or its territories, which would then remain secure.

Griffiths finally broke his silence when sentenced to death, and he spoke to the astonished council of chiefs in their own language, assuring them that there was no spying expedition and no planned invasion of their territories. The outcome was a change of heart and the six intruders were spared and lived with these white-skinned, Khumric-speaking nation for eight months. Of their history they reported that they knew nothing apart from the fact that they had come up a river from a very distant country. They lived in a tract of land fifty miles long on the banks of the Missouri, and where three tributary rivers fell into the Missouri. They were hunters who dressed in skins, and they had no iron, but used bows and arrows. They were numerous, and Griffiths estimated that there must have been some fifty thousand men capable of bearing arms, so they were indeed a formidable nation.

Maurice Griffiths made no mention of the religion practised by this white-skinned nation, apart from stating that they possessed no books or records of any kind. The lack of comment upon customs is unfortunate. So, is it a traveller's tale, or is it true?

In 1842 one Thomas Hinds, a noted antiquarian, wrote to the editor of *The American Pioneer* and detailed how six skeletons, each wearing a brass breastplate, had been dug up near Jeffersonville. These metal plates were reported as being emblazoned with a Welsh coat of arms specified as a mermaid and a harp, which will be news to Welshmen. The 'Mermaid' figure could perhaps be the half-man half-snake figure of Ea-Oannes, who became Yah or Jah, and Yahweh or Jehovah, but until one of these breastplates is recovered the story again gets any enquiry precisely nowhere. Jim Michael has a lead on one possibility, but so far has not yet tracked down its possible present owner.

Mr Hinds quoted an account of a Mr MacIntosh who reputedly claimed to have witnessed a Welshman in discussion with a Native American far up the Missouri. To this was added the note that the Mohawk tribe had a tradition of the White Nation, presumably the British Khumry, being cut off in a war at the Falls of the Ohio. This matches with the Algonquin, Delaware, and Cherokee traditions of this event, and the finding of six skeletons wearing some form of breastplates near the Falls of the Ohio River in 1799 is clearly being linked to this long-ago battle at these Falls.

Chapter 15 - British Coelbren Inscriptions in America

A further account of contact with Khumric-speaking Indians was given to Edward Williams in Glamorgan by a Mr Binon, who lived at Coyty (now Coety), who had spent more than thirty years in America. Binon stated that around 1750 he was trading with the Indians out of Philadelphia, and with five or six others he ventured much further west than usual. They encountered a nation that actually spoke Khumric. Binon claimed to have seen crude stone-built houses, ruinous buildings, which could have been a castle and a church, and an ancient book which contained their language and their religion. Binon was shown the book but was unable to read it. When he told them that he came from Wales, and in Khumric he would tell them he was a Kumro, speaking Khumraeg, and was from Khumry, these Native Americans said that they recognized the place as being that from where their ancestors came. They would of course not recognize the English word 'Wales'.

Finally, these accounts of meetings ceased to be reported. Whether diseases to which they had no resistance wiped out these populations, or whether they were Mellungians, is not known. Five instances of ancient books, presumed to be Bibles, led to two being in the hands of the French Governor of Quebec, but none are now available. All that remains is disused, dismantled hill forts, huge snake mounds, cor-like religious circles, grave mounds, and the priceless inscriptions in caves, on rocks and stones, and on artefacts. Twenty-five reputedly authentic accounts of meetings with Khumric-speaking Natives are known, and of these people there is now no trace.

Chapter Sixteen

American Inscriptions

Jim Michael had flown over from the U.S.A. to visit Baram Blackett and Alan Wilson in early 1991, and whilst he was accustomed to academic intransigence at home, he was shocked at the savagery of the situation confronting his contacts in Wales. In 1992 the Ancient Kentucke Historical Association arranged for Alan Wilson to fly over to Kentucky where a series of lecture engagements had been set up, and arrangements made to allow him to visit some of the more important American sites. Despite the flow of information sent over through the mail, nothing could have prepared Alan for what he encountered in the U.S.A.

Alan's cataract problems were worsening and he was suffering from an untypical loss of confidence resulting from this. Out of doors in daylight he could generally cope, but evenings and nights were a different matter. He was unable to read, and he could not see the slides shown to illustrate any lectures that he was to give, and he would have to rely upon his memory. The fact that he could not read the notices of flights at the airports or see the numbers on buses was a source of worry to him, and at the last minute on the day before departure he decided not to go to the U.S.A. Two friends of Alan and Baram, Pete Sunman and Karen McRobbie, would have none of this, and they packed his suitcases and then literally first shoved him protesting into a taxi, and then pushed him aboard the bus to the airport. So, Alan Wilson set off for the U.S.A. feeling like a real-life version of the totally myopic cartoon character Mr Magoo.

He made it to St Louis, and somehow caught the connection to Louisville, where he was met by Jim Michael. The first task was to put together a double act between Jim Michael and Alan to make a presentation at the I.S.S.A.C. conference in Columbus, Georgia. I.S.S.A.C. stood for 'Institute of Scientific Study of American Culture', and its headquarters were in Columbus. So, a few days after Alan arrived in Kentucky, he set

Chapter 16 - America Inscriptions

off with Jim Michael on the twelve hundred-mile drive to Columbus, Georgia, where they arrived, on 9th October 1992. The venue for the week's events was the Old Opera House, with its fine auditorium and its typically western saloon-style bar, where a Hollywood western movie could easily have been made with Errol Flynn or John Wayne without hardly changing a thing.

The first thing they did on arrival was to visit a cultural festival organised by local Native American tribes. Here they witnessed an extraordinary event at a fenced square enclosure, which, as Dr Joe Mahon pointed out, was constructed to conform to the Bible description of the Festival of the Booths. The booths set on each of the four sides of the enclosure were square structures made from poles, which were roofed with leafy branches. Heavy timber logs were laid out in the form of a cross in the centre of the enclosure, presumably to indicate Betelgeux in Orion the Man, Aldebaran in Taurus the Bull, Regulus in Leo the Lion, and Altair in Aquila the Eagle.

Other logs were laid to surround this timber cross. Then the participants from the Yuchi nation lined up in pairs in descending order of height, with no regard for either age or sex. The tallest pair was at the front and took the lead followed by the others right down to tiny children. It was almost impossible not to recognize the impressive symbolism as this procession slowly circled the arranged logs chanting 'Yahweh, Yahweh, Yahweh'. The whole representation was that of a comet with its long tapering tail circling around through the skies.

As with British Khumric records, the name of God was uttered by the deity as IO U or I AU, which became Iahweh (in English pronunciation and spelling 'Yahweh'), and was the dreaded screech of the comet. As for the squared area of the Booths Festival Alan Wilson already knew of similar sites in Wales which he had never before equated with this well-recorded festival.

Later in the week Alan and Jim attended a lecture on Philosophy given by Dr John Ross of the Lakota Sioux. Anyone who mistakenly thinks that Native Americans do not have a good sense of humour has never had the pleasure of listening to Dr John Ross, who, wearing his national dress complete with feathers, was at the same time, authoritative, easily understood, informative, instructive, and highly entertaining. Alan Wilson sat spell bound as Dr Ross spoke of the Sioux beliefs, and described the circles of the continuity of life and creation, which appeared to very closely match the doctrines of ancient British Druidic Circles of Inchoation. It is doubtful if anyone else who heard Dr Ross or his kinsmen speak had ever heard of the Druid Circles of

Inchoation, and would be able to see the possible parallels between the two cultures.

One of the many presentations at the Old Opera House was given by the Rev. Jim Burchall, from near Manchester, Kentucky, who, after he had heard what Jim Michael and Alan Wilson had to say, got into conversation with them. The Rev. Burchall and his colleague Hezekiah Hemsley had knowledge of several rock-cut inscriptions close to Manchester that were not identifiable with any commonly known alphabet, and he now thought that they might match the British Coelbren as described by Alan and Jim Michael. Arrangements were made for a visit to Manchester in Clay County to see these inscriptions, some of which were very recent discoveries.

The whole week in Columbus, Georgia, was taken up with a kaleidoscopic variety of presentations by generally remarkably well-qualified independent researchers. Some able mathematicians were investigating the fact that the layout of some of the circle and squared earth-bank and stone mounds of North America indisputably showed that the ancients were mathematically able to square the circle. They, and others, were working on the similarity between the ovals of British and American stone 'circles' which are based on combining two overlapping, different-sized circles. Another clever researcher was examining the detail of mix and content in Roman bricks in Europe, and bricks found in an area of South America. He had located fifty-one identicalities. Yet another researcher was diligently creating a catalogue of all the ancient Iberian inscriptions from ancient Spain that, sadly for him, did not assist in the deciphering of the North or South American Coelbren inscriptions. He is probably correct in believing that they are written in ancient Irish Gaelic. In ultra-conformist dog-trained Britain, where ability and success are feared, and mediocrity is the most prized value, Alan Wilson and Baram Blackett often felt isolated and alone in conducting research which contradicted and challenged authority. Yet here was a whole assembly of hard-working, non-conformist and dedicated researchers, all doing their own thing.

The first major target for Alan Wilson was to visit the famous Pig-Pen site in Eastern Kentucky. The site is at a low cliff, an outcrop of rock between two farms in a generally heavily wooded area. The land above the cliff to the edge is owned by one farmer, and the land below the cliff reaching to the base is owned by the neighbouring farmer, and rumour has it that the two don't get on together. The Pig-Pen itself is an overhang - a low, wide cave reaching back some twenty-five feet under the cliff at the base. So, is the Pig-Pen the property of the farmer who owns the land above the cliff, as it reaches in under his land, or is the Pig-Pen the property of the farmer who owns

Chapter 16 - America Inscriptions

the land abutting right up to the base of the cliff, as access is only through his property? Alan immediately felt that he was back in Britain, and particularly Wales, where these problems are endemic. Access to the secret walled-up Cave of the Cross at Nevern is gained from the cliff face from Church of Wales land, but the cave then stretches back underneath another property.

Above the cliff is a large plâteau of cleared and fairly flat land of around fifty acres. This would be an eminently suitable area for raising crops. So, after the long drive through wooded areas and meeting the landowners and a few of their friends, at the isolated farm above the cliff, Alan Wilson, Jim Michael and their escort descended the cliff to take a look at the Pig-Pen. The site is called this because the farmer at one time used this cave-overhang as a ready-made pigsty, by simply fencing off the entry and herding his swine to shelter under this deep overhang. In most areas the cave roof is around three feet high, and it is necessary to crouch and crawl to get to the areas of smooth, flat, horizontal rock some twenty-five feet in at the back of the overhang to get to the inscriptions.

So Alan Wilson came face to face with the inscriptions, which he had only previously seen from photographs sent over by Jim Michael. A careful examination showed that the photographs which Jim Michael had sent across the Atlantic to Baram and Alan were clear and accurate, and there was no discrepancy, or anything unclear. The writings are in three groups, and the first to be examined are arranged in four groups set in the angles around a large Christian Cross. The texts read from left to right, as all Coelbren inscriptions appear to do in the Christian epoch.

This section of the inscriptions appears to be a straightforward Harvest Prayer or even a Harvest Thanksgiving statement. Immigrants in a strange new land, totally dependent upon their own, perhaps limited, resources and seed for crops, and with no possibility of help from either neighbouring people or trading partners in the event of a crop failure, would write this. Jim Michael suggests a reading of: 'Tarry here on high fat (= bountiful) corn plough-land on high here.' This is as good a rendering of the intended message as is possible, but given the 'AA' and 'I' signs in the lower right quarter, we may have: 'Tarry here on high, fat (= bountiful) corn plough-land, rejoice towards on high.'

Jim Michael with the Pig-Pen inscriptions in Kentucky

Chapter 16 - America Inscriptions

Detail of Pig-Pen inscriptions in Kentucky

Second detail of Pig-Pen inscriptions

Chapter 16 - America Inscriptions

Third detail of Pig-Pen inscriptions in Kentucky

The King Arthur Conspiracy - Wilson & Blackett

Fourth detail of Pig-Pen inscriptions

Chapter 16 - America Inscriptions

Either way the inscription is obviously in Coelbren, and it follows naturally that the language employed is simple Khumric-Welsh. The interpretation being that these statements were carved into the rock by members of the Arthur II and Madoc expedition of *c.* AD 574. The full reading is shown in the Pig-Pen illustrations and suggests a reading of: 'Tarry here on high, fat (bountiful) corn plough-land on high here'.

With Jim Michael carefully highlighting the ancient lettering with chalk, and debating with Alan over any possible natural clefts that might confuse matters, the process of on-the-spot decipherment of the Pig-Pen texts proceeded. The centre section of the texts lies to the left of what Alan and Jim recognized as a Chi-Rho sign, and, as with the other groups of inscriptions, it was accompanied by known Coelbren signs. These were identified and their modern equivalent letters identified. This section deciphers and is shown in illustration 16-2: *The Pig-Pen Central Area inscription* and appears to give the message -

'What impels (god or nature) to grow verdant it shall be on high a deluge (rain) to break in (the) furrows.'

The obvious vital preoccupation with the growing of crops and good harvests is again evident. This is perhaps something we have tended to forget and overlook in our modern industrialised world. A whole group of Welsh words commences with- 'ire-', indicating the regeneration of plant-life in the spring and summer seasons. In this sense this inscription adds little to our knowledge of the life drama of the writers, apart from revealing a probable harvest prayer.

When they had first arrived at the farm above the Pig-Pen Alan Wilson had noticed that there was a possible grave-mound near the top of the hill and close to the cliff. A farm building stands on top of this obviously well-drained and raised area, making any positive identification difficult. There also appeared to be vestiges of banks and ditches around the hilltop area, and Jim Michael estimated that some fifty acres of good arable land stretched away across the plâteau. It appears that no one had previously given any thought to looking for any other physical remains of habitation or sepulchre that might be associated with the carved inscriptions in the cliff overhang.

These possible vestigial remains above the cliff may in fact be associated with a third section of inscriptions in the Pig-Pen below the cliff. This appears to be a carving and a short text that is a resurrection statement. A mound is shown, which appears to represent a typical tumulus or grave-mound, and under this mound is a small number of Coelbren letters which may be three words of a short statement. The full reading is shown in *illustration 16-3: The Pig-Pen Grave Mound inscription.*

The first letter or two letters is difficult to assess because there are two strokes which are both almost vertical. It appears to be/ I that gives Ffei for 'subtle, or cunning', but it is possible that I \ is intended, which would produce 'ill' meaning 'they'. Less likely it might be I / giving 'if' meaning 'to cast down'- and this is the least likely reading.

A reading of 'They cry out the secret name of god' from within a tomb mound makes sense, as does 'Subtle they cry out the secret name of god.' The third alternative may be associated with the ancient practice of sometimes carving grave memorials in Latin, and commencing with 'Hic Iacit', which means 'Here is cast down', and which is almost invariably misread as 'Here lies...' The third alternative would give us "(they or he) who is cast down cry out the secret name of god."

This raises a very important issue, for ancient Khumric epic poetry is specific that the desiccated body of King Arthur II was kept through the winter under a 'bargoed' or 'bargod' before it was transported back across the continent and the Atlantic in the spring and summer, and a 'bargod' is a cavity under a cliff which is not exactly a cave. This is precisely what the Pig-Pen in Kentucky is. This then brought matters to the inscription which other researchers have dubbed the Chi-Rho inscription. This is again a clear Coelbren statement of a Christian nature and it also appears to relate to the sixth-century AD adventures of Arthur II and his brother Madoc Morfran. The style of the lettering is similar to that of the other inscriptions discussed.

This statement implies a belief in some form of Christianity, and it is doubtful if it refers to the Resurrection story at the core of the belief of most branches of the Christian religion. The text appears to read as: -

'In a state of being in Christ (= salvation) taken out into the strong light, a long time having been in the tomb, outwards thou art.'

The archaic nature of these Coelbren writings appears to favour the sixth-century expeditions, and it is difficult to see what other source or origin they might have. This Chi-Rho inscription again appears to directly relate to the momentous event of the

Chapter 16 - America Inscriptions

Illustration 16-1: The Pig-Pen, Kentucky, U.S.A.

One prominent set of inscriptions in the Pig-Pen consists of four short statements set around the four quarters of a Christian cross. This reads straight into Coelbren from left to right, as do all inscriptions of the Christian epoch.

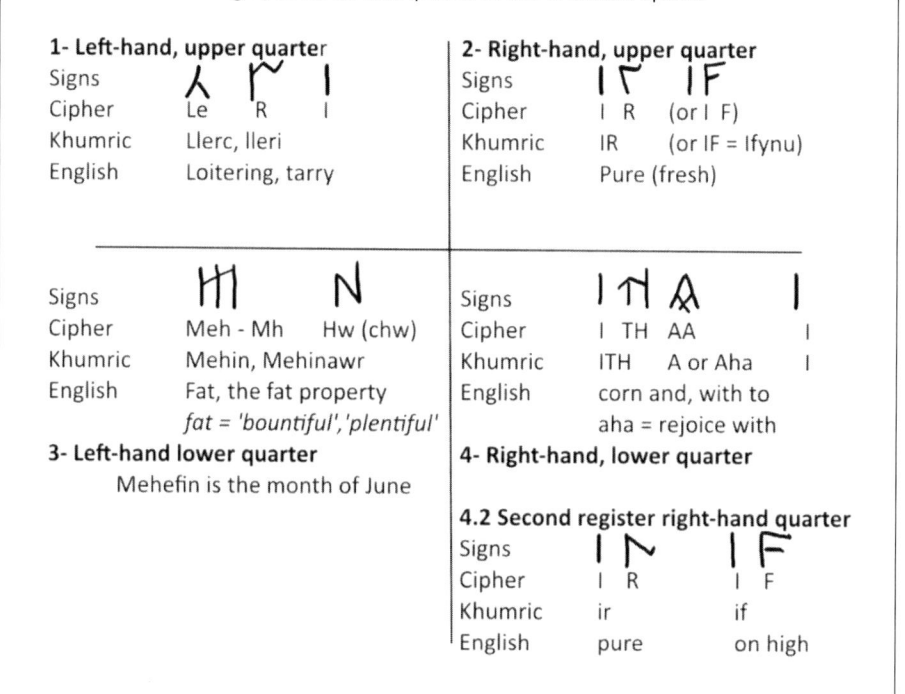

1- Left-hand, upper quarter

Signs			
Cipher	Le	R	I
Khumric	Llerc, lleri		
English	Loitering, tarry		

2- Right-hand, upper quarter

Signs		
Cipher	I R	(or I F)
Khumric	IR	(or IF = Ifynu)
English	Pure (fresh)	

Signs		
Cipher	Meh - Mh	Hw (chw)
Khumric	Mehin, Mehinawr	
English	Fat, the fat property	
	fat = 'bountiful', 'plentiful'	

3- Left-hand lower quarter
Mehefin is the month of June

Signs		
Cipher	I TH	AA
Khumric	ITH	A or Aha
English	corn and, with to	
	aha = rejoice with	

4- Right-hand, lower quarter

4.2 Second register right-hand quarter

Signs		
Cipher	I R	I F
Khumric	ir	if
English	pure	on high

The inscription reads as a Harvest Prayer or a Harvest Thanksgiving statement. Immigrants in a strange new land some five thousand miles from home, and entirely dependent on their own resources, with no possible aid from anywhere in the event of crop failures. James B. Michael of Louisville, Kentucky, suggests of 'tarry here on high, fat (bountiful) corn ploughland on high here'. This is probably as good a rendering as any, but given the 'AA' and 'I' signs on the Right-hand lower we may have 'tarry here on high, fat (bountiful) grain ploughland, rejoice towards on high.'

Either way the inscription is very definitely written in British-Khumric Coelbren and the language of Khumric-'Welsh'.

Illustration 16-2: The Pig-Pen Central Area inscription

As with the other Pig-Pen inscriptions and other messages left around in Kentucky the inscription is written in the British Coelbren Alphabet and the language is Khumric.

American Cipher	R WY F	I R E	I E	I F
Khumric	rhwyf	irdu	ie	if
English	what impels a ruler	to grow juicy verdant	it shall be	on high

American Cipher	Lli F	B(a)	Lli	I
Khumric	Llif	bali	(balc, balcio)	
English	a flood, deluge	to break into furrows		

The text appears to read: 'what impels (God) to grow verdant it shall be on high a deluge (rain) to break in furrows.'

The obvious overriding preoccupation with, and the necessity to grow crops and to get good harvests in, a new land is evident. The inscription adds little of historical value to the great life drama being enacted by the writers apart from revealing a harvest prayer.

When first attempting decipherment from photographs, Alan Wilson and Baram Blackett had no idea of the nature of the site that they were dealing with. Up above is a large fairly flat area of good farmland, and there appears to be vestigial remains of mounds and ditches around this open hill-top area. There is a possible mound on the top of the hill above the cliff and overhang, but a farm building stands on top of this raised area and it is difficult to determine whether or not this is the mound shown in the rock-cut inscriptions in the overhang below. Other soldiers were killed in the fighting that took place before the assassination of King Arthur II and their bodies were not returned to Britain. This mound could well be their grave. Jim Michael estimates about fifty acres of good arable land on this hill-top area.

Ancient epic Khumric poetry records that King Arthur's corpse was placed in an overhang over the winter to await transport to Britain in the spring or summer of the next year and some of the overhang inscriptions may confirm this.

Chapter 16 - America Inscriptions

Illustration 16-3: The Pig-Pen Grave Mound inscription

One carving and inscription in the Pig-Pen appears to be a resurrection statement. It shows a mound of typically tumulus or grave-mound style, and there is a three-part short statement.

The first word is difficult to make out as both strokes are almost vertical. We may have 'Ffe I', giving giving 'ffei', or instead we may have 'I Ll', giving us 'ill', and meaning 'they'. It could also be 'cast down' which is the normal British burial statement. In Britain the Latin version is 'hic iacit', meaning 'here is cast down' and this is routinely mistranslated as 'here lies'.

The statement beneath the grave mound is as follows:

American Cipher	╱ I	⊣ I	╱I╲
	Ffe I	HW I	AWEN sign
Khumric	Ffei	hwi	
English	subtle cunning	to hulloo to shout/cry out	the secret name of God

American Cipher	I ╲	⊣ I	╱I╲
	I LL	HW I	AWEN sign
Khumric	ill	hwi	
English	they	cry out shout/hulloo	the secret name of God

The reading of 'they cry out the secret name of God', associated with a tomb mound, makes good sense. Whether we have subtle to cry out the secret name of God' or 'they cry out the secret name of God' or 'they who are cast down cry out the secret name of God', is open to interpretation. The general intent is fairly clear.

The mound on the hill top above the overhang is important as others were killed in the fighting after which King Arthur II was assassinated, and this might well be the grave of those that fell.

paramount British king being assassinated in America. Very few of the ancient British kings are recorded as suffering violent deaths, and the majority died peacefully in old age. Their sons and grandsons, or otherwise the Wledigs (Legates), routinely led the armies in warfare, unless as in the case of Arthur II, who had no sons, or their sons were too young. This text clearly states that a corpse is being removed from a tomb after a prolonged period to be taken outwards - away.

These Coelbren inscriptions certainly appear to match with the story told in the epic sixth-century poetry, mostly ascribed to Taliesin son of St Henwg, the Merlyn figure. These poems have in modern times been dubbed as being 'mystical', when they are nothing of the sort. Instead, they are detailed and accurate accounts of momentous events in sixth-century history. It is ironic that these supposedly lost or unrecorded missing accounts of allegedly forgotten British history have been written down in great clarity and always available from the allegedly unrecorded times.

This now moves matters forward to a remarkable inscribed stone discovered by Andrew Smith on 20th May 1987 in Jackson County, Kentucky (illustration 16-4). This stone appears to be of tremendous importance, and the site and surrounding area may contain archaeological evidence that might serve further to corroborate the ever-accumulating evidence supporting British-Khumric records. This inscription can be deciphered and translated as follows:

The word 'dwy' is one of a large number of Khumric words with dual meanings, and this otherwise unexplained duality is the key which is vital to understanding the method of unlocking the door to decipherments extending back to before 2000 BC. The word 'dwy' means both 'two' and also 'the ruler'. This text has a typical cross with a bar or foot, and it appears to be Christian, and it is most certainly written in Coelbren. The Andrew Smith inscription from Jackson County appears to read literally as:

'Unlucky the ruler mighty this place distinctly the end (for him).'

This might be better expressed in English as: 'Unlucky for the mighty ruler this place distinctly was his end.'

We have no name for the mighty ruler, but it seems to be unavoidable that this stone marks the place where King Arthur II ap Meurig was assassinated in ancient Kentucky.

Chapter 16 - America Inscriptions

The stone was found near to the site of what appears to be a remarkable natural fortress, and the inscription is on a low boulder. The Khumric record states that Arthur was sitting - perhaps on a boulder or rock - inside an enclosed area surrounded by a palisade, after a day's fighting. A 'naked savage' crept up through bushes and brakes and unexpectedly struck him with either a javelin or an arrow. The location is one from where it would be quite a straightforward matter to transport the body down the Kentucky River to the Ohio. There are also other inscriptions in overhangs nearby.

At all times Jim Michael, Alan Wilson, and Baram Blackett have been careful never to reveal the Coelbren ciphers to anyone in America. So which sign corresponds to what modern letter is kept as secret as is possible. This has to be done to avoid allegations of forgery, although the majority of Coelbren inscriptions in America have been well known for very long periods and were never before identified as British Coelbren. It also serves to try to prevent any 'helpful' forged inscriptions being made.

If this stone recording an unlucky ruler relates to Arthur II, and the Pig-Pen is the Bargod or Bargoed = overhang where the desiccated body was kept over the winter before being transported back to Britain, then there is an obvious link with the stone found at Yarmouth Bay in Nova Scotia. This inscribed stone was found on his estate at Yarmouth Bay in 1812 by Dr Richard Fletcher. The stone was at the high-water mark near the shore, at the head of a cove on the north-west point of Yarmouth Harbour.

This rock or stone is an irregular hemisphere, and around two feet in diameter (about 60 cm.). It has one naturally smooth surface upon which an inscription has been cut, and it may have once stood on the bank above the shore where it was found. The stone has been examined several times by academics, and on 15th April 1948, the Welsh magazine *Y Drych* carried an article written by a Dr William Evans that positively identified the inscription as being written in the British Coelbren alphabet:

> 'The lettering on the Yarmouth Stone (Nova Scotia) is undoubtedly ancient Welsh, resembling no other alphabet on earth.'

Close-up of Yarmouth Stone inscription

The inscription on the stone was made using a sharp, pointed instrument, and some form of mallet or hammer. The marks of the successive blows are clearly visible, and the resulting grooves extremely shallow. Sadly, Dr William Evans was totally inept when it came down to the translation of the text.

This inscription can in fact be read with a fair degree of confidence *(see Illustration 16-5)*, and Alan Wilson and Baram Blackett base their decipherment on the large number of similar texts which they have read in Britain, Etruria, Asia Minor, America, and elsewhere, over the years. Wherever two identical sign/letters are found together there is an invariable intention of 'dwy' = 'two' = 'the Ruler', as 'dwy' means both 'two' and 'ruler'. The Yarmouth Bay Stone introduces this concept with Ti + Ti, and then with C + C.

It may seem extraordinary that no one has translated this inscribed text before, and Dr William Evans made a dog's dinner of his attempt by attempting to conjure the name of Madoc out of the letters and the date of around AD 1170. He was also unfortunate as he faced the difficulty of the insane campaign of Griffith John Williams at its height. A wild onslaught of absurdities was spewing out unchallenged across the BBC airways that labelled all South East Wales History as forged. The ancient Coelbren Alphabet was being derided as a forgery of AD 1800 and academics fearful of their reputations, and their places on the career ladder, were steering well away from the allegedly tainted matter. They should instead have confronted the idiot from Cellan.

So, the decipherment of ancient Coelbren texts in Britain, and also mixed Latin and Coelbren texts, became a taboo area for those seeking to make a comfortable, safe,

Chapter 16 - America Inscriptions

and protected academic career. Where inscribed Latin texts contained Coelbren letters to give otherwise difficult Welsh sounds and meanings to names and words, the British-Khumric letters were now deliberately misidentified as ancient Irish. Trying to explain how or why Irish would be written on the monumental stones of the kings in Wales led to quite remarkable re-writes of history. This turned the Latin- En- Ni - Ac - Un- into an alleged 'Einion' and allowed the memorial stone of King Theothuric-Theoderic or Tewdrig, the Uthyrpendragon who was mortally wounded in AD 509 at Tintern Ford, to be concealed. The same process was applied to the stones of King Teithfallt-Theodosius, the father of Tewdrig, and to that of the Bishop Cuhelyn, a son of King Tewdrig.

Common sense - a rare commodity - demands that the Yarmouth Bay Stone should be seen as clearly marking the place from which Taliesin son of St Henwg-the Merlyn figure, and Myrddyn Wyllt-Martin the Wild, along with five others, sailed in AD 579. They took with them the desiccated corpse of King Arthrwys ap Meurig ap Tewdrig, their purpose being to return him to his native land of Britain. Sixth-century epic poetry and other historical records, in the *Life of St Illtyd* and in Nennius' *History of Britain,* detail their arrival at the estuary of the Ewenny River in Glamorgan in 579- 580. Poetical records tell of the King's corpse being wrapped in a bag or pouch made by three ladies of the court from three North American deerskins. The Yarmouth Bay inscription matches with these records. It is not impossible that the grave of Arthur II might contain scraps of North American deerskins, which might be DNA-tested. There might also be pollen peculiar to the Mid-West of the U.S.A., and which is well-nigh indestructible.

This now introduces some other solid evidence, and it comes inadvertently from North Wales, where the mixed Welsh, Irish, and Strathclyde population has run riot for many years in attacking the impeccably genuine South-East Wales histories. As late as 1580, over a thousand years after the death of King Arthur II in America, the North Wales bard named Rhys Cain, who was then living in Oswestry, travelled to an Eisteddfodd in Powys. An Eisteddfod is a bardic meeting for competitions in poetry, literature, music, and song, and related events. In 1580, during the reign of Elizabeth I, Rhys Cain was shown a Glamorgan Bard's wooden Peithynen, and he mocked it. This is an upright wooden frame that holds sticks cut triangular in cross section and slotted horizontally across the frame. The faces of the sticks forming a horizontal rack are cleaned and smoothed. The straight stroke lettering of the Coelbren Alphabet is cut into the flat surfaces of the triangular sticks set horizontally in the frame, allowing rows of writing to be shown as on three printed pages of a book.

It is in line with all North Wales negative activity that mockery would be anticipated from Rhys Cain in 1580, but what he mocked is more than interesting. Rhys Cain not only jeered at the Coelbren Peithynen frame, but he went so far as to write a satirical poem about it and the contents of its text. He made fun of a story of the death, the embalming, and the transportation of the sixth-century King, Arthur II of Glamorgan and Gwent. This is part of what Rhys Cain from Merionethshire wrote in *An Englyn on a Wooden Book*:

> 'A skeleton in a bag. It is not a wise lip that praises it. The song-book of a purblind bard, it is difficult to understand it rightly, it will suit one who is blind.'

An Englyn is a Grave Elegy, and it is well known that by its very nature a Peithynen text in Coelbren could be read in the dark or by the blind. Straight strokes that are cut into a smooth wood surface with a knife or axe, can indeed be read by a person using his fingers. It is the first form of Braille. But Rhys Cain is here confirming the existence of a Peithynen frame and Coelbren writing in 1580. This is over three-hundred and sixty years before the modern North Wales academics, and Griffith John Williams of BBC fame, declared that all South-East Wales genuine histories, along with the Coelbren alphabet and the Peithynen frame, were inventions of the most honourable and honest Edward Williams, *alias* Iolo Morganwg in around 1800. In addition, Rhys Cain is unwittingly proving and confirming the antiquity of the stories of the Body in the Bag, which are also derided as modern forgeries. He also confirms South-East Wales as the centre of the ancient Coelbren writing.

Neither Jim Michael nor Baram Blackett nor Alan Wilson anticipated that there would be written supporting evidence of the epic of King Arthur II in the U.S.A. and Canada. That there were Coelbren inscriptions in North America had been long known to Alan and Baram, but their locations, numbers, and contents were never anticipated. That only the most important events would be set down would be natural, and that memorial stones - as in other ancient cultures - invariably were set up by, or concerned, the kings, was expected. The corroborative evidence in the U.S.A. was beyond all expectations and imagination. It is no exaggeration to say that the enigma of the end of King Arthur II son of Meurig (pronounced My-rigg) could not be resolved without the American evidence. A great deal is owed to all those who plod hopefully through the trackless woods, scrambling up and down slopes, pushing through thickets, and venturing into holes and caves, to find the priceless texts.

Chapter 16 - America Inscriptions

Overhang inscription

Further up along Bar Creek, a few hundred yards from a roadside farm, there are inscriptions in an overhang under a rocky cliff. These inscriptions are in unmistakeable Coelbren, and the texts state

'Towards my reward (from) the warrior, the ruler, what exists, the ruler fine/subtle he is.'

Immediately opposite this cliff face is a large flat field of good arable land and beyond that is the river. The farmer regularly finds quantities of fine flint arrowheads here, and it is clear that a dim distant forgotten battle was fought here on this fertile bottom land. Who the ruler was is not stated, but it appears that he gave the land to someone.

Two ancient Caucasian-type skeletons were discovered nearby, both teenaged, one male and the other female. These exhibited a venereal disease, and an ancient Khumric poem does mention such diseases implying that these diseases resulted from the impact of the comet debris of AD 562.

The discovery of the Burchall Hemsley Stone

Chapter 16 - American Inscriptions

Rev. Jim Burchall uncovering inscriptions

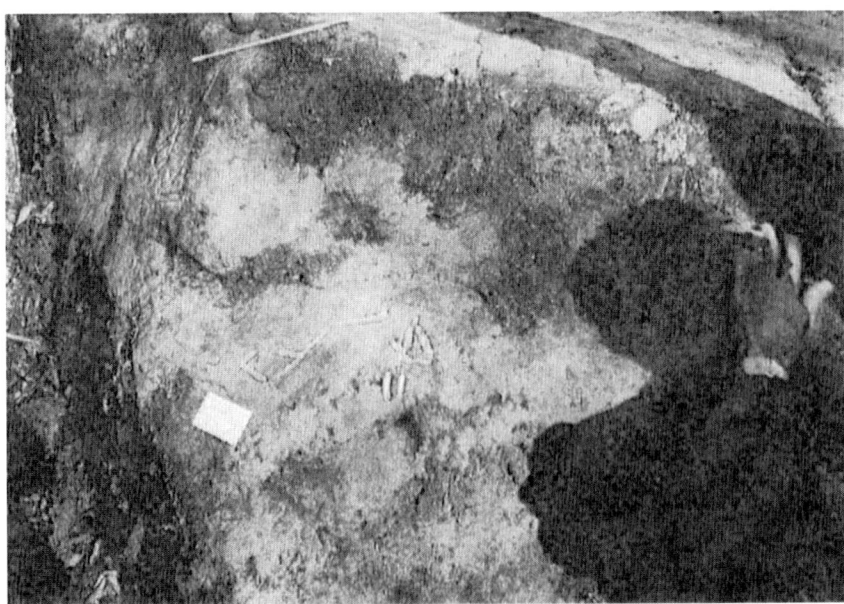

Newly uncovered inscriptions on the Burchall-Hemsley stone

Chapter 16 - American Inscriptions

Illustration 16-4: The Bar Creek Slab in Clay County, Kentucky

Top Side horizontal face inscription

American	↑	↾	│	ⱪ
Coelbren	↑	↾	│	ⱪ
Khumric	ti	rha	i	ffe
English	you are	the power	towards	to go / outward

The text reads: ' You are the power to go towards.'

There is a coiled sign below this inscription that is most probably the Snake Sign of Jehovah. There is also a tall-stemmed cross and a wheel cross carved on this slab face. A cross is 'croes', and 'croeso' means 'welcome'. The 'Wheel' is 'rhod' and 'rhod' also means 'gift', and so we have 'the welcome gift'. The other word for cross is '"ryws', and the tall uncircled cross may be 'crwys-hir'"for 'cross-tall', and phonetically gives giving 'crwydr', that is 'to wander', implying wanderers or migrating people. Putting both crosses together would give 'the welcome gift to the wanderers.'

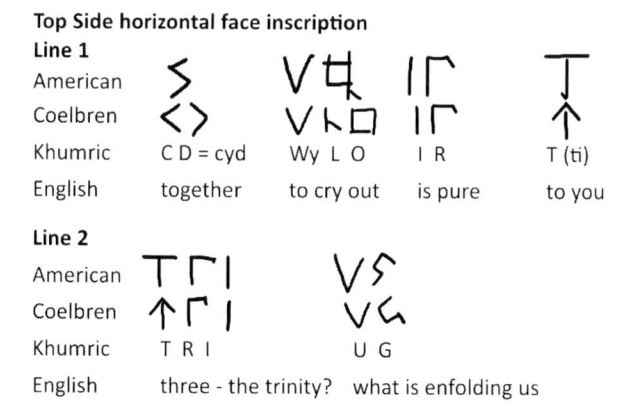

Top Side horizontal face inscription
Line 1

American	⟨⟩	V♯	I⌐	T
Coelbren	⟨⟩	V⊾□	I⌐	↑
Khumric	C D = cyd	Wy L O	I R	T (ti)
English	together	to cry out	is pure	to you

Line 2

American	T⌐I	V⌠
Coelbren	↑⌐I	V⌠
Khumric	T R I	U G
English	three - the trinity?	what is enfolding us

The text reads: ' - "together to cry out to you the trinity that is enfolding us.'"

Reversed this produces D and C, and 'dych' meansing 'a groan, sign'. Another combination sign already encountered elsewhere is the L plus 0, with the 'O' frequently appearing as a diamond or square shape.

North Side - vertical face

American	⌀	I<	+I	<I
Coelbren	⌀	I<	+I	<I
Khumric	Y N G	I C	LI I	C I
English	in the	acute	stream / flood	holdfast

The text reads: '- "In acute (flash) flooding (this is) a holdfast.'"

CI and CA in the 1848 Dictionary have the same meaning of ' "a holdfast, a keep, hold'.." The message is that this is a safe place from violent flooding of the valley and its river. Sadly, in early 1992 a flash flood drowned four people in this same Bar Creek valley just a few miles upstream. Yet here is a fourteen hundred years old warning and a guide to a safe area when just such a flash flood occurs.

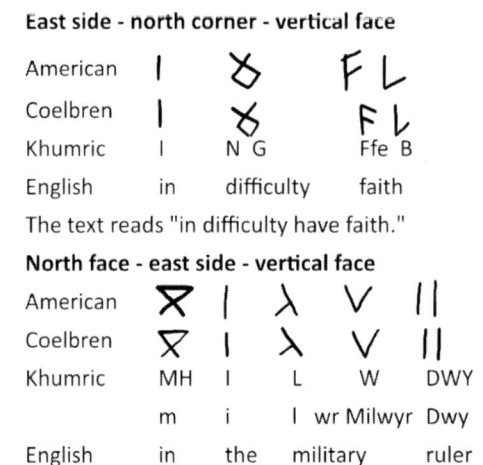

East side - north corner - vertical face

American	I	⌀	F L
Coelbren	I	⌀	F L
Khumric	I	N G	Ffe B
English	in	difficulty	faith

The text reads "in difficulty have faith."

North face - east side - vertical face

American	⌅	I	⋋	V	II
Coelbren	⌅	I	⋋	V	II
Khumric	M H	I	L	W	DWY
	m	i	l	wr Milwyr	Dwy
English	in	the	military	ruler	

The two II signs indicate Two = dwy, and dwy is also = ruler

Chapter 16 - American Inscriptions

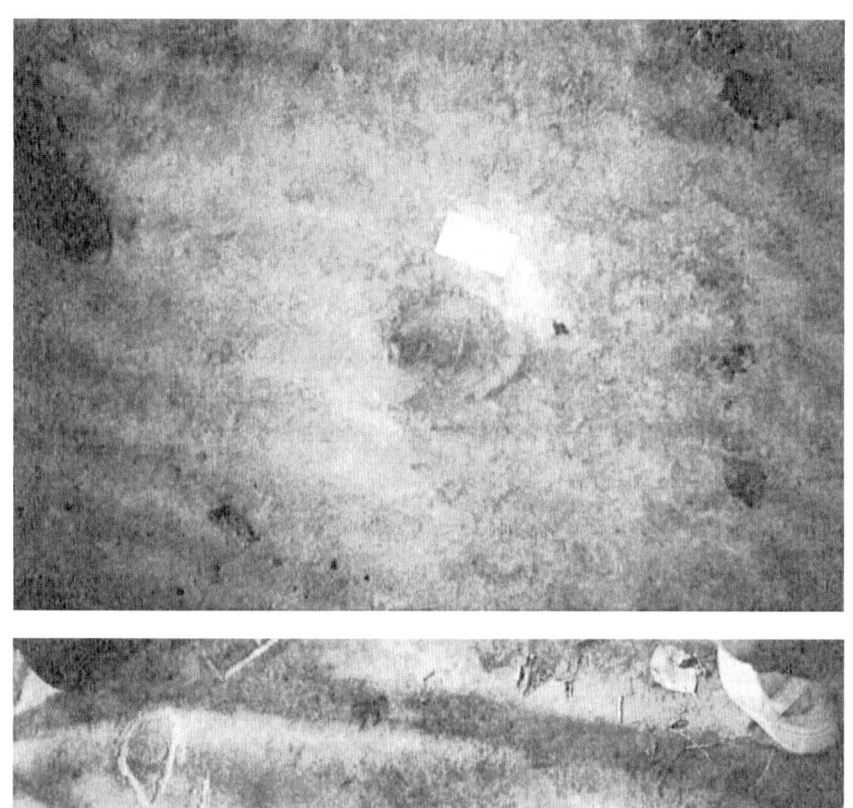

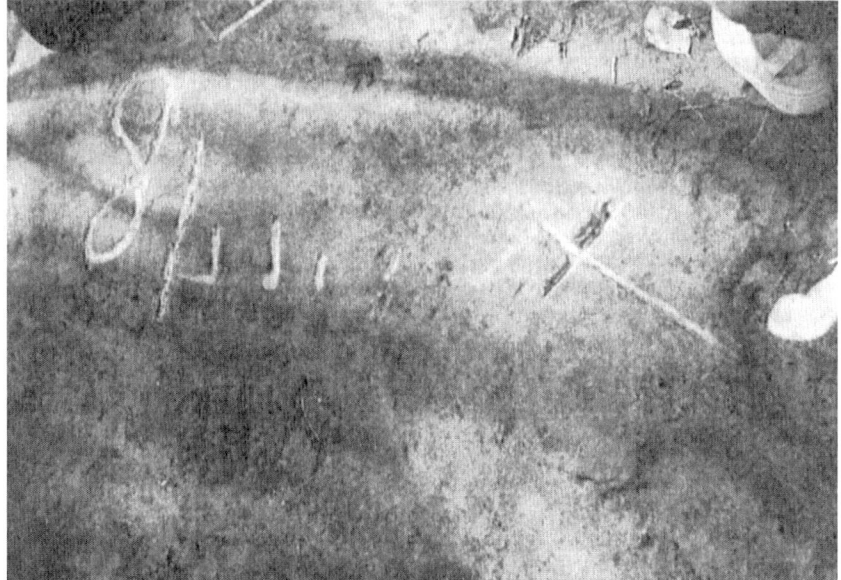

Further uncovered inscriptions on the Burchall-Hemsley stone

The Visit to Bar Creek, Clay County, Kentucky

On Saturday the 26th of October 1992, Jim Michael and Alan Wilson were up and about at 5.30 in the morning, preparing for the long journey to Manchester, Kentucky.

Arrangements had been made to visit sites near Manchester where inscriptions had been discovered, following the discussion with the Reverend Jim Burchall, the local preacher and minister, at the I.S.S.A.C. conference in Columbus, Georgia. *En route* to Manchester, Jim and Alan stopped at the home of Dr Clark, a member of the Ancient Kentucke Historical Association, who would accompany them in his own car, and the party arrived at Jim Burchall's home long before noon.

They were joined by the Rev. Jim Burchall and his friend and co-researcher Hezekiah Hemsley, and Jim Hays, a local teacher who was researching the ancient Warriors' Trail. After a drive along ever-worsening tracks, through woods and across rivers and streams, they came to a halt in the thickly wooded area miles from anywhere, and where the track runs close alongside a river. After having met no one at all on the journey, along came a local inhabitant, bumping along the track in a battered old truck as soon as they got out of the cars. This happy, very drunk character was more than surprised to see two cars parked along the lonely roadside, and he stopped to enquire why. The consensus opinion was that he probably had a whisky still somewhere nearby around the area and he preferred solitude.

Everyone then moved off north, up through the heavily wooded gradual slopes of the hill and after climbing for around a hundred and fifty yards, the party arrived at a large flat boulder lying flat on the ground. The stone is roughly square, some ten feet long and ten feet wide, and around two to three feet high above the ground. The upper table-like surface is naturally flat, and at that time around two thirds of this flat surface area was thickly overgrown and covered with a very thick layer of moss and detritus.

On the clear areas of the top surface of the stone on its north side were clearly visible carved letters and signs. Some were very clearly graffiti of the modern era, being the dated names and initials of early settler generations, but the other carvings were very different. These were now familiar ancient letters and emblems to Alan Wilson and Jim Michael, and were not, as had been speculated, precursors of the modern, Latin-derived alphabet. It was these very unusual inscriptions that had first attracted the attention of Jim Burchall and Hezekiah Hemsley, when they discovered this flat rock slab in the woods. When the Rev. Jim Burchall saw and heard Alan

Chapter 16 - American Inscriptions

Wilson and Jim Michael's presentation at the Columbus Conference, he immediately realised that the British Coelbren alphabet, which they were demonstrating, might well be that used to inscribe this Bar Creek stone with which he was familiar.

The first sign of Line 1 is familiar from inscriptions deciphered in Britain, Etruria, Etruscan Empire (*c.* 650-100 BC), Lemnos (*c.* 500 BC), and Phrygia (Asia Minor *c.* 650 -100 BC) and in the USA. It is a combination of the signs for C and D, producing 'cyd'.

There were in fact two identifiable Coelbren inscriptions visible on the exposed flat surface of the slab, and both were deciphered and translated coherently, as Alan Wilson, who had come prepared, was able to demonstrate on the spot. There were also two three-sided snake signs, which are identifiable as 'Yahweh' or 'Jehovah' snake symbols, and a drawing of what appeared to be a strange house. Alan then asked if the very thick ancient layer of moss could be removed from the rest of the surface of the slab, and willing hands rolled back the three-inch-thick growth which came away unbroken, just rolling up like a carpet. When this ancient layer had been peeled back, more Christian symbols were found, a cross in a circle (of the type misnamed as the 'Celtic' Wheel-Cross), and another tall cross sign. There were no other inscriptions on this top flat surface of this very large boulder.

Alan Wilson then turned his attention to the vertical sides of the stone, and suggested that it might be worthwhile to pull away the moss that covered the vertical sides of the stone on the north, the west, and the east sides. When this was done, Coelbren lettering began to appear from under this heavy growth as soon as the first patches were pulled away. Three short Coelbren inscriptions were found, and these remarkable discoveries were totally unexpected by everyone in the party. They had all had been more than rewarded and satisfied with the find of the clearly visible two crosses under the moss on the top of the rock.

Everyone photographed these new groups of letters, and each other, and themselves on site, and Alan Wilson drew careful sketches of the lettering to assist himself in the translation procedure whilst Jim Michael finally marked the letters in silver paint to get detail photographs. The great rock had yielded a total of no fewer than five short Coelbren inscriptions, and it confirms the remarkable discovery made by Rev. Jim Burchall and Hezekiah Hemsley. Six men of good repute, who generally did not know each other, had come together to make a find mutually. Jim Burchall and Hezekiah Hemsley knew only each other well, and Jim Hays, the schoolteacher, had never ever met any of the other five until a few days before. Jim Michael knew only Dr Clark well, and Alan Wilson was unknown to anyone other than his newly acquired colleague Jim Michael. Everyone was of scant or zero acquaintance.

The inscription, which they identified as Figure 1.A reads:

'Thou art the power to go outwards.'

Text Figure 1.B. reads:

'Mutually together to cry out is pure to you the trinity what is enfolding us.'

Figure 2 reads: 'A holdfast from acute flooding', and

Figure 3 reads: 'In difficulty have faith'. Finally

Figure 4 poses a problem and appears to read: 'lightning (is the) governor/ruler.' or 'military ruler.'

Alan Wilson and Jim Michael were surprised, when after making these readings, the locals in the party immediately explained that they made sense. Flash floods occur in the area, and only three months earlier three unfortunate people had been drowned in just such a flash flood very close to this spot. Anyone making for this huge flat slab of rock would in fact be in a safe place.

On the way back from this inscribed stone the party stopped at a bridge across the narrow river to view a huge boulder lying in the river bank which had numerous line carvings, and which closely resembled some form of calendar in stone, a seasonal clock, a sun dial, or a measuring table. This was a well-known stone, but apparently it has attracted little or no academic interest, probably as it may contradict the other politically correct theories.

Then they all went on to view the very well-known, extensive, and quite magnificent rock-carvings in the cliff above the main road to the east from Manchester, Kentucky. These quite remarkable carvings are deserving of some funded study, and again they appear to be some form of seasonal calendar measurement device. Sadly, these quite extraordinary rock-carved remains have long been frequently used for target practice by local riflemen. The basic idea of protecting sites which are probably of very significant historical and archaeological importance is a difficult matter, given the American concept of the rights of the owners of private property. What laws there are do not seem to be either well defined or enforced.

Chapter 16 - American Inscriptions

These ancient calendar carvings are important, no matter who carved them in antiquity, and they are remains that might be tackled using the Coelbren stroke numbering systems.

The party then drove off, turning left to cross a simple planked wooden bridge over the river again, and once again they traversed track roads until they suddenly emerged from the woods into a small cleared area and a small farmhouse. It was a plain, single-storey wooden building with a simple open bare-planked veranda along the front, where an amply proportioned lady was sitting peeling vegetables, surrounded by three children. The group in the two cars stopped about fifty yards short of the buildings, and they just caught a fleeting glimpse of the farmer vanishing around the corner of the rear of the house. Hezekiah Hemsley explained that he was distantly related and knew the farmer, and so he went forward to talk to him whilst everyone else waited in the cars. After a few minutes he returned and said that everyone was invited to the farm.

The objective of the visit was to look at some locally famous inscriptions written on a rock face under a cliff overhang. The necessary introductions were made and the nature of the general interest, and Alan Wilson's visit to the U.S.A., was explained. The couple were genuinely surprised that their inscriptions could interest anyone from such a distance. If the carvings were a form of writing, then they were interested in having them read.

So, a small procession formed up and everyone, including the children, went up past the farmhouse and along the dirt road towards a steep, wooded hill where the road curved around the base. Finally, they arrived at an exposed area of rocky cliffs flanking the road, where there is a large overhang cutting back in under the cliff. A mound of fallen stones and rocks tumbles forward out from under the overhang and the areas of relatively smooth rock faces at the back of this nearly-a-cave are reached by scrambling up over this shifting loose pile, which is about twelve feet high. With some difficulty, as the loose stones slipped and slithered from under their feet, Hezekiah Hemsley and Alan Wilson made this uncertain ascent followed by Jim Michael.

When they finally reached the top of this wobbling pile of stones, and were able to see and touch what were very clearly man-made cuts forming lettered inscriptions, the good lady from the farm advised them: "You all be careful up there now. There's plenty of rattlers up around there." Alan Wilson, who was slipping and sliding and trying to keep himself upright, and was wearing low-sided walking shoes, sighed: "Now she tells us." To which the cheerful Hezekiah responded, "Don't worry, if we've scared them, they won't do anything until we move to go down." It was obvious why no one else had bothered to climb up to see the carvings: either they were having a joke, or if they were serious then down on the dirt road was the best place to be.

Once again, the groups of symbols were copied on a note pad and photographed, and after making certain they hadn't missed anything, everyone adjourned back to the farm. With everyone lounging around the veranda, Alan offered the opinion that the inscriptions indicated that at some time a major battle had taken place near the cliff overhang. This sparked interest, because a few quite large fields lay on the other side of the dirt track away from the cliff area, bounded on their far side by the river. The farmer explained that he was constantly finding ancient arrowheads when ploughing these fields, and he went inside the house and returned with two large jars filled with a remarkably fine collection of arrow-heads from the fields. He then confirmed to Jim Michael that it was in these fields, on the side close to the river, that two very ancient skeletons of Aryan-type teenagers had been exhumed. Jim Michael already knew of the reports of these skeletons, which had been Radio Carbon 14 dated to the sixth-century AD era, and which exhibited skeletal evidence of syphilis, but he was previously unaware of the exact site. Alan Wilson confirmed that he and his partner had identified an ancient Welsh poem, reputed to be of the sixth century, in which there was definite mention of venereal disease.

The very clearly cut inscriptions, although smooth with all the signs of considerable antiquity, were protected from weathering by virtue of being placed well back away under the sizeable rock overhang. They appear to read:

'To me towards my reward (from) the warrior who/what exists the ruler, fine subtle he is.'

This would seem to indicate that the carving commemorated and confirmed a land grant, probably for military achievement.

These overhang inscriptions in relatively close proximity to other inscriptions, and two major calendar computation sites, along with quantities of ancient arrow heads, and along with other yet to be inspected inscriptions, all combine to point to a British-Khumric presence in this area in antiquity. Hezekiah Hemsley and Jim Burchall had been told of other similar inscriptions on rock on one of the steep hills

Chapter 16 - American Inscriptions

over on the south side of Bar Creek by local Native Americans. They had not at this time located these, but were trying to make arrangements to get to visit the site.

The same party of six, which was led by the Rev. Jim Burchall and Hezekiah Hemsley, then went on to a remote woodland area some twenty miles south of the town of Manchester. This led to another scramble up very steep slopes and through heavily thicketed woods.

Set on the south-facing side of a very steep hill, and deep in the tangle of woods, is a small cave. The smooth sides of this narrow cleft in the rocks at the top of the hill is quite literally covered with inscriptions and carvings, which again appear to be in some way associated with calculations of some kind. The first impression is that whoever made these markings may well have been using this cave to construct some kind of seasonal calendar, or to calculate the position of the cave geographically on planet Earth. Whether the method used was to calculate the position of the Sun at dawn and sunset by placing rods in set positions in front of the cave to cast shadows and then observing the fall of the shadow is not certain.

The Coelbren letters, lines, and the diagrams and numbers are so many, and so detailed, that only a major study will resolve their purpose. As might be anticipated, others had found this cave in the outcrop of rocks on the summit of the steep hill, and there were modern names carved alongside and over the much more ancient markings.

Jim Burchall admitted that his first impression had been that some of the lettering might have been Greek, and this is not surprising given that the Greek got their letters from the ancient Khumry. There is a basic similarity between ancient British Coelbren lettering and Greek and Julius Caesar drew the comparison between ancient British Coelbren and Greek lettering, and Ammianus Marcellinus explained the similarity by the Greeks obtaining the alphabet from the migrating British-Brutus people. That the educated Khumry knew Greek and Latin is well attested, and there is the story of St Cadoc leaving his copy of Virgil on Echni Island in Cardiff Bay, and then sending two young monks back across the dangerous waters to get it. Both were drowned. The records of Morgan-Pelasgius, the leading sage of the era around AD 400, and the letters of the Sicilian Briton also support this, as do the writings of Strabo. It is a fact that Alfred of Wessex, realising that no one in his kingdom could read or write, sent to the Khumry for Geraint y Fard Glas (known as Asser), and for John Menevensis, and John Erigena in around AD 870 to build a foundation for the education of his people.

Either way, this strange cave requires a thorough investigation that might determine whether it is associated with geographical or calendar studies, and by whom it was made and when. The presence of a sketch of a strange building on the flat stone in the woods at Bar Creek may indicate the site of an ancient hall building nearby, probably at the top of the hill, and the learned men set to carry out solar, lunar, or stellar, observations would probably not be too far away from the centre of power in the area.

The Threshing Floor

With the evening drawing in, a dash was made to yet another hilltop site, where yet another alphabet inscription had been found by the Rev. Jim Burchall. The site was at an open area on top of a wooded hill, where a bare patch of smooth rock lies exposed. A track road runs through this site and farm vehicles are unavoidably driven through the area and across the bare smooth rock.

The bare flat rock surface was used by the first settlers in the area as a ready-made threshing floor, where the wheat or corn could be winnowed and separated from the chaff. Jim Burchall explained that the marks on the rock have been known locally down the generations for two hundred years since these first settlers made use of it as a threshing floor, so there was again no question of any modern provenance.

There are, in fact, two sets of letters carved into the surface of this flat hilltop outcrop of bedrock. One set of letters runs horizontally in the conventional manner, and the other group is set out in a vertical manner. The inscriptions are clearly in some danger as modern motorised heavy tracked vehicles are faster and much heavier than horses and slow carts, and the modern motorised vehicle can pull heavier trailer loads. There are in fact signs of these vehicles tearing at and damaging the rock surfaces. Inevitably these inscriptions will in time be destroyed. This will be a loss, not only for the County and the State of Kentucky, but also for the wider world, and for future generations. Formerly the practice in Britain was for farmers to be paid a small fee or grant to protect any ancient monument on their land, and this encouraged them to pass around it, and thereby to protect and preserve the site. The more important monuments are registered, and are protected by law regardless of property ownership, and it is a serious offence to damage or to interfere with them.

Chapter 16 - American Inscriptions

The inscriptions on the old settlers' threshing floor are in Coelbren and can therefore be deciphered and translated into Khumric. As they are almost certainly related to the King Arthur II and Madoc-Morfran migration expedition of AD 562, they may well be around fourteen hundred and fifty years old. Along with the Bar Creek stone and the overhang inscriptions, these are priceless relics of evidence of culture and inheritance.

The inscription can be read as:

'A reproach, a cry he/him (to) god mutually together (for) good/profit to intercede'.

The last word is probably 'intercede', but it may, less likely, be 'scanty'.

It is not impossible that this old bare rock surface could have been used as a threshing floor by the settlers of the Arthur II and Madoc expeditions long centuries before the modern generations of Kentuckians first moved into the area. The only difficulty with the inscription is whether the last Coelbren letter is a 'B' or an 'L'. If it is a 'B', we have the word 'rhib', meaning 'scanty', emerges. If it is an 'L'' the word 'rhil', for an 'interstice, interceding' emerges, which would indicate a plea to God to act on behalf of the supplicants.

Back at Jim Burchall's house, where Jim Michael and Alan Wilson stayed overnight, the Rev. Burchall showed them an arrow-rest, which is inscribed on both sides. The stone is not recognised as being local, and is finely shaped and grooved. An arrow-rest is a small grooved stone held against the bow, across which the arrow runs, so absorbing the heat from the friction generated at release. The inscription on the arrow rest reads:

'A roebuck of the female kind.'

Perhaps this animal is what the hunter was seeking. The consensus is that this curious object needs further assessment since it may have had another purpose, perhaps also being used in rubbing down deerskins. The fact is, however, that it is indisputably inscribed in Coelbren lettering.

The Grave Creek Tablet

Museums are set up to preserve cultural artefacts. Some of the bones from the grave-mound, which may be those of Madoc Morfran, were placed in the Smithsonian, and could be DNA-tested and compared with bones from the grave of King Tewdrig, the father of Madoc at Mathern. The Bedd Morgan Mwynfawr, the Grave of King Morgan, who succeeded Arthur II, could also be examined for DNA remains for comparison. The body of Arthur II could be exhumed for the same purpose. At this time the bones from Grave Creek cannot be found in the Smithsonian Museum, but they do have a hundred thousand stuffed parrots. The two smelted copper bracelets may also be of European provenance, but they also are difficult to find. The inscribed stone tablet found at Grave Creek in 1838, which started all this, has also gone missing. It is all a little too much like the Court Case for murder in which the vital evidence of a wound in a skull went missing because someone cut the piece out of the skull and then succeeded in losing it.

Fortunately, the Grave Creek Tablet was widely copied and examined in the august scholarly circles, so we still know exactly what is on it. We set down the Ancient American text, then we set down the equivalent Coelbren signs, then we set out the letters corresponding to the Coelbren signs to get words on Khumric, then we set down the equivalent English words that are expressed in Khumric.

Chapter 16 - American Inscriptions

Illustration 16-5: The Grave Creek Tablet

Grave Creek tablet - line 1

Sign/letter	ᛘ /	┼	✕	∧ 4|	✕
Coelbren	┌ V	+	Y ✕	∧ 4		✕
Cipher	P W	+	Y X	A MH I	X
Welsh	pwff	croeso	y croes	a mi	croes
English	wind, gust	welcome	the crossing	over with me	crossing over

Line 2

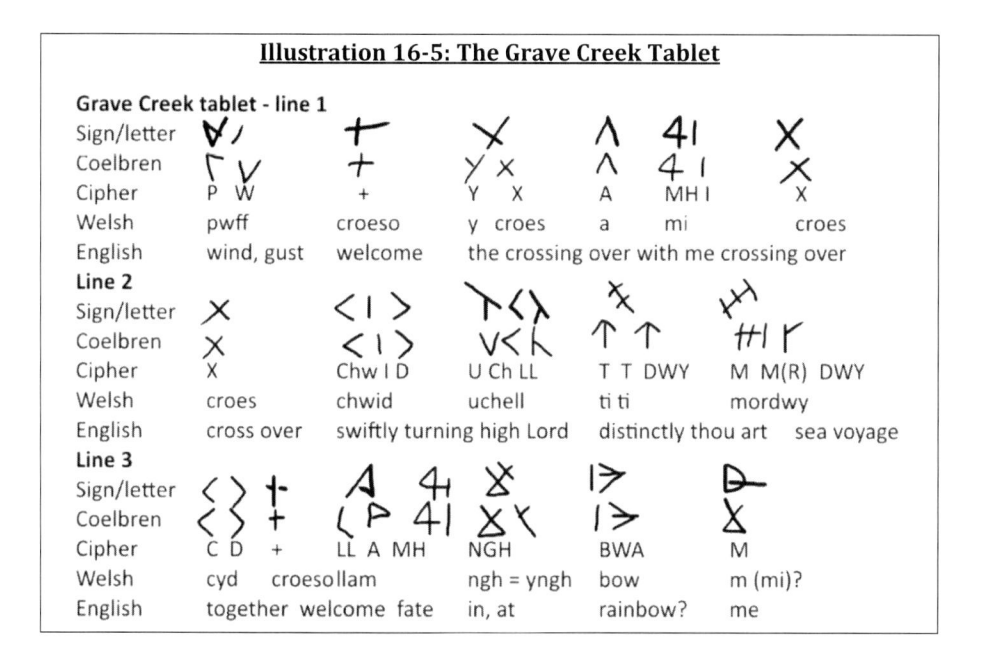

Sign/letter	✕	<I>	⊤⟨⟩	✳ ↑	⊞ ⌐
Coelbren	✕	<I>	V< ʎ	↑ ↑	⊞ ⌐
Cipher	X	Chw I D	U Ch LL	T T DWY	M M(R) DWY
Welsh	croes	chwid	uchell	ti ti	mordwy
English	cross over	swiftly turning	high Lord	distinctly thou art	sea voyage

Line 3

Sign/letter	<> ┼	A 4| ✕	|>	⊖
Coelbren	<> +	⌐P 4| ✕⟨	|>	⌐
Cipher	C D +	LL A MH	NGH	BWA	M
Welsh	cyd	croesollam	ngh = yngh	bow	m (mi)?
English	together	welcome fate	in, at	rainbow?	me

Illustration 16-6: Inscribed Stone from Bat Creek, U.S.A.

America	||	⊿ ✕ ∃⩘<	У⌐|
Coelbren	||	⌂ ∧ ∃⩘<	⌐>|
Khumric	|| = dwy (2)	M A E F U C	Y D I (ydi)
English	the ruler	Madoc	he is

The inscription reads 'The ruler Madoc he is.' Presumably Madoc ap Meurig the brother of Arthur II.

The word for 'two' is 'dwy', and 'dwy' has the dual meaning of 'ruler'. These dual words are common, and they are of immense value in decipherment of hieroglyphics. There is nothing difficult in this decipherment once the tablet is turned upside down to get it the right way around.

> **Illustration 16-7: Inscribed stone from the Mammoth Mound, Grave Creek, U.S.A.**
>
> | | | | | |
> |---|---|---|---|---|
> | American | < I | Y △ | | ∧⊗ ⟟ |
> | Coelbren | < I | Y △ | | ∧⊗ ⟟ |
> | Khumric | C I | Y N | | A M H A D |
> | English | a stronghold | in a state of being | | to sow with mixed seeds (many types.) |
>
> | | | | | |
> |---|---|---|---|---|
> | American | ⨉ | <I> | + | ∧/୮ |
> | Coelbren | ⨉ | <I> | + | ∧/୮ |
> | Khumric | N | C I D (cyd) | Croesaw | A F R |
> | English | we, us | mutually | welcome | flowing principle (water, rain) |
>
> | | | | |
> |---|---|---|---|
> | American | L I | Y ▷ | ⟟ ୮ / |
> | Coelbren | (I | Y ▷ | ⟟ ୮ / |
> | Khumric | LI I (Lli) | Y D (yd) | P I Ff (piff) |
> | English | flood, stream | corn, grain | sudden blast = the wind to blow. |
>
> Any people crossing the Atlantic from Europe would have basic problems in initially timing the seasons for the sowing of seeds and crops. This is the burden of this text that in correct Khumric-'Welsh' appears to read:
>
> 'A stronghold being established (and) sown with many kinds of seeds, we together welcome (pray for) rain (the floods) for com and the winds to blow.'
>
> Clouds bring rain, and clouds are invariably accompanied by winds.
>
> 'distinctly' and two signs means 'dwy' = 'two' = 'ruler'. A bow is 'bwa', and a drawn bow is 'bwa'r arch', or a rainbow. The text appears to read:
>
> 'crossing over the welcome winds with me crossing over, crossing over and swiftly turning in the sea voyage a high lord distinctly thou art, mutually together a welcome hand (to) me in a rainbow (to) me.'
>
> 'Swiftly turning' may refer to the swinging due west through the Florida Strait, and then due north up the Mississippi and the Ohio rivers. The fourth line on the Tablet shows only an elongated cross laid on its side, with what looks like a familiar map at the west end or top of the cross.

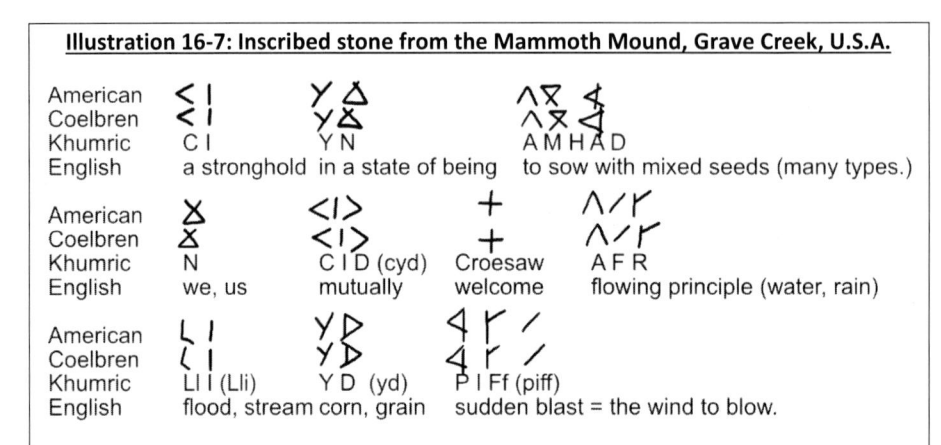

Chapter 16 - American Inscriptions

Illustration 16-8: The Bar Creek Stone Inscriptions, Clay County, Kentucky

Figure 1A - top side, horizontal surface
Sign
Cipher
Welsh   Ti   Rha   I   Ffe
English   Thou art   the power   towards   to go / outwards
"Thou are the power to go towards (to approach.)"

Figure 1B - top side, horizontal surface
Sign
Cipher
Welsh   C + D = Cyd   Wy L O   I R   Ti
English   Mutually together   to cry out   is pure   (to) thee
... "mutually together to cry out in purity to thee."

Line 2
Sign
Cipher
Welsh   T R I   U G
English   Three (trinity)   what is enfolding us
"mutually together to cry out is pure to thee the trinity which is enfolding us."

The first sign of line 1 is the familiar C + D combination giving 'cyd'. This is seen in numerous inscriptions previously translated in Britain, Etruria, on Lemnos, and in Asia Minor, and it reappears in several instances in the U.S.A. The third sign of line 1 is yet another combination of lettering also found elsewhere. It appears as I = L, plus = 0, and the Coelbren <> diamond shape is frequently found as a square in Etruria.

Illustration 16-9: The Heavener, Poteau, and Shawnee inscriptions. USA.

These three texts, known as the Heavener, the Poteau, and the Shawnee inscriptions, are all in the style and alphabet that is known as 'Anglo-Saxon', but more correctly it is probably Old British. The same script appears on the Franks Casket that exhibits five scenes that are all part of the British historical experience. These scenes include the Siege of Troy, the Siege of Jerusalem, the founding of Rome, and the beheading of John the Baptist. These scenes are accompanied by words that translate into Khumric.

1- Heavener - Oaklahoma

American Cipher	G L OE	M E D A	E L
Khumric	gloes	med	ael
English	escstacy/pain	reaped close to,	near

2- Poteau - Oaklahoma

American Cipher	G L NG	I D	AE L TH
Khumric	glen	id	aelth
English	purity/splendid	is drawn out from	woe, sadness
			aele = grief/sadness

3- Shawness - Oaklahoma

American Cipher	M A D O E C
Khumric	mad o ech-echu
English	good what goes to go aside, to retire

It is perfectly logical that people from Lloegres, now England, would have accompanied the Khumry on their expeditions to America.

There can be very little doubt that the word in the text known as the Shawnee inscription reads as 'Madoec', and the ancient Khumric versions of Madoc, Maedoc, and so on are all thought to mean 'a good man who went aside/away'. Possibly this meant 'one who has migrated.' A language can be expressed in any alphabet.

Chapter 16 - American Inscriptions

Illustration 16-10: The Grave Creek Tablet

Grave Creek tablet - line 1

Sign/letter	∨		+	Y X	∧	4₁	X
Coelbren	Γ	V	+	Y X	∧	4 I	X
Cipher	P	W	+	Y X	A	MH I	X
Welsh	pwff		croeso	y croes	a	mi	croes
English	wind, gust		welcome	the crossing over	with	me	crossing over

Line 2

Sign/letter	X	< I >	` < ⋋	⚹	⋈
Coelbren	X	< I >	V < ʞ	↑ ↑	ℋ Γ
Cipher	X	Chw I D	U Ch LL	T T DWY	M M(R) DWY
Welsh	croes	chwid	uchell	ti ti	mordwy
English	cross over	swiftly turning	high Lord	distinctly thou art	sea voyage

Line 3

Sign/letter	< >	+	L P 4 X	I >	X
Coelbren	< >	+	L P 4 I X X	I >	X
Cipher	C D	+	LL A MH NGH	BWA	M
Welsh	cyd	croesollam	ngh = yngh	bow	m (mi)?
English	together	welcome fate	in, at	rainbow?	me

The text appears to read:

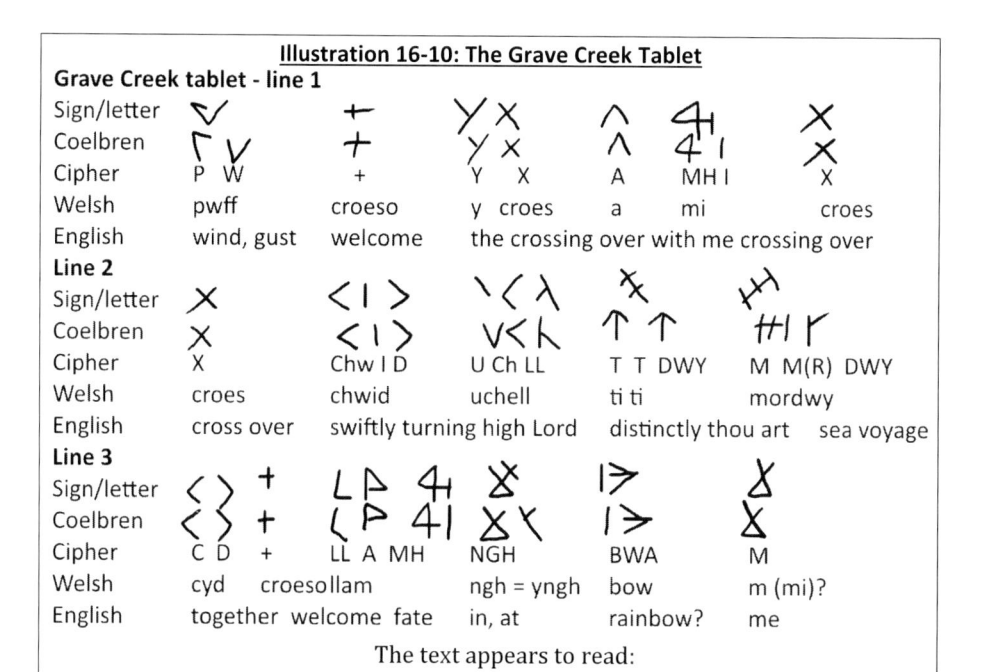

'... crossing over the welcome winds with me crossing over, crossing over and swiftly turning in the sea voyage a high lord distinctly thou art, mutually together the welcome fate in/at me.'

The 'swiftly turning' phrase may refer to the swinging due west through the Florida Strait, and then due north up the Mississippi and the Ohio. The fourth line on the tablet shows only an elongated cross laid on its side, with what looks like a familiar map at the West end or top of the cross.

A bow is bwa and a drawn bow is a bwa'r arch or a rainbow. With rainbow included, the text appears to read:-

'... crossing over the welcome winds with me crossing over, crossing over and swiftly turning in the sea voyage a high lord distinctly thou art, mutually together a welcome hand (to) me.'

507

Illustration 16-11: The Bar Creek Stone Inscriptions, Clay County, Kentucky

Figure 1a – Top side – horizontal surface
Welsh	Ti	Rha	I	Ffe
English	Thou art	the power	towards	to go/outwards

'Thou are the power to go towards (approach)'

Figure 1b – Top side – horizontal surface
Welsh	C + D = Cyd	Wy L O	I R	Ti
English	mutually together	to cry out	is pure (to thee)	

'Mutually together to cry out in purity to thee'

Line 2
Welsh	T R I	U G
English	Three (trinity)	what is enfolding us.

'Mutually together to cry out is pure to thee the trinity which is enfolding us'.

The first sign of Line 1 is the familiar C + D combination giving 'cyd', seen in numerous inscriptions previously translated in Britain, Etruria, Lemnos, and Asia Minor, and it reappears in several instances in the U.S.A. The third sign of Line 1 is yet another combination lettering also found elsewhere. It appears as I = L, plus O, and the Coelbren < > diamond shape is frequently found as a square in Etruria.

Figure 2 - North side, vertical face
Welsh	YNG	I C	Ll I	C I
English	in the	acute	stream/flood	a holdfast

'A holdfast in acute flooding'

Figure 3 – East side, north corner, vertical face
Welsh	I NG	Fe B
English	in difficulty/in a straight	(have) faith

Figure 4 – North face, east side corner, vertical face
Welsh	M I L W R	2 = dwy = the ruler
English	military (milwyr)	ruler

'The military ruler'

Museums are set up to preserve cultural artefacts. Some of the bones from the grave mound which may be those of Madoc Morfran were placed in the Smithsonian, and could be DNA tested and compared with bones from the grave of King Tewdrig, the father of Madoc at Mathern. The Bedd Morgan Mwynfawr - Grave of King Morgan who succeeded Arthur II, could also be examined for DNA remains for comparison. The body of Arthur II could be exhumed for the same purpose. The bones from Grave Creek cannot be found in the Smithsonian Museum. But they do have a hundred thousand stuffed parrots. The two smelted copper bracelets may also be of European provenance, but they cannot be found either. The inscribed stone tablet found at Grave Creek in 1838, which started all this, has also gone missing. It is all a little too much like the Court Case for murder, in which the vital evidence of a wound in a skull went missing because someone cut the piece out of the skull and then succeeded in losing it.

The British Iceni Inscriptions

This may well be a suitable point at which to introduce some of the other strange and ancient evidence found in North America, which in all probability supports the extensive number of clearly British-Coelbren inscriptions.

As has been pointed out earlier, the Welsh histories state that the language which prevailed amongst the swirling mixture of Dark Age peoples in what is now England was the language of the Icinglas. The entry is made around AD 826 when some kind of uniformity might have emerged. This means that modern English is founded upon the language of the Iceni people of Eastern and Central Britain. Correctly it is very Old British stemming from the ancient Albyne Chaldean invasion of around 1600 BC; and it is neither German Angle nor German Saxon. The Iceni were of course the nation which fought the Romans under their Queen Boudicca in the time of Nero in AD 56.

It is perfectly reasonable and understandable that folk from the Eastern territories in Britain, which later became known as England, would have accompanied the western Khumry in the seven-hundred strong migration fleet of AD 574. In fact, it would be strange if there were none of these people present amongst the migrants, and there should be no surprise at finding ancient relics of their writing in North America.

Three inscriptions have been found in North America which are in the same alphabet as that found on the ancient Franks Casket (named after an owner named

Franks Casket – Prophecy scene, Founding Rome, Jerusalem falls

Chapter 16 - American Inscriptions

Franks) and the Ruthwell Cross, and many other ancient relics, and manuscripts. Perhaps a little more notice should have been taken of the six essentially British connected scenes carved on the Franks Casket, (a) the Siege of Troy, (b) the founding of Rome, depicting Romulus and Remus and the wolf, and birthplace of Brutus, (c) the Sack of Jerusalem by Titus, (d) the beheading of John the Baptist, (e) the Magi presenting gifts to the infant Jesus, (f) the robing and election of a leader, Brutus.

Another scene of an armed warrior standing before a female figure, who is wearing a deer's head with birds' wings, depicts Brutus before Diana the huntress goddess. After Brutus sacrificed a bull to her at her Lemnos Island temple, she directed him to sail to Britain, and so on. The bull to be sacrificed is shown choosing itself by eating cakes from a plate on an altar. The scene of the Siege of Troy shows a number of significant details, with the slain Hector pursued by Achilles, and the word Agili written above the archer Paris, and an old Welsh word 'agili' means to go around or surrounded, and besieged. The word 'Magi' is written above the scene of the three Magi presenting their gifts. Strangely, the scenes carved on the Franks Casket are alleged to be of Germanic Anglo-Saxon origin by virtue of comparisons made with unrelated Scandinavian and Norse mythology, which appears to be somewhat illogical.

The Stone from Bat Creek, Tennessee

All this brought Alan Wilson, Baram Blackett, and Jim Michael, and his associates back to their initial start point. The simplest and perhaps easiest of all the many Coelbren inscriptions sent over from the U.S.A. was the first. A short text scratched on a stone found in a grave mound in Louden County, Tennessee.

In 1885, the largest of three grave mounds found near Bat Creek was excavated. This tomb mound was found to be intact, and it had never been previously interfered with or robbed. Nine skeletons were found in the mound, together with a number of artefacts. Seven skeletons lay at the north end of the mound with their heads to the north, and feet towards the south. Another two skeletons lay south of this group, in the centre of the mound, with their feet to the north and heads to the south. Under the head of the skeleton, which appeared to be that of the most important person, was a small inscribed stone.

Again, given the welter of supporting evidence surrounding the British histories of the Khumric Prince Madoc migrating from Wales to America around 562, it is astonishing that in a hundred and twenty years no one ever thought to try reading the inscription from Bat Creek into Welsh. Someone, somewhere, in the nineteenth century, must surely have known of the existence of the widely published and well-evidenced ancient British Coelbren alphabets, and been alerted to the possibilities. *The Barddas*, which details every aspect of the Coelbrens, was published in 1852, and so was available.

Instead, the Bat Creek Stone has been the subject of an array of bizarre theories. These range from attempts to slot it into the relatively modern Cherokee alphabet, to ancient Hebrew. The breath-taking Hebrew theory postulates an unrecorded fleet of Jewish ships sailing over five thousand miles through the Mediterranean and across the Atlantic Ocean. Others blessed with a total ignorance of the existence of the Madoc histories and evidence, and knowing nothing of the Welsh language and the Coelbren alphabets, have developed equally remarkable ancient Phoenician theories. Using simple and straightforward British Coelbren and the Khumric language the inscription appears to read:

Cipher	2=dwy	M A E F-U C	Y D I	or T + T = Ti, Ti
Welsh	dwy	Maefuc-Madoc	ydi	Ti, Ti
English	the ruler	Madoc	he is distinctly	thou art

The only difficulty is that posed by the final letter, which is either an 'I', or a double 'T'. In the case of T + Twe would have Ti + Ti, and 'Ti' has two meanings, 'you are', and 'distinctly'. In older inscriptions of the 300 to 2150 B.C. era, this Ti + Ti occurs with great frequency.

The find is remarkable, and the stone - usually placed upside down - is now in the Smithsonian Institute listed as U.S.N.M. Archive No. 134902. The inscription reads from left to right. All this led Wilson and Blackett to run a check on the description of the grave site of Madoc as in the *Songs of the Graves*, and again the Bat Creek site appears to match the description given.

The Mammoth Mound Stone from Grave Creek, and the Braxton Stone

The wheel having turned circle, Alan Wilson and Baram Blackett, along with their American colleagues were right back at Grave Creek and the inscribed tablet found by Abelard Tomlinson in 1838 in the Mammoth Mound, at Grave Creek in Moundsville, West Virginia. On 21st April 1940, Mrs Innis C Clark, the West Virginia State archivist, announced that her department had purchased the Braxton Stone

Chapter 16 - American Inscriptions

from Mr Blaine Wilson. The Braxton Stone was discovered by Blaine Wilson on 10th April 1931 at Triplet Creek, eight miles from Gassaway in Braxton County. This inscribed stone, found in the bed of a stream in West Virginia, bears inscriptions in what is clearly the same alphabet as the Grave Creek Stone. The finding of this small stone tablet, measuring four and one eight of an inch long and three and three sixteenths of an inch wide, revived the whole almost forgotten alphabet enigma beginning with Abelard Tomlinson in 1838. Newspaper coverage of the purchase of the Braxton Stone stated that 'the alphabet and the language employed on both these stones is not known to scholars in the U.S.A.' Sad, as at least fourteen million modern Americans are estimated to have Welsh origins.

That the Grave Creek Tablet carries the British Coelbren alphabet is clear. Also clear is the fact that the letters are so arranged as to convey a written message, in a very similar manner to the arranged display of the basic alphabet shown in the Bodleian Manuscript No. 572 in Oxford, England. That the Braxton Stone also carries the British Coelbren alphabet is unmistakeable. Once again there is a tablet that deciphers and translates using the Coelbren alphabet and the Khumric language.

The problem facing the 'experts' in 1940, and ever since, is that they had already made it an article of faith that no one on the North American continent had ever had an alphabet or the ability to write before Christopher Columbus found his way to the West Indies islands. Their problems are compounded by the very uncomfortable fact that two smelted copper bracelets were found in the Grave Creek Grave mound. As the Native Americans are not known to have smelted metal, these bracelets are very difficult to explain away. The bracelets actually contain 69% copper, 27% zinc, and 4% lead, which again points to a European provenance.

> **Illustration 16-12: The Braxton Stone**
>
> | | | | | |
> |---|---|---|---|---|
> | American | < I | Y △ | ∧ ⊽ ⊰ | |
> | Coelbren | < I | Y △ | ∧ ⊽ ⊰ | |
> | Khumric | C I | Y N | A M H A | D |
> | English | a stronghold | in a state of being | to sow with mixed seeds (many types.) | |
>
> | | | | | |
> |---|---|---|---|---|
> | American | X | <I> | + | ∧/Γ |
> | Coelbren | X | <I> | + | ∧/Γ |
> | Khumric | N | C I D (cyd) | Croesaw | A F R |
> | English | we, us | mutually | welcome | flowing principle (water, rain) |
>
> | | | | |
> |---|---|---|---|
> | American | L I | Y ▷ | ⊲ Γ / |
> | Coelbren | L I | Y ▷ | ⊲ Γ / |
> | Khumric | LI I (Lli) | Y D (yd) | P I Ff (piff) |
> | English | flood, stream | corn, grain | sudden blast = the wind to blow. |
>
> 'A stronghold being established (and) sown with many kinds of seeds, we together welcome (pray for?) rain the flood streams for grain/corn and the winds to blow.'
>
> Clouds bring rain, and rising winds are inevitably associated when rain clouds fill the skies, and so the text is all very logical.

> **Illustration 16-13: The Dighton Rock in Massachusetts.**
>
> At first sight the Dighton Rock appears to resemble a disaster area in a modem city where a horde of ancient graffiti artists who for long centuries lacked spray paint and so resorted to hacking, cutting, and carving in a frenzy of identity markings. The only way to deal with this mess is to eliminate the obvious modern and non Coelbren markings and pictures and to then see what is left to deal with. Ancient Coelbren would have been written in horizontal registers and so anything either at an angle of vertical could be ignored.
>
> Amongst the maze of marks and graffiti that sprawl all across the flat landward surface of the Dighton Rock there are fourteen areas that appear to have horizontally arranged registers of the straight-line sign lettering of Coelbren writing. These inscriptions appear to read as follows:
>
> | | | |
> |---|---|---|
> | Section 1 | from afar off | I A R |
> | Section 2 | fresh/verdant it is ploughland | IR E AR |
> | Section 3 | from afar off with | I A R A |

Chapter 16 - American Inscriptions

Section 4	in difficulty/in a straight the army	I N O Ll (lli)
Section 5	the army (of the ruler) crosses over	LL XX (2 = dwy = the ruler)
Section 6	going over it shall be sure /certain	A D B I SIC (sicr)
Section 7	the sea multitude?	M O R
Section 8	pure/fresh	I R
Section 9	mutually together the court	C Y D Ll Ys (llys)
Section 10	defiled	H A L W G
Section 11	it is	E
Section 12	god (secret name) in motion cross over nearby outwards	IOI CHWIM X WNGH W(wo)
Section 13	in terror fright	Dy Ch RE
Section 14	cornlands towards	I D I

It is a simple statement that relates to the destruction of Britain by débris from the great comet that caused pollution and terror, and then the fleet expedition transporting the army across the seas to find new fresh arable lands/cornlands.

Dighton Rock
Photograph by Davis 1883 – Public Domain

515

Chapter Seventeen

Other American Inscriptions

Historical research is sometimes aided by luck and often dogged by sabotage. In that strange fortunate, blundering, accidental way which characterises the progress of this type of seminal pioneering research, fate or luck, or whatever had brought the King Arthur Research and the Ancient Kentucke Historical Association together. Two groups that were operating four thousand miles apart on different continents had conducted research that complemented each other. The result has been to exhibit the certainty that a large group of British Christian people migrated across the Atlantic in the late sixth century AD, to settle in the Mid-West of what is now the U.S.A.

As with every other facet of the ever-expanding octopus-like Arthurian Project, this investigation into the linked Khumric and American histories now spawned yet another major project. What happened to the powerful white nation, which had settled for some time in and around ancient Kentucke? By good fortune some unexplained data had been researched by Alan and Baram in the early 1980s which now began to make sense, and opened up yet another panorama. There was no need to get side-tracked and to follow the fools' trail north to the Mandan Indians, as the correct area was already targeted.

Not all the Coelbren inscriptions of North America or South America have yet been deciphered, and a large number of scattered texts remain to be dealt with. Some of these texts are published and well-known and were not recognized as British Coelbren in the general ignorance surrounding the alphabet and Khumric history. Some researchers try to read texts as 'Celtic' and speak of the 'Celtic' language. Whether by this they mean the totally different and unconnected Irish Gaelic and Scots Gaelic, or the British Khumric is not clear. As none of these three nations were, or are, 'Celtic' the matter is yet another nonsense. Numbers of scholars have wasted large parts of their careers in futile attempts to match and blend the irreconcilable, and the prevailing theory is that the two Gaelic tongues are 'Q'-Celtic, and the Khumric is 'P'-Celtic. None of them is any form of 'Celtic' and the languages labelled 'Q' and 'P' types are totally unrelated.

Legions of scholars all trooping down the wrong path of 'Celticism' have striven

Chapter 17 - Other America Inscriptions

mightily to correlate Irish and Scottish Gaelic with Khumric without any success. Irish histories claim a national origin in the area around the upper Tigris, and a migration first south to the Egyptian Delta, and then west along the North African coast. The direct result of 'Celticism' is that the Irish also appear to have lost their history.

As explained earlier there are problems associated with the Ogham inscriptions that are found in Wales and southern areas of Ireland. The Book of Ballymote is claimed to contain seventy Ogham alphabets, and ancient monks are said to have known of a manuscript containing over one hundred and thirty of these 'alphabets'. This has to be complete nonsense, as any literate society only requires ONE alphabet, be it Arabic, Greek, Latin, or anything else. ONE alphabet is all that is required to write anything and everything in any language. The existence of seventy, or one hundred and thirty alphabets, is nothing short of ludicrous.

Even more ludicrous is the statement that alphabet No15 is the best and preferred alphabet to use. The very layout of these Oghams speaks of music and finger arrangements for five stringed harps and crwyths (guitars), and flutes. That Ogham might be pressed into use as an alphabet is possible. The point needs to be made as many of the ancient American inscriptions, which, as a child can see, bear little or no resemblance to any Ogham, have nonetheless been labelled as being Ogham. As has been explained earlier, no one ever claimed to be able to 'read' Ogham until modern times. The problem is an emotive and nationalist one, where one group wants to see every inscription as Irish-derived Ogham, citing St Brendan, and another wants to see every inscription as Viking-derived runes, citing Leif Ericsson, regardless of the fact that the majority of the inscriptions are obviously neither Irish nor Scandinavian.

As Alan Wilson put it to Jim Michael -"You cannot decipher and translate ancient written prose messages using musical scores for Strauss waltzes and operatic arias."

It seems that generalists have taken Herodotus, the Greek historian who wrote around 450 BC, far too simplistically and seriously. Herodotus simply stated that the people who lived furthest west in Europe were the Celts. Actually, a large number of quite diverse nations lived in Western Europe, which Herodotus never visited. In addition, none of the Irish, the Scotti, or the Khumry were living in Europe at all, as they all lived in the British and Irish islands. Even the American scene is therefore confused by these unfounded theories, and the emotive hype employed to further the ambitions of national self-interest groups causes many scholars to avoid these matters entirely. What should be of major academic concern and interest then becomes an arena of unwelcome fringe research and important artefacts are not protected. Taken as a group the Coelbren inscriptions in the U.S.A. are amongst the best preserved and written available.

The Brandenburg Stone

This intransigent and negative attitude of officialdom and academia towards evidence brings in the Brandenburg Stone. The stone was found in 1912 by a farmer named Greg Crecelius on his land in the Brandenburg area of Indiana. The Crecelius farm was near the Ohio River in Paradise Bottoms, just west of Battletown, Kentucky, some forty miles from the Falls of the Ohio. At first, Greg Crecelius kept the stone in his barn for several years. He thought that the stone might be of value, but failed to find anyone who could recognize the writing on the stone. Finally, he gave permission for the stone to be moved to the Brandenburg Library in the 1960s, and Alan Wilson examined it there in 1994.

Failing to get any academic or official interest, Greg Crecelius decided to exhibit the stone at State Fairs. The stone clearly might contradict the dogma of 'Columbus Only' and 'No One Else Ever Before Columbus', and so official and academic avoidance was obligatory. The problem facing Greg Crecelius was that the stone was large and heavy, and lifting it into and out of his cart was difficult. So, he solved this problem by breaking this priceless artefact into three pieces.

Chapter 17 - Other America Inscriptions

In fairness to the owner, he did realise that his stone was valuable regardless of any opinion to the contrary, and he did ensure its preservation. In breaking it up into three parts he also did a careful job, and very little of the inscription carved on the stone was damaged. Would-be 'experts' attempted to dismiss the long, complex lettering of the inscription as plough marks, which would convince no one who actually saw the stone, and finally the stone found its way into the Brandenburg County Library. It does, in fact, carry one of the best Coelbren inscriptions yet found in the U.S.A., and in 1998 the Brandenburg Stone was put on show in the new museum at the Falls of the Ohio.

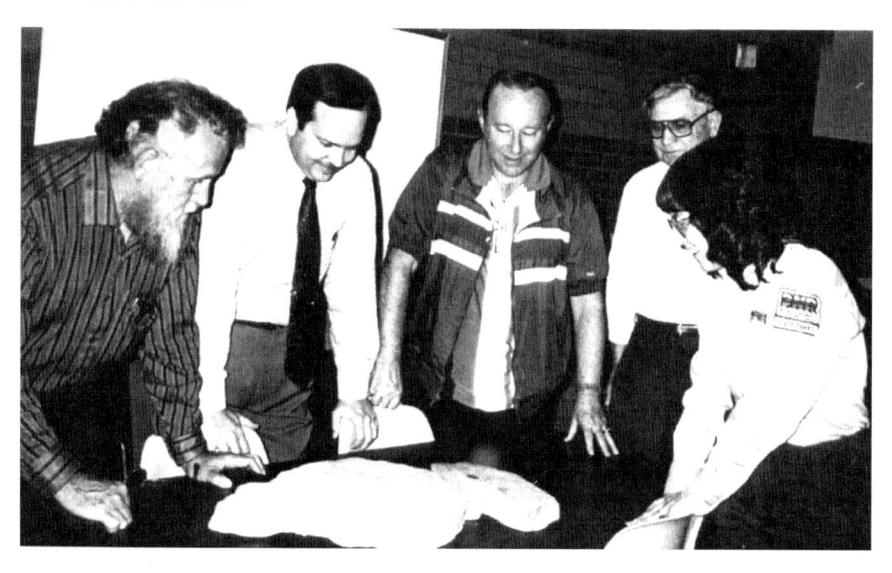

The Brandenburg Stone is examined (from left) by Professor Lee Lennington – *Jefferson Community College*; Troy McCormick, Past Property Manager- *Falls of the Ohio Interpretive Centre*; James Michael, President – *Ancient Kentucke Historical Society*; Robert E. Gallman, President – *Clark's Grant Historical Society* and Brett Etenohan, Interpretive Naturalist – *Falls of the Ohio Interpretive Centre*.

(Photograph kindly supplied by Lee Pennington)

Jim Michael had sent photographs of the Brandenburg Stone over to Alan and Baram in 1991, and they were able to easily decipher the text. Alan Wilson was able to see and examine the Brandenburg Stone during his six-week tour of the U.S.A. in 1994, when he first visited Boston, to deliver the annual Bemis Lecture. A long line of words in Coelbren lettering runs neatly right across the centre of this large flat slab of stone. It is in fact one of the most interesting texts, and carried sentiments that are similar to those on the Perugia Cippus in Etruria. The written message shows a clear recognition of the need to preserve unity amongst the migrants.

It is laughable that the 'experts' attempted to dismiss this remarkable inscription by claiming that the letters were made as a result of plough marks. No one who actually examines the stone will support this weird assertion. Columbus was nine hundred and eighteen years late.

Illustration 17-1: The Brandenburg Stone

The farmer who owned the stone got no help from the authorities and so he cut the stone into three sections to make it possible for him to load it onto a cart and take to the State Fairs as an exhibit. He realized that the stone was important and as a result he wanted to preserve it, and he was careful to avoid damage to the inscription when cutting it.

American					
Coelbren					
Cipher	I	Ffe R	Y Ll I	T I R	U F
Khumric	I	Ffer	ylli (ylliad)	tir	uf
English	towards	strength	parting/dividing	the land	what is spread over

American				
Coelbren				
Cipher	P U R	S I L	Ff U R	
Khumric	pur	sil	ffur	
English	pure	offspring	wise, wisely	

Chapter 17 - Other America Inscriptions

The Dighton Rock

The Dighton Rock is an enormous boulder found on the beach at the water's edge in a bay in Massachusetts, some thirty yards from the main shoreline. The flat surface of this stone measures around ten feet long and some five feet high, and the stone is plastered with carved inscriptions and graffiti cuttings. The location is on an 'Indian' Native American Mission station, and the tides lapped around the Dighton Rock as it sat in low water. In a careful exercise of sanity, which should be an object lesson to others, a short causeway was built out from the shoreline and a small artificial island was created where the stone had been lying. A small circular museum was then built and the Dighton Rock was placed inside a large reinforced glass case in this purpose-built museum. Care was taken to position the stone in the exact location above the spot from where it had been taken on the beach.

Dighton Rock
Photograph by Davis 1883 – Public Domain

It is with the study of this confusing Dighton Rock that the study of North American inscriptions began. The problem with this Dighton Rock is that it is plastered with dozens of drawings, letters, pictographs, and graffiti, both ancient and modern, which makes it extremely difficult to disentangle one from the other. Added to this is the unavoidable competitive scramble to claim the inscriptions on the rock for several nationalist groups of immigrants. The usual theories of the rock being inscribed in ancient Phoenician and Carthaginian, attributed to the abortive voyages of Harnmo and Hanno around 500 BC, are advanced. Other claims are made that the markings are Portuguese. The completely different script of a Portuguese inscription made in Africa on the Congo River in 1498 supports these *(Geographical Journal, 1908, xxxi. 590)*.

521

There is no point in going into the history of all those who have published drawings and theories about the Dighton Rock, other than to point out that everyone who made a drawing of the markings saw something different. It has been differently described and endlessly 'translated', ever since Cotton Mather sent a drawing and description to the Royal Society in London in 1712, and the Society published it in 1714. Whole books have been written cataloguing the multitude of theories and 'decipherments'. So totally different are the conflicting claims made about the Dighton Rock that it has in fact become a translator's graveyard and nightmare.

Alan Wilson, whose first inclination was to avoid this incredible muddle of marks, consulted Baram Blackett, and they decided that they might as well have a crack at the Dighton Rock along with everyone else. What was encouraging were two quite good photographs of sections of the Dighton Rock surface showing clear Coelbren lettering which had by some miracle been read as 'Miguel Cortereal'. The reading was plainly wrong, but at least the marks were recognized as alphabetic. In fact, the photographs appeared to show two horizontal registers of Coelbren.

There is an incredible tangle of sea- and weather-worn cuts and grooves, some curved, some straight, and most of them entwined, that it is almost impossible to make either head or tail of the overall picture. Assuming that there is an overall picture drawn on the Rock or perhaps a map, Alan Wilson decided that if there was any chance of identifying and reading an inscription on the Dighton Rock, then it would be necessary to try to isolate what might be straight line letters of a stroke alphabet from the rest of the twisting mass of shapes and curves on face of the rock. This meant eliminating or ignoring all curved or bent shapes, and concentrating only on those areas exhibiting groups of straight lines in horizontal order. As Coelbren consists of straight lines only when cut or carved, all curved lines could be ignored, and only the marks laid out in horizontal sequence need be considered.

Alan Wilson was taken to see the Dighton Rock by Mrs Ruth Dimancescu of Lincoln, Massachutsetts, when he was invited to deliver the prestigious annual Bemis Lecture in 1994. The Bemis Lecture is an annual event, and given by such luminaries as John Galbraith, Margaret Meade, university presidents, senators, and others. Both Baram and Alan had seen photographs of the Dighton Rock some ten years earlier, and had formed the opinion that there was a Coelbren text on the stone. Their letters to the author of the book containing the photograph went unanswered, however, as this Scots author sadly saw every mark on every stone as Ogham' or Carthaginian.

Chapter 17 - Other America Inscriptions

> **Illustration 17-2: The Dighton Rock in Massachusetts**
>
> At first sight the Dighton Rock appears to resemble a disaster area in a modern city where a horde of ancient graffiti artists who for long centuries lacked spray paint and so resorted to hacking, cutting, and carving in a frenzy of identity markings. The only way to deal with this mess is to eliminate the obvious modern and non-Coelbren markings and pictures and to then see what is left to deal with. Ancient Coelbren would have been written in horizontal registers and so anything either at an angle of vertical could be ignored.
>
> Amongst the maze of marks and graffiti that sprawl all across the flat landward surface of the Dighton Rock there are fourteen areas that appear to have horizontally arranged registers of the straight-line Sign Lettering of Coelbren writing. These inscriptions appear to read as follows: -
>
> | | | |
> |---|---|---|
> | Section 1 | from afar off | I A R |
> | Section 2 | fresh/verdant it is ploughland I | R E AR |
> | Section 3 | from afar off with | I A R   A |
> | Section 4 | in difficulty/in a straight the army | I N O Ll (lli) |
> | Section 5 | the army (of the ruler) crosses over | LL XX (2 = dwy = the ruler) |
> | Section 6 | going over it shall be sure/certain | A D   B I   SIC (sicr) |
> | Section 7 | the sea multitude? | M O R |
> | Section 8 | pure/fresh | I R |
> | Section 9 | mutually together   the court | C Y D   Ll Ys (llys) |
> | Section 10 | defiled | H A L W G |
> | Section 11 | it is | E |
> | Section 12 | god (secret name) in motion cross over nearby outwards | IOI CHWIM X WNGH W(wo) |
> | Section 13 | in terror fright | Dy Ch RE |
> | Section 14 | cornlands towards | I D I |
>
> It is a simple statement that relates to the destruction of Britain by débris from the great comet that caused pollution and terror, and then the fleet expedition transporting the army across the seas to find new fresh arable lands/cornlands.

Mrs Dimancescu not only took Alan to see the Dighton Rock, but she had also obtained permission for Alan to be allowed inside the huge glass case to examine the stone. This was necessary as control of the lighting is necessary when trying to read a badly eroded and graffiti overladen stone. Strong direct light simply bounces back from the surfaces and actually serves to obscure and confuse man-made and natural grooves. It is best to have light shining across the face of the stone at acute angles so as to highlight the proper shapes of the carvings, and the custodian and Mrs Dimancescu duly obliged, patiently switching lights on and off and holding flash-lamps at desired angles. After about two hours Alan felt that he had been able to disentangle the modern overlay of names and initials from the original text, and something intelligible might emerge.

In total there appear to be fourteen areas of the landward surface of the Dighton Rock that carry horizontally arranged straight line lettering of Coelbren inscriptions. These appear to read as shown in illustration 17-2.

It is a simple statement which relates to the destruction of Britain by the comet which caused pollution and terror, and then the fleet expedition transporting the army across the seas to find new fresh arable land/ cornlands.

The Bourne Stone from Komassakunkanit, Cape Bay, Massachusetts

The famous Bourne Stone was found at Komassakumkanit, on Cape Cod Bay, also in Massachusetts. There appears to be one line of writing in Coelbren lettering inscribed on the Bourne Stone, which reads from right to left and left to right; an infrequent occurrence but not unknown to the ancient Bards.

The Bourne Stone is one of the best-known inscribed stones in North America and it has been the subject of much speculative writing, some of which theorises that the text commemorates a voyage to America by the Carthaginian Hano. This is, to say the least, a tenuous theory, as the writing is in a style of alphabet that is not found in association with ancient Carthage or Phoenicia. What we appear to have, is a text that reads from left to right and we have re-set this to read left to right as follows:

Illustration 17-3: The Bourne Stone from Massachusetts

American Coelbren	Cipher	Khumric	English
Y K I	Y Ch I	Y Chi I	the
	DH	dh=chwith	quick turn
	MH U	mu (mudo)	to remove
	A Dh R E Ff	adreff	to return home
	E W A	ewa	smoothly

When any great discovery was made, such as a British fleet discovering America,

Chapter 17 - Other America Inscriptions

there would a necessity to turn around as quickly as possible to get home with the news. This may be why this stone was left on the east coast of North America.

The Bourne Stone was the first American inscription to be deciphered by Alan Wilson and Baram Blackett in 1984. At the time they had no interest at all in the Madoc voyages as they were embarking on other important research. They did write to Barry Fell, the author of *Ancient America*, three times, but got no response and it became clear that if Fell saw a Latin or Greek inscription in the U.S.A., or a Chinese or Egyptian Hieroglyphic text, he would instantly and automatically claim it to be Irish Ogham, and actually Ogham was also used in Wales and was not peculiar to Ireland anyway. So, avoiding the green fog being manufactured by Fell, Wilson and Blackett were steering east and not west in 1984.

St Brendan went to America AFTER he heard of the voyages of the Teyrn = the Monarch, so it was clear that a king had sailed to America in the sixth century AD, BEFORE St Brendan's voyage.

The Pe + Wa giving 'what causes fluid motion' and meaning 'sailing' is found in several other texts in Etruria and America. The 'su' is identical with 'si', as noted in Welsh dictionaries. It would appear that the Dighton Rock was inscribed in one of the fleet expeditions of Madoc or Arthur II in the mid to late sixth century

There are, or were, other inscribed shoreline rocks. Four inscribed rocks on the west of Rhode Island, known as the Portsmouth Rocks, near Melville, which were seen and recorded by Ezra Stiles on 17th June, and on 6th October 1767. Ezra Stiles subsequently made drawings of these inscribed rocks, describing their writing as: 'their inscriptions of the same kind as those at Assonet, though not so distinct and well done'.

Unfortunately, the United States Navy later built coal depot wharves right over these rocks, without bothering to move and preserve them. Another inscribed shoreline rock is the much-photographed Mount Hope Rock near Bristol. All texts in all four areas read from left to right which indicates that this is an inscription of the AD era. The style of the Coelbren also indicates a late developed date rather than an early BC dating.

The Metcalf Stone

Once it is proved that the correct method of decipherment and translation has been established there is an inevitable urge to decipher everything available in the targeted alphabet and language. This is precisely what happened with Alan Wilson and Baram Blackett, who, lacking funds for travel, resorted to any clear photographs available in books on the subject. Studying photographs with a magnifying glass is not as perfect a method as actually seeing the stone and touching it, but provided that the photographs are of good quality a great deal can be done.

The Metcalf Stone

On Page 70 of Dr Joseph Mahan's book *The Secret* there is an illustration of the Metcalf Stone, which is a typical example. The lettering is somewhat crude, and is scratched onto an uneven surface.

The statement appears to read: 'a piece/fragment swiftly together with the ruler, to pray for he shall be out from it.'

The 'piece or fragment' would be the part of the nation seeking new lands.

Spread across the centre of the stone, and through the inscription, are six dots or small holes. These are placed to resemble the major stars in the constellation of the Bear. It may be significant that in Khumric the Bear is 'Arth',.

The decipherment presents no real problems as you can see, but a thorough examination to check the alignment of the dots/holes should be made to see if they match with the constellation of the Bear.

Chapter 17 - Other America Inscriptions

Illustration 17-4: The Metcalf Stone

Top left to right
American   ⟩ᴍIL   ᴦ
Coelbren   ⟩ᴦIᴋ   ᴦ
Cipher   D R I L   R
Khumric   dryll   rhe
English   a piece/fragment   swift/rapid

Centre, Left to Right
American   ⟩   ⟩   o
Coelbren   ⟨ ⟩   ⟨ ⟩   ◊
Cipher   C + D   C + D   (dwy = two = the ruler)   0
Khumric   cyd   cyd   dwy   o
English   united   together   the ruler   out of, from

Lower centre, left to right
American   I O ʟ I
Coelbren   I ◊ ʟ I
Cipher   I O L I
Khumric   ioli
English   to pray

Bottom, left to right
American   ʟ   ᴋ   o
Coelbren   ʟ   ᴋ   ◊
Cipher   B   CH   O
Khumric   Bi Ch = Biach   o
English   it shall be   out of, from, he

The Spratt's Farm Site

One site, the name of which constantly recurred in conversations with Jim Michael and several members of the Ancient Kentucke Historical Association, was that of Spratt's Farm. This unusual site has attracted interest from a variety of persons, some seeking for a long-lost silver mine and others after archaeological treasures. Any visit to the farm and the most cursory examination shows that there are ancient signs of human activity scattered everywhere at the site.

Realising the importance of the Spratt's Farm site, Professor Lee Pennington and his wife Dr Joy Pennington visited the area on several occasions, with the permission of the owner, and began making a quality film record of the site. This is a particularly valuable undertaking as it does several valuable things. First, it preserves a record of the site in the almost certain event of it being destroyed by vandals. At least it will show what was at the site that will allow for future study and reference. Secondly, it overcomes the barriers of distance and expense, by allowing others to get at least a partial view of the site as far away as Britain and elsewhere. Thirdly, it places on record what has been handed down over the generations and the years to the present owner Mr Spratt, now well in his seventies, in a first-hand account of what he knows.

When making their film, the Penningtons identified a number of long stone cairns which had the appearance of probable grave mounds in an ancient cemetery. They have visited ancient sites in Britain and they know what they are looking at. In fact, these long low piles of stones bear an uncanny resemblance to the graves in the ancient cemetery at Oldbury where Arthur I son of Magnus Maximus (Mascen Wledig) is buried in Warwickshire where 'multitudes of the illustrious dead of the British are buried'. There also appears to be a long, winding, twisting, stone rubble-built serpent mound typical of the old Christian-Israelite religion.

There are stretches of cliffs at Spratt's Farm and some caves and a number of deep over-hangs under these cliffs. It was whilst Lee Pennington was showing Alan Wilson a video film of some of these caves and overhangs that Alan asked Lee to stop the film and run it back a few seconds. The pictures were of the entrance to a large cave, and the camera had panned clear across a long row of strange markings cut into the rock. These markings had not been seen or recognized by the Penningtons or Mr Spratt, and it was simply one of those fortuitous situations where the camera picks up on what the human eye fails to detect. These markings cut into a horizontal row across the rock surface caught Alan Wilson's eye as soon as he saw the film, and by freezing the frame the row of Coelbren letters was suddenly obvious to Lee and Joy Pennington, and Jim Michael, who was present. They had not been either looking for or expecting to see any ancient inscriptions and had passed by a neatly cut row of unfamiliar letters without even seeing them.

Near to this inscription, the outline of a human hand had been carved out on a rock boulder, and it was this that had drawn the Penningtons to this particular location. This well-known ancient eastern religious motif of the human hand had been recently neatly chiselled out of the rock, leaving only a bare space. Sadly, this desecration of what is almost certainly a fourteen hundred-years-old archaeological site of some importance to the cultural heritage of the state and nation, was actually believed to have been carried out by a person employed to safeguard such important sites. Private collectors, secretively gathering their hidden hoards, like the collectors of rare birds' eggs, proliferate in the U.S.A.

This matter of private collecting for personal home collections is a threat to most of these unprotected, remote, and vulnerable sites. Whilst private collectors will see something as plainly obvious as the carving of a human hand, they will almost certainly miss other things, in the same way that the Penningtons missed the long Coelbren inscription. Apparently, anyone is free to bulldoze what are always termed 'Indian Mounds', provided he or she owns the land or has the owner's permission, just as British farmers routinely plough over ancient fort sites and burial mounds. Ancient monuments are sometimes registered as such in the U.S.A., but the majority are not. Perhaps it is because they reveal awkward evidence that overthrows the politically correct Columbus Only Theories. As stated before, Christopher Columbus never actually reached America and he did not even know of the two continents' existence when he died.

The freedom to do whatever a person likes with his or her own land is a fundamental principle as a right, but this liberalised anarchy does not extend to ancient monuments in Europe, other than Wales. In the case of Spratt's Farm, the owner, Mr Spratt, was most anxious to see the area protected and preserved. Yet even he allowed a man to bring in a bulldozer onto the site and to winch it up on top of the cliffs, where a major destructive attack was made on an area of caves and overhangs in a vain attempt to locate the fabled lost silver mine. Whether this destroyed any inscriptions or anything else will never now be known. Fortunately, the bulldozing miner ran out of cash and the destruction ceased.

The Pennington Inscription found on Spratt's Farm can be deciphered and translated into British Khumric quite easily, which should surprise no one given the existence of the cemetery of long grave cairns and the serpent mound in this same area. The carving of the hand is missing from the boulder near to the rock inscription, but at least it is known to have existed there until the early 1990s. This is as much as needs to be said about this site at the moment, and there appear to have been at least two linked sites in close proximity to each other. One is the cemetery and the other seems to have been a religious site, and that both relate to the Arthur and Madoc expedition of *c.* AD 574 appears to be certain.

Not until this entire site has been thoroughly examined and filmed from the air and surveyed at ground level, and comparisons made with British sites and historical records, will any possible story emerge.

The deliberate toppling of marker boulders from the cliff tops does not and will not assist evaluation, and at this time no further comment needs to be made. No attempt is made in this volume to detail the precise locations of rock inscriptions, as these quite remarkable relics are unprotected. At least two other remarkable rock-cut inscriptions have been used for rifle target practice by morons, and given the prevalent custom of the clandestine amassing of meaningless private collections, it is best to try to limit the possibilities of destruction.

The reading of the Pennington Inscription from Spratt's Farm makes it virtually certain that there is a monumental ancient graveyard that has distinct similarities with the cemetery of 'multitudes of the illustrious dead of the British' at Oldbury ('Old Burial Ground', where the remaining part of a memorial/accession stone that appears to relate to Arthur I was found), near Atherston, in Warwickshire, England. The Pennington inscription reads as:

'From below/under/ in a state of going down, in need/want, all the whole of what is outward it shall be a place revered, the ruler in God the power the end manifest.'

The presence of the long winding stone mound as a Yahweh-Jehovah snake makes this identification complete. That this is a major ancient British Christian site in the Mid-West of America that dates from the Arthur and Madoc expedition appears to be very possible and to the authors it is demonstrated beyond any reasonable doubt.

The Pennington Inscription from Spratt's Farm, Kentucky

The Coelbren inscription video-filmed by Professor Lee and Dr Joy Pennington at Spratt's Farm runs across a large piece of fallen rock, which was dynamited out of its original position in the cliff face by treasure-hunters searching for an alleged lost silver mine. It is reported that a large part of the original inscription is still intact and is visible *in situ* and as yet unread. The section, which has been read is as set out below.

There are minor problems with this text, such as 'hyd' meaning 'revere' which might possibly be 'hwh', meaning 'effort' or 'push', and 'eisi', meaning 'want' or 'need' might instead be 'ei', meaning 'its' or 'his', and 'si' meaning 'hiss' or 'buzz', and referring to the comet or the winds.

Chapter 17 - Other America Inscriptions

```
Illustration 17-5: The Pennington Inscription from Spratt's Farm, Kentucky
American    IK          EIKI        OK              KE IΓ
Coelbren    IK          EI+K        ΘI              EE IΓ
Khumric     O  IS       El  SI (eisi)  OL                      FfE    IR
English    frombelow, under in want/need  of all / whole  of what is  outward
                        in a state of                    whole   what is pure
                        going down
American        LI      K           H I             II
Coelbren        LI      K           H L             II
Khumric         B I     Lle         Hw B (hyb)      Dwy = two = the ruler
English         it shall be a place of reference    the ruler

American        ४   DV      Γ           ナ                  Ł
Coelbren        ४   DV      N           +L                  Ł
Khumric         Yng D W (duw)  Rha      crwys + B = crwyb   Ffe
English         In  god         the power  the end manifest / outward
```

There are some indistinct marks after the signs for 'ffe' which appear to be 'ir' for 'what is pure'. This section of this text then reads:

> 'from below/in a state of going down, in want need all that is outward what is pure it shall be, a place of reverence (to) the ruler in God the power, the end manifest/outward.'

The experience gained in dealing with Etruscan inscriptions proved invaluable in the decipherment and reading of these American inscriptions. The whole inscription needs to be carefully examined, drawn, photographed, and filmed, before what appears to be an inevitable destruction occurs.

The Davenport Stele

Amongst other strange artefacts found in North America is the Davenport Stele, and like many other inscribed stones it has not received the attention that it deserves. Probably the lack of information of the facts and the evidence held in the British-Khumric historical records has made academics over-cautious in their attitudes. The Davenport Stele is an inscribed stone and is on display in the Putnam Museum as specimen No. A.R.15338 Cremation Scene, and No. 15339 the reverse side. Also, in this museum, there is the Calendar Stone as specimen No. 15341, found in the same mound.

There is a difference between Coelbren that is *scratched onto* a stone surface and Coelbren writing that is *cut into* the surface. The scratching action involves wrist action and so it tends to automatically produce a cursive script as opposed to the straight lines of a cut that is chiselled or chipped out. Anyone with any knowledge at all of industrial methods Time Measurement or Predetermined Motion Time Study techniques will know this. In the case of the Davenport Stele the straight lines of the lettering have tended to curve.

This inscription is cursive and appears to follow hand and wrist movements as opposed to straight line Coelbren cut into wood or chiselled into stone. The first thought was to avoid this inscription but then it was decided to make some attempt at decipherment.

It appears certain that this text tells of the death in America of King Arthur II son of Meurig, and the decision was taken to send his body home to Britain wrapped in a bundle, through the Appalachian Mountains ('place falling snow'), to the coast of 'this place' (the U.S.A.), and across the 'flood' that is the Atlantic, to go by sea back home. This text fits with every other piece of evidence so far amassed.

The inscription can be arranged into areas and lines for decipherment and translation.

Alan Wilson and Baram Blackett first thought to omit this stele from their range of studies, as the style of the Coelbren writing is not the conventional straight cut stroke design. It is, however, worth the hazard of offering some explanation of the text as its authenticity appears to be beyond dispute. The Davenport Stele was discovered by the Reverend Jacob Gass, who was born in Oltingen in Switzerland in 1842, and who studied theology in Basel before emigrating the United States in 1868.

He continued his studies at Wartburg Seminary, at Strawberry Point, in Iowa, and finally arrived at the first Lutheran Church in Davenport in 1871. Here he preached and taught in German to the largely German population

It was here in the thriving, growing, bustling community of Davenport that Jacob Gass launched himself into a career of almost frantic digging. Commentators on his life and efforts make it plain that Jacob Gass was crude beyond even the most primitive ideas of archaeology in his own times. He also had a further handicap in communicating with the vast majority of academics who were struggling to come to terms with American pre-Columbus history and archaeology, as he spoke very little English, and his brief accounts of his activities were written in German.

The Davenport Academy was the stronghold of the English-speaking community who mostly hailed from New York and New England, and who were it seems generally contemptuous of the later German immigrants who had moved into

Chapter 17 - Other America Inscriptions

Davenport in very large numbers. The Reverend Jacob Gass did not help himself with his hot temper and somewhat insulting manners. He had taken interest in ancient lake-dwelling sites in his native Switzerland, which archaeologists had labelled as Neolithic, and this probably aroused his interest in the ancient American mounds. Somehow, he managed to get elected to the academy in 1876, where he is said to have accused academy members of being lazy when digging into ancient mounds. It is probable that they were working slowly and methodically attempting to act in a more scientific and careful manner than Jacob Gass did himself. Jacob Gass had no compunction in hacking and slashing his way down through any later post-Columbus burials and relics in a totally destructive manner to get down to earlier archaeological remains. He made few notes and left only the scantiest records.

What happened was that in 1874 Jacob Gass, along with his brother-in-law Borgelt, and two theological students, were reported to have made discoveries when they excavated several mounds on Cook Farm, then on Davenport's outskirts. Dr Robert Farquharson, a prominent Academy member, then visited the site and persuaded Jacob Gass to turn over his finds to himself, so that a scientific report could be published. Much of the report centred around the ancient copper axes which had been found, and the result was that Dr Farquharson was able to persuade prominent Academy sponsors to back the nomination of Jacob Gass to the Davenport Academy. Thereafter most of what Jacob Gass found passed by purchase or donation into Davenport Academy and on to the Putnam Museum.

To quote from Marshall McKusick, who wrote *The Davenport Conspiracy*:

'In view of the debacle that developed over fraudulent artefacts, it is important to emphasis here that the specimens found by Reverend Gass in 1874 were genuine. I have personally examined the artefacts, and they represent a collection of great rarity etc.'

The real drama ensued when in 1877, not long after being elected to the Academy, Jacob Gass returned to dig at Cook Farm in the depth of winter. The lease on the farm was due to expire, and the new tenant had sworn never to allow Jacob Gass onto the property. When this was reported to Jacob Gass, several supporters urged him to dig again immediately in what had become a 'now or never situation'. Alan Wilson and Baram Blackett are themselves well aware of this type of dilemma, and can sympathise with Jacob Gass.

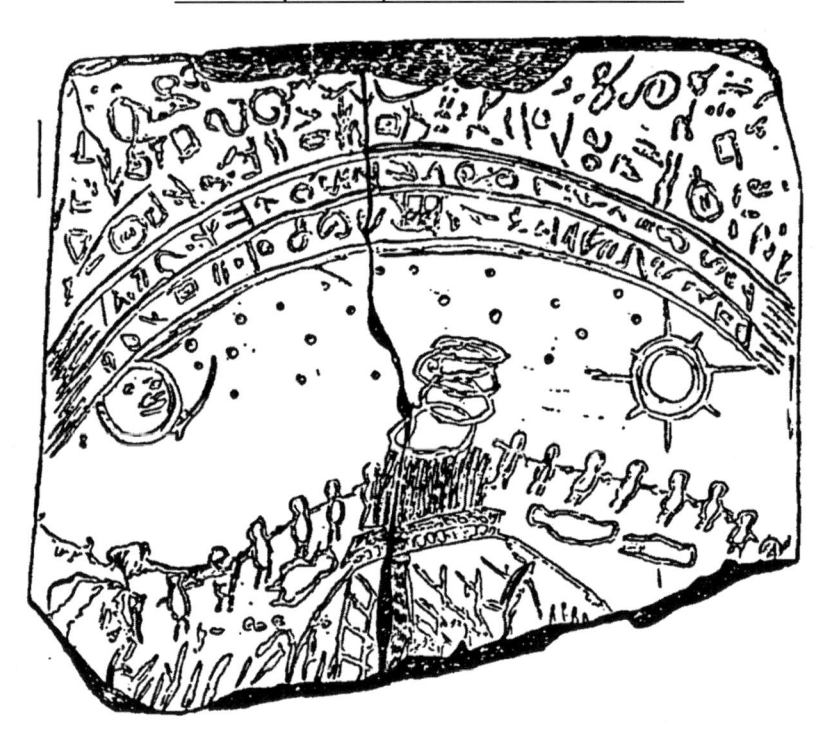

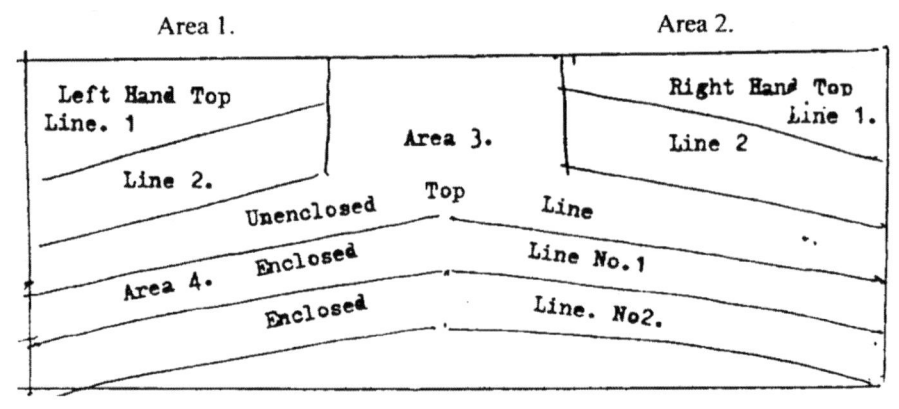

The Davenport Stele, now in the Putnam Museum

Area 1.   Area 2.

Left Hand Top Line. 1
Line 2.
Area 3.
Right Hand Top Line. 1
Line 2
Top Line
Unenclosed
Area 4. Enclosed
Line No. 1
Enclosed
Line. No2.

Chapter 17 - Other America Inscriptions

Illustration 17-6: The Davenport Stele, U.S.A.

This inscription is cursive and appears to follow hand and wrist movements as opposed to straight line Coelbren cut into wood or chiselled into stone. The first thought was to avoid this inscription but then it was decided to make some attempt at decipherment.

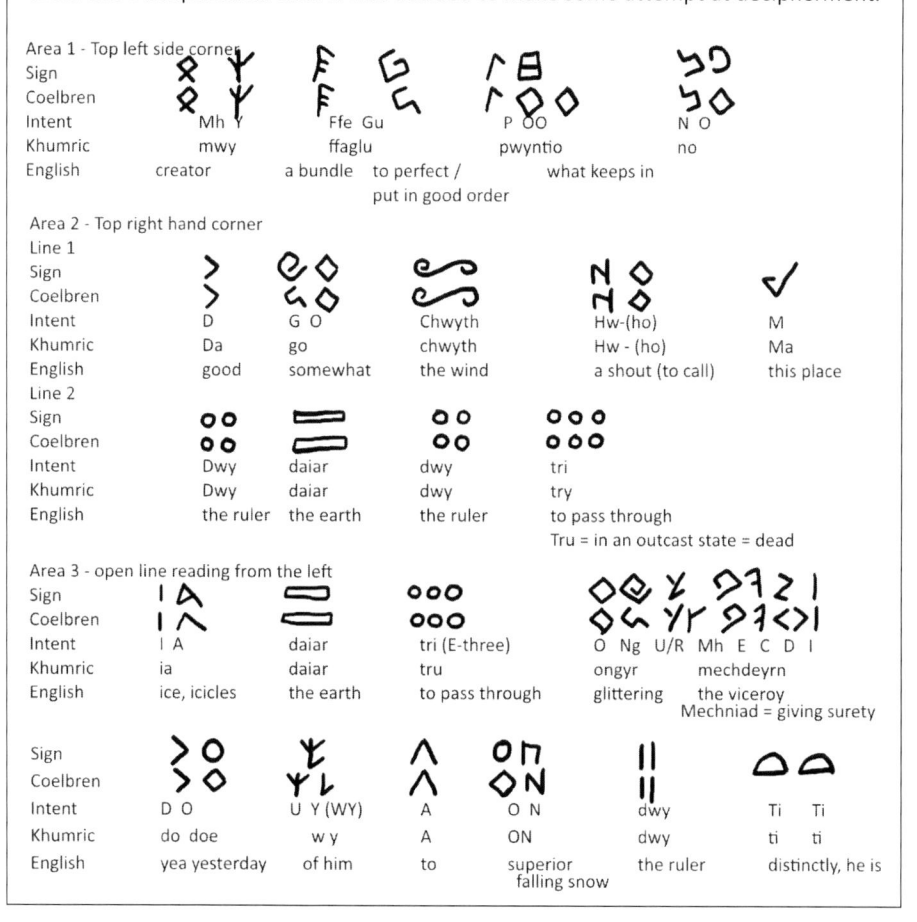

Area 1 - Top left side corner

Sign				
Coelbren				
Intent	Mh	Ffe Gu	P OO	N O
Khumric	mwy	ffaglu	pwyntio	no
English	creator	a bundle	to perfect / put in good order	what keeps in

Area 2 - Top right hand corner
Line 1

Sign					
Coelbren					
Intent	D	G O	Chwyth	Hw-(ho)	M
Khumric	Da	go	chwyth	Hw - (ho)	Ma
English	good	somewhat	the wind	a shout (to call)	this place

Line 2

Sign				
Coelbren				
Intent	Dwy	daiar	dwy	tri
Khumric	Dwy	daiar	dwy	try
English	the ruler	the earth	the ruler	to pass through
				Tru = in an outcast state = dead

Area 3 - open line reading from the left

Sign				
Coelbren				
Intent	I A	daiar	tri (E-three)	O Ng U/R Mh E C D I
Khumric	I A	daiar	tru	ongyr mechdeyrn
English	ice, icicles	the earth	to pass through	glittering the viceroy
				Mechniad = giving surety

Sign					
Coelbren					
Intent	D O	U Y (WY)	A	O N	dwy	Ti Ti
Khumric	do doe	w y	A	ON	dwy	ti ti
English	yea yesterday	of him	to	superior falling snow	the ruler	distinctly, he is

535

The King Arthur Conspiracy - Wilson & Blackett

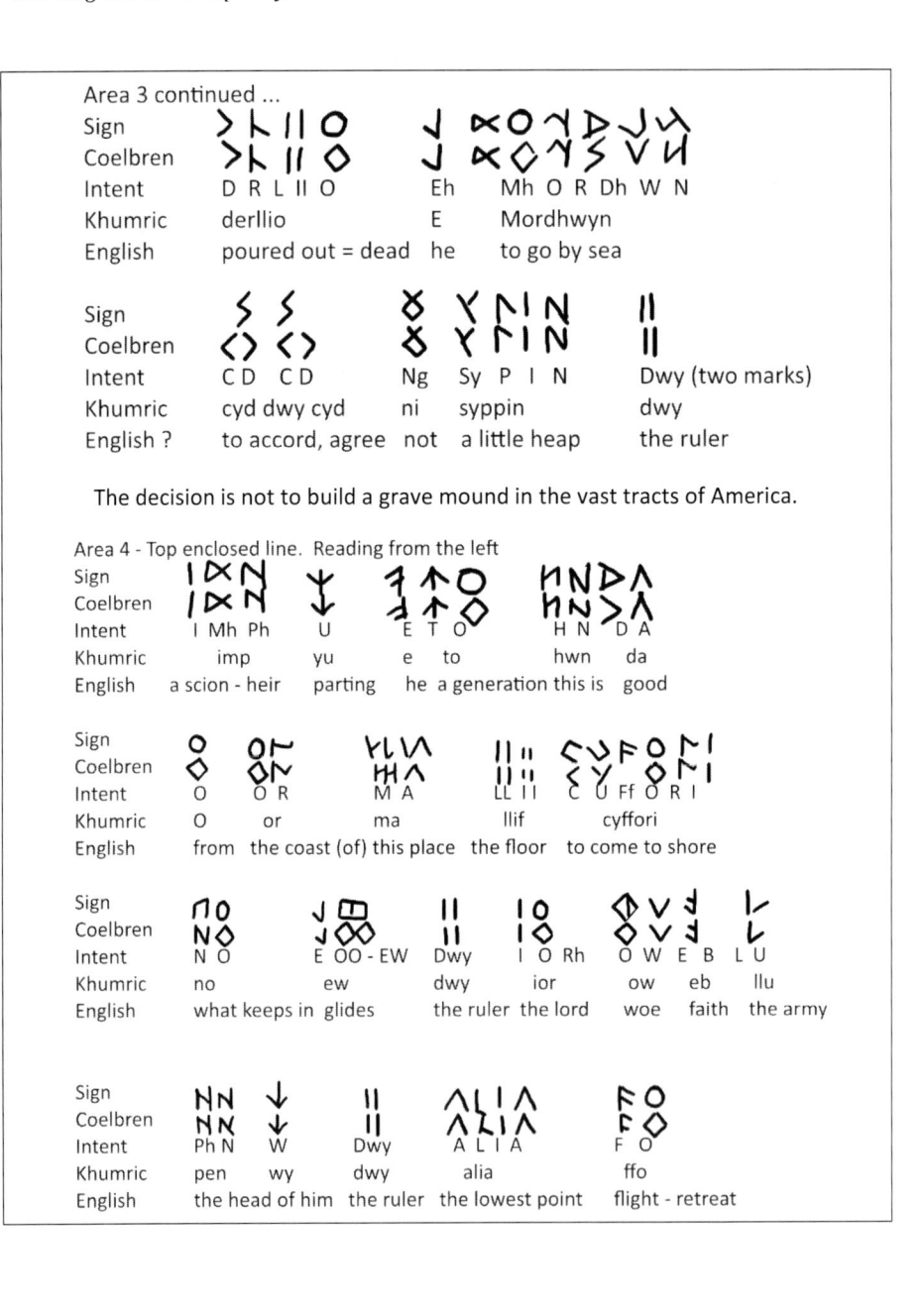

Area 3 continued ...

Sign			
Coelbren			
Intent	D R L ll O	Eh	Mh O R Dh W N
Khumric	derllio	E	Mordhwyn
English	poured out = dead	he	to go by sea

Sign				
Coelbren				
Intent	C D C D	Ng	Sy P I N	Dwy (two marks)
Khumric	cyd dwy cyd	ni	syppin	dwy
English ?	to accord, agree	not	a little heap	the ruler

The decision is not to build a grave mound in the vast tracts of America.

Area 4 - Top enclosed line. Reading from the left

Sign					
Coelbren					
Intent	I Mh Ph	U	E T O	H N D A	
Khumric	imp	yu	e to	hwn da	
English	a scion - heir	parting	he a generation	this is good	

Sign					
Coelbren					
Intent	O	O R	M A	LL II	C U Ff O R I
Khumric	O	or	ma	llif	cyffori
English	from	the coast (of)	this place	the floor	to come to shore

Sign					
Coelbren					
Intent	N O	E OO - EW	Dwy	I O Rh	O W E B L U
Khumric	no	ew	dwy	ior	ow eb llu
English	what keeps in	glides	the ruler	the lord	woe faith the army

Sign				
Coelbren				
Intent	Ph N	W	Dwy	A L I A	F O
Khumric	pen	wy	dwy	alia	ffo
English	the head of him	the ruler	the lowest point	flight - retreat	

536

Chapter 17 - Other America Inscriptions

So Jacob Gass, with seven German friends, set out in an Iowa winter to hack through two-and-a-half feet of frozen ground to create a hole in what remained of Mound No. 3 on Cook Farm. First, they found a disturbed Native American burial of the recent post-Columbus era, identified by the presence of European trade goods. Deeper down they found two layers of shells, and underneath a burial pit filled with loose black soil and human bone fragments and pieces of slate. This was very different to the complete skeletons previously excavated from the southern half of Mound No.3. The disturbed skeletons and the loose black soil were noted by Jacob Gass:

'These circumstances arrested particular attention, and caused me to proceed with more caution, until soon after, about five o'clock in the afternoon, we discovered two inscribed tablets of coal slate.

'The smaller one is engraved on one side only, and the larger on both sides. The larger one was lying with that side upward which was somewhat injured by a stroke with the spade.

'Both were closely encircled by a row of limestones. They were covered on both sides with clay, on the removal of which the markings were for the first time discovered.

'It should also be remarked that I did not leave the mound after penetrating through the frost until the tablets were discovered and taken from their resting place with my own hands.'

So the Davenport Stele and the Calendar Stone came to light during a frantic day of digging on a bitterly cold winter's day, and in a shambles of an excavation. Initially the discoveries were greeted with great acclamation. Enter one William Pratt, who visited the site alone the next day. He claimed to have found a concreted animal-shaped object that had two glued-on quartz crystals for eyes. William Pratt now alleged that the eight diggers had all missed this object. As it was quite incorrectly believed that any form of glue would have to be modern, this then cast doubt on the tablet discoveries. All this then led to suggestions that Jacob Gass was set up by conspirators who had 'salted' the Mound No. 3 site with fake artefacts.

It was the same old 'here we go again' situation, as it was alleged that none of the Native American people had a written alphabet, and therefore the slate tablets could not be ancient. It was then alleged that the incisions were not weathered, and this is both illogical and irrelevant as buried objects do not weather.

Professor F. W. Putnam, described as 'one of Harvard's legendary founders of

North American archaeological research', was naturally alarmed at the prospect of any find that included alphabet writing, and which therefore meant that there had been a pre-Columbus migration from Europe. So he visited his cousins, the Davenport Putnams, and wrote to Dr Farquharson stating that the slate tablets were forgeries. If they were not forgeries, then they showed a link between ancient America and the Old World and his theories were in tatters. As for William Pratt, well he was one of the first three founder members of the Davenport Academy that was heavily criticised by Jacob Gass and was rewarded with his appointment as the first curator of the Putnam Museum.

It is therefore against the usual acrimonious and negative background of allegations of forgery from the 'No Europeans ever before Columbus' academics that Wilson and Blackett agreed to look at the Davenport Stele. The false allegation of forgery, to get rid of awkward evidence, was nothing new to them in their investigations. There is a scene shown roughly drawn on the Davenport Stele. In the centre of the picture is a large fire with smoke curling upwards from it. To the left of the fire is a representation of what might be the moon, and to the right of the fire a drawing of the sun. Scattered around the sun and moon and across the top of the fire are smaller circles, which undoubtedly represent stars. Ranged on either side of the fire are two rows of crude human figures with hands joined together. There are eight of these figures on the right, and seven on the left. Below the row of human figures on the right is another such figure lying prostrate alongside a coffin. Another figure also lies prostrate on the left-hand side.

The impression is one of a funeral pyre, or perhaps a fire to dry out a corpse, with a human-shaped coffin, or human-shaped bag, lying waiting on the right hand side. The prostrate figure on the left-hand side has no coffin and may or may not be the murderer.

Set across the top of this scene are five rows of writing. The area in the centre of the top two rows may have been damaged, so if there was writing in this central area, it has now been lost. A sketch plan of the layout of the lines of written text was first constructed, just as with the Etruscan Stelae and the Lemnos Stele. This makes control of the decipherment much easier.

The pattern was area 1 consisting of line 1 and line 2 of the left-hand top section; area 2 consisting of line 1 and line 2 of the right-hand top section; area 3 consisting of the unenclosed line 1 of the central section; and finally area 4, consisting of line 1 enclosed, and line 2 enclosed. All texts in all four areas read from left to right.

'Side of the head, to pass through, spear, the viceroy/regent Yea, yesterday of him to superior/or falling snow. The ruler he who is poured out (=dead) he to go by sea.

'To accord not a little heap (to) the ruler (the decisions not to build a grave mound)'

Area No. 4, top line 1:

'A scion/heir departing with him he a generation is good. From the coast of this place the flood (=ocean) to come to shore.'

Bottom line 2:

'What keeps in what glides (=sailing) the ruler the lord/governor we faith the army the head of him the ruler the lowest point flight or retreat.'

It seems certain that this text tells of the death and embalming of King Arthur II ap Meurig in America, and the decision to send his body home wrapped in a bundle 'through the place of falling snow' (either the winter or the Appalachian Mountains) 'to the coast of this place' (North America) and across the flood, to go back home by sea. The text fits with every other piece of evidence so far amassed.

That the sudden death of the king on this great voyage and expedition would be a happening of such magnitude in the minds of his kinsmen and followers as to cause them to record the events on stones and in epic poetry should be no surprise. Arthur II ap Meurig was the ruler who had preserved the nation in the aftermath of the colossal destructions of the comet, and the king who had led the armies to a series of victories over the invaders who then tried to seize lands in Britain. He was a heroic figure in his own time, and the national version of Alexander the Great, or Napoleon, a saviour figure in what Winston Churchill would have called 'their darkest hour'.

The Calendar Stele, found by Jacob Gass, is inscribed with a well-drawn circle, which is then surrounded by three other successively larger outer circles. In the second inner circle there are four Awen, Broad Arrow /|\, signs. These are evenly spaced at what might be north, east, south, and west, or at 3, 6, 9, and 12 o' clock. In the outermost circle there are twelve groups of signs, again evenly spaced, and probably resembling a Zodiac arrangement. Several of these signs contain clearly identified Coelbren letters. Whoever made this, whether ancient relic or modern fake in 1877, knew the Coelbren alphabet; and it has to be pointed out that loose earth beneath two or three feet of frozen ground should be no surprise.

The Wiggins Point Stone

Illustration 17-7: The two sides of the Wiggins Point inscribed stone, U.S.A.

The style of the writing on this stone is clearly cursive, where the lettering is scratched rather than cut, or carved, or hewn, with straight line strokes as the British Coelbren would be when cut into wood. The word 'Coelbren' implies writing on wood, and the letters were cut into the wooden strips or staves with a knife or an axe. This automatically required that the alphabet was entirely constructed of straight strokes cut at various angles.

It is not known if this Wiggins Stone is genuine or not, but on the presumption of innocent until proven guilty the interpretation of the pictographs at the top of both sides and the decipherment of the texts was attempted.

Most people will remember that when they were young and were first taught to read and write, they first learnt the alphabet as plain generally straight-line signs before progressing to what children in Alan Wilson's early days called 'real writing' by joining the letters together in longhand. To do this capital letters are generally abandoned in favour of half-uncials. Something like this process appears to have occurred with the Davenport and Wiggins Point stones as the lettering has tended to become curved instead of remaining straight-stroked. By straightening out the curved lines of these letters that were so shaped, the reading of the texts of both stones presented very little difficulty as written in the Coelbren and the Khumric language. There may even be a case for investigating whether half-uncials evolved out of the Coelbren Alphabet.

The importance of these texts is that they are comparatively long statements. The Davenport Stele appears to record the embalming of the body of an unnamed but clearly very important man. The text tells of the death of this leader from a head wound, and of the decision not to bury him in America, 'in a little heap', tumulus grave mound, but rather to wrap him up for transport. The decision is to send the body home across the seas for burial. It is not clear whether the person making this decision is the Mechdeyrn = Viceroy, taking charge after the death of the leader, or whether the dead person is the Mechdeyrn. The involvement of the term 'Mechdeyrn' implies that a major king is involved. As Nennius states in his *History of Britain*, compiled by AD 822, Arthur was not yet king when he led the armies in battle. His father, King Meurig, lived to a great age (perhaps near a hundred). Although the date of his death is unknown, it was almost certainly after AD 572. So, Arthur II would have been a viceroy for most of his life.

The Wiggins Point Stone is a form of declaration monument, which records the great voyage of sailing across the oceans, driven by the winds to this spacious land. It tells of the intention of ploughing and farming this new land, and like the Davenport Stele, it mentions the crossing of 'the great flood', which is, presumably, the Atlantic. As the Davenport Stele clearly identifies the dead leader = ruler as the Head of the Army, and makes it clear that his loss is a catastrophe, it is difficult not to identify the dead man as Arthur. As this text also talks of a bundle, again, presumably, the leather sack made by three ladies of the court to wrap the body, it is again difficult not to see the deceased as Arthur II. In both cases there is a clear resolution to stay in the new land, and the sending home of the body seems to imply a decision to maintain contact with the old homeland.

Each side of the Wiggins Point Stone carries a pictograph at the top, and even these drawings may relate to the events described.

When Alan Wilson and Baram Blackett first saw photographs of both the Davenport Stele, and the Wiggins Point Stone they were disinclined to regard these as being written in the British Coelbren alphabet as many of the letters are curved. It is well known, however, that wrist action when a person is scratching marks onto a tough surface with a scraping or cutting instrument has a natural cursive effect. This would contrast with the straight strokes made when Coelbren letters were cut into wood with knives or axes, and chiselled into stone.

The choice was very simple, they could either do nothing or they could make some attempt and see what emerged. So Blackett and Wilson decided to straighten out the curves in the lettering on both the Wiggins Points and the Davenport Stones. The result was the emergence of clear Coelbren writing.

Most people will remember when they were young and they were first taught to read and write, they first leant the alphabet as plain generally straight-line signs before progressing to what children in Alan Wilson's early days called "real writing" by joining the letters together in longhand. To do this the capital letters are generally abandoned in favour of half-uncials. Something like this process seems to have occurred with the Davenport and Wiggins Point stones as the lettering has tended to become curved instead of remaining straight stroked. By straightening out the curved lines of these letters that we so shaped, the reading of the texts of both stones presented very little difficulty as written in the Coelbren and Khumric language. There may even be a case for investigating whether the half-uncials evolved out of the Coelbren alphabet.

The importance of these texts is that they are comparatively long statements. The Davenport Stele appears to record the embalming of the body of an un-named, but clearly important, man. The text tells of the death of this leader from a head wound, and of the decision not to bury him in America – "in a little heap" – or tumulus grave mound, but rather to wrap him up for transport. The decision is to send the body home across the seas for burial. It is not clear whether the person making this decision is the Mechdeyrn – Viceroy, taking charge after the death of the leader or whether the dead person is the Mechdeyrn. The involvement of the term Mechdeyrn implies that a major king is involved. As Nennius states in his History compiled by AD 833, Arthur was not yet king when he led the armies in battle. His father, King Meurig, lived to a great age (perhaps near 100) although the date of his death unknown, it was almost certainly after AD 572. So Arthur II would have been a Viceroy for most of his life.

The Wiggins Point Stone is a form of declaration monument, which records the great voyage of sailing across the oceans, driven by winds to this spacious land. It tells of the intent to plough and farm this new land, and like the Davenport Stele clearly identifies the dead leader – ruler as the Head of the Army, and makes it clear that this loss is a catastrophe, it is difficult not to identify the dead man as Arthur. As this text also talks of a bundle, again, presumably, the leather sack made by three ladies of the court to wrap the body, it is again difficult not to see the deceased Arthur

Chapter 17 - Other America Inscriptions

II. In both cases there is a clear resolution to stay in the new land, and the sending home of the body seems to imply a decision to maintain contact with the homeland.

Each of the Wiggings Point Stone carries a pictograph at the top, and even these drawings may relate to the events described.

The possible meaning of the pictograph on side 1 of the Wiggins Point Stone.

Jim Michael had long felt that the strange pictures on the top of both sides of the Wiggins Point Stone might have a meaning that could be interpreted. He pointed out that there were seven circle-dots on the picture, and the clear representation of a boat with a box in it. This inevitably invites comparison with the ancient British poetry that relates that King Arthur was brought back across the oceans in a boat manned by seven other persons.

Having successfully deciphered large numbers of ancient British, Etruscan, Phrygian, and Egyptian texts Alan Wilson and Baram Blackett were persuaded to offer a possible interpretation.

Pictograph on the top of the Wiggins Point Stone

Pictographs require a measure of interpretation to allow for an attempt at decipherment. The reader must bear this in mind as this attempt made to decipher the Wiggins point pictograph. Starting at the bottom left-hand side of the signs and reading clockwise.

C + D = Cyd	cyd = mutually together
Two dots = Dwy	dwy = the ruler (dwy almost means ruler)
One dot = un	un = one, an individual
Snake sign = nadr	naddu = to cry out = neidr
One dot = un	un = one
Wind sign	wind

There are seven dots, and in ancient Khumric Epic poetry there were seven people in the boat that brought the embalmed corpse of Arthur II back to Britain.

The emerging statement is:

'mutually together (we seven) with the ruler, one in a coffin, in a ship/boat, in an outcast state (or to pass through) mutually together with one, to cry out for wind.'

It could be slightly variant and also mean:

'mutually together (we seven) with the ruler monarchical, in an outcast state (or, to pass through) mutually together as one to cry out for wind.'

This interpretation and decipherment would appear to be a statement concerning the transportation of the body of the dead king in a boat. The British King was to Britain what the Pharoah was to Egypt, and his death by assassination with a relatively small number of his people in a distant foreign land was an awesome event. The news had to be carried back to Britain to the regents Ffrioch (Rioch) a brother of Arthur II, Urien Rheged a cousin and the one hundred and eighty Mayors.

'mutually together (we seven) with the Ruler (one) in a coffin in a ship/boat, in an outcast state (or, to pass through) mutually together with one the wind/ or to cry out.'

Alternatively it could mean:

'mutually together (we seven) with the Ruler monarchical in an outcast state (or, to pass through) mutually together as one to cry out.'

It would appear that this statement also concerns the transportation of the body of the dead king in a boat. The British king as head of the First Holy Family was to Britain as the Pharaoh was to Egypt, or the early Emperors to China. The death of the King by assassination in a foreign land was an awesome event. The news and proof of his death had to be carried back to the Regents, Frioch his brother, Urien Rheged a second cousin, and Maelgwn Gwynedd, and to the hundred and eighty Mayors of Britain.

Pictograph on Side 2 of the Wiggins Point Stone

At first sight this picture appears to be even more cryptic that the scene which shows a boat with a box on board. As is evident, the picture shows something that might resemble a dial or a gauge on a piece of modern electrical equipment, with a tuning knob below the curved scale.

This picture shows what appears to be the curvature of the earth with twelve marked divisions to represent the daylight hours, there being twelve hours of night and twelve daytime hours. If the left side is taken as the west or sunset and moon area, and the right as the east or sunrise area, then the picture may start to make sense. There is a circled dot on the sight to represent the sun, and a crescent on the left to represent the moon, and in between is the circle, representing planet Earth.

The arc curving above the earth circle represents the passage of the sun across the skies from east to west. There are six marks or divisions to the east, and then a circle representing the sun, and five more marks to the west. The sun is therefore at the seventh mark, or the seventh hour. If the beginning of this curved measure on the right is taken as representing sunrise as it occurs in Britain, then the message is seven hours' time difference from the eastern point which is Britain. This is correct for the time difference from between Britain and Kentucky.

The crescent shape on the left may be a moon, but it also has the Cloak symbol shape, and 'segan' means 'cloak', giving 'segru' = 'to secrete', 'to set apart', whilst 'seguru' means 'to loiter', 'to stay a while'.

There are several words that generally mean 'circle, wheel, ring, round', and so on. These are 'cylch', 'cylchwy', 'amgant', 'cant', etc. 'Cant' also means 'orb', 'horizon', and 'rim', and so the circle below the large curve may be telling us that the curve is the horizon of the earth. This supports the proposition that the evenly spaced marks along the large curve represent hours. The smaller circle on the right at sunrise may also have a dual meaning, for 'amgant' may imply 'amgau', meaning 'a place of minstrelsy', which would be Britain. The words for mark or stroke, which are 'nod', 'arwydd', and 'man', bring in further wordplay. 'Man' has the dual meaning of 'place', whilst 'nodfa' means 'refuge'/'sanctuary', and 'arwyl' means 'funeral'. Perhaps we are being told that the king died at longitude seven hours from Britain, and that there was a secret place of refuge, and that this concerns a funeral.

It is admitted that this is interpretation and conjecture, but the general import of the messages scratched underneath these pictographs corroborates these suggestions. It might also be worth noting that Alan Wilson and Baram Blackett have used just such interpretations for several years to locate a number of as yet undisclosed important sites in Britain. As Alan says, "You have to try to learn to think in the same way as they thought."

Illustration 17-8: Wiggins Point Stone decipherment – front side

Line 1
American Coelbren	BO⊃	YɅ←	⁄VJ⊃
Intent	B O D	S U W	H E D
Khumric	Bod	Suwr	Hed
English	the being	one who hushes	tranquility

Line 2
American Coelbren	KJL	⫯↑	V Y
Intent	C E Bi	S/T W	R
Khumric	Ebystyr		
English	tehtered (sheltered, protected by)		

Line 3
American Coelbren	JL	⋉	⁄VI⊃	T↑
Intent	E B	Ni	Ni d	Ti
Khumric	eb	Ni	nid	Ti
English	issuing out going forth	we	what is impending	you are

Line 4
American Coelbren	⋎⋎	▷⋎	ⱡ
Intent	U NG	D W	Se
Khumric	un	Duw	Se
English	one	God	fixed, established

Chapter 17 - Other America Inscriptions

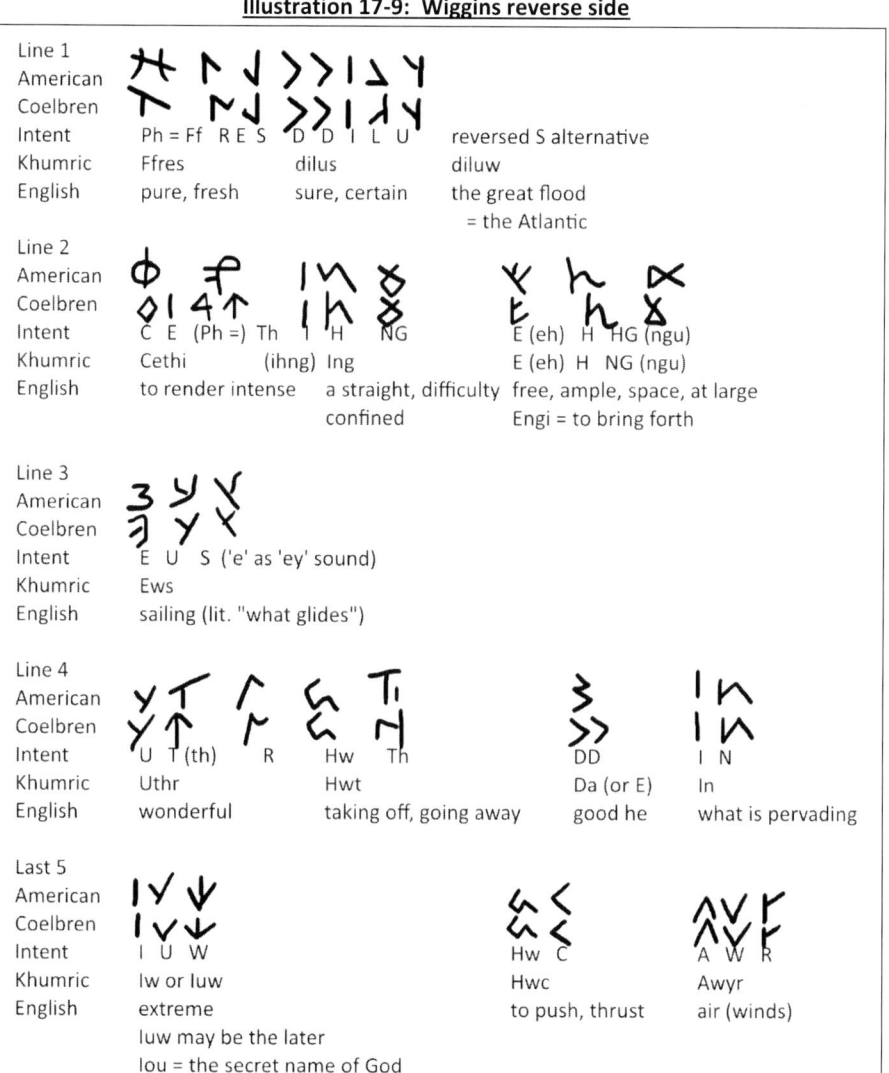

Illustration 17-9: Wiggins reverse side

Line 1
American Coelbren Intent: Ph = Ff R E S   D D I L U   reversed S alternative
Khumric: Ffres   dilus   diluw
English: pure, fresh   sure, certain   the great flood = the Atlantic

Line 2
American Coelbren Intent: C E (Ph =) Th   I H NG   E (eh) H HG (ngu)
Khumric: Cethi   (ihng) Ing   E (eh) H NG (ngu)
English: to render intense   a straight, difficulty confined   free, ample, space, at large   Engi = to bring forth

Line 3
American Coelbren Intent: E U S ('e' as 'ey' sound)
Khumric: Ews
English: sailing (lit. "what glides")

Line 4
American Coelbren Intent: U T(th)   R   Hw Th   DD   I N
Khumric: Uthr   Hwt   Da (or E)   In
English: wonderful   taking off, going away   good he   what is pervading

Last 5
American Coelbren Intent: I U W   Hw C   A W R
Khumric: Iw or Iuw   Hwc   Awyr
English: extreme   to push, thrust   air (winds)
luw may be the later
Iou = the secret name of God

Illustration 17-10: Wiggins reverse side continued ...

Line 6
American Coelbren: M A O NG
Khumric: Maon
English: the peipole, multitude, subjects.

Line 7
American Coelbren: I R W
Khumric: Irwr
English: Anointed

Line 8
American Coelbren: E T I
Khumric: Eti or Erifedd
English: yet again the heirs to

vertical - T W Y Ph = Th
Twyth
springing, with celerity

Line 9
American Coelbren: A M O
Khumric: Amo
English: Covenant

or

A R U C
Aruo
to plough, to till

An alternative for the second word of line 8 would be 'twcll', meaning a 'cutting off' or a 'docking', as with docking or trimming a horse's tail, and to some it might imply circumcision.

Chapter 17 - Other America Inscriptions

This appears to be a Christian statement, and as such it may again relate to the sixth-century expedition led by Arthur II ap Meurig and his brother Madoc Morfran, in their attempt to seize and establish an empire in the Americas.

The (apparent) front side of the Wiggins Stone reads:

'The being who hushes (consoles?) in tranquillity sheltered by, issuing out we. What is impending you are one God established.'

The reverse side reads:

'Fresh certain the great flood (Atlantic) to follow, an intense difficulty, to bring forth (by) sailing, wonderful the taking off he what is pervading in that extremity, to push with winds the anointed people/multitude yet again with celerity a covenant to plough.'

This inscription is in the Coelbren alphabet and reads directly into Khumric-'Welsh'. Combined with the other examples such as the 'Chi-Rho' inscription shown in Chapter 16, the style favours association with the sixth-century voyages.

The Problems of Too Much Evidence

One of the major difficulties that confronted Alan Wilson and Baram Blackett in their efforts to co-operate with the American researchers was the sheer volume of potential evidence that poured out from all sides. It proved to be almost impossible to convince them that deciphered inscriptions are the most powerful and conclusive of all evidence, and that unless this could be done everything else was relegated to the level of conjectural comparisons until DNA might offer some assistance.

It is the Coelbren inscriptions and their correct decipherment that prove the truth of the Arthur and Madoc expeditions of the mid to late sixth century AD.

There are in the Mid-West of the U.S.A. over eight thousand tumulus mounds, and only a small fraction of these mounds can be attributed to the British colonising expedition. It is hardly possible that all of these mounds are associated with British Dark Age migrations. The same exclusion may apply to a great deal of other very early remains found in the U.S.A.

Alan Wilson and Baram Blackett were basically solely concerned with establishing the plain fact that British inscriptions in the ancient British alphabet and language existed in North America. In this respect there is already much damage to repair in the U.S.A. If remains found at Woodstock, Vermont, and the surrounding areas can be taken as an example, it may be possible to illustrate the confusions that have been set in motion. In relation to an inscribed stone found at South Woodstock this has led to such fantasies as 'the precincts of the gods of Iargalen'. Yet this stone - described as a '"eltic milestone' - bears a clear Coelbren inscription on one side and a Christian Cross and one letter on the other. The text reads: 'the place of the ruler, the host (army) in a state of being the ruler'. The Christian Cross on the other side is 'croeso', which well before the Christian era meant 'welcome'. The single letter with the cross is either an 'E', meaning 'he', or an 'I' meaning 'towards'.

Almost unbelievably the upright Christian Cross has been interpreted as the Roman numeral 'X' (ten), carved at an angle of 45%, and the 'I' as the numeral I (one), giving a puzzling 'eleven'. From this weird deduction the writer then inferred that this 'Celtic milestone' recorded eleven 'Celtic' miles from somewhere in some direction. What length a 'Celtic' mile was is not stated, but certainly the writer has no notion of the ancient British-Welsh mile, which in no way equates with the Roman mile as is optimistically stated. It seems that reverse reasoning operates, as a ruin was found some ten to eleven statute miles away. This ruin has another cross incised on a ceiling slab (in this instance identified as somehow representing the Phoenician goddess Tanith, and 'she spreads her arms like wings') but a cross is a cross is a cross.

There is an inscription at this second site that is also claimed to be written in 'Celtic' Ogham. As the Khumric-Welsh are provably Trojan, and the Lloegrian-'English' are equally provably ancient Chaldean-Syrian, and the Irish are Gaels from the Upper Tigris, and as Ogham is a system of musical scores, it is very difficult to understand why these alleged Phoenician - Carthaginian goddess Tanith inscriptions are allegedly written in 'Celtic' Ogham. In Coelbren the text simply reads:

'the power to cross over mutually together we to this place.'

The 'Power' is routinely a reference to God.

The site is then labelled as 'the Temple of Byannu'. Worse follows as yet another inscribed stone, found ten miles north of this site, also carried a very clear upright Christian cross, which is a totally unmistakeable symbol by any standards. On the left side of this cross is a single vertical stroke cut 'I' meaning 'towards'. In addition, there was another inscription in very clear Coelbren, and this again was declared to be Ogham musical scores, and read as Phoenician. Again, it was alleged to read 'Tanith'.

Chapter 17 - Other America Inscriptions

The researcher concerned made a guess that the legendary voyages of the Carthaginian admirals Hammo and Hano, who reportedly sailed west out into the vast wastes of the Atlantic before turning back, had actually reached America. No such claim was ever made by the rulers of ancient Carthage, and so it is conjectured that the discovery was kept secret, so that only the Carthaginians could profit from this alleged discovery around 400 BC. A Carthaginian named as Annon or Hanno did circumnavigate Africa and he wrote an account of the voyage in Punic, which was translated into Greek. This account still survives in an alleged copy; see Vossius *The Histories of Greece*.

It is not unnatural that, confronted with such misidentifications and conjectures, the academic establishment seeks to distance itself from the matter. Signs which are very clearly Coelbren (and unlike Ogham musical scores, are said to be in the 'Celtic' language which appears to be unrelated to Irish Gaelic and British-Khumric), are said to be inscriptions left by ancient Phoenicians writing in 'Celtic' Ogham. This is more than enough to deter any serious researcher from becoming involved.

British ancient histories tell of migrations from Chaldea-Syria around 1600 BC and from Western Asia Minor around 504 BC. The second migration, from Asia Minor, has a common link with the Etruscan migration to Italy from Asia Minor around 650 BC. The same Coelbren Alphabet is found stretching back along the ancient migration trails from Britain, Etruria and Switzerland to Asia Minor and on back to Assyria and Palestine. A very similar alphabet is found in Iberia, and this may decipher into Irish Gaelic. None of the peoples of Britain and Ireland are Celtic, and these American inscriptions are plainly in Coelbren and not in Ogham, and there is no apparent justification for attempting to decipher Khumric Coelbren into Irish Gaelic.

Anyone who holds that the Scots, Welsh, or Irish are 'Celtic' has clearly not taken the trouble to read the histories of these nations. Nor will they have they made even the most elementary study of the evidence available.

In the wake of political propaganda from London, Oxford, and Cambridge, designed to re-label the Irish, the Scots, and the Welsh as 'Celtic', hordes of scholars have blindly followed this Pied Piper of Hamelin path, and like Don Quixote and Sancho they have laboured mightily over the imaginary 'P' Celts and 'Q' Celts, in attempting the impossible by trying to reconcile the irreconcilable in these very different language groups. This ridiculous theorising runs contrary to all the histories and it becomes necessary to totally abandon all the histories in order to accommodate this nonsense. The cancer has spread to America.

Alan Wilson and Baram Blackett are only interested in the RECORDED British-Khumric voyages of discovery and migration in the period circa AD 562-574. Hopefully scholars will examine the evidence on its merits and abandon the polarised views which currently prevail, and give their much-needed support to these on-going investigations.

Chapter Eighteen

Snakes, Forts, Pottery and Symbols

The Wallam Olum and Leni Lenape histories of the Delaware nation contain a number of cryptic references to a people who are identified as the 'Snake People', who appear as the enemies of the Delaware. These strange mentions are perhaps identifications of the people who built the serpent mounds that have been found in the Mid-West regions. Long, winding mounds of stone and earth were constructed so as to resemble great serpents with a circle or globe in their jaws as if it were about to be swallowed.

The largest known serpent mound is the enormous earthen effigy on the east bank of Brush Creek, in Adams County, Ohio. Some idea of the size of this great earth mound serpent can be gained from the fact that the distance from the centre-point of the head to the centre-point of the tail is three hundred and seventy-nine feet, four inches. Very detailed studies have been carried out to ascertain the orientation of the centre line of this effigy, which is precisely north to south, and the complex mathematics used in its symmetrical construction. The work of William F. Romain of Brooklyn, Ohio, gives extraordinary insights into the geometry of this remarkable site and many others.

These serpent mounds may well have British, and even Irish, connections. Everyone knows the old tale of how the Welshman St Patrick left Wales in AD 434 to commence his Christian missionary work in Ireland. One of the earliest and the most decisive of Patrick's actions was the casting out of all the serpents from Ireland, and there is a description of how he carried out this action. St Patrick simply went to the ceremonial circles set out in the jaws of the huge winding stone mound serpents and lit his own ceremonial fires in the circles before the Irish holy men arrived to light their fires. He had therefore desecrated their sites and rendered them unusable for their religious ceremonial services. St Patrick of course had leanings towards the Roman Church persuasions, and was not in line with those of the Apostolic British Church, founded in 35-37AD. This would explain his vandal assaults on the serpent mounds.

The common idea that Patrick somehow ejected all the live snakes from Ireland is of course nonsense, and it is belied by the known fact that numbers of common grass snakes still live in Ireland. Alan Wilson and Baram Blackett well remember being at Shannon Castle when a visitor picked up a four-foot grass snake in the field on the west side next to Shannon Castle.

There are no poisonous snakes in Ireland, and Britain only has the viper or adder, the grass snake, and the smooth snake, so on the face of things there seems to be little logic in any interpretation of St Patrick casting out live serpents. If, as is evident, he was engaged in tearing apart the great winding snake mounds of earth and stone, usually six feet wide and three feet high, and often stretching for hundreds of feet, the story makes sense. It links together with the ceremonial circles at the jaws of these snake mounds where the ritual fires were lit. These effigy serpents were probably intended to represent a great comet with its vast, coiling and sweeping tail, thousands of miles long, which most nations remembered as appearing to threaten to swallow the sun and to damage the earth in antiquity. Whether the comet represented God, or an agent of God in the form of an archangel, is unclear.

So, the St Patrick story may be quite sensible after all, and it was the older religion that he was endeavouring to cast out by destroying their 'snakes'. This more ancient religion with its great symbolic serpents has also left vestigial remains in mediaeval stories in Britain. Fourteen strange stories survive in Britain where named mediaeval knights went out armed to destroy these great serpents, known as worms, which were terrorizing their local areas. The most famous of these tales are those of the Lambton Worm and the Laidley Worm, but there are others. Old British religious ideas and practices did not die out easily or swiftly, and from one end of Britain to the other all manner of strange local and village customs, which relate to the older religion, were preserved right up until the twentieth century and many still survive. Best known is the November Bonfire Night.

Chapter 18 - Snakes, Forts, Pottery and Symbols

These monstrous and dangerous serpents were everywhere, and there were plenty of them known as worms. In the Library of Durham Cathedral there is a broadsword, which by tradition is the sword that the knight Sir John Coyners used to kill the great Sockburn Worm, which was a terrible dragon. As a reward for this feat Sir John was made Lord of Sockburn around 1350. A boulder in a field near Sockburn Church marked the spot where he slew this dragon worm. Thereafter, every new Lord of Sockburn met new Bishops of Durham at Croft Bridge on the river Tees and offered his sword. This old custom was discontinued after 1826, but the sword at the service of the church and the boulder near the Sockburn church are significant survivals. The worm was seen as a threat to the Christian religion, and it was routine practice to set up a Christian church on the site of the older religion that was being forcibly suppressed and displaced.

A similar old story tells how the Lambton Worm, in County Durham, caused chaos in the village of Penshaw, close to Lambton Castle. Around 1300, the youthful heir to Lambton Castle caught a strange worm whilst fishing, and he threw it into a well close to the castle. Years later, as a young man, the heir went on a crusade, and when he returned, he found that the Lambton Worm had grown so large that it coiled around Lambton Hill no fewer than three times. The soldier heir, fresh from the crusades in Palestine, covered his armour with razor blades, and went out to confront the giant worm. The great worm duly coiled itself around him and in so doing, it cut itself to pieces on the razors, and its remains were swept away into the river.

A similar tradition surrounds Sir Walter de Teyes, who died in 1325, and whose effigy lies on top of his table tomb in Nunnington village church. Local tradition here actually claims that the tomb belongs to one Peter Loschy who killed a great dragon worm in Loschy Woods, and again the pieces of this fearsome creature were carted off and disposed of. It all sounds very much like the dismantling of the great worm mounds of the old religion. One can imagine the local Christian priest arriving at the manor of the local lord or squire, and complaining bitterly that they, the villagers, were not attending church and that they were all up at the hilltop every Saturday night. Finally, the pestered local dignitary would go up and tear the mound apart to get some peace.

Another very strange story, with echoes of Snow White and the Wicked Witch

Queen, concerns the Laidley Worm that terrified the district around Bamburgh Castle, a huge stronghold, said to be founded in 547. This worm or dragon was the bewitched daughter of the King of Northumbria, who was transformed into the great worm by her stepmother the Witch Queen. For this reason, the worm refused to fight the king's son, Child of Wynde, and exchanges of identity broke the spell. Another great dragon is recorded as being slain in Lower Stanks field, on the north side of Brinsop church in Herefordshire. Around the year 1100, one Piers Shanks, the Squire of Pelham, Hertfordshire, also slew a great dragon serpent in Great Pepsells field. The effigy on the tomb of Piers Shanks shows a great coiled serpent belching flames like a comet dragon. So it goes, on and on, all around the country. The sixth-century St Leonard is reputed to have killed a great dragon in a forest near Horsham in Sussex. In the Orkney Isles the Meister Stoor Worm was killed by a local hero, and in Wales the dreaded Alfane and the Llamigan-y-dwr filled the Dragon-Worm role.

In Brittany and Llydaw (Normandy), where the British-Khumry re-conquered and settled in 383AD, there are innumerable folk-tales of great serpent dragons being driven out by ardent Christian saints. Frances M. Costling wrote travelogues of Brittany in 1908, and described the very ancient crypt of the church at Lanmeur, where the sad boy-heir to the throne was buried after his mutilation and murder around 550. Here in the crypt two large squat pillars support the floor of the church above, and writhing many-headed serpents are carved, entwined all around them. Possibly these represent the comet of AD 562.

What has this to do with American links? A lot, because huge, coiled, winding serpent mounds with egg-circles in their jaws have been found scattered across the Mid-West of the U.S.A. In Britain some great snake mounds survive. Ignatius Donnelly noted the surviving snake mound at Glen Feechan (also spelt Feochan) in Argyllshire, Scotland, in his book titled *Atlantis - The Antediluvian World*, published in 1882. See page 204-205. Another very large snake mound survives in Wales. Remarkably, the re-founded Druid order in Wales erected a large, newly built snake mound, complete with a circle in the jaws, on the hilltop west of Pontypridd in Glamorgan in 1908. One Christian minister involved abandoned his thirty-two-years' ministry and became a practising druid. Periodic attacks are made on this snake mound, allegedly by enraged local

Chapter 18 - Snakes, Forts, Pottery and Symbols

'He struck a violent blow upon the monster's head'
C.E. Brock 1893

Christians. It is this fear and religious rivalry which have perhaps motivated the attacks made by Calvinist and Methodist groups on Edward Williams - Iolo Morganwg (a founding member of the Unitarian Church) and the Khumric histories.Ignatius Donnelly compared the Argyllshire serpent mound with the serpent mound in Adams County, Ohio. He wrote:

> '*Serpent-worship in the West.* —Some additional light appears to have been thrown upon ancient serpent-worship in the West by the recent archaeological exploration of Mr. John S. Phené, F.G.S., F.R.G.S., in Scotland. Mr. Phené has just investigated a curious earthen mound in Glen Feechan, Argyleshire, referred to by him, at the late meeting of the British Association in Edinburgh, as being in the form of a serpent or saurian. The mound, says the *Scotsman*, is a most perfect one. The head is a large cairn, and the body of the earthen reptile 300 feet long; and in the centre of the head there were evidences, when Mr. Phené first visited it, of an altar having been placed there. The position with regard to Ben Cruachan is most remarkable.'

'As reported in the Pall Mall Gazette'.

The proposition being investigated and proved by Wilson and Blackett is that there are alphabetic, linguistic and religious cultural links between a people who were in Egypt until *c.* 1350 BC, when a great comet serpent shattered the Egyptian state. They then lived in Palestine from around 1300 to 720 BC, and were subsequently moved forcibly to the region around north Armenia to help guard the southern end of the Caucasus, like a stopper in a bottle. They left this area around 687 BC, taking advantage of the turmoil in Assyria following the murder of Sennacherib. These same people migrated west for fifteen hundred miles to the Dardanelles, where *c.* 650 BC half of them migrated to Italy to found the twelve-city Etruscan League. In 508 BC the remaining half of the people took ship and sailed in a great fleet to Britain. One thousand years and more later, some of them sailed the Atlantic to North America in a fleet of seven hundred ships in AD 574. They left Britain because much of the great state had been shattered and left in ruins by débris from a great comet serpent in the skies in AD 562.

It is necessary to restate this in order to bring in the snake element of ancient Israelite worship. The transfer of this idea of the great destructive serpent in the sky is part and parcel of the evidence of their migrations. The serpent mounds are emphatically not the vestigial signs of an unhistorical 'Celtic' druid religion and worship. Sky-serpent ideas played a major role in the ancient Khumric-Israelite religion, and the evidence still remains for all to see, despite persistent attempts by pious forgers to sanitise and wipe out this past record. T. C. Robinson in his *Decline and Fall of the Hebrew Kingdoms* puts his finger on the pulse, when on page 73,he discusses the religious reformations of King Hezekiah son of Ahaz of Judah. We quote:

II Kings 18:3-4.

'And he did *that which was* right in the sight of the LORD, according to all that David his father did. He removed the high places, and brake the images, and cut down the groves, and brake in pieces the brasen serpent that Moses had made: for in those days the children of Israel did burn incense to it: and he called it Nehushtan.'

As the Ten Tribes of Israel had already been deported far away to the north some forty years before King Hezekiah began his religious reformation, it is not unreasonable to assume that they took with them the original ideas of 'Druid' worship involving oak groves, standing stones, and great serpents.

The bronze serpent figure is mentioned in the Book of Numbers 21:8-9.

'And the LORD said unto Moses, Make thee a fiery serpent, and set it upon a pole: and it shall come to pass, that every one that is bitten, when he looketh upon it, shall live. And Moses made a serpent of brass, and put it upon a pole, and it came to pass, that if a serpent had bitten any man, when he beheld the serpent of brass, he lived.'

The great detail on serpents and rods, beginning with the serpent and the 'Garden of Eden' story, is best discussed elsewhere. Everyone is familiar with the story of the 'Rod of Moses' transforming itself into a serpent and devouring the two serpent-rods of the Egyptian priests. Also, there is the story of Solomon setting up two brass serpentine pillars before the Jerusalem temple, and then decorating the building with 'cherubims', which were great four-legged winged dragon-like creatures, exactly like the Dragon emblem on the Welsh national flag.

Robinson pointed out that in Numbers 21, the serpent was identified as the Saraph, and says:

'This, it will be remembered, is the name given by Isaiah to the attendants of Jahveh when he saw his great vision in the temple. The word Saraph, however is not applied to it in the present passage (II Kings 18) the more general term serpent being employed. All things considered, it would seem that no objection was felt to the worship of this emblem of Jahveh until the time of Hezekiah, and it is interesting to find that we have no record of protest made by Hezekiah against its use.'

Earlier Robinson states:

'This seems to have been an ancient object of reverence, and was probably associated with Jahveh himself.'

So he saw Jahveh or Jehovah or Yahweh as a great fiery serpent, which accords with the well-known theories of many authors that Jehovah was a great fiery comet which wound through the heavens with writhing trailing tails like a great serpent. This great comet could and did periodically wreak massive destruction on Planet Earth when it came too close, and this was seen as a

Chapter 18 - Snakes, Forts, Pottery and Symbols

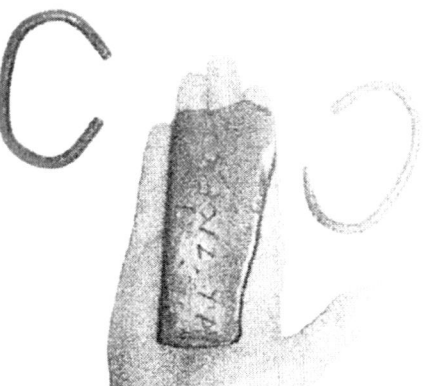

Grave Creek Madoc Stone and copper bracelets

Christian Amulets

punishment of floods, earthquakes, inundations, and pestilences upon mankind. This theory of heavenly punishment was a huge and very profitable blackmail weapon in the hands of the priesthood.

Gnostic Christian literature believed to have been buried around 400 was found at Nag Hammadi in Egypt in 1945, and includes a document which details the seven-headed serpent comet. This same seven-headed serpent comet is described in the *Brut Tysilio* and the *Brut Gruffydd ap Arthur*, and the effigy of the seven-headed and seven-tailed fiery heavenly dragon is clearly carved upon the stone dug up in St Paul's Churchyard in London in 1852. The *Book of Marsanes*, from *The Nag Hammadi Library*, also describes an alphabet which is identical to Khumric. This makes it ever more difficult to give any credence to the objections from North Wales and England, which seek to label the alphabet as a forgery of around 1800.

In the American Mid-West, pioneer trailblazers came across a huge effigy of a Welsh-type dragon carved on a cliff face. Sadly, American rifle owners defaced this priceless effigy out of all recognition. Fortunately, early artists had taken the care to copy the carved dragon and to exhibit its shape. Despite this, a recent funded attempt to restore a picture of the dragon at the site resulted in a total farce as the 'restorer' appointed decided to introduce a totally changed Chinese-style dragon, which is markedly different in a number of ways. Strange, as the Welsh national flag still exhibits the Red Dragon, complete with huge leathery bat-shaped wings, a coiling single-point serpent's tail, a wolf's head with a long single-pointed tongue, and a lion's body, and eagle's talons. Fortunately, drawings of the original dragon carving still survive.

That this tradition continued is obvious from the large number of Yahweh medallions of the Maccabean period from roughly 200 BC to AD 60, which have been found to depict the god Yahweh as half-man and half-serpent. The Greeks also frequently depicted their chief god Zeus as half-man and half-serpent in statuary and in paintings, and the notion of a great, but sometimes capricious, sky-god in the guise of a serpent dragon or fearsome comet was widespread.

There is a difference between a serpent and a snake. The Biblical word is 'saraph' for the Great Serpent that is legged. An 1848 Khumric dictionary gives 'sarff' for a 'serpent', and 'sarddan' for 'a creeping thing', while a 1688 dictionary gives 'sarph' for a 'serpent'. Very close to the Hebrew 'saraph'. A snake in Khumric is 'neidr' or 'nadr' and is different as being 'legless'. A serpent would be a lizard, or crocodile, or an iguana; a legged reptile.

There is no shortage of surviving serpent mounds and effigies in North America, and there was a *Serpent Mound Research Project* with headquarters at West Chester, Ohio. This project was designed to gather and disseminate information about the serpent effigy mounds, and any related subjects. They list:

1 - The Great Serpent Mound;

2 - The Kern Effigies 1 and 2;

3 - Spruce Hill;

4 - Stubbs Mill 1 and 2;

5 - The West Chester Effigy;

6 - The Blue Ash Effigy, all in Ohio;

7 - Tithe Ashville Serpent;

8 - the Spratt Farm site;

9 - The Bell County Effigy;

10 - The Cumberland Gap Effigy;

11 - the Maysville Serpent - all in Kentucky;

12 - The Logan No. 1 and 2 in West Virginia;

Chapter 18 - Snakes, Forts, Pottery and Symbols

13 - The Stone Mountain and Gwinnett Falls in Georgia

14 - The Rice County Intaglio in Kansas;

15 - The Blythe Effigy in California;

16 - The Parker Rattler in Arizona;

17 - The Snyder Mound in Illinois;

18 - The Afton Effigies in Minnesota;

19 - The Rice Lake Serpent in Ontario; and possible effigies in New York, Wisconsin, and Iowa States.

Perhaps not all of these serpent carvings and mounds will be immigrant relics; some carvings will perhaps be those of Native American origin. The serpent mounds however are of major interest in any study of possible contact with or origin in Arthurian Britain.

The Indian Head in the Rhondda

Alan Wilson and Baram Blackett are firmly of the opinion that most researchers fail in their attempts to discover the truth in British history because they invariably pay little or no attention to detail. In the bad old days of animal massacre, no professional hunter went out looking for a lion or tiger, or a buffalo or whatever. They employed trackers who went out and looked for tracks, footprints, and animal droppings, or the carcass of a recently killed herbivore being eaten by a predator, and they followed clues of bent or broken grass and twigs. None of the legions of popular authors writing about 'King Arthur' ever gets anywhere by routinely grabbing all the other books from the library shelves and searching the indexes for references under the name of Arthur.

While sitting in discussion with Jim Michael in 1994, Alan Wilson was looking at a nineteenth-century print in a book dealing with South American relics. Two explorers were pictured standing before a crumbling stone wall, where a gigantic carving of a human face was set. This six foot-high face, set high in the wall, was carved with a heavy beard, and it is a fact that Native American people do not have heavy beards. The face of the ancient carving was distinctly Aryan. Alan looked carefully at the picture and then drew Jim Michael's attention to the manner in which the beard was carved.

The beard on the face had been exhibited by a series of generally downward strokes, which to the casual observer would represent facial hairs. What in fact was shown was a cleverly constructed Coelbren inscription of straight and angled lettering. This simple discovery is in the same genre as the alleged King Lists, which are not lists of names at all; they are nothing other than a list of Khumric words forming a message. There are many other camouflaged messages in other styles littered everywhere. No one else ever sees these messages until they are pointed out to them.

The message in the beard immediately stimulated Jim Michael's interest, as he knew of three other smaller stone carvings of the same type of bearded head which had been found in North America. He knew that one such carving had only recently been found, on a flat slab of stone on the steep slopes of a hill beneath an ancient fort near Louisville, and he had already set about obtaining a photograph. The photograph duly arrived, and Jim and Alan had the pleasure of meeting with two of the discoverers of this carving for lunch together.

Alan Wilson also asked Jim to set up a quiet meeting with Colonel Russell Burrows of Burrows Cave fame. This was arranged, and Jim Michael drove Alan Wilson to a quiet roadside café in Indiana where a very productive discussion was held. Nothing had been said of the bearded heads to Colonel Burrows, but fortuitously he had brought some photographs with him, which he generously gave to Alan Wilson. One photograph showed the same style and type of heavy-bearded Aryan head as that on the stone found beneath the hill-fort. Again, there was a string of Coelbren letters arranged around the cheeks and chin of the face, which give the general impression of facial hairs. Here was yet another message

Chapter 18 - Snakes, Forts, Pottery and Symbols

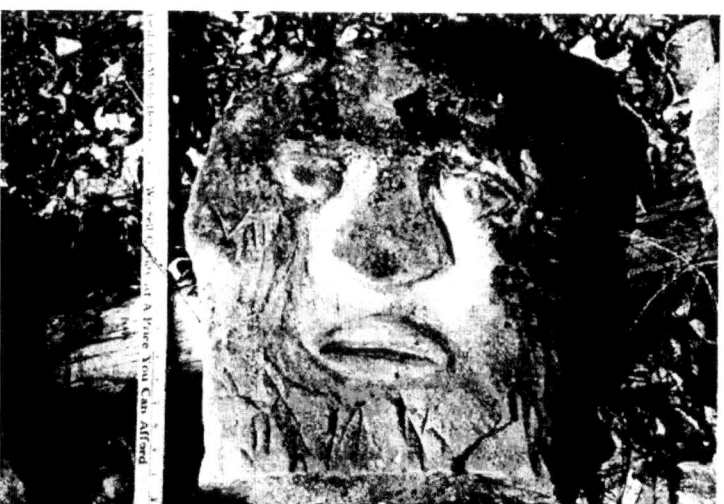

Indian's Head, Rhondda, Wales, and Bearded Head, U.S.A.

written in Coelbren right out in the open and totally unnoticed.

At this stage Alan Wilson was racking his brains to try to remember where he had seen this message in the beard before. He knew that he had seen a photograph, or drawing, or something very like these bearded faces, years before, in times when he had no great ambition to get involved in asinine arguments with blinkered British academics. He just could not recall where or when he had seen and noticed all this before.

It was not until he was back home, in 1995, that he was taken by Dewi Bowen and Brian Davies to see several interesting sites near Clydach Vale in the Rhondda Valley, and made the connection. The party left an old Welsh longhouse farm and moved on through the woods towards an open area where on one side of a tiny rivulet were the remains of ancient dwellings, and on the other side was an ancient burial ground. Right above this site was an outcrop of rock that had long ago been carved into the shape of a human head complete with a beard. The features on the face are distinctly those of a Native North American. Admittedly there are many people in Wales with the same high cheekbones and hawk noses, and some of Alan Wilson's own forebears have these features. Suffice it to say that this effigy is known locally as 'The Indian's Head'.

Alan Wilson was naturally fascinated by the obvious string of Coelbren straight stroke letters which cleverly constructed the beard, in exactly the same manner as the beards on the heads in the Americas. That this practice of portraying a bearded head, and using the peculiar letters of the same straight stroke alphabet to convey a disguised message in the beard, could be a coincidence is beyond belief. The fact that the same face and beard stares out from a crumbling wall in an ancient ruined city in an American jungle has to be seen as a link, and a matter to be addressed seriously. Naturally nothing can be done as 'what postures as 'British' history is in fact simply English history writ large.' (Long Article, Western Mail, Cardiff. 1987).

Chapter 18 - Snakes, Forts, Pottery and Symbols

The messages in the beards appeared to tie in with other ancient artefacts. One item, which may or may not be genuine, is a small piece of limestone about three-and-a-half inches long, and carved into a shape of three heads or faces. Two appear to be human, and one perhaps animal. This stone was found four feet down in a mound at Unzicker by a Mr. Cooper, in the presence of others, on 11th June 1865, and is therefore called the Cooper Stone. One side of the stone was partly eroded and the other better preserved and polished. Curiously there are letters written across the forehead of one of the human faces. The presence of these letters on the stone must be a major factor in the academic practice of totally disregarding the stone. Academic dogma demands that all pre-Columbus artefacts must be identified as Native American, and the same dogma insists that no Native American ancient people had an alphabet. It automatically follows that any inscribed ancient artefact which may be pre-Columbian must be labelled a fake.

The stone was photographed three times in 1868, by George W. Chase of Newark, and it was not until 1978 that Chance Brockway, of Buckeye Lake, Ohio, got active and took photographs that the stone began to be known. It was the Cooper Stone which got Jim Michael more than interested when Alan Wilson showed him the surviving triple-faced stone in Llandaff Cathedral in 1990. These triple-faced carvings were prohibited by the Bishop of Rome around 1450, but one survives in Cardiff, and there are others in England, at Leicester. The three faces are joined and cleverly carved so that they share only four eyes. Taken left to right eyes 1 and 2 serve the outer left face, eyes 2 and 3 serve the centre face, and eyes 3 and 4 serve the outer right face.

In the strange way of progress in these meandering projects, Alan Wilson received a letter from a Mr. Brian Slade, President of the Sheppey Archaeological Association in Kent. Mr. Slade is a historian/archaeologist who had interested himself discovering the site of the ancient local nunnery, which appeared to date back to early Saxon times, being named for Seaxburh, the daughter of King Anna who died in 654AD. The topographical and historical researches of Brian Slade proved to be remarkably accurate, and the nunnery site was located. At the nunnery were ancient drainage ditches, and an ancient well that had been filled in over the centuries, and it was an obvious target for excavation to Mr. Slade. Not only did things get dropped into wells by accident, but in times of crisis, when some ancient Saxon or later Viking crews were seeking a soft target, they attacked the churches, monasteries, and nunneries, close to shorelines. Objects of value might be thrown into the wells for later retrieval by monks and nuns, who might not have survived the attack themselves. Alternatively, raiders might throw anything they did not want into the wells.

Mr. Slade also reasoned that the Monasterium Seaxburh might stand on top of an earlier pre-Saxon British church foundation, which is almost always the case. This of course would not make him popular with the English church authorities.

So, Brian Slade excavated the well all the way down, and near the bottom he found some strange pottery, which exhibited three human heads or faces. This interested Alan Wilson and Baram Blackett, who immediately informed Jim Michael. Mr. Slade was also at odds with the Establishment in Britain, mainly because he exhibited and published the fact that the Abbess of Seaxburh possessed her own gallows, stocks, pillory, and ducking-stool. These she used freely, and woe betide the man whose land she fancied owning, and who did not gift it to her abbey. One false trumped-up charge of heresy or witchcraft, and the victim was swiftly swinging in the breeze, and his land confiscated by the Abbess. This was re-confirmed by a Royal Charter of 1343. This was nothing unusual in mediaeval times, as detailed writings by Walter Map and others exhibit. The publication of these simple facts caused outrage on the part of the Church against Brian Slade, and his twenty booklets, which he sold to aid the building of a new church hall, were all banned from the church hall, which they helped to build. Brian Slade was then forced out of his Curatorship of the Abbey Museum, which was his brainchild and creation, stemming from his many discoveries.

Chapter 18 - Snakes, Forts, Pottery and Symbols

Being denied all accurate knowledge of British history, along with the rest of the population, Brian Slade and his associates dubbed the three-headed figure as an image of the totally imaginary British goddess Coventina. The three-headed figurine vase actually bears the sign of a cross, and this makes it likely that it represents Mary the Mother, Mary Magdalene and Mary Cleophas, or alternatively Mary the Mother, Mary Magdalene, and Salome. There are the usual confusions over 'Celts' and 'Celtic' gods, which characterise all the thirty-three known surviving ancient three-headed images mostly found in church decoration. Not until the 'Celtic' nonsense is removed can sanity be restored.

Not far from Sheppey lies Lullington 'Roman' Villa, at Eynsford, near Dartford. Here a deep, cellar-like room contains a fresco depicting three ladies. A Christian chapel and associated rooms were added to this villa in 360-370, and the deep room still continued in use. It seems to be forgotten that all the earliest Christian worship was underground.

Brian Slade had acquired the same mutual mistrust of the Establishment which is all too frequently encountered. This was partly because of a slight upon the work of one of his forebears. In 1674 workmen unearthed a part of the lost abbey at Athelney. In 1801, Colonel John Slade had been the first person to locate and identify this refuge of King Alfred, the cake burner, at Athelney. He erected a large squat stone obelisk as a monument on the site to commemorate this first original modern historical research and excavation, and set it behind ornamental iron railings right in the middle of the abbey ruins. Some hundred and ninety years later, the Channel 4 Time Team made a TV programme that actually appeared to pretend that their research and programme was original, and marked the identification and the discovery of the site. All through the one-hour film the squat obelisk, set up to commemorate Colonel Slade's work a hundred and ninety years earlier, kept popping up in the background of camera shots, despite studious efforts to avoid it. Not a word was said of 1674 and Colonel John Slade's pioneering work of the actual discovery and identification, and his name was never mentioned. Once you know what the truth is, it really is quite comic to observe these persistent archaeological antics.

This was seen as duplicity by Brian Slade, and he was incensed by what he saw as this deliberate ignoring and avoidance, indeed the usurpation, of his forebear's achievements. So there was yet another of the growing army of people totally discontented with the performance of academia and the archaeological establishment. Anyone would sympathise with Brian Slade in this matter. To say that the misguided and generally Roman-mad academic establishment is completely and absolutely out of touch with the needs and aspirations of the British public has to be a major understatement. The very idea of known and proven British Christianity and its different theology existing for five hundred and sixty years before Austin arrived from Rome in 597 to convert the Saxon and Jute immigrants, is of course poison to the establishment Church, and Mr. Slade's digging in the bottom of the ancient abbey well was very unwelcome.

There was, however, the reward of three-headed pottery. Whether this is some form of early representation of the Christian Trinity, and some continuance of much older ideas, or otherwise associated with foreign Roman deities like Janus, is not known. The basic fact is that a three-faced item was found buried four feet deep in a mound in America in 1865, and this artefact carried a British Coelbren inscription. Brian Slade found three-headed figures dating back to around 400, in the bottom of an ancient nunnery well in Britain. Added to this an ancient three-headed and linked faced carving has survived in Llandaff Cathedral along with several others elsewhere. It is another link.

Chunkee Stones

Some of the links between the New World of America and the Old World in the West are so mundane as to be easily overlooked. Jim Michael showed Alan Wilson and Baram Blackett a photograph of a small, neatly-shaped circular stone with a hole in the centre. This, he explained, was a strange type of stone artefact, occasionally found in the Mid-West, and which was called a 'Chunkee Stone' by

Chapter 18 - Snakes, Forts, Pottery and Symbols

Native Americans. Neither the new American whites nor the Native Americans knew what these chunkee stones were or who made them, or for what purpose. This interesting feature of the stone that Jim Michael was exhibiting was that it was very clearly marked with the ancient British Awen sign of the Broad Arrow.

Alan and Baram burst out laughing when they saw the stone, and Baram quickly flicked through the files to produce a photograph of six near-identical 'chunkee stones'. A number of these stones were found by Heinrich Schliemann in his excavations of Troy at Hissarlik in Turkey, which began in 1876. All six are now in the British Museum, and all six are equally clearly marked with the Awen sign, the symbol of the ancient British Coelbren alphabet. Why no museum employee has noticed this very obvious British Trojan connection is not known.

These stones marked with the British Broad Arrow cipher are in fact simple light stone weights, known as spinning whorls, used to weigh down threads in the process of spinning, and at least one surviving ancient Greek drawing shows a woman spinning wool or cotton using these 'Chunkee Stones'. It is almost hilarious that when several similar stones were found in North Wales in the nineteenth century, they were guessed as being wheels from an ancient child's toy.

The Native Americans are not known to have ever spun either cotton thread or wool, and so these simple artefacts represent a major piece of archaeological evidence of migration links. That the American spinning-weights should be marked identically with those from ancient Troy, the city from which Brutus led the people, is not something that the academic fraternity can easily sweep away under the carpet. This cannot possibly be either ignored or dismissed as coincidence. The Native Americans did not spin or weave; yet someone was spinning either wool or cotton in ancient America, and that someone knew the Awen or Broad Arrow holy sign of the British alphabet.

Another piece of American evidence that was hotly pursued by Jim Michael, was a pair of ancient smelted copper bracelets now in the Smithsonian Museum.

Chunkee stones from Kentucky and Troy

Chapter 18 - Snakes, Forts, Pottery and Symbols

Again, as the Native Americans are known not to have smelted metals, there is the unanswered question of who did smelt these copper bracelets. The problem in America is no different from that in Britain, and academia is extremely selective in choosing what evidence is allowed to be acknowledged and exhibited, and what overwhelming mass of evidence is to be ignored and deliberately obscured. In fact, there is very little to support the academic stance apart from a negative attitude and an unproven theory.

For many centuries academics preached with great certainty and authority that there was nothing smaller than an atom, and they went on doing it long after the atom was split by two Englishmen in 1932. Now we know that all sorts of electrons, neutrons, and protons, or whatever, are buzzing around inside atoms. They preached that no vehicle heavier than air could ever fly. They preached that a vacuum could not exist, and thousands and thousands of other non-starters, and they have been wrong, wrong, and wrong. If the original egg-heads of mankind were right then the human race would be still living in caves, that is if the egg-heads had allowed our ancestors to come down out of the trees. They get out of the problem of exposure with "We will have to revise our ideas", and the key word is 'ideas' and not 'FACTS'.

Facts in an investigation means all the facts, and not a carefully chosen selection of bits and pieces which suit and support any particular preferred emotional, political, religious, or nationalist idea or argument. The 'Chunkee Stone' spinning-whorls incised with the Awen signs at Hissarlik (Troy) and in ancient America are facts, and so are the smelted copper bracelets which have a content mix matching that found in Europe.

The Fox Field Mound

In the spring of 1917, a grave mound at Fox Field, close to Augusta, in Kentucky, and near to Portsmouth, Indiana, was carefully excavated by a qualified archaeologist, Mr. William Webb, the first Professor of Archaeology at the University of Kentucky. In the mound a skeleton was found, and on its breast was a shell gorget with two holes, presumably made for a cord to hang the gorget around a person's neck. The gorget was clearly inscribed with a Maltese type of cross set at a slight angle within a circle, rather like the tilt of the poles of Planet Earth. Also marked on this gorget, and outside the circle containing the Maltese cross, were four sets of three small circular indentations. Three sets of these groups of three-dot indentations are placed in positions at 3 o' clock to 7 o' clock. The remaining fourth set of three tiny holes is placed at 9 o' clock to 11 o' clock, and a line of six more dot indentations runs from the uppermost hole at 11 o' clock to the opposite uppermost hole at 3 o'clock. The gorget appears to be a form of sundial or clock, and perhaps a calendar stone.

Also found in this same grave mound at Fox Field was an inscribed bear's tooth. On one side this bear's tooth is marked with a very clear Maltese cross, and also with three lines of dot indentations forming the sacred and alphabetic Awen Sign of the Broad Arrow. There are two other groups of dot indentations on the left side of the cross, which may represent stellar constellations. The reverse side of the bear's tooth had another very clear Maltese style of cross incised on it.

Later Mr. Webb discovered another incised Christian artefact in the form of a shell with a square set cross set inside a circle upon it, and each angle of the cross in the triple form of chevrons. In the segments between the four angles of the cross and the outer enclosing circle are numbers of dot indentations, which may indicate star constellations. Around the outside of the circle containing the cross is shown an encircling serpent, with its tail being seized by its own mouth. The entire body of the serpent is covered with dot indentations, as if to indicate that a stellar purpose is intended. Above the serpent at the top of the design are letters that clearly appear to be Coelbren.

Jim Michael is inclined to identify the chevrons on the shell with the triple chevrons that form the badge and coat of arms of the Glamorgan kings. These well-known heraldic devices still ornament public buildings in Cardiff in Wales, and were used by King Iestyn ap Gwrgan who was deposed in 1091. Taken together, there are (1) Christian Crosses; (2) the Coelbren Alphabet Awen sign; (3) Coelbren lettering; and (4) chevrons. This surely is too many parallels in symbols and signs to be either coincidental or accidental. No trace of Native American occupation of this area was found by the earliest French and English settlers. To excavators unfamiliar with the Awen sign and its significance, their failure to recognise a probable early British presence is understandable.

In 1992, Professor Lee Pennington, Jim Michael, and Alan Wilson visited the ancient religious mound and ditch circle at Mount Horeb in Kentucky, a very well-preserved site in the care of Kentucky University near some of the world-famous Kentucky horse farms. A simple guide to ancient sites is that a fortress site has a ditch on the outside and the earth banks on the inside, but a religious site has the earth banks on the outside and the ditch inside. The Mount Horeb site is very definitely a religious cor.

At the Mount Horeb cor site Alan Wilson asked Lee Pennington if he had brought a compass. The ever-well-prepared Lee had a compass, and so Alan took it, and after aligning things, he pointed in the precise direction of some farm buildings and said, "If this place conforms with Wales and the Midlands, and there are any ancient burials around here, then that's where to look." Lee Pennington took the compass and followed the line of the bearing, and replied, "That is exactly where some ancient burials were found." Everything in ancient Britain follows precise patterns, and by identifying these patterns, Alan Wilson and Baram Blackett have been able to find extraordinary things. It saves a lot of time and energy to know where custom dictated that things should be placed. The fact that the same patterns of culture seem to exist in ancient America is important. As Baram says, "It is much easier to go to an area and know just where to start looking for what."

There are many ancient religious cor sites still existing in England and Wales, and the Khumric word 'cor' can mean 'religious circle', 'choir area of a church',

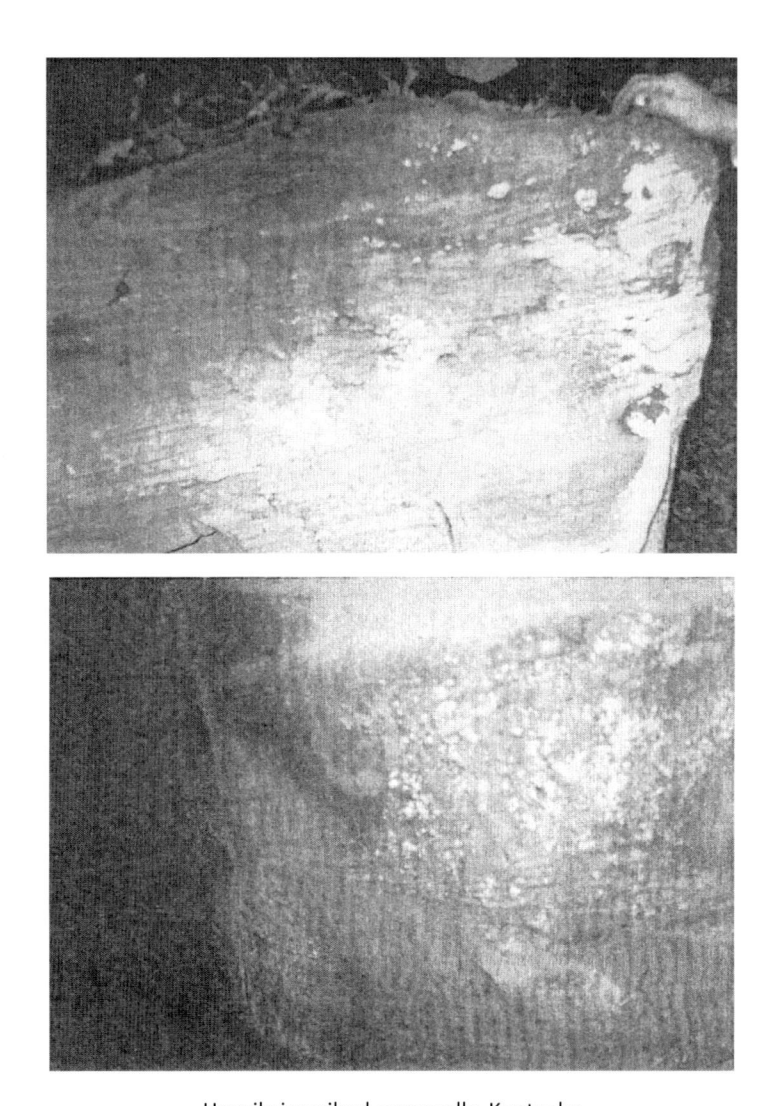

Heavily inscribed cave walls, Kentucky

Chapter 18 - Snakes, Forts, Pottery and Symbols

Manchester roadside inscriptions & thresher floor

and 'choir'. There is a good example at Trefran (Manor of King Bran) in Glamorgan, and several others, near Atherston, in Warwickshire. When the Khumric armies under Magnus Maximus invaded Gaul in 383, the regions of Brittany, and Llydaw (later Normandy) became the British Kingdom of Brittany or Lesser Britain, with Conan Meriadoc as the first King. Not surprisingly, religious cor circles were built in new Brittany.

Confused English archaeologists saw the cors in Normandy and assumed that they were Norman-built, and then seeing similar sites in Wales they decided that these cors were also built by the Normans. This disregarded all ancient historical records identifying these cors of nearly two thousand years old, and all other evidence, but it was in line with political correctness. Standing everything on its head and causing pandemonium is par for the course in this Alice in Blunderland asylum. The knock-on effect was that all ancient pottery and other artefacts found at these cors were classified as twelfth-century Norman. There has been chaos ever since, with no identification of any native Welsh pottery between 100 and 1200, as it has all been re-labelled as twelfth-century Norman. This total farce of incompetence is then used to 'prove' ancient Welsh barbarism. The result is that according to the Establishment dictate, the only people on planet earth incapable of making simple pottery were the Welsh.

In pursuit of following manuscript information and establishing cultural patterns, and so knowing where to look for exactly what, there is the matter of Guy of Warwick, an eponymous Midlands folk hero. Legend has it that Guy of Warwick (which in Welsh is 'Gwyr o Caerwythelin', and can be construed as 'Man of the Castle with the Military Retinue') invaded Europe and fought against the Emperor of Constantinople. This mysterious Guy is Gwyr = Man, and is obviously none other than Arthur I, son of Magnus Maximus. Arthur I, misidentified as Andragathius in Latin texts, did invade Europe in 383, and he did defeat and kill Gratian, the Emperor of Rome, and he then went on to fight the Emperor of Constantinople in Yugoslavia. The entire folk tale of Guy mirrors the military epic of Arthur I. This identification was made by Edward Llwyd, as well as by

Chapter 18 - Snakes, Forts, Pottery and Symbols

Baram and Alan, and they noticed this on the page of Llwyd's *Itinerary* which detailed the Lords of Coed Y Mwstyr in Cardiff Library.

A fragment of what appears to be an accession stone, or memorial, to Arthur I was found at a tumulus mound in the ancient burial ground of the British at Oldbury near Atherston (Arthur's Twyn), in Warwickshire. It is part of what appears to have been a rectangular block of stone. Fortunately, there is a sufficient indication on the inscription to give the significance of the relic. The remaining words in Latin are: ARTORIV ... IACIT IN ... MAGL ... The first word is almost certainly 'Artorivs', and below is IACIT for 'here is cast down', meaning 'here lies' or 'is buried'. Whether MAG and the partial letter 'I' is Magnus following the custom of naming the father, is conjecture. There is a similarity with the famous Bodvoc = Budic stone at Margam Abbey, both in the shape of the stone and the style of letters. This, and the stone of Arthur II, is discussed in *The Holy Kingdom* and in *Artorivs Rex Discovered*.

Chapter Nineteen

Possible Dark Age Christian Relics in Arizona

Before recounting the story of a group of what are very probably Dark Age Christian relics found in Arizona it is advisable that a few cautionary notes be made for readers. In the treacherous world of research, investigation and discovery, the vast majority of those involved are not employees of universities or colleges. It is a fact that the great majority of worthwhile discoveries have been made by people who are not employees of universities or similar institutions. It matters not how intelligent, learned, well-educated, or honourable, hard-working, capable, and dedicated the non-university employee may be, he or she will always be mislabelled as being amateur. The fact is that a great many amateurs know far more about the chosen subject to which they are dedicated than almost all university employees, who for some strange reason are regarded as professionals, and not as teachers.

Most university employees spend long days for most of the year delivering routine and politically acceptable lectures to students, holding tutorials and seminars, and marking long repetitious essays and papers. They have in fact very little time available for any genuine research, unless they quit work for a year and take a sabbatical period.

This then brings us to the insane set of rules under which research and discovery are governed. These are very simple and are as follows:

1.   Any discovery made by any university employee in any field of expertise regardless of the expertise professed by that employee, is classified as 'existing'. Therefore, it exists.

2.   However, if it fails to conform to currently accepted theory and dogma the discovery may be discarded and ignored completely. It may not even exist and can be ignored.

3. Any discovery made by someone not working for a university is classified as 'amateur', and therefore it does not exist, because it was not discovered by a university employee. It is, therefore, inadmissible evidence.

4. A discovery made by an amateur may however be legitimised and declared to exist if it supports current university guesswork and theory.

5. An amateur may have his or her life's work accepted as existing, if he/she finds and agrees to share the credit with a university employee who has played no part in the research and often does not properly understand it. As the vast majority of the human race are not university employees, or even schoolteachers at any level, these rules inhibit and restrict research and discovery.

In order to illustrate this absolutely vital dictum and demonstrate the ease with which frightened academics can crush and obliterate discovery for decades, there is the salutary story of the Spanish nobleman Don Marcellino de Sautuola. Ten thousand or more such tales can be told, but this one should suffice.

It was on the estate of Don Marcellino in 1858, that a dog chasing a fox fell into a crevice. In order to save his dog, the huntsman forced his way into the crevice after and discovered a large cave, which was partly blocked by fallen stone. Nothing happened at this blocked cave at Altamira until 1875, when Don Marcellino and some of his workmen cleared some of the stone blocks away and had the cave entrance enlarged. Inside, Don Marcellino found several animal bones, which he handed to a friend, one Juan Villanova, who was a Professor of Geology. The very surprised Juan Villanova found these bones to be those of Ice Age animals, including bison, wild horses, deer, and others. Even more startling was the fact that these ancient bones had obviously been split by men to get at the marrow.

Nothing happened for several years, and Don Marcellino toured other known caves, searching the débris that they contained, excavating and salvaging the contents. This was the era when the theories of Charles Darwin were first exciting people to seek out old and fossilised bones, and the religious ideas of the world being a creation of around 4000 BC were being challenged for the first time. Don Marcellino visited Paris to see the bones found by Lartet and Christy at Périgord in France, which had drawings scratched upon them. He studied this Paris exhibition. Then, suitably prepared, he set about excavating the floor of his own private cave at Altamira, unearthing stone tools, blackened areas where fires had been lit, more ancient bones, scattered mussel shells, and something else which he at first failed to comprehend, encrusted deposits of black and red colouring agents in the mussel shells which lay amongst the ancient refuse.

It was not until Don Marcellino took his five-year-old daughter to the cave with him, that the little girl lost interest in her father's labours in the cave floor. She began playing around in the inner recesses and passageways of the Altamira cave, and a great discovery was made. The child saw figures and forms painted upon the roof of the cave and along the high walls. Figures of bison, deer, woolly rhinoceros, horses, and all manner of animals covered the uneven surfaces.

Professor Villanova persuaded Don Marcellino to catalogue and record in detail all of his findings. To assist him in this Don Marcellino employed an impoverished French painter to make accurate drawings and paintings of the ancient cave art for his report. Amongst a great number of visitors, the King of Spain, Alfonso XII, came to see the cave but the academics stayed away. It probably never occurred to Don Marcellino that he was threatening to destroy countless phantom herds of much loved academic sacred cows of theory with his discoveries. Edouard Harle, an engineer and a self-styled pre-historian, visited the cave, but fled in haste when he heard that a poor artist had been employed to copy the paintings for Don Marcellino's report. Harle, exhibiting monumental ignorance, promptly declared the Ice Age paintings to be fraudulent.

In 1880, a congress of pre-historians (whatever they may be) met in Lisbon and solemnly pronounced the Altamira cave paintings to be inauthentic. The whole gang, the archaeologists, the anthropologists, and the pre-historians, combined to condemn the Altamira discovery. The negatively destructive Rudolf Virchow, the Englishman John Lubbock, the Swede Oscar Montelius, and the Frenchman Cartailhac, followed like a baying pack. All spurned the paintings, and Cartailhac described them as 'a swindle, a joke, and caricatures'. They all enjoyed the tremendous advantage of never having seen the paintings at Altamira, which they publicly ridiculed. The authentic very ancient animal bones found in the cave were disregarded and forgotten in the rush to destroy.

Don Marcellino was frozen out, and he was denied the opportunity to speak at a later Congress of Pre-Historians in Berlin in 1883, and for years he was prevented from making any public presentation in any forum. Five years later he died, a man unfairly shamed and mistreated. Even whilst Don Marcellino was alive, however, the cancer was spreading. In 1881 on 6th May, peasant people at the village of Marcamp, in the Gironde, found a hole which led into a large cave, and when late in 1883 the pre-historian François Dalcau made a thorough investigation of the cave he dared not mention the twelve Ice Age paintings which he found on the cave walls. Then, when a clergyman enthusiast excavated the Marsoulas cave near Sailes-du-Salat in Haute-Garonne between 1881 and 1883, he also found painting after painting, all across the cave walls. This discoverer was also afraid to dare to mention his find. Neither man was willing to run the risk of uncivilised academic libel and slander that would ruin their public lives and reputations. Nothing has changed.

The incredible Cartailhac ruled the roost and succeeded in frightening everyone from his dominant position as the President of the Prehistoric Society of France. When on 11th April 1895, a schoolboy named Gaston Barthoumeyrou squeezed through a narrow crevice in a walled cave known as La Mouthe, near Les Eyzies, which was used by M. Berniche as a storage chamber, he discovered a series of strange engravings on the walls of the cave beyond. Caution had to be exercised by these amateurs, and the information went from the boy to his schoolteacher, and then on to an archaeologist Emile Rivère. When Rivère examined these paintings, he found that some parts of them disappeared beneath layers of chalk and stalagmite, and as he knew that these layers would take thousands of years to form, their antiquity became unmistakable. Now the genie was out of the bottle, and the antiquity of these marvellous Ice Age cave-paintings could be unquestionably proved.

Emile Rivère by-passed Cartailhac and approached the Paris Académie des Sciences. This caused the Abbé Henri Breuil to go to M. Berniche, who owned the cave, to visit another cave on M. Berniche's property, known as Les Combarelles. Here M. Berniche had seen more ancient paintings. On 9th September 1901, Henri Breuil, with Peyrony and Capitan, began the systematic exploration of Les Combarelles. In this cave they found painting after painting of long-vanished animal species, and Peyrony then went on to discover more cave paintings at the Font-de-Gaume cave near Les Eyzies and called in Breuil and Capitan to help him to study these discoveries.

Finally, the weight of evidence was too much for the Abominable No-Men, and the entrenched opposition to honourable progress finally collapsed. For well over twenty years, and at great harm and cost to others, the academics had protected the most useless and fragile entities on earth - their own reputations.

The final effect was a long-overdue total revision of the whole approach to the matter of mankind's ancient history and our ancestors. The tale is a typical one, and follows a pattern familiar to any capable researcher. It is familiar, in the inevitable vicious attacks on the character and reputation of the persons, and not on their work and discoveries. Don Marcellino did not employ a penniless artist to forge cave paintings at Altamira, instead he sought to make an accurate record of the find, and the persecution and denigration of Don Marcellino served to force others into silence.

With this in mind and knowing that this is still normal everyday misconduct practised by academics, we can approach the matter of discoveries made near Tucson in Arizona. There is nothing on Planet Earth that is more dangerous than the thwarted, cornered, academic grant farmer, protecting his funds and grants of public money.

On a September afternoon in 1924, one Charles E. Manier, of Tucson, in Arizona, was out with members of his family when they walked to take a look at an abandoned nineteenth-century limekiln. The limekiln had been built in an excavated area of desert limestone known as caliche. This rock-like substance is formed from the slow dissolution of calcium carbonate out of the desert soil, and builds up into rock-hard deposits over the centuries. The caliche in this area where the limekiln had been constructed had built up to a depth of six feet or more. Reports of this site state that the caliche was so hard that dynamite had to be used to make holes for fence posts.

The important facts about the limekiln are that it was built in 1884 and abandoned in 1914. During the thirty years of its working life, a pathway had been worn in the caliche leading to the kiln. This worn-down path exposed the bank alongside the trail to weathering and erosion. When Charles Manier and his father walked along this track towards the abandoned kiln on the September afternoon in 1924, Charles Manier saw a metal object lodged in the side of the eroded bank. Determined to get this metal object out of the rock-hard caliche, Charles fetched an army entrenching tool from his car and he hacked away at the caliche to get it free. What he recovered was a thick lead cross some one-and-a-half-feet high and one foot across the horizontal arm. The cross was roughly moulded, and the vertical and horizontal sections were four inches wide and two and a half inches thick. It weighed sixty-two and a half pounds (nearly four and a half stone).

This was not all, however, for when Charles Manier cleaned the cross down at his home, he found that it was constructed of two crosses riveted together. With natural

Chapter 19 - Possible Dark Age Christian Relics in Arizona

curiosity Manier opened out the rivets and took the two fitted crosses apart. He then found that the inner surfaces had been covered with wax, and when he removed the wax, he saw that there were inscriptions on both surfaces.

When a neighbour told Charles Manier that these inscriptions were in Latin, they immediately took the crosses to Frank H. Fowler, then a Professor of Literature at the University of Arizona in Tucson. Frank Fowler's readings of these Latin texts are: 'We are carried forward on the sea', and 'In memoriam'. As Wilson and Blackett already knew that a major migration fleet set out for America from Deu-Gleddyf (Milford Haven) in *c.* AD 574, the presence of Latin inscriptions on Christian artefacts buried in Arizona was very interesting, but not altogether surprising.

Charles Manier went straight back to the limekiln area the next day, and this time he found a triangular piece of roughly formed caliche with a smoothed area. Here were inscribed the names of 'Theodorus' and 'Jacobus', along with a roughly drawn human figure and what appeared to be the date DCCC or 800 that would perhaps be AD 800.

These crosses and the names Theodorus and Jacobus could perhaps belong to Spanish missionary priests pushing up northwards into Arizona in the early period following the rediscovery of the Americas in 1492. Equally, anyone familiar with the Khumric royal genealogies and cathedral charters will instantly recognize the name Theodorus=Teithrin, as with Theoderic=Tewdrig, Theodosius=Teithfallt, and Theodore=Teitfal, and so on. The Khumric Jacob is Iago as there is no 'J' in the alphabet, but important clerics named Jacob appear in the Latin texts of Dark Age Welsh Cathedral Charters.

It was not long after Charles Manier's finds that a friend, Thomas W. Bent, joined him in a partnership further to excavate the caliche deposits around the limekiln. They started work on 28th November 1924, and within days they had unearthed yet another split and riveted lead cross that weighed twelve pounds. This cross again revealed waxed inner surfaces, with more, apparently mediaeval, Latin inscriptions. This time the letters appearing to give the dates of 790 and 900(AD) were found, together with a name of a king of Israel who reigned sixty-seven years. Also named were other kings named Israel II and Jacob, and a deadly war. The letters 'Oe' also appeared.

Now, Wilson and Blackett have no idea whether all this is some pious religious fake in the long tradition of Christian fakery of thousands of saintly bones, countless gallons of duck's blood masquerading as Holy Blood, and enough timber splinters from the 'True Cross' to build the Spanish Armada.

Reverting to historical records, it is perhaps possible to get some indications. King Solomon, the son of David, had at least five names. Of the five names known, one is Ithael. In the late sixth and mid-seventh century AD two kings named Ithael ruled over Morganwg = Glamorgan - Gwent, etc. One was King Ithael the brother of King Morgan Mwynfawr, the direct successors of Arthur II ap Meurig. This Ithael left a nine-foot high, seven-ton memorial stone at Llanilltydfawr, in Glamorgan, naming himself as Ithael Rex, and St Illtyd, the soldier turned abbot who buried his first cousin King Arthur II; and Arthmael-Iron Bear was the common appellation of Arthur II. King Morgan Mwynfawr was succeeded by his son who was also named Ithael. Names like Prince Ithael son of Eddilwyrth, and these kings called Ithael, were common in Dark Age Wales. In fact, Hebraic names abounded, with Ismael son of Budic, Bishop Joseph, Jacob the Priest and Charter witness, and so on. Admittedly, Ithael is not Israel, and there is no person named Israel known to Blackett and Wilson in the ancient Khumric records.

In Arizona in 1925, Thomas Bent took legal possession of the land where the caliche deposits and the limekiln lay, under the Homestead Act, to prevent any contention over the ownership of the artefacts discovered there. It appears that Charles Manier had withdrawn from the venture, which was not proving to be profitable, and the active pursuit of the search passed over entirely to Thomas Bent and his brother John Bent. Thomas Bent had to live for a specified time on the site to meet with the provisions of the Homestead Act, and apparently this was a rough experience.

The digging by the Bent brothers recovered at least twenty further lead items from the concreted Caliche deposits. The general conclusion, drawn from the inscriptions and the decor of these articles, was that they seemed to represent a combination of Christian and Hebrew symbolism - which is exactly what might he expected from a Christian ethnic group from Dark Age Wales, who had Ten Tribe Israel ancestry.

There were several more split and riveted crosses with waxed inner surfaces and underlying inscriptions. These inscriptions are said to record leaders named as Jacob and Israel, and Benjamin, and tell of a great battle involving Jacob and Israel, and a strange event referred to as the freeing of the Toltezus. Again, Khumric has no 'Z', but

Chapter 19 - Possible Dark Age Christian Relics in Arizona

Latin texts do. Once again there appear to be dates written, and these give the years 880 and 896. The Khumry did count and number the years, as did the people of ancient Israel and Judea. As well as crosses, an assortment of spears, swords, maces, and processional standards was found, and several were embellished with snake images. Several items had drawings depicting men, and these were then thought to be the Joseph and Benjamin of the Latin texts. A domed building - possibly a temple like Santa Sophia in Constantinople - a possible town map, and a personage riding on a cloud, also appeared in drawings.

Back in South-East Wales there are only two fairly crude carvings of early kings, notably one of Gorddyfwyn the Exile that shows a king carrying a sword and a sceptre or ceremonial mace. The prohibition against depicting the human image made in the likeness of the god himself is well known.

These Arizona maces show scenes that include ray-like symbols descending from a crescent shape, which is exactly how the Awen Sign or Broad Arrow triple strokes appear from a cloud-shaded sun. Rays also descend from beneath a sketch of what is called a thunderbird in North America, which is possibly a dragon. A sword also carries the figure of a reptile that resembles a dinosaur, which has been suggested to be a diplodocus, but which may equally be the Welsh dragon.

Perhaps someone should look at the tall headless effigy of a fully armoured Templar Knight at Margam, where a diplodocus-like dragon is carved gnawing away at the bottom of the warrior's shield. The Templar Knights ceased to exist in most areas in 1308, following the murderous programme against them engineered by the King of France and the Bishop of Rome. Strange tales of dragons were told, and the last dragon was apparently slain under the walls of a South Wales castle some five hundred years ago. The Welsh national flag is the Red Dragon, and dragon emblems abound in Wales. In Cardiff a large statute of a coiled dragon sits on top of the domed roof of the City Hall. Rows of carved dragons front the Temple of Peace, now part of the Welsh Office; a dragon carving sits on top of the old Technical College; and a huge Red Dragon figure decorates the front of the newly built International Centre. There is Red Dragon Radio, and all manner of companies style themselves as Red Dragon, painters, builders, cleaners, taxis, and so on.

Inevitably these remarkable artefacts dug out of the caliche had to be brought into the academic forum, and it is a constant wonder to Blackett and Wilson that the amazing thing about history is that no one ever seems to learn anything from it. It is a form of a reversed Cassandra syndrome. Just what did Byron Cummings, the Head of Arizona University's Archaeology Department, expect when he took ten of the artefacts dug up by the Bent brothers to meeting of the American Association for the Advancement of Science at Kansas City in December of 1925? What did he expect from a similar meeting at the Smithsonian Institute? And what did he anticipate from further visits to Cornell and Princeton Universities?

The only efforts made were the inevitable efforts to discredit the finds. The possibility of ancient Christian Hebraic style artefacts in the U.S.A. did not fit, and were in no way compatible, with the current theory. These artefacts were outside the narrow limitations of the current historical knowledge and research. Events that cause academic revolutions are even more unpopular with the incumbents of soft, easy, well-paid academic positions than they are with the incumbents of political positions in revolutions. Against all logic, all manner of frantic efforts were made to totally discredit these unprecedented finds from Tucson.

It is hardly worth describing in detail the antics of the detractors anxious to get rid of unwelcome and disturbing evidence, but some comment is required. Neither the Bent brothers nor Charles Manier could be fitted up as forgers because their excavations were too well known and were patently honest, and so a scapegoat had to be found. The chosen victim was one Vicente Odohui, an eighteen-year-old Mexican youth, whose family arrived in Tucson in 1886, TWO YEARS AFTER THE LIMEKILN WAS BUILT over the top of the caliche. The fact that caliche takes centuries to form in depth bothered no one.

The Mexican Odohui family were alleged to have arrived in Tucson with some books in burlap sacks. Young Vincente was then alleged to have copied out mediaeval Vulgate Latin mixed with Hebrew phrases from these remarkable, unrecorded, never seen or produced books. This multi-talented eighteen-year-old was then allegedly also a sculptor, who set up an unseen, undetected furnace process, and proceeded to cast all these objects. He then allegedly carved scenes on some items, cut the inscriptions, and fitted the riveted sectional crosses together. Then it was alleged that with great and unknown ingenuity, Vincente Odohui proceeded to scatter these artefacts, which he had made, deep down throughout the rock-solid caliche deposits.

He even managed to scatter some of them deep down UNDERNEATH THE LIMEKILN, which was built two years before his family arrived in the Tucson area. These astonishing feats, which credit Vincente Odohui with very remarkable abilities,

Chapter 19 - Possible Dark Age Christian Relics in Arizona

did not lead to one single offer of a college scholarship.

If the question of 'How did Vincente Odohui achieve all this?' is left aside, there is then the question of 'Why did Vincente Odohui do all this?' There was not a single scrap of evidence of any kind to support this remarkable series of unproved allegations, which were published in three Tucson newspapers. There is nothing unusual about this bizarre style of press witch-hunt and character assassination as Blackett and Wilson can testify.

The overall and desired effect was to provide the die-hards and negative sceptics the platform from which to denigrate these discoveries. One political historian announced that the use of AD initials did not come into use until after AD 1000, but this is something that is not proven and is in fact not provable. Others scoured Latin texts and phrase books to try to match the inscriptions and to cry "forgery", if texts seemed to match. The eminent Cyclone Covey and Dr Joseph B. Mahan, experts in more modern times, both recorded how a George Hawley spent many years 'proving' that the Tucson inscriptions were taken from volumes which were first published several years after the initial discoveries by Manier and the Bents, and long after the limekiln had been built over the top of the Caliche layers and directly over several artefacts.

In the rush to crucify a victim, no one bothered to notice that Charles Manier was not the first discoverer. It escaped everyone's notice that two lead objects had been dug out of the caliche layers in 1884 when the foundations of the limekiln were being dug. This was of course when Vincente Odohui was fifteen or sixteen years old, and two years before he arrived in Tucson, and thirty long years before Charles Manier made his 1924 find.

The theory propounded in an attempt to explain away these swords, crosses, spears, maces, and processional standards is weak past the point of being preposterous. The theory that is proposed to support the genuine nature of the discoveries is no better. This holds that the Emperor Charlemagne, King of the Franks, prevailed upon the then Bishop of Rome, in around 755, to expel all the Jews living in Rome. These Jews, who were expelled from Rome, then took ships and sailed through the Mediterranean and across the Atlantic to North America. Sadly, Dr Cyclone Covey published this hilarity in 1975 in a volume entitled *Calalus*, exhibiting this untenable, not provable, hypothesis, much to the great delight of all those who do blindly and rigidly adhere to N.E.B.C. – 'No Europeans Before Columbus'. Unrecorded

Jews fleeing from Rome would hardly make Christian crosses, and it is not clear how or why they would have been ruled by kings. Why is it impossible for academics to simply say, "I don't know"? Dr Cyclone Covey had successfully re-opened, or, more accurately, initiated, the first fair and open debate, and a major enquiry could have followed.

Whether these artefacts at Tucson are genuine or not is not yet known. Certainly, there has been no attempt to examine them fairly and impartially without prejudice. At least Dr Cyclone Covey was prepared to recognize a Dark Age migration from Europe to America. The Latin-inscribed texts bearing traces of 'Hebrew', and Vulgate Latin at that, are possibly likely to be Latin texts with mixed Coelbren lettering, which is precisely what can still be seen on the Dark Age stones of kings in South Wales.

The dinosaur dragon symbol on the blade of a sword appears to match the pre-1308 carving of a dragon at Margam Abbey, in Wales, and the dragon remains the national symbol of Wales to this day. It is on the flag, and in statues and carved forms on public buildings, and in all manner of badges and decorations. The Khumric nation of Ten Tribe Israelite origin adopted Christianity in AD 35-37, 'in the last year of Tiberius', and practised the early form of Christianity for over ten centuries, and thereafter secretly. The Christian symbols of the Tucson discoveries do not stand alone. Other representations of the cross symbol exist in ancient form in North America. The cross symbol appears on rock-cut inscriptions in Kentucky. It appears unmistakably carved on shells found in Dark Age environments.

If hasty British writers had not made crude blunders, and had not misdated the Madoc voyages for fawning royal political patronage, and misrepresented the epic voyage of Arthur to Preiddeu Annwn, 'the migration to the other world', and if they had not failed to recognize the 'voyage of the Teyrn' associated with the Life of St Brendan and meaning 'the voyage of the Monarch', then all this acrimonious angry dispute would perhaps have been cleared up years ago. Perhaps the finds of Charles Manier and Thomas Bent would have been universally hailed and applauded. Young Vincente Odohui would not have had his reputation smeared, and his name slandered and libelled, and we could have all been doing much more constructive and useful things. This then is how matters slide into buffoonery. Civilised enquiry and unprejudiced discussion figure nowhere. Deliberate misrepresentation, allied to misquotation and character assassination, are the first and only weapons still automatically employed whenever the wall of silence is breached.

Chapter 19 - Possible Dark Age Christian Relics in Arizona

Why did Dr Cyclone Covey shoot himself in the foot after demolishing the scandalous conspiracy to discredit the discoveries of Manier and Bent? There is no record of any Jewish fleet sailing from Rome, and the theory is bizarre, and it does even more damage to a shambles of an affair. Why on earth did Covey think that Jewish people would make Christian crosses? By contrast, a multi-record account of a major Dark Age migration from Europe to America is recorded in the Madoc histories, which came out from the first Christian state in the world, so why has no one ever attempted to examine the possibility of a Khumric connection with these lead crosses and other artefacts found in Arizona? It seems that some histories are simply politically popular, and that others are politically and religiously embarrassing.

Evidence that is not admissible evidence

The situation surrounding the strange discovery of lead crosses in Arizona and the lack of any organised approach towards solving the mystery is not peculiar to America. Time and again new discoveries are brought to nothing by the iron curtains of the academic mindset. Nothing is allowed to interfere with the ramshackle edifice of paper-thin theories that masquerade as facts, and which are in fact articles of faith and not proven facts. This can be illustrated by recent finds made in Britain.

The ancient British histories confirm the arrivals in Britain of the fleets of the advanced Chaldean-Syrians under Albyne around 1600 BC and the highly culturally-advanced Brutus led Khumric Nation around 508 BC. The archaeologists in Britain confirm these arrivals and identify two sudden eruptions of highly technically advanced metal-working cultures in Britain at around 1600 BC, which they call the Wessex Culture, and another around 600-500 BC. It is a total paradox that whilst the archaeologists clearly identify evidence corroborating the historical records, the historians persist in blindly denying these records. In *The Holy Kingdom*, published in 1997, Alan Wilson and Baram Blackett with Adrian Gilbert, let out some information on the gigantic ancient harbour on the Afallach-Orchard levels off the east Cardiff shoreline. This aroused no archaeological or historical interest from anyone in the universities. The discovery in 2002 that the three ancient ships that were found in the mud of the Humber in 1937 are radiocarbon 14 dated to around 1600 BC,also sparked no interest whatsoever in the Albyne history of 1600 BC.

On 18th September 2002 *The Guardian* reported that archaeologists had made totally unexpected discoveries at Poole Harbour in Dorset on the south coast of

England. They found that the many thousands of oak tree trunks that had been driven down into the mud to stabilise the masses of rocks and rubble in the ancient quays, were radiocarbon 14-dated at 250 BC. The person leading the discovery team stated, 'The scale of the construction work was astounding, and implied a large, skilled and organised workforce'. It is described as 'startling evidence', and one wonders why, unless of course the ridiculous phony versions of British history, as invented around the 1840-1860 era in Oxford and Cambridge on behalf of the London political and religious establishment, are still being believed.

Two eighty-metre-long quays, both eight metres wide, with paved flagstone surfaces, reaching out into the deep water. Astounding? Not really, when anyone takes the trouble to read our native British histories that were politically and religiously assassinated in Oxford - Cambridge - London in the mid-nineteenth century. This huge Iron Age construction is a tiny- mini harbour when compared with the enormous Great Stone Port built at Cardiff. The archaeologists admit that the Romans did not build this harbour two hundred to two hundred and fifty years before Julius Caesar attempted to invade Britain, and they claim that it is the oldest harbour in Britain. Correctly, it is the oldest harbour yet found and excavated. So, it is the oldest yet known in Britain, and the search has not yet begun.

Oh dear - what a catastrophe! Poole Harbour was built three hundred years before the Romans arrived in Kent. This does not however deter the intrepid archaeologists involved, and they are quoted as fervently hoping to discover a Greek or Roman trading vessel in the silt and mud. Is this not just a little peculiar? As the harbour is in Britain, might it not be reasonable to hope to find a BRITISH ancient ship in this BRITISH ancient harbour? If not a British ship, why not an Etruscan or Carthaginian ship? But surely as British citizens and nationals they should hope to discover a British ship of our British forefathers.

Professor Tim Darvill of Bournemouth University: "I'm not asking for much, a nice Greco-Roman trader complete with its cargo would satisfy me." Incredible: why does he not hope to find a British trading vessel? Unless of course the professor wishes to avoid finding himself totally out of step with the bemused academic herd mentality, and in step with the politically incorrect historical unreality. Are we all being asked to believe, once again and for the ten thousandth time, that British evidence is not evidence? Are the 'experts' suggesting that imagined Greek, Roman, or other traders came here to Britain and proceeded to transport over ten thousand tons of rocks and to cut down thousands of oak trees, and laboured to build a harbour in Britain? Is it not time to realise that this ancient harbour in Britain was built, and used by, and belonged to, the highly civilised and culturally advanced Ancient British? Why on earth would anyone who is British want to find a foreign Greek or Roman ship instead of an ancient British ship?

What we have is very clear evidence of the academic mind-set with the rubberoid brain firmly set into Roman concrete. The Chaldean-Syrian arrival of *c.* 1600 BC and the Brutus arrival of *c.* 508 BC brought people from the most culturally advanced areas of the Near East into Britain to found the new nations of Britain, and the research of Wilson and Blackett are proving this to be true. It was our British ancestors who built and traded out of these British harbours.

The fact is that the existence of this very large, well-built, ancient harbour demonstrates that our British ancestors were a technically advanced and highly cultured race, exactly as our native British histories record that they were, and as Strabo and others faithfully recorded.

The existence of huge ancient city walls underneath 'Roman' London is an academic embarrassment. The discovery of the remains of a huge pre-Roman triumphal arch at Ludgate in London, at exactly where British native histories state that King Lud built a monumental triumphal arch, is another embarrassment. In fact, there are embarrassments all over the place, but who needs evidence when there are plenty of unfounded nineteenth-century theories available?

The Angel Stone in Manchester Cathedral.

There is a difficulty in persuading readers that the evidence of Britain's past is not hidden away and hard to come by, but instead it is often readily available. In 2000, the Angel Stone in Manchester Cathedral was brought to the attention of Alan Wilson and Baram Blackett by Tim Matthews. This stone bears a carved figure of a winged being and a very clear ancient British Coelbren inscription. The stone is on display in the cathedral in a prominent position and it is known to be ancient. This alone destroys the disgraceful allegation and fabrication that Edward Williams forged the ancient British Coelbren Alphabet in around 1800.

The lettering of the inscription is a mixture of several old British Coelbren alphabet letters and a small number of hybrid Latin alphabet letters. For example, the British < > diamond shaped sign representing 'O' is replaced by the circular Latin

The Angel Stone, Manchester Cathedral, England

Chapter 19 - Possible Dark Age Christian Relics in Arizona

'O'. Mr. Tim Matthews made the identification that this Angel Stone is inscribed with the British Coelbren and informed Wilson and Blackett of this fact.

The main feature of the carving is that of a remarkable figure shown on the stone. The human-like figure wears the long garments associated with the ancient clergy, the nobility, and wealthy classes, and it has a long cloak draped across the shoulders. The carving is worn, and the being appears to have a tall hat on its head. Most remarkable however is the representation of large wings on this humanoid figure. The wings give the figure the appearance that is commonly associated with angels in European cultures, and it is obvious that this is a heavenly entity and not an earthly being.

The angel has its arms outstretched and is holding a very thick and large staff or rod in its hands. These are huge, which is an important feature. Until the nineteenth century, and in a few cases up into the early twentieth century, statues and carvings of the Angel of Death, known as L'Ankou, stood in almost every church in Brittany. Brittany and Llydaw were the twin-brother colonies of the British-Khumry re-established by Mascen Wledig (Magnus Maximus) in 383. The L'Ankou figures were mainly represented as skeletal, and they had huge hands just like those of the Angel being in Manchester Cathedral.

The Angel figure is holding the large, thick staff at the top, and the action appears very clearly to be one of pounding downwards as if to crush things with this huge weapon. The staff itself is also winged and the wings are placed at the top just above the huge hands of the Angel being. The whole scene is we believe a representation of a huge heavenly body, which would probably be the AD 562 comet shown as the angel itself, and the staff pounding downwards would be the comet débris smashing down and pounding the sixth-century Arthurian kingdom of Britain into devastation.

As the learned Immanuel Velikovsky demonstrated in his works in the 1950s and 1960s, the historically recorded catastrophes of the ancient world, which we know of as 'Noah's Flood', and the 'Flood of Ogyges', and the later disasters of the Hebrew *Exodus*, were recorded around the world by virtually every nation on every continent as being caused by the near-approach to earth of massive extra-terrestrial objects. Both Ignatius Donnelly and Velikovsky identified planetary disturbances in our solar system and giant comets as being responsible for catastrophes on our planet Earth. Velikovsky identified the archangel Gabriel as a planet responsible for moving into a dangerous position when shifting into a new orbit around the sun, and as another planet when Mars endangered Earth. Both events were remembered in Hebrew tradition as actions performed by the archangels Gabriel and Michael, who were in fact planets shifting into new and dangerous orbits. All ancient nations preserved the dread and fear of giant comets and shifting planets which when in motion resembled comets.

In 1900, Frances A. Gosling published *The Bretons at Home* and included a description and a photograph of one of the last surviving statues of *'Ankou'* that was then in the church of Ploumilliau in Brittany. Frances Gosling was interested in L'Ankou after reading the collection of superstitions in *Legende de la Morte*, by Anatole le Bras. Carvings of the death angel were at Bulat, Roche, Maurice, and elsewhere, but only at Ploumilliau had a statue of L'Ankou survived. The statue is remarkable for its disproportionately huge hands. The old statues of Brittany were proving to be an embarrassment to the nineteenth- and early twentieth-century church, and so they were being removed and either destroyed or hidden away. Frances Gosling records how the local people at Ploumilliau called the statue Ervoanik Plouillo. Whether Ervoanik is the Khumric 'erfyniad' meaning 'the striker', or the one who strikes down, is not certain.

The likelihood is that this Death Angel depicted in Manchester Cathedral is a British version of the Breton L'Ankou, with both deriving from a common origin of belief, and is being shown as the terrible force of the comet débris that struck the powerful Arthurian Kingdom of the British in AD 562. The devastation of Arthurian Britain was certainly caused by a scatter of débris from a comet as stated in the historical records, and here is a picture of how this vast disaster was seen by at least some of the survivors.

This brings us to the matter of the inscription on the Angel Stone that is set out in three lines of old British Coelbren lettering, with a few Latin alphabet letters also used.

Chapter 19 - Possible Dark Age Christian Relics in Arizona

The Decipherment of the Angel Stone

The determination is that the Angel Stone in Manchester is inscribed in the ancient British alphabet. This alphabet is generally known as Coelbren as it is designed to be inscribed on wood. The alphabet is also found on ancient stones and other artefacts, and where this occurs the Coelbren straight strokes can be sometimes modified as curved lettering. This has occurred with a few of the letters shown on the Manchester Angel Stone, where the diamond shaped British <> for 'O' has been replaced by the Latin Alphabetic 'O' as used today. With only three such discernable exceptions the remainder of the letters are those of the ancient British Coelbren.

The inscription is set into three lines that run vertically down on the left side of the Angel Stone. The stone has to be inverted so that the right side becomes the bottom, and the inscriptions are then presented horizontally. The two lines of inscriptions that are the horizontal at the top of the stone are read from left to right. The inscriptions on the great staff or club pounding downwards appear to read from left to right when represented in this position.

The top line of the inscription

Symbol	ꓥ Ƨ	O ◁	O	Y	⌐ I	⌐ H
Coelbren	E S	O D	O	Y	B I	B Hw
Khumric	ES	OD	O	Y	Bi	BHW (Bw)
English	since	strange thing from	the		mockery	the fear / bugbear

The second (centre) line

Symbol	O O	⊃ ⊬ I	ꓢ Y Ᏸ	⌐
Coelbren	O O	Ch E I D L	S W D (sud)	Ff
Khumric		Wy	Ceidl	saviour	Fe
English	their	saviour (ceidwal)	form/manner	He / him / it

(The written OO consistently produces an "W" sound as in "Who" in other inscriptions. Therefore, we are attempting to maintain a consistency in interpretation.)

Symbol	ҟ Ϟ ∧	H √	V ⊢I
Coelbren	L(e) S A	N(e) B	V=Ffe HI
Khumric	Lesad	Neb	Ffel (ffehl)
English	the good advantage	no one	knowing

With no obvious or marked break points between the words inscribed there is obviously scope for alternative interpretations. Wilson and Blackett have been deciphering Coelbren in Asia Minor, the Aegean, Italian Etruria, Swiss Rhaetia, Britain and North America since 1984 (see *Volume 1*), and this had allowed us to accumulate a certain understanding of the methods and thinking processes of our British ancestors. We would welcome any constructive comment on this quite difficult inscription.

Line 1. Strange (or deceive) the mockery (or information) the bugbear fear

Line 2. Their saviour   a form / a manner he/it

Line 3. Good / advantage to one knowing.

It seems that the bugbear of fear in the comet was seen as a mocking deception of the saviour by appearing in this form or manner, and that no one knew of any good or advantage coming from this.

The great comet passing close to earth is seen as the Death Angel, and the shower of débris scattered across Britain like a rain of atomic bombs, is seen as the huge staff held by the Death Angel pounding down upon and crushing the Kingdom. This gives us a pictorial representation of the most awesome event in British history, and one that has been deliberately erased from the sanitised records taught to the unsuspecting people. When on several recorded occasions in history stones fell from the sky before a crowd of people the scientific and religious dictat held firm: 'it is impossible for stones to fall from the sky'. When on 7th November 1492 a stone identified as an aerolite fell close to the Emperor Maximillian and his Court at Ensisheim in Alsace, the religious diktat still persisted, that stones cannot fall from the sky and strike Planet Earth. Not until another unmistakable shower of meteorites fell at Aigle in France on 26th November in 1803 was the academic and religious dogma, which preached that it was impossible for stones to fall from the sky no matter what the evidence or record, finally overthrown. The fall of meteorites was investigated by Biot and the matter was finally admitted that stones can and do fall

Chapter 19 - Possible Dark Age Christian Relics in Arizona

from the sky.

The important fact as pointed out by Velikovsky, was that 1492 to 1803,was the era of the great pioneers of modern astronomy, when Copernicus, Galileo Galilei, Kepler, Newton, and Huygens, and others all lived. Throughout this entire era the whole scholarly world refused to believe even the ancient Roman accounts of stones falling from the sky. So the authentic and accurate records in the ancient British histories that were preserved in Wales had no chance in the face of such blind obstinate intransigence and flat refusals to accept visible facts. We all know the answer: the British histories, which recorded the near-total devastation of the powerful British kingdom by a huge scatter of comet débris in AD 562, were automatically dismissed and ridiculed. After all, every conceited smug, self-satisfied academic knew that 'stones cannot fall from the sky'. So, all British ancient history had to be labelled as a fake and a forgery, because all the 'experts' knew that 'stones cannot fall from the sky'.

It is remarkable that ancient British records carry identical accounts of the aftermath of such an impact as happened when the extra-terrestrial object struck Tunguska in Siberia at seventeen minutes past seven on the morning of 30th June 1908. The old British records state that for nine days it was noonday bright for twenty-four hours a day. For nine days in 1908 people all over northern Europe played tennis, sat in their gardens by night and day, made films, and took photographs in conditions of twenty-four hours-a-day brightness exactly as the ancient British records describe. At Irkutsk five hundred miles away from the epicentre of the impact at Tunguska, the seismograph shook violently for over an hour when the object from outer space hit Earth on 30th June 1908. The old British records of impeccable antiquity tell of the 'terrific blast' in AD 562 and are disregarded. The dictat that 'stones cannot fall from the sky' allowed the academics to despise and to ridicule these perfectly accurate records, and the religionists were delighted to have the weapons with which to attack the older religion of Britain.

In this climate of biased opinion, the question was: "How could there ever have been a great powerful Arthurian kingdom, ruled by Arthur II the son of King Meurig, which was destroyed by stones from the sky causing titanic devastations?" The whole matter was impossible and there never ever could have been any Great Wastelands in Britain where nothing could live for many years. Despite there being an array of ancient records of aerolites and meteorites, and other phenomena, all falling from the sky and causing immense devastation on earth, the experts all 'knew' that 'stones cannot fall from the sky'. The dinosaurs would not have agreed with this expert view. The Angel Stone in Manchester Cathedral is we believe a refutation of that very foolish belief that flew in the face of known and recorded facts. We see that it records the great catastrophe that devastated Britain in AD 562. The victim that was sacrificed to that academic and religious foolishness was the immensely valuable authentic ancient histories, the culture, and the heritage of the British nation.

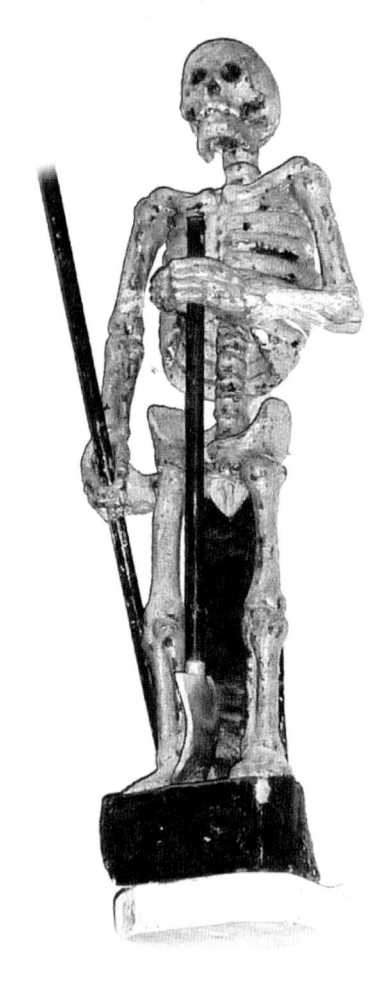

L'Ankou Statue, Ploumilliau, Brittany.

Chapter Twenty

The Dead Sea Scrolls

In 1947 a Bedouin youth named Mohammed el-Dib (the Wolf) was searching for a stray goat when he found a cave in a ravine near Khirbet Qumran. Inside this cave Mohammed el-Dib discovered a great treasure of inestimable value that had lain undisturbed for almost two thousand years. Mohammed had found ancient manuscripts which men of piety and faith had stored in clay jars for preservation in a time of crisis, against the day when someone would rediscover them and value them instead of destroying them.

Khirbet Qumran is near the north-western shore of the Dead Sea, close to the mouth of the River Jordan. It is a wilderness place, a desolate, ravaged land of rock, crags, sand, and cliff, where the sun weighs heavy with a slow and merciless heat. Here on a rock plâteau, several hundred feet above the shores of the Dead Sea, lie the ruins of a settlement once occupied by the Judean religious sect of the Essenes. It is a certainty that the written scrolls found by Mohammed el-Dib, and the subsequent discoveries made largely by his kinsmen in at least twelve other caves in the rocky ravines, were hidden by the long-forgotten scribes of the Essenes, around AD 62-100.

As is the case with such finds the first scrolls were not identified at their true worth, and they passed through the hidden labyrinth of the antiquities black market. The story has been told often enough of how the whole region was in a state of turmoil, with the discoveries in 1947 coinciding with the British decision to renounce responsibility for maintaining law and order in Palestine. Armed conflict was imminent and inevitable, and the anticipated war was fought in 1948 when the new-born state of Israel fought with the neighbouring Arab states. It was against this background of tumult that in 1949 a joint expedition of Jordanian and French archaeologists began a systematic exploration of the first cave of scrolls. In 1952 Bedouin Arabs found a second cave, and then a third, below the rock terrace where the ruins of the dwellings of the ancient Essenes lay. By 1956 no fewer than eleven caves containing ancient manuscripts had been found.

In the third cave something very unusual was discovered. Here were two rolled-up scrolls of copper. All the other scrolls found were of writing upon leather, parchment, or papyrus. In total, parts of some six hundred scroll manuscripts are estimated to have been found. Many are fragmentary, and indeed most are a mass of tiny pieces of crumbling bits. Only eleven are almost complete and intact. One leather manuscript of the Book of Isaiah is of rolled leather measuring twenty-six feet long and a foot wide.

It was these badly corroded rolls of copper with their strange inscriptions which attracted the attention of Alan Wilson and Baram Blackett when they saw a rare photograph of a scholar leaning over a desk with part of these texts spread out before him. For forty years a small group, who did not themselves discover the Dead Sea scrolls, exercised an unhealthy and unprofessional monopoly over access to the scrolls, and the few photographs made public were generally deliberately of very bad quality. This prevented any close examination of these carefully guarded texts by anyone outside the tiny tightly closed circle monopolising the study of the Dead Sea texts. Here, however, was a colour photograph of very good quality of the 'scholar' and there were very clear texts in the background, which were intended to be incidental.

Blackett and Wilson were instantly aware that they might well be looking at a very early form of Coelbren writing. This was quite logical and indeed possible, as the trails of historical evidence which they were following led back from the U.S.A. to Britain, and then back following the Brutus and Albyne sea-borne migrations to Etruria, and Trojan lands in Asia Minor. The people of this alphabet and language were the same 'Welsh' Khumry, who emerged as the Asia Minor Kimmerians or Kimmeroi, and were known to the Emperors of Assyria as the Khumry around 740-690 BC. The Khumry in Britain had maintained their claim to be the lost Ten Tribes of Israel down through the centuries, and the Khumry recorded in the Assyrian texts were very clearly the same deported deported Ten Tribes of Israel.

It followed that the Khumric language and its Coelbren alphabet were essentially the ancestral language of these ancient Lost Ten Tribes with roots leading back to Israel and to Egypt. Other extensive studies of the evidence in the Khumric Triads, set down, as presently existing, some one thousand years ago, had already proved correct the ancient claim that ancient Egyptian hieroglyphics could be read into

Khumric. A professorial thesis written in 1898 by Sir John Morris Jones explored and confirmed the syntax of both ancient languages as identical and pointed to this as correct. What emerged from this was overwhelming, even monumental, evidence to support this, and Alan Wilson and Baram Blackett had leap-frogged over the question of Israel and had gone straight to Egypt in 1984. They were in fact spending more time on this project than on anything else. If the Ten Tribe people had been in Egypt for centuries, and had then left under the leadership of Moses, there should be some Egyptian links. So, Alan Wilson and Baram Blackett got out their magnifying glasses to get a better look at the accidentally photographed text, and later they had the photograph enlarged.

Letters were written and attempts made to get co-operation with various scholars, scholarly magazines, and language study societies, which as usual produced a majority of zero responses, and a minority of rejections refusing to accept papers or in any way to review evidences. The best response came from one scholar who claimed to be very busy, and could Wilson and Blackett perhaps write again in another six months. In order not to waste precious time, energy, and money, the matter was 'put on ice' and stored away.

It was all hugely frustrating, as it was well known that the two copper scrolls from the Qumran caves were very different from the whole of the rest of the six hundred or so texts which had been wholly or partly discovered. The copper scrolls alone were not written in Hamatic Aramaic of the era around 50 BC to perhaps AD 100: they were written in a very different alphabet and in a different language. The fact that the language and alphabet were said to be 'unknown' to the scholars was a very exciting prospect to Alan Wilson and Baram Blackett. They already knew that the listing of 'all' the known ancient alphabets of the world printed in every university history or manual and in every scholastic text or encyclopaedia, always routinely excluded the ancient British Coelbren alphabet. Every one of these weighty tomes also published the hilarious and gross error that the 'Welsh' Khumric language was 'Celtic', which of course is manifestly untrue.

In describing the search to try to read the Egyptian hieroglyphics it is always claimed that every known language was tried, which is not true as Khumric was ignored. The same false claim was made about attempts to decipher Etruscan, and again only the Khumric language was excluded from decipherment attempts. It is incredible in the light of the evidence already listed that the history enshrining this very ancient language and alphabet should have been ignored. The fear in London and in Rome is evident. There was also the matter of the ongoing Napoleonic Wars between Britain and France to consider in Champollion's time, and he could never have even considered that the ancient Egyptian hieroglyphics could be read using an enemy British language. The race to try to decipher the Egyptian hieroglyphics was an affair of huge national pride. As is always the case, politics disfigured the attempted researches.

The Egyptian hieroglyphic studies did however provide a remarkable information spin-off or by-product for Wilson and Blackett. The presence of the Khumric language in ancient Egypt caused them to take interest in the Gnostic Christian Library discovered at Nag Hamadi near Chenoboskian in Egypt in 1946. In this case an Arab named Mohammed Ali was seeking for firewood, when he found a five-feet clay jar in what turned out to be an ancient Gnostic cemetery. The five-feet clay jar contained fourteen leather satchels, and these leather satchels contained an entire Gnostic Christian library. This collection of early Christian manuscripts, which had apparently been buried around AD 400, consisted of gospels and other religious treatises written from around AD 50 to 350.

Some of these Gnostic gospels were known to have existed from mentions made in early Christian writings, but had been lost. Considering the evidence that they contain, it is not surprising that they were 'lost'. Several of these Nag Hammadi texts mention an unnamed alphabet which appears to bear an uncanny resemblance to the Khumric. The same seven vowels - A, E, I, 0, U, W, Y, - which match both the same seven Ancient Egyptian and Khumric vowels, are listed.

It was not until November 1992, when Alan Wilson visited Kentucky and made journeys to several other states, that he opened up the subject in discussion with Dr Ray Hayes. Immediately, Dr Hayes produced a volume containing translations of all the Nag Hammadi texts and loaned it to Alan Wilson, who had by now all but forgotten the idea of reading either the copper scrolls from the Dead Sea, or the Nag Hammadi texts. Unlike the Dead Sea Scrolls, the Nag Hammadi Library had not attracted much publicity or interest. This probably stemmed from the unease of 'established' Christian churches over the discovery of the major rival 'non-conformist' Apostolic Christian church. Ancient texts which pre-dated the uniform texts and gospels chosen from the Lyons catalogue around AD 500, and the gospels edited by Eusebius around AD 324 which contradicted and refuted the established dogmas, were most certainly unattractive, if not downright unpopular. The Moslem population of Egypt were not too interested, and no great fuss was made over this entire ancient Christian library.

Chapter 20 - The Dead Sea Scrolls

It is a fact that the Christianity that was permitted and adopted into Britain in AD 35-37 was almost certainly Gnostic Christianity. In fact, the records make this clear to almost a virtual certainty. This would have preceded the religion later invented by Paul of Tarsus. This accounts for, and is exhibited in, the records of the antagonism and dislike of the British Church for its later offspring in Rome.

What Alan Wilson found interesting in November 1992, was the fact that one entire Gnostic book from the Nag Hammadi Library was devoted to the subject of the alphabet. The text is known as *Marsanes*, and typically the scholars have been wondering who this person 'Marsanes' was. In fact, 'Marsanes' is not a person at all, for in Khumric 'mar' means 'laid flat', 'san' means 'wrought by hand', and 'es' means 'a wonder'. It seems that 'Marsanes' simply describes the wonder, even the miracle, of writing anything and everything by using a concise workable modern alphabet. The entire text, from start to finish, details the construction of the alphabet and exactly how it works. The one thousand, eight hundred-year-old Marsanes text matches the British Khumric descriptions of the origin and development of the Coelbren alphabet of Britain recorded in *Barddas*, published 1852 and in the Iolo Manuscripts published in 1825. There can be no doubt in any unprejudiced mind that the same alphabet is being detailed.

So, the earlier suspicions of Alan Wilson and Baram Blackett dating back to around 1978 were confirmed with Dr Ray Hayes in Kentucky in 1992. The 'unknown' Coelbren alphabet of Britain had turned up yet again, and this time in ancient Egypt. How Edward Williams, alias Iolo Morganwg, forged this alphabet before AD 400 and buried it in a clay jar in Nag Hammadi needs to be explained. Pre-AD 400 is at least one thousand, four hundred years before the allegations of an AD 1800 forgery made by the ridiculous Griffith John Williams. Coelbren is the tool to decipher 'indecipherable' Etruscan and Rhaetian, it unlocks the door to read ancient 'Pelasgian', and it leads back and points directly at the two copper scrolls found at Qumran. Yet this same alphabet is deliberately ignored and excluded from every catalogue of ancient alphabets in the world.

These 'experts' actually seem to believe that

(a) almost all British history was forged around AD 1800;

(b) the same history and allegedly forged alphabet appear on ancient stones all over Britain as far back as AD 200, and on coins back to 200 BC;

(c) the allegedly 'forged' history is written in a massive array of centuries-old venerable forged manuscripts;

(d) the forgers numbered thousands collaborating together from at least 800 to 1800, spread all across north, south, east and west Wales to produce a vast interlocking forgery including ancient forged graves, battlefields and huge war cemetery mounds, ancient churches, fortresses, and hundreds of ancient forged inscribed stones.

(e) the Nag Hammadi evidence can be ignored; and the fact that the British, Etruscan, Rhaetian and 'Pelasgian' Asia Minor alphabets are near-identical, and can be deciphered and translated, should also be disregarded.

The 'Mind-Set' in Britain is one that refuses to tolerate and recognise a vast mass of physical and manuscript evidence.

Wilson and Blackett are waiting to see just how the Nag Hammadi book with the detailed Marsanes text describing the Ancient British alphabet will be disintegrated and dematerialised and made to become invisible. This should be very interesting to observe.

The Two Copper Scrolls from Qumran

To reiterate slightly, of all the six hundred scroll documents found at Qumran, only two are not written on parchment, leather, or papyrus, and these two are not in Aramaic. These are the two copper scrolls found in jars in Cave No. 3. Some scholars believe them to be one split scroll and refer to them as one scroll. The most peculiar feature of these copper scrolls is that they carry inscriptions in a totally different 'unknown' alphabet and a different unknown language from the rest of the six hundred scrolls. Unknown, that is, to the few who claim to have studied these scrolls for the past fifty years.

The vast bulk of the Qumran scrolls are written in Aramaic, probably in the period between 50 BC and AD 100. This has led investigators to assume that the two copper scrolls are (1) of this same time period, (2) written in some form of Aramaic, (3) therefore written in a local Aramaic dialect, (4) written by an illiterate unskilled scribe, because these scrolls do not conform with the uniformity evident in the rest of the six hundred-odd scrolls.

Chapter 20 - The Dead Sea Scrolls

A section from the replica of the copper scrolls of Qumran

In order that the readers may assess the situation for themselves, we can quote from a lecture presentation by a Professor P. Kyle Carter Jnr. who was intending to write a book on these scrolls. The numbering of these quotes are additions to make explanation simpler.

Professor J. Kyle Carter Jnr states that:

1- 'The Copper Scroll is an anomalous part of the story we are telling today. That is, it does not fit into any of the categories we have been discussing except that it is rolled up (or was rolled up) and it came out of one of the caves' (*i.e.* No. 3, at Qumran).

2- 'It is written in a language that is different from the language of any of the other scrolls.' (Note - it is therefore NOT Aramaic.)

3- 'It is written in a script that is not like the script of any of the other scrolls.' (Note - it is therefore in a different alphabet.)

4- 'It is written on a material that is different. The other scrolls are leather, a few are written on papyrus, but this is on a sheet of copper.'

5- 'And its content has no parallel. That is, in content it does not resemble any of the other Qumran scrolls - or anything else, except pirates' treasure-maps in Hollywood movies. It is an unusual phenomenon, an anomaly.'

How on earth Professor Carter can state that the content of a document written in an unknown alphabet and in an unknown language, has no parallel with other documents is beyond the comprehension of Wilson and Blackett. If neither the alphabet nor language is known, then logically the text cannot be read. It follows that the content of the unread text cannot be compared to 'pirates' treasure-maps in Hollywood movies'.

If we look at these comments made by Professor J. Kyle Carter, we can find interesting points. He refers to the two scrolls found together, side by side, as one scroll, and this is not strictly accurate. In the context of the origin of the Copper Scrolls it could be downright misleading. Rolling up a long strip of leather or papyrus would be a natural method of storage in the period around 5 BC to AD 100, but this would not be the case with plates of copper. Rolling up two sheets of solid copper would be an unnatural method of storage, particularly as both these copper scrolls clearly exhibit regularly spaced nail holes, and regularly spaced tear marks ripped from these nail holes, all along the length of the top and bottom of both scrolls. This indicates that almost certainly these two copper plates were once attached flat onto a wall with fairly evenly spaced-out nails. Of this there can be no doubt.

The Polish priest, J. T. Malik, who monopolised these two copper scrolls for over forty-six years, produced what he alleged was a complete translation of these scrolls, published along with very poor-quality and almost indistinguishable black-and-white photographs. That it took forty-six years to read two hundred and eight lines of writing is astonishing. So, Professor Carter was certainly opening a can of worms. The method adopted by J.T. Malik, if it can be so described, was to assume that the quite different non-Aramaic letters on the two copper scrolls were in fact Aramaic. He then looked for the nearest similar Aramaic letter, or letters, to each copper scroll letter, and replaced the letter in the unknown alphabet with Aramaic. J. T. Malik often employed considerable ingenuity and imagination in this strange comparative exercise and he frequently made use of two Aramaic letters for one unknown letter, and *vice versa*. The majority of these alleged comparisons are not comparisons at all, and letters in the Aramaic alphabet bear no resemblance to their supposed identified counterparts in the 'unknown' alphabet.

The result is that the number of letters per line varies in J. T. Malik's alleged translation of the texts, with remarkable variations from the number of the letter symbols marked into the surface of the Copper Scrolls. The shapes of the 'unknown' alphabet have to change considerably to accommodate the switch from the quite different script and the different language into J T Malik's imagined Aramaic. There is no need of professional expertise to identify shape changes and differing numbers of symbols and letters per line. Anyone who can see and count can do it.

If we proceed with these very different copper scrolls, we find further very interesting points raised by Professor Carter. In relation to these texts on the Copper Scrolls, he states:

1- 'Now let me list the peculiarities and problems in working with this text. It is written in Hebrew.'

2- 'It is a form of Hebrew that has a lot in common with Mishnaic Hebrew, but it is not Mishnaic Hebrew.' (He proceeds to note that Mishnah is an early Rabbinical text of around AD 200.)

3- 'It is unlike any Hebrew that we know, probably because this text was not written by a professional scribe.'

4- 'It is probably a village dialect of Hebrew.'

5- 'This was a time when Aramaic speaking was the rule, but Hebrew was still spoken in villages, and so the author of the Copper Scroll, whoever he might have been, presumably wrote his own dialect with all its idiosyncrasies.'

6- 'To continue, the spellings of individual words are often peculiar.

We can pause for a while here and take stock. Professor Carter states that the texts are Hebrew, but not in Hebrew of around AD 200. He actually admits that it is unlike any Hebrew which he, and presumably the other investigators, actually know. If they do not know the alphabet or the language, then he cannot honestly state that the language is Hebrew. Nor can he state that the 'spellings of individual words are often peculiar', as he does not know either the alphabet or the language, and therefore he does not know any of the words. Neither can he state that the scribe was probably not professional, nor that the text is written in a local dialect.

What the professor does not know, and the question he totally fails to address, is the age of the Copper Scrolls. There is in fact no justification whatsoever for assuming that the Copper Scrolls were written at the same time as the leather and papyrus scrolls from Qumran.

The proposal that the alleged Hebrew of the Copper Scrolls is a local village dialect is untenable and in fact illogical. So also is the proposal that this alleged Hebrew was set down by an untutored unskilled scribe in a remote village. Copper scrolls or inscribed plates are hugely more expensive than either parchment or papyrus, and it appears incongruous that the professional and skilled scribes would have been given the cheaper leather and papyrus to write upon, yet the humble village semi-literate would be given the immensely more expensive copper. If, as Professor Carter states, Aramaic speaking and writing was the rule around 50 BC to AD 100, is it not probable that these copper scrolls are many centuries older than the leather and papyrus found at Qumran?

Chapter 20 - The Dead Sea Scrolls

Is it not also probable that the so-called dialect idiosyncrasies and alleged peculiar spellings are the direct result of these copper scrolls having been written some eight hundred years earlier than the other Qumran texts? Is it not equally likely that this unfamiliar form of alphabet and writing is not the surviving oddity of a mangled village Hebrew dialect found in an unknown, unnamed village, but is instead simply a much more ancient form of Hebrew from around 850-800 BC? The Hebrew that was lost by 50 BC and mangled by the deportations of the Judeans to Babylon by Nebuchadnezzar, may exist on these scrolls.

There is not one single scrap of evidence to support the hypothesis that an unknown scribe sat in an unnamed village and wrote in an unidentifiable local dialect. The fact that copper was vastly more expensive than parchment or papyrus, and is a most unsuitable material to use in a rolled scroll, should mitigate against this.

The obvious likelihood is that the two copper scrolls are several centuries older than the other Qumran soft and flexible parchment and papyrus scrolls becomes even more apparent if we further examine Professor Carter's hypothesis. He states that:

1- 'We know a variety of spelling systems, a variety of kinds of orthography (handwriting) as it is called, from the various Qumran scrolls and from other manuscripts, but no orthographic system quite matches the one used in the Copper Scroll.'

2- 'Sometimes this seems to be because mistakes are being made.'

3- 'Other times it may be that it is not a spelling peculiarity but a grammatical peculiarity that we are not familiar with.'

4- 'Next the script is unusual. If you or I were to take a sheet of copper and attempt to write upon it with a chisel or some other sharp object, the result would be different from our normal handwriting.'

5- 'In part therefore the handwriting is peculiar because the scribe is working on an unfamiliar material, but again this seems likely that this is not the hand of an expert scribe such as those who wrote most of the leather manuscripts in the Qumran archive.'

The orthographic system is identified as being very different from the texts of 50 BC to AD 100. Instead of recognising a highly probable antiquity in the two copper scrolls, the alleged orthographic strangeness, the spelling peculiarities, and other differences, these differences are simply attributed to untutored inefficiency, an inability to spell, and to bad grammar. Amazingly it is concluded that the scribe was unaccustomed to writing on copper, and was therefore not an expert.

Every Biblical scholar should know of metal plates being placed on walls, and of these metal plates being inscribed with texts. The following hypothesis is offered as the most likely explanation of the origin of the Copper Scrolls from the Qumran cave near the Dead Sea.

When King Solomon built his temple at Jerusalem around 930-850 BC he had the walls covered with sheets of gold. Upon these golden plates Solomon had the holy texts inscribed. So we have a beginning of the practice of nailing metal plates inscribed with holy texts onto the walls of the temple in Jerusalem. When Solomon died, his son Rehoboam was only able to secure sovereignty over the two Tribes of Judah and Benjamin, and the area of Judea. The other, larger areas held by the vastly numerically superior Ten Tribe Israel were ruled by King Jeroboam. This division was obviously part of a 'divide and conquer' policy of the Egyptian Pharaoh 'Shishack', and when this pharaoh appeared with his army at Jerusalem, King Rehoboam had little option but to surrender all the treasures of Solomon's Temple to save the city. These treasures, which are stated to have included Solomon's golden plates from the temple walls, were then carted off to Egypt.

This happened in the era around 900 BC, and the impoverished King Rehoboam replaced the surrendered golden plates with plates made of copper, and he had these fixed to the Temple walls in Jerusalem. This practice of plating the walls is recorded in I Kings 10:16-17:

> 'And king Solomon made two hundred targets *of* beaten gold: six hundred *shekels* of gold went to one target. And *he made* three hundred shields *of* beaten gold; three pound of gold went to one shield: and the king put them in the house of the forest of Lebanon.'

This forest of Lebanon is thought to have been the Hall of Cedars in Solomon's palace.

In I Kings 14:25-27, we learn of Shishack's raid into Judea:

> And it came to pass in the fifth year of king Rehoboam, *that* Shishack king of

Egypt came up against Jerusalem: And he took away the treasures of the house of the LORD, and the treasures of the king's house; he even took away all: and he took away all the shields of gold which Solomon had made. And king Rehoboam made in their stead brasen shields, and committed *them* unto the hands of the chief of the guard, which kept the door of the king's house.'

The Jerusalem Temple lost its accumulated treasures for the second time when king Amaziah of Judah made war against King Jehoash of Israel. Amaziah had placed idols in the holy central shrine of the Temple of Yahweh, and there are clear indications of a religious war between the pagan Amaziah of Judah and the religiously orthodox King Jehoash of Israel. Ten Tribe Israel refused to recognize the sanctity of the polluted Jerusalem Temple and set up temples in Israel territory, and so a vast source of annual income dried up in Jerusalem as the Ten Tribes ceased to visit the city for worship. The result of the war is told in II Chronicles 25:23-24:

'And Joash the king of Israel took Amaziah king of Judah, the son of Joash, the son of Jehoahaz, at Bethshemesh, and brought him to Jerusalem, ad brake down the wall of Jerusalem from the gate of Ephraim to the corner gate, four hundred cubits. And *he took* all the gold and the silver, and all the vessels that were found in the house of God with Obed-edom, and the treasures of the king's house, the hostages also, and returned to Samaria.'

As has been pointed out earlier, in II Samuel 6:10 we are told:

'So David would not remove the ark of the LORD unto him into the city of David: but David carried it aside into the house of Obed-edom the Gittite.'

Whereas all went well at the house of Obed-edom, the Ark caused disasters in almost every other location, and it seems obvious that King Jehoash of Israel was merely reclaiming the Ark from the Jerusalem Temple polluted by Amaziah, along with every other decoration and implement. As Jehoash removed the guardian family of Obed-edom, he clearly also removed the Ark of the Covenant. That he would have taken Rehoboam's plates away around 790 BC is almost a certainty, unless someone else removed some of them.

The third major despoliation of the Jerusalem Temple was at the hands of the Chaldean Emperor Nebuchadnezzar in *c.* 598 BC; and it is not impossible that the copper scrolls found at Qumran were thin plates hurriedly torn down from the walls of a temple and unnaturally rolled up to be hidden away safely. The hypothesis that these copper plates were originally laid flat and nailed to a temple wall is far more likely than the theory that they were always intended to be rolled-up scrolls. There were later despoliations of the Jerusalem Temple in the times of the Seleucid king-emperors, and finally the Romans.

Antique copper plates hurriedly ripped from a wall and rolled up to be concealed easily and smuggled away for safekeeping, is the most obvious conclusion. The very clear and evenly spaced nail holes running along the whole length of the top and bottom of these scrolls, and the obvious tearing of the metal ripped up on the edges of the plates from each of the holes, are unmistakable. Antique copper plates inscribed and fixed centuries earlier to temple walls would account for the unusual orthography, and the imagined spelling and grammatical errors, and the supposed dialectical peculiarities.

The significance is this. If these two Copper Scrolls date from some time before 598 BC, which appears to be the case, and perhaps even back to around 790 BC, then they date from the era when huge numbers of the Ten Tribes of Israel, the people of Omri, were deported by successive Assyrian Emperors to the regions around Armenia to the north of Assyria around 730-700 BC. This means that the Ten Tribes took the original language and alphabet, and religion with them. The remaining two Tribes of Judea were later deported to Babylon by Nebuchadnezzar, and it is known that they lost their language and came back with new religious ideas. The Ten Tribes kept the same ancient language and alphabet, which can be traced back from Britain, Etruria, Rhaetia, and Asia Minor to Assyria; and this then may be the alphabet and language of the two Copper Scrolls. Therefore, the means exist to decipher and translate these enigmatic scrolls.

This possibility is made all the more obvious with the idea, prevalent amongst scholars, that the Copper Scrolls contain strange letters which look like Greek. It has even been suggested that these 'Greek' letters form some sort of code within the general texts. It is worth recalling that Julius Caesar in his war diaries, *De Bello Gallico*, recorded that the Greek alphabet was similar to that of the Khumric-British. Add to this the fact that Ammianus Marcellinus noted that the British and Greek Alphabets were very similar, and that the Greeks obtained their alphabet from the British, presumably *via* the sage Abaris who taught the Greeks philosophy and sciences, and the presence of these British 'Greek' type letters is not so strange.

Chapter 20 - The Dead Sea Scrolls

Why on earth would any ancient scribe in Israel or Judah use Greek? These allegedly unusual letters support the distinct possibility that these copper plates are of the era prior to the deportation of the Ten Tribes of Israel to northern regions of the Assyrian Empire beginning around 730 BC. In this event all the letters on the Copper Scrolls should be identifiable. We have the alphabet and the language available.

Baram Blackett and Alan Wilson were not alone in following this line of reasoning. It was for this reason that Jim Michael took Alan Wilson out for a drive on a dark Friday evening in November 1994. They were off to look at black-and-white photographs of the famed copper scrolls. They arrived at the Baptist Seminary College in Louisville at around 7.00 pm, and there were very few people around in the College Library, as might be expected. The librarian assisted Jim to get the required volume, and Alan Wilson chose a quiet corner, well away from anyone else, in the near-deserted library. Finally, they were going to take a first look at photographs of the whole of these copper scrolls found at Qumran.

As had been reported the photographs that were published were far worse than poor quality, and extremely indistinct. Matters were not helped by the fact that Alan Wilson had cataract problems in both eyes, but Jim Michael, with no such difficulty, was not able to make out the letters sufficiently well either. A reader could be excused for thinking that the author of the volume was less than anxious to allow others to see these scrolls clearly. As Alan Wilson put it: "These shots look as if they were taken with a damaged, cheap box-camera at midnight in a thunderstorm sometime around 1920. I don't think this guy wants anyone to look too carefully at this." Jim Michael agreed: "You can bet your life on that, buddy."

Jim Michael had anticipated poor-quality, blurred and indistinct photographs, and had brought magnifying glasses with him. With these simple aids it was possible to examine some few lines of the texts in these muddy photographs. As an automatic first exercise Alan Wilson simply began by counting the number of letters that appeared cut into the individual lines of script on the copper scrolls. Then he counted the number of letters in the Aramaic text offered in the transposition on the opposite page, comparing each line with its supposed Aramaic identity. The numbers of letters did not match.

The next step was to examine the shapes of the letters on the copper scrolls and then to attempt to compare them with the shapes of the alleged counterpart shapes of the Aramaic letters. This was not possible as the shapes were not the same, and coupled with the fact that the numbers of letters on each line did not tally, there was clearly a major problem. It appeared that the author of this 1962 volume had chosen to compare the letter symbols on the copper scrolls with letters of the Aramaic alphabet as it was known around 50 BC to AD 100. The fact that the letters were quite dissimilar was obvious and this should have dissuaded any reputable scholar from this procedure. Having converted these Copper Scroll letters to quite different Aramaic letters, and in several cases used two Aramaic letters for one Scroll letter, and *vice versa*, the author then proceeded to 'translate' the texts as if the language that they had been written in was Aramaic.

There is no justification whatsoever for any assumption that Aramaic letters had somehow changed beyond recognition down the centuries and therefore it was perfectly in order to convert the Scroll letters into completely different shapes which would match Aramaic letters of the desired era. Professor J. Kyle Carter was right in saying that the text was Hebrew, even though he offered no evidence to support this. The lame excuses of an alleged semi-literate scribe, who was a poor speller, bad at grammar, unskilled in orthography, and unaccustomed to writing on copper, are illogical. So, also, is the assumption that these copper sheets were originally intended for a scroll instead of being nailed flat onto a wall.

Whether the famed golden shields of Solomon were actually copper, and became transformed into gold as stories passed through the centuries no one knows. Whether these are rolled-up sheets of copper hurriedly torn down from a temple wall to save them from Pharaoh Shishack, or King Jehoash, or Nebuchadnezzar, or the Seleucid emperors, or the Romans, may also be impossible to know. The first thing to do is to take sheets of copper of the same dimensions and thickness and to nail them to a wall, in the same manner as the holes in these Dead Sea scrolls indicate, and then to tear them down quickly but as carefully as possible without removing the nails, using perhaps a sword to prise or rip them away. Some pious person many centuries ago tore them down from a temple wall and hid them under his garments as he rushed away before the enemy soldiers arrived, and then he rolled the copper scrolls up and put them into clay jars to preserve them for future generations.

The possibility that these two Copper Scrolls are inscribed in very early Coelbren at some time between 830 BC to 600 BC was always worth investigation. It was upon this premise that Alan Wilson and Baram Blackett decided to attempt a decipherment if they could get good-quality photographs. It was to be many years later, however, before they first saw even reasonable quality photographs of these texts.

On the Friday night in Louisville in November 1992 Alan and Jim settled for scanning the pages of murky photographs to see if there were lines here and there which were clear enough to offer some degree of confidence. Alan Wilson looked for what might just be familiar groupings of letters or repetitive groups, and finally he decided that it might be worthwhile to attempt five lines of the texts. This first brief overlook indicated that the texts were probably an early form of British Coelbren and that there was an apparent lack, or at least a scarcity, of vowels. The only thing that Alan knew of early written Hebrew was that it was thought not to involve the use of written vowels, so Professor Carter was on the right track in that respect.

The letters in the five lines selected were not altered in any way or combined together making two into one, but it was accepted that if there were no vowels in the writing, then vowels might have to be inserted. The lack of vowels probably results from the transition from a pictorial writing using short root words, for example, rha, or rhe, or rho, or rhu, or rhi, and so on, where the slight differences in the 'r' letter indicated the vowel to be assumed. This much is confirmed by the Book of Marsanes found at Nag Hamadi. The omission of vowels was in itself a transitional phase.

It was puzzling to try to understand why it had taken so many years to accomplish so little in reading a mere two hundred and eight lines of writing. It was not until 1994 that leading scholars finally lost patience with the very limited information being issued, and the exclusive access to the Dead Sea Scrolls being limited to only a few, and a major academic row erupted on an international scale, and spilled over into the popular press, radio and television. The archaeological convention is that the discoverer of a document, or other artefact, is allowed to be the first to publish on that discovery. This disregards the fact that the discoverer may not be the best person to decipher anything, and may not chose to publish anything for decades, if ever. In the case of the Dead Sea Scrolls a small group were exercising the rights of discoverers, when they had in fact not personally discovered anything at all. It is clear that by imposing and exercising a secretive monopoly these few were guaranteeing themselves a soft life for several decades, and often without actually accomplishing anything at all. The subject was therefore live when Alan Wilson visited Jim Michael in 1992 and 1994.

Trial Decipherment of Lines of the Dead Sea Copper Scrolls

The lines which were first attempted for decipherment do not appear to bear any correlation with the alleged decipherment made by John Allegro in 1956, which led to the popular idea that there were vast caches of ancient treasure buried all around Jerusalem. The text reads from right to left and so it needs to be reversed in order to read it conventionally. Armed with both the correct language and the alphabet ciphers it is a fairly straightforward text *(see illustration 20-1)*.

Page 1. Line 1.

The text appears to read:

'Good we towards you, you towards (is) good with the hidden/veiled one amiable good, to hold good with slippery (way) to go out, (with) the god mine the living spirit what is pure.'

Page 1. Line 2.

The text appears to read:

'Father who exists in us to take off/go away towards glittering corn (lands) supreme lord to cry out sublime/beautiful.'

Page 1. Line 3.

The text appears to read:

'Arable land there will be (the promised land) a holdfast (stronghold) to cry out arable land towards it (we) the forcibly ejected distinctly with velocity fixed/established towards (it) choose.'

Page 9. Line 9.

The text appears to read:

'We (with us?) swiftly turning you are (the) danger towards you of being immersed outwards to go outwards god smoothed out.'

Page 9. Line 10.

Chapter 20 - The Dead Sea Scrolls

The text appears to read:

'(To follow) one's own path outwards dry what is opposite/ before us, to traverse over.'

Lines 9 and 10 combined state:

'We a number separated (from) you are swiftly turning danger towards you to go outwards immersed towards god, our own track smoothed out towards dry (places) to what is opposite before us, to traverse over you are the power you are.'

It appears to describe the crossing of the Red Sea by the Hebrews, where they are at first confronted with drowning - being immersed - and the god turns their danger towards himself and then a dry pathway through the waters is opened up before them by God for them to 'traverse over', 'outwards' (away from Egypt) and god is the power which is.

Two short lines towards the centre of the texts were the first to be attempted for decipherment, and they tell of two tribes and ten tribes, which appears to indicate that the Copper Scrolls are from the post-Solomon era. Ancient peoples were not careless, stupid and forgetful, and they did not lose and neglect their records, alphabets, and histories, as those in academic sinecures would have us believe.

We have to remember that when English-speaking peoples migrated to North America, Australia, New Zealand, South Africa, India, and elsewhere, in modern times they took their language, their literature, their alphabets, their culture, and religion with them. We are following the migration trail of a people who were first in Egypt until Moses led them out *c.* 1360 BC. Then they dwelt in Israel until the Assyrian emperors deported them around 730-700 BC and placed them up north in the region of Armenia, and called them the Khumry. Then around 687 BC they took off in a mass going westwards through the whole length of Asia Minor, arriving at the Dardanelles around 650 BC, and the Greeks called these Khumry the Kimmeroi. From here, half the nation went to Etruria around 650 BC and the other half finally sailed for Britain under Brutus around 508 BC. In Britain they remained as the Khumry and today after two thousand, five hundred years they are still the Khumry. They preserved their language, and they preserved their alphabet; and it is this language and alphabet which allow us to trace them along the ancestral migration trails. This is what this part of the project is all about.

Illustration 20-1: Dead Sea Scroll translation 09/04/2022

Page 1 Line 1

Sign / letter	꜂	⊓	T	I	T	I	꜂	∧	K	꜂	N	
Coelbren	>	N	↑	I	↑	I	>	∧	K	>	N	
Cipher	D	N	T	I	T	I	D	A	(K) Cu	D	L	
Welsh / Khumric	da	ni	ti	i	ti	i	da	a	cu	d	l	cuddliwr
English	good	we	thee	towards	thee	towards	good with	hidden,	veiled,	curtained

Sign / letter	K	꜂	꜂N	꜂	∧	I∧	Ł	Y	꜂↓
Coelbren	K	>	>N	>	∧	I∧	Ł	Y	>↓
Cipher	(K) Cu	D	D L	D	A	I A	F Fe	Y	D W
Welsh / Khumric	cu	da	dal	da	a	ia	ffe	y	duw
English	amiable	good	to hold	good with	slippery	outwards	the	god to go out

Sign / letter	꜀I	Y	꜂N	⊓H
Coelbren	꜀I	Y	꜂N	⊓H
Cipher	P I	Y	E N	N TH
Welsh / Khumric	pi (au)	y	en	nith
English	mine	the	living spirit	what is pure

Text - 'Good we towards thee towards (is) good with the hidden (one) amiable good to hold with slipper (way?) to go out. (with) the god mine the living spirit what is pure'

Page 1. Line 2

Sign / letter	꜀꜂	V V	I	ꞃ	꜀꜂	I	Hꜞ Y
Coelbren	↑>	V V	I	ꞃ	꜀>	I	N↑ Y
Cipher	TH D	W W	I	N	H D	I	LL TH Y
Welsh / Khumric	tad	yw	i	ni	hwd	i	llatheu
English	father	what exists	towards	us	take off go away,	to	glittering towards

Sign / letter	Y꜂	꜀ꞁ	H ꞁ	∧ ꜂I꞊
Coelbren	Y>	꜀N	H ꞁ	∧ꞁ>Iꞁ
Cipher	Y D	P N	H(w)	A R D I N
Welsh / Khumric	yd	pen	hw	arddin = arddun
English	corn (lands)	chief (supreme lord)	to cry out	sublime / beautiful

Text - 'Father who exists to us (to) take off/go away towards glittering corn (lands) supreme lord to cry out sublime beautiful.'

Chapter 20 - The Dead Sea Scrolls

Illustration 20:1 continued ...

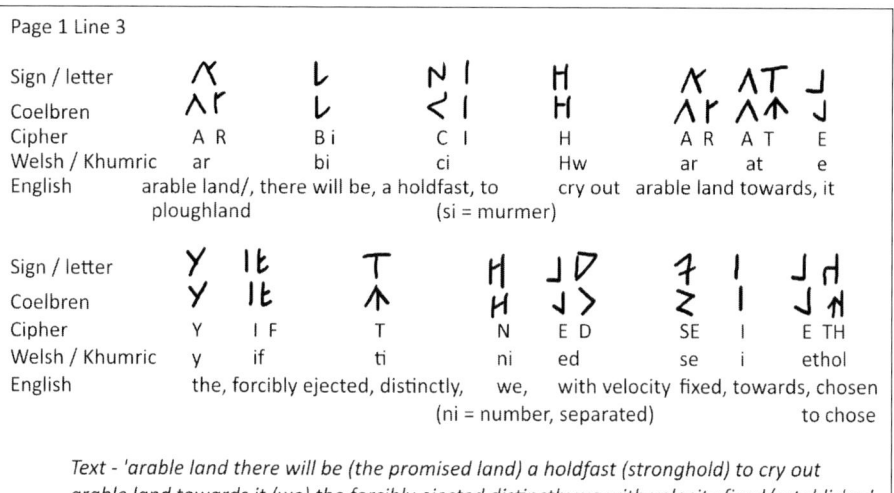

Page 1 Line 3								
Sign / letter								
Coelbren								
Cipher	A R	B i	C I	H	A R	A T		E
Welsh / Khumric	ar	bi	ci	Hw	ar	at		e
English	arable land/, there will be, a holdfast, to			cry out	arable land towards, it			
	ploughland		(si = murmer)					

Sign / letter								
Coelbren								
Cipher	Y	I F	T	N	E D	SE	I	E TH
Welsh / Khumric	y	if	ti	ni	ed	se	i	ethol
English	the, forcibly ejected, distinctly,			we,	with velocity	fixed,	towards,	chosen
				(ni = number, separated)				to chose

Text - 'arable land there will be (the promised land) a holdfast (stronghold) to cry out arable land towards it (we) the forcibly ejected distinctly we with velocity fixed/established toward (it) chose.' Combination letters A + R and S + E are problems.

Too Many Migrations

The major problem which has confronted epigraphical researchers and archaeologists in the U.S.A. is an apparent set of evidences which seem to indicate that there were a number of voyages of discovery made to America in remote antiquity. A large number of claims have been made alleging that several ancient nations had contact with the Americas, and it is an understatement to say that this has caused confusions and has made the professional archaeologists wary of the matter to the point of hostility.

In fact, there is an explanation for this apparent confusion. Anyone who has made a thorough study of ancient British history will know that the discovery of what looks like a possible Carthaginian and North African presence might be anticipated in ancient America.

1. In AD 406 the German confederation of the Vandals, the Sueves, and the Alans crossed the Rhine into Gaul and they proceeded to smash the Roman army, and then commenced the wholesale destruction of Gaul.

2. The British King Constantine III, who had succeeded Arthur I son of Magnus

Maximus, assembled the British army and with his general Geraint, he invaded Gaul, just as British armies were compelled to enter Gaul-France in 1914-1918 and again in 1939-1945. The objective was to restore the Western Empire and to keep the German hordes away from the Channel and Britain.

3. The British army decisively defeated the Vandals, Sueves, and Alans and penned them into the south of Gaul, and General Geraint blocked the passes of the Pyrenees.

4. In AD 411, Geraint opened the passes and the whole horde crossed south into Spain. The Sueves and Alans seized much of Spain, and the Vandals went further south and in AD 422, led by their King Gaiseric, they crossed the Straits of Gibraltar into North Africa.

5. The Vandals quickly seized all of North Africa and made the cities of Carthage and Hippo their main bases. Gaiseric built fleets and in a very short time the Mediterranean became a Vandal lake. Rome was forced to surrender itself to the Vandals and the Vandal German kings became known as the kings of Africa.

6. For over a hundred years the Vandals dominated the Mediterranean until in AD 532 the Emperor Justinian of Constantinople seized an opportunity and sent his general Belissarius to attack Carthage. The entire Vandal army and fleets were away conquering Sardinia, and Belissarius had only boys and old men to oppose him.

7. The Vandal king returned home with his army and found that he could not enter his own capital of Carthage. For fifteen years a savage war was fought that devasted North Africa, and finally in AD 548 the Vandal king gathered his huge fleets and put his entire nation of some one hundred and sixty-five thousand persons on board and sailed to Ireland. Vandal war fleets in excess of five hundred ships were commonplace.

8. King Arthur II assembled the British army and crossed over to southern Ireland to assist kings descended from Ceredig son of Cuneda. After one battle with the Irish army the Vandals boarded their ships at night and crossed over into Wales leaving the British King Arthur II and his armies behind them in Ireland.

9. The British army followed the Vandals back to their homeland, and a savage campaign of pursuits followed as the Vandals had split up into nine groups to try to get enough food as they moved eastwards across South Wales towards Lloegres.

10. The remnant of the Vandals finally got across the River Severn and moved east to settle in the East Midlands of what is now England, and they became known as the Mercians.

11. The Vandal-Mercian arrival in AD 548 means that there were large numbers of European people from Carthage and North Africa present in Britain when the great Island was devastated by comet débris in AD 562 just fourteen years later.

12. It is logical that some of these people would have been amongst the immigrants who sailed to North America with the fleet in AD 574.

13. All this is clearly set out in *Artorivs Rex Discovered*, written and published by Blackett and Wilson in 1986. The discovery of what appears to be a North African or Carthaginian presence in North America is both logical and expected. There was not a succession of migrations of discovery into North America in antiquity, but simply one well-recorded and fully-explained migration.

14. The politically correct Establishment version of Ancient British history invented in Oxford and Cambridge in the 1714-2004 era is total rubbish and hugely destructive.

The Egyptian Connection with North America

We have seen how a large part of the British at the time of the comet catastrophe in AD 562 were descended from the Ten Tribes of Israel, and it is quite easy to establish an Egyptian connection for these people.

1. The fact is that Ancient British History is very well and precisely recorded, but it is neither studied nor researched.

2. The journey of the Ten Tribes is outlined in this volume and it is simple to see that if the British were from the Ten Tribes, then before they moved to Palestine under Moses, they were in Egypt.

3. The very strong Egyptian connection is fully dealt with in the volume *Moses in the Hieroglyphs*, and there is a guide to learning how to read and write hieroglyphs for yourself in *Cymroglyphics by K.R. Broadstock*.

4. American researchers should not be surprised when they discover pictographs and rock carvings that appear to have a clear Egyptian provenance.

These again probably result from the migration to North America from Britain recorded in AD 562, 573 and 574.

5. To offer one clear example, modern American researchers have found an assembly of pictographs on rocks that are known as the Rochester Creek Hieroglyphics. These very old pictures bear a recognizable resemblance to ancient Egyptian figures, and of that there is no doubt.

6. These Rochester figures also bear a resemblance to a very ancient and very similar scene carved on a rock face in Britain. There is therefore a possible link between Egyptian style pictures and Britain and then on to North America.

7. This constantly brings matters back to the well-recorded discovery of America by the British in the person of Madoc son of Meurig in AD 562, followed by the exploratory voyage of Admiral Gwenon, and the sailing of a large fleet under King Arthur II son of Meurig in AD 574.

8. Given the close association of the British with the Roman Empire for a few hundred years, instead of claims of large number of unrecorded 'discovery' voyages made by Romans, Carthaginians, Egyptians, 'Hebrews', and so on, that have perplexed and angered many academics, there was probably only one well-recorded set of voyages.

9. The cultural links that created the illusion of a long succession of successive discoveries can be demonstrated in detail.

10. The blame lies squarely at the door of the London Establishment who were hell bent on creating a new and vainglorious history suitable to the promotion of the imperial monarchy of the nineteenth century.

As for 'Celts' in America, there were no 'Celts' in Britain, and so there were none in America. An over-enthusiasm for imaginary 'Celts', and for vowelless Ogham, has created a situation in which professional academics are unable to work with well-intentioned epigraphists. It may be worth remembering that without epigraphy we would know next to nothing of the ancient world as we would not be able to read the records. An amateur, Georg Freidrich Grottefend, accomplished the near-impossible by deciphering Cuneiform. Another amateur made the first identification of Cleopadra and Ptolemy, allowing another amateur, Champollion, to make the first in-roads into deciphering ancient Egyptian hieroglyphics. Another amateur, an army

Chapter 20 - The Dead Sea Scrolls

Sample of Rochester Creek rock artwork

engineer named Rawlinson, deciphered Persian Cuneiform. Another amateur, an architect named Michael Ventris, deciphered Linear B on Crete. It is no accident that Wilson and Blackett are regarded as 'amateurs' and yet they can read Etruscan, Rhaetian, Pelasgian, and other indecipherable records.

The study of Ancient History would be in a sorry state without the dedicated labours and the accomplishments of the 'amateur' epigraphists.

Chapter Twenty-One

Conclusions

One of several main planks in this renewed and rebuilt platform of correct "Dark Age" history is the demonstration that in the mid sixth century of the Christian era a hugely populated, culturally advanced, and powerful state in Britain was devastated by what appears to have been débris falling from a comet around AD 562. When Wilson and Blackett first published this in 1986, they estimated the date at around AD 555 using the British data then available.

This has now been confused in a late stage of the research by dendro-chronological claims that the devastations were caused by the massive eruption of a volcano on the island of Krakatoa off the coast of Indo-China in circa AD 535 - 537. This frail and 'politically correct' volcanic proposition, which claimed that this was the cause of the destruction of Arthurian Britain, can only survive if the massed array of historical records of the comet is ignored. Wilson and Blackett's position is that although around AD 535 a volcano exploded on Krakatoa and threw massive dust discharges up into the atmosphere which darkened the skies of the earth for three years, it was impossible that only Britain and Ireland on the other side of the world would have been seriously selectively affected by this Krakatoa eruption. The devastations of Britain and Ireland in the AD 562 era the comet débris devastated Britain in a quite separate event.

Professor Michael Baillie, of Queens College, Belfast, published that the clear signs of stagnation in tree-growth for several years were caused by the Krakatoa volcanic eruption in the Pacific. He guessed that this great blight of plant growth was the cause of the great wastelands of Arthurian sagas. He took the currently popular, but totally inaccurate date offered for the Battle of Camlann at AD 535 and fixed his dendro-chronological patterns onto that date. Alan Wilson and Baram Blackett wrote to Baillie and told him that a volcanic eruption in the mid-Pacific would have affected other countries besides Britain and Ireland. They also told him of the evidence of a comet striking Britain, and that their own research showed that this was the cause of the disaster. Baillie then amended his publications and switched from the Krakatoa volcano to the comet. He did not however amend his anchor date of AD 535, which he had chosen whilst wrongly believing that the Battle of Camlann was so dated.

Baillie later got much publicity over the comet causing plant destruction and retarded growth in the sixth century AD, and he lectured at the Royal Society on this. He never mentioned the correspondence with Wilson and Blackett. Readers of Wilson and Blackett's several books, and visitors to their internet sites, often query their reluctance to divulge information. The answer should be obvious.

Fortunately, there are other generally ignored sources that throw light upon this very simple situation. Wilson and Blackett turned again to the reliable and accurate Arab historians of the Dark Ages and mediaeval era. The Bodleian Library manuscripts Hamilton no. 1 and no. 52, the work of Gregory Bar Hebraeus (Gregory Abu'l Faraj), who died in 1286, were translated by Ernest Wallis Budge. Gregory wrote and studied at the library of Maraghah, which contained a collection of many ancient Arabic, Syriac, and Persian manuscripts. The tombs of Gregory Bar Hebraeus and his brother Bar Sawma are in the north wall of the monastery of Mar Mathai, on Jabal Makub. The chronography of Gregory Bar Hebraeus has information on these momentous sixth-century events, using the records of John of Asia amongst other sources. He records in Volume II page 74 that in the year AD 537:

> 'The Sun went dark for eighteen months, and nothing like it had ever been seen before.'

This would match with the aftermath of the Krakatoa explosion. Gregory then records that later 'in the eleventh year of Justinian,' which is AD 539, a terrible comet appeared.

Moving on to the twenty-seventh year of Justinian, which is AD 554-555, Gregory states that the sixth-century writer John of Asia reported a description of

> 'The world shaking like a tree before the wind for ten days.'

This event slots into the time frame of AD 562 arrived at by Blackett and Wilson for the destruction of Britain. Significantly John of Asia describes earthquakes graphically, but he does not identify the enormous shaking of the whole world for ten days as an earthquake. The violence of events portrayed by John of Asia in the era from AD 544 onwards is peculiar. Whole nations and cities are recorded as having been hit by a 'rod', and this sounds rather like a comet tail.

It could imply massive electrical discharges between planet Earth and a close heavenly body. The result was the sudden and savage death of countless humans and animals, and John of Asia is clearly describing the British catastrophe. That Gregory knew of Britain is clear and he calls it Brutonia after Brutus. *(Vol II, page 57.)*

John of Asia recorded that the 'shaking of the whole world for ten days' was so violent that the huge double walls of Constantinople collapsed. In this same twenty-seventh year of Justinian, AD 554-555, John of Asia (as reported by Gregory Bar Hebraeus) recorded huge inundations along the coast of Lebanon and Palestine, and along the coast of North Africa. Many cities and countries were flooded by the rising seas, and the great city of Alexandria in Egypt sank beneath the waves. Modern under-water archaeologists explore these sunken harbours and cities all around the Eastern Mediterranean without discovering the written record of John of Asia through Gregory Bar Hebraeus.

These Mediterranean disasters mirror the inundations in Britain where extensive land in the Scilly Islands sank beneath the waves, as did the Lost Cantref in Cardigan Bay, and land at Henwy between the Conway estuary and Menai. The Great Stone port in the sea, sitting on Aballach = Orchard ledge at Cardiff, subsided beneath the waters and was swallowed up by mud.

Between Cardiff and Newport and further east along the banks of the Severn, two thousand, four hundred monks laboured under the direction of St Illtyd to build the still-present dykes to protect valuable land, as recorded in *The Life of St Genovesius*. At the same time large areas of Heligoland off the German and Dutch coasts sank beneath the cold waters of the North Sea.

At this time also a large number of ancient harbours in the Eastern Mediterranean sank beneath the rising seas. The oceans do not lie uniformly over the surface of Planet Earth, and the level or depth of a body of water is affected by how near or far it is from the equator or the poles. Whatever happened in *c.* AD 562, and what were the cause and effects of the ten days of the shaking of the world, has never yet been fully investigated by oceanographers, astronomers, or historians. Ancient British 'prophecies' tell of distortions in the perspective of the heavens, and the pre-AD 562 Christian churches are out of alignment with East.

Accompanying these catastrophes was a strange and terrible pestilence, which John of Asia described and Gregory Bar Hebraeus re-recorded. The sequence of events fits with the mass of the population, who worked out of doors in the fields, dying almost immediately. The rich and powerful, who spent much more of their time indoors in their mansions and palaces, were affected later. Wilson and Blackett make no claim to any medical expertise, hut they offer the thought that the symptoms of the pestilence which accompanied this world-shaking event appear to match those of radiation poisoning, which would not have been known to Wallis Budge, writing almost a hundred years ago. People had severe evacuations of diarrhoea, all manner of tumours, and many had blood and skin disorders - cancers?

Contrary to the received wisdom of the colleges, there are extant (through Gregory Bar Hebraeus) the contemporary sixth-century accounts and records of John of Asia, who described both the effect of the massive eruption of the Krakatoa volcano which darkened the skies around the earth, and the impacts of the comet débris on Britain and in the oceans. The much-derided and abused British histories have support in the corroboration available from these records of John of Asia who was a contemporary sixth-century historian.

In France, Gregory of Tours wrote of earthquakes which severely damaged towns, and of whole cliffs falling into rivers. In a year which scholars date as AD 555, Gregory of Tours also wrote:

> 'at this time too, a fifth star, moving in the opposite direction, was seen to enter the circle of the moon.' Book IV, Ch .9.

Later Gregory of Tours states:

> 'Before the great plague which ravaged the Auvergne, prodigies terrified the people of that region in the same way. On a number of occasions three or four great shining lights appeared around the sun, and these, the country folk also called suns. "Look," they shouted, "there are now three or four suns in the sky." Once, on the first day of October, the sun was in eclipse, so that less than a quarter of it continued to shine, and the rest was so dark and discoloured that you would have said it was made of sackcloth. Then a star, which some call a comet, appeared over the region for a whole year, with a tail like a sword, and the whole sky seemed to burn and many other portents were seen.'

The idea of a comet filling the skies for a year matches exactly with the constantly abused and ridiculed British records that tell of a huge comet filling the skies and stretching across from Britain over Gaul for a whole year.

After then digressing into a superstitious tale about a lark, Gregory of Tours returned to the major event:

'When the plague finally began to rage, so many people were killed off throughout the whole region and the dead bodies were so numerous that it was not even possible to count them. There was such a shortage of coffins and tombstones that ten or more bodies were buried in the same grave. In Saint Peter's church alone on a single Sunday three hundred dead bodies were counted. Death came very quickly. An open sore like a snake's bite appeared in the groin or the armpit, and the man who had it soon died of its poison, breathing his last on the second or third day,' Book IV Ch 32.

This event, dated by scholars at AD 562-563, now appears perhaps to need some further thought. Gregory of Tours does not employ any dates in his *Histories*, which were written retrospectively, and these have to be calculated. It would be strange for Gregory first to describe four extra sun-like stars in AD 563, and then to write of a fifth star being seen in AD 555, and to talk of a great comet also in AD 562.

It is not impossible that in collecting data, often retrospectively, from the four Frankish kingdoms and elsewhere, in what was a chaotic and turbulent era, Gregory of Tours made some chronological mismatches. The indisputable fact is that there is another impeccably authentic contemporary record of floods and earthquakes, of great comets and of plagues. Earlier, in this same chapter (no. 32), Gregory of Tours describes how an earthquake caused the side of a mountain to collapse into the river Rhône and blocked the river. The waters finally broke through causing massive flood damage as far downstream as Geneva.

There were other events described by Gregory of Tours, which involved comets linked with plagues. In Book VI, Ch 13, in what appears to be AD 583, Gregory writes:

'In the seventh year of Childebert's reign, which was the twenty first of both Chilperic and Guntram, there were torrential downpours in the month of January, with flashes of lightning and heavy claps of thunder. The trees suddenly burst into flower. The star, which I have described as a comet, suddenly appeared again and the sky appeared particularly black where it passed over the heavens. It shone through the darkness as though it were at the bottom of a hole, gleaming so bright and spreading wide its tail. From it there issued an enormous beam of light, which from a distance looked like a great pall of smoke over a conflagration. It appeared in the western sky during the first hour of darkness.'

Chapter 21 - Conclusions

In the city of Soissons on Easter Sunday the whole sky seemed to catch on fire. There appeared to be two centres of light, one of which was bigger than the other, but after an hour or two they joined together to become one single enormous beacon, and then they disappeared.

In the Paris region real blood rained from a cloud, falling on the clothes of quite a number of people and so staining them with gore that they stripped them off in horror. This portent was observed in three different places in that city. In the Senlis area a man woke up one morning to find the whole of the inside of his house splattered with blood.

This year the people suffered from a terrible epidemic, and great numbers of them were carried off by a whole series of malignant diseases, the main symptoms of which were boils and tumours. Quite a few who took precautions managed to escape. We learned that a disease of the groin was very prevalent in Narbonne this same year, and 'once a man was attacked by it, it was all up with him.' (Narbonne was in Visigoth territory.)

It becomes a familiar story of comets coinciding with plagues and pestilences. In Book VII, Ch.11 there is another comet:

> 'All this happened in the tenth month of the year. New shoots appeared on the vine stalks, misshapen grapes formed, and the trees blossomed a second time. A great beacon traversed the heavens, lighting up the land far and wide some time before the day dawned. Rays of light shone in the sky, and in the north a column of fire was seen to hang from on high, with an immense star perched on top of it. There was an earthquake in the district of Angers and many other portents appeared. In my opinion all this announced the coming death of Gundovald.'

Strange that there is a mediaeval romance poem of Sir Cliges finding a cherry tree blossoming in December and taking a branch from it to the Uthyrpendragon at Cardiff Castle during this same, mid sixth-century era. (See The Cardiff Records).

In Book V. Ch 23. Gregory again tells of a comet and a plague:

> 'When I was celebrating mass on St Martin's eve which is 11th November, a remarkable portent was seen in the middle of the night. A bright star was seen shining in the very centre of the moon and other stars appeared close to the moon, above it and below. Round the moon stretched the circle, which is

usually the sign of rain. I have no idea what all this meant. This same year the moon often appeared in eclipse and there were loud claps of thunder just before Christmas. The meteors which country folk call suns and which were seen before the plague in Clermont Ferrand, as I told you in an earlier book, appeared around the sun. I was told that the sea rose higher than usual and there were many other signs and wonders.'

In yet another account Gregory Florentius of Tours describes a massive ball of fire in the sky. Book VI. Ch 25:

'In the city of Tours on the 31st January in the eighth year of King Childebert, this day being Sunday, the bell had just rung for matins. The people had got up and were on their way to church. The sky was overcast and it was raining. Suddenly a great ball of fire fell from the sky and moved some considerable distance through the air, shining so brightly that visibility was as clear as high noon. Then it disappeared once more behind a cloud and darkness fell again. The rivers rose much higher than usual. In the Paris region the river Seine and the river Marne were so flooded that many boats were wrecked between the city and the church of St Lawrence.'

Common features occur in all these accounts. Great lights and high tides and floods that may indicate gravitational pull exerted by this heavenly ball of fire, or something plunging into the ocean, and accompanying or subsequent pestilences.

As stated earlier, Gregory of Tours mentions two islands destroyed by fire. This is in his Book VIII, Ch 24, and he links the event chronologically with the elevation of a cleric Desiderius to be Bishop of Albigeois. The whole style of Gregory's writing is that he is dictating his recollections to another person. Frequently he says 'As I told you before' and 'As I have told you many times.' This would account for many of the apparent chronological deviations in the text. He names a Bishop Desiderius of Verdun appointed in 548, who would have been around at the era 555–562. One later bishop, Desiderius of Albi, appears to date around 580. The name Desiderius appears for six different people in *The History of the Franks*, five of them clergymen, and it is not possible to reconcile the burning of Britain and Ireland with the current dating of this later figure.

'This same year two islands in the sea were consumed by fire which fell from the sky. They burned for seven whole days so that they were completely destroyed, together with the inhabitants and their flocks. Those who sought refuge in the sea and hurled themselves into the deep, died an even worse death in the water into which they had thrown themselves, while those on land who did not die immediately were consumed by fire. All were reduced to ash and the sea covered everything. Many maintained that the portents which I said I earlier that I saw in the month of October, when the sky seemed to be on fire, were really the reflection of this conflagration.'

It must have been a colossal conflagration to be seen inland at Tours.

This account by Gregory of Tours has a remarkable similarity with the account of St Gildas in *De Excidio et Conquestu Britanniae*, which describes the almost total destruction of Britain by a comet. The British records very clearly have support from Gregory Bar Hebraeus citing John of Asia, as well as from Gregory of Tours.

The Beowulf Legend of England is clearly an allegorical account of the sixth-century comet disaster, as has been noted by several scholars, and identified as such by Blackett and Wilson. So also is the account identified by Michael Baillie in the Book of Leinster, where in the time of St Columkille (mid to late sixth century) a vast sea-monster washed ashore at the foot of Croagh Patrick mountain. Michael Baillie, quoting Joyce, states:

> 'He (the monster) was able to vomit in three different ways three years in succession. One year he turned up his tail, with his head buried deep down, he spewed the contents of his stomach into the water, in consequence of which all the fish died in that part of the sea, and curraghs and ships were wrecked and swamped. Next year he sank his tail into the water, and rearing his head high in the air, belched out such noisome fumes that all the birds fell dead. In the third year he turned his head shoreward and vomited towards the land, causing a pestilential vapour to creep over the country that killed men and four-footed animals.'

That this is a comet with its tail swinging around towards the sun under the sun's gravitational pull is unmistakable.

Too Much Evidence

Quite apart from the 'red herring' of dendrochronology, which caused Michael Baillie to allege that the Krakatoa eruption of 535-537 in the Pacific Ocean was the selective cause of the 562 comet destruction of Britain, there were other major problems. A major difficulty is that there is simply too much evidence available, and this volume only exhibits an overview to establish a correct scenario, and a working hypothesis. Huge areas of valid information remain unpublished, since books of three thousand or four thousand pages are impossible.

The intention is to stick as rigidly as possible to tracing the alphabet and matching the historical migration stories and trails to the areas where the alphabet is found. There was a major problem with American friends and associates, who were unable to restrain themselves from deluging the project with masses of unrelated data. Apart from the records of the Wallam Olam and the Leni Lenape, the detailed customs and cultural histories of dozens of native American tribal nations is generally totally unrelated to this study, and where it is related it can be dealt with later. Unless the alphabet links are proved correct, and DNA becomes a possibility, then all else remains speculative.

The result of the ongoing campaign of attrition being waged against the remarkably successful research project was a decision to slim down the project and to cut away from most contacts. Only a tiny number of associates would be kept. Two of the three offices in Alan's large house were stripped down in mid-1997, and when a removal skip was full, the remaining material, which was the most sensitive and useful material of the projects being abandoned, was burned over a period of three weeks. This left only the major core projects to be dealt with, some parts of which are in this volume.

Near and dear to Jim Michael's research heart are the Mellungians. Here there is yet another well-known but little-publicised mystery. When the first white explorers began pushing west out from the original colonial states along the Eastern Seaboard of the U.S.A. in the late eighteenth century, they were astonished to encounter large numbers of white people living scattered through the mid-west areas which became West Virginia, Kentucky, Tennessee, and Indiana, descended from white people who had lived there for centuries. These white people were known as the Mellungians, and they spoke a form of mixed dialect intelligible to English speakers. Problems over voting rights for these Mellungians arose in the late nineteenth and early twentieth centuries, as they were very clearly not native Americans (misnamed Indians), and neither were they new migrant white settlers of the modern era.

The question of where the Mellungians came from remains unanswered. One theory is that they descended from survivors of Sir Walter Raleigh's ill-fated settlement of 'The Lost Colony' of Roanoke in West Virginia in 1587. These settlers were landed and planted inside a fortified coastal stockade with some food supplies, and left for a year until a re-supply and a supporting relief fleet arrived from England to expand the colony on an annual basis. When the ships arrived in 1588, however, the houses behind the stockade all stood empty and the entire group had vanished without trace. Alan Wilson noted that the Mellungians still make a box guitar, identical with the ancient Welsh crwyth. Examples of the crwyth in Welsh museums and in an illustration in a book of 1784 were pointed out by Baram Blackett. There is literally no space even to attempt to examine the Mellungian mystery in this volume, but a main theory, with some substance, is that the settlers in Raleigh's attempted colony ran short of food. They were building up some links with some Native Americans at that time, and news of their arrival filtered inland. This resulted in their being contacted by some friendly but unknown groups or tribes, who for totally unexplained reasons, were motivated to travel to visit them and to assist them. The settlers then all left their desperate starvation situation at their fortified compound at Roanoke and went inland to live with these other unidentified groups. This much is known.

Whether they were visited and assisted by white descendants of the Arthur and Madoc expedition is conjecture, and investigations into the Mellungian origins have so far been limited. The Mellungians live in scattered communities in the more remote hill areas, and they are by nature somewhat reclusive and quiet folk. A private people, they were discovered by Daniel Boone and the early explorers of the mid-West wilderness, the mountain men. They still make and play the distinctive ancient style of Welsh crwyth, which was known over a thousand years before Columbus, and Alan Wilson had the pleasure of visiting and talking to some of the Mellungians in 1994. No Welsh academic could be found who had ever even heard of the Mellungians.

The *Tennessee Anthropologist* Volume XV, No 1. of 1990, published a survey of a 'Comparison of Gene Pool Frequency Distributions' which attempted to obtain matches with Mellungian and other national gene pools using the five basic blood type groupings. This concentrated upon probable Portuguese and English origins, and the survey included a group from Wales. The reliability of such a worthy attempt is compromised, however, by the huge population shifts and mixtures which have occurred in England and Wales since the dawn of the industrial revolution in 1760 and the present day, with intermarriage between the many races in Britain accelerating to an all-time peak in the mobile twentieth century. Alan Wilson is typical in having two very Welsh grandparents, one from North East England, and one of allegedly mixed Irish and Welsh descent. From the North East alone the mixture might be Old British, plus Angle, plus Danish Viking, and possibly Norman. How anyone could hope to get a representative native Welsh group of people with distinctive genes, unmixed with Ealde Cyrcenas, some Roman, Angles, Saxons, Irish, and others is difficult to see.

Conclusions that a mixture of 90% 'English' (which would be a mixture of Ealde Cyrcenas, Angles, Saxons, Jutes, Irish, Welsh, Scots, Danes, Normans, and a few others,) with 5% Native American, and 5% black blood types and genes might match the Mellungians do not appear to be solidly based. Particularly as the Mellungians do not have the genes which make sickle cell anaemia possible, as in black races. As the Mellungians are themselves possibly a mixture of the sixteenth-century mixed English stock of Raleigh's expedition, then further mixed with the mysterious group that adopted them, the situation is confused to say the least.

Wishing history

It took some time for Alan Wilson and Baram Blackett to grasp some of the prevailing problems in America. First, there is the residual antagonism of orthodox Roman-style Christians to the Mormon religion, which has given rise to a desire to obliterate any form of early pre-Columbus migrations from Europe to America that might support the Mormon faith. Then there is the more rational view that, as sites and artefacts still exist in numbers, it is unacceptable to pretend that they do not exist.

In order to make these sites and artefacts acceptable, even to themselves, a suitable origin has to be devised. This inevitably led to recourse to the 'lost' Ten Tribes of Israel, and theories were devised allowing for historical inventions of unrecorded Jewish fleets sailing over two thousand miles across the Mediterranean from Haifa, and then a further three thousand, five hundred miles to America. These wild theories depended largely on the strange stroke alphabet found in the Americas being likened to, and then identified as, ancient Hebrew.

Another line of thinking developed, which got around the problems raised by Joseph Smith and Mormon religion, resulting in Christian unease and conflict. This more ambitious theorising proposed that the inscriptions in America were pre-Christian, but instead of being Hebrew, they were Carthaginian-Phoenician, from five hundred years before the dawn of Christianity, or otherwise 'Celtic' from non-Celtic Ireland or Britain. Everyone wants history to have been be the way they wish that it had been, and not as it actually was. Rather like Edwin Guest at Cambridge and Bishop Stubbs at Oxford.

Into this stew of theorising came an expansion of the factual reality that Leif Ericsson, the son of Eric the Red, had reached Labrador and Nova Scotia, and had sailed south to a place somewhere near Maryland. Therefore, all the strange stroke alphabet inscriptions could be claimed as Viking runes, despite the fact that they are plainly not Viking runes. Scots and Irish wanted the inscriptions to be

Ogham and Irish, even 'Celtic', despite the fact the Ogham is also found widely in Wales, and the inscriptions are plainly not Ogham at all. Portuguese immigrants then wanted to see all the ancient symbols as having an ancient unrecorded Portuguese origin. It is in fact a 'Tower of Babel' situation.

The result is a frantic searching in all directions, for any and all manner of scraps of possible evidence or ancient quotations which might give some form of support to each and every cause. For Alan Wilson and Baram Blackett, it was like trying to walk in a straight line across a crowded dance floor with everyone else gyrating and milling around in all directions. The straight line is the pursuit of inscriptions, which are carved or scratched in the ancient British Coelbren alphabet, and the decipherment of those inscriptions in a consistent coherent manner that stands up to examination.

It is said that the Americans, having broken Japanese secret codes, were in possession of every detail of the planned attack on Pearl Harbour in December 1941, before the attack took place. They had so many thousands of other pieces of decoded information of all sorts flooding in daily however, that they were not able to 'sort the wheat from the chaff' quickly enough to put the picture together. Presumably someone failed to establish any system of classifying incoming information in A – Urgent, B - Important, C - Interesting, D - Routine, or whatever, by early recognition of source and to a vitally important, type. Trying to sort out an ancient historical picture or scenario in America poses exactly the same problems. There is, for most researchers, far too much peripheral information clouding the mind.

Both sides of the Atlantic having parallel-style 'snake mounds', 'hill forts', and 'grave mounds' is front-line information. They are clearly similar, but they could still be of independent parallel development. Artefacts that have incised crosses are not necessarily Christian, as the design of the cross as simple ornamentation, or even as spelling, are not solely peculiar to Christianity. The cross appears on very early Egyptian hieroglyphic inscriptions, and elsewhere around the world. Skeletal differences are evidence, but the argument has been stood on its head by archaeological somersaults that now claim that there must have been two Native American racial types, one of Siberian-Mongolian extraction, and the other of Caucasian original American. Mummies and woven cloths, and copper smelting, not done by ancient Native Americans are evidence, but can be ignored. The only thing that is conclusive and decisive is the complex alphabet and its decipherments in a developed and surviving language, supported by native histories in both Wales and America.

Next, there is academic chicanery that seems to be directed at damage limitation. There can be no doubt whatsoever that Leif Ericsson reached Northern America as is being proved by archaeological investigations at L'Anse Aux Meadows. So, the second line of defence is Leif Ericsson before Columbus and no one else at any costs. Vikings only, is the new position. To support their collapsing edifice of theory the academics at Yale University authenticated a remarkable 'discovery' in 1965. In a manuscript book, said to date from 1449, was found what was said to be a contemporary fifteenth century map of the Atlantic, which showed the areas of Newfoundland, Nova Scotia and the eastern seaboard of North America, described in the Icelandic Vinland Sagas. Here was proof positive of Viking achievement before Christopher Columbus, and no one else, except of course Columbus some four hundred years later. Viking voyages and Viking histories are popular.

The manuscript is titled *The Tartar Relation*, and it bears signs of worm holes, but it took some time before a brave soul pointed out that the worm holes in the Vinland Map and the worm holes in the manuscript book did not match up. Yale University was in receipt of this 'evidence' at a moment when perhaps too coincidentally, it also received a copy of an earlier work titled the *Speculum Historiale*, which also happened to have worm holes similar to those in *The Tartar Relation* and its Vinland Map. So, the 'experts' at Yale University formed the opinion that the Vinland Map was almost certainly authentic.

However, when the Tartar Relation and its Vinland Map were published, numbers of people raised doubts and criticisms. Three years later, under mounting pressure of this criticism, Yale appointed an independent team of investigators, and in 1974 Yale was forced to admit that the Vinland map was a fake. Tests showed that the inks used in both manuscripts were made of ingredients used in mediaeval times. The inks used on the Vinland map however, also showed elements that were not in use until after the 1920's.

Then there is the case of the Kensington Stone, which was once proudly exhibited in the Smithsonian Museum. This is a stone weighing two hundred pounds, or over fourteen stone, which bears a runic eight-line inscription claiming to detail a fourteenth-century Viking expedition to America. This expedition is not recorded in European sources. This stone was 'discovered' by one Olaf Ohman in 1989, entangled in the roots of a tree on his farm near Kensington in Minnesota. The academic opinion is almost wholly that this stone is a hoax, and in 1974 the ageing children of Olaf Ohman's neighbour confessed that their father had helped Ohman to carve these Runic inscriptions.

Chapter 21 - Conclusions

The first experts to see this stone instantly labelled it as a fake, and accusations of fraud were made against the Scandinavian Ohman and his neighbours, who were clearly trying to promote their own ancestry. Linguistic experts insisted that certain colloquial expressions only developed in nineteenth-century Minnesota. This did not prevent the Smithsonian Institution from displaying the stone in 1948-49, and it is presently kept in Douglas County Museum in Minnesota. Anyone who has looked at and handled large numbers of anciently inscribed stones would be compelled to have the gravest doubts over this inscription, which is far too neatly set out. In stating this, it is a fact that several sixth-century stones, known to be authentic, retain sharp incisions in the lettering which look as if they could have been carved within the past decade.

Nothing matching either of these alleged frauds has ever been exposed against British Khumric history, yet in stark contrast to the mistreatment of the British records and artefacts, these frauds have done no damage at all to Viking histories. Alan Wilson had the quite extraordinary experience of re-reading American reports on the Vinland Map fraud and the Kensington Stone fraud on 15th November 1999, and then, later that same afternoon, watching a programme on the Sky TV History Channel extolling the wonders of the proven forgery of the Vinland Map and Viking achievements.

The inaccuracy of the 'experts' on these television history channel programmes is of course legendary. Unfortunately, most people get their ideas on history from television and films. One programme, on Richard III of England, hilariously labels Henry VII Tudor as the son of the English Henry VI, when every schoolchild knows he was the son of Edmund Tudor and grandson of Owen Tudor, who married the dowager Queen Catherine of France, the widow of Henry V. Another television offering on British castles, made by academics, asserts that Britain's second largest castle, built at Caerphilly in South East Wales by Gilbert de Clare in 1268, was never taken. Llewellyn ap Gruffydd demolished it in 1270, and of course Owain Glyndwr captured this immense structure in *c.* AD 1406. It is all part of the same centuries'-old negative propaganda campaign.

Most remarkable is the widely shown television programme which several times makes the provably incorrect claim that the use of the Native American Navajo language by the United States Marine Corps as a base for their encoded messages, is the only instance of an unbroken military code in World War II. In World War I the English recruited large numbers of educated Welshmen into their Intelligence Corps, and their military codes were all made using the Khumric Welsh language, which they so despised and had sought to obliterate for centuries.

The Germans were totally baffled by Khumric, and they were completely totally baffled by encoded Khumric, and right throughout the four years of warfare these codes were never broken. One would think that someone might have learned something from this.

These Viking promotional fakes in America have done absolutely nothing to damage the unfounded ideas of Viking interior exploration and settlement in the USA; they have, paradoxically, served to support the propaganda alleging everything else to be faked. It is entirely similar to the scandal of the huge nineteenth-century Ossian forgeries by Macpherson that could have resulted in immense harm being done to both Irish and Scots ancient History, and perhaps resulted in their being consigned to the dustbin. Instead, neither Irish nor Scots heritage suffered any damage at all as a result of these colossal forgeries. Paradoxically it was the authentic, never forged, and remarkably accurate British-Khumric histories that were deliberately targeted for destruction. Laughably some American researchers still quote the known and admitted Ossian forgeries as if they were genuine. The problem now in America is that a number of known forgeries made by Viking and Christian enthusiasts have served to damage the entire field of study in every other direction.

It took some time for Wilson and Blackett to realise that some ardent Christians saw the opportunity of solving the apparent problem of the disappearance of the lost Ten Tribes of Israel at one fell swoop, and were prepared to give their belief a helping hand with the time-honoured practice of forgery. What happened to the lost Ten Tribes? Well, they sailed straight off to America and here is a carved inscription to prove it.

It was absolutely extraordinary for Wilson and Blackett to read on Page 11 of the Volume *Ancient American Inscriptions* by five members of the Early Sites Research Society published in 1993:

> 'Schoolcraft noted the resemblance of the inscribed characters to a number of Mediterranean alphabets, but he thought that they were closest to the Bardic alphabet of the Celts, known from the so called 'Stick Book', an analogy noted by others.' (Barnhart 1986: 106).

This 'Stick Book' can only mean the British Khumric Coelbren alphabet and the Peithynen wooden stick frame. Thereafter, in four hundred and thirteen pages, no attempt whatsoever is made to investigate this in any way. Instead, there is a concentration on Ogham despite a passage on Page 119 quoting McManus:

'The history of Ogham has to be tentative in many respects owing to the nature of the evidence available to us.'

'Where, when, and by whom the Ogham alphabet was invented is not known. What can be said, however, with certainty is that Ogham existed already in the fifth century (AD) as a monumental script.'

'The nature of the Ogham script is such that it is impossible to pinpoint its source of inspiration or to identify its formers in time and space with any degree of accuracy.'

'...had the (Ogham script's) inventors set out with the intention of completely covering their tracks and presenting an enigma to modern scholarship they could scarcely have been more successful.' (McManus).

The facts are that Ogham appears on stones in those areas of Ireland and Wales that appear to have been influenced by the Cuneda in Wales, and his sons, notably Ceredig in Ireland.

After AD 434, Ceredig is the prince heavily criticised by St Patrick for his mistreatment of the Irish. This would account for the absence of any traditional pedigree for Ogham as an alleged alphabet. In addition, very few of the American inscriptions bear any resemblance to Ogham at all, and everything points to Ogham having a probable musical rather than a linguistic origin. Furthermore, an origin in the fifth century AD is hardly ancient at all given the current progress of investigations.

A number of areas remain to be explored, and most are well known to researchers. These include the lighthouse of Newport Tower, at Newport, Rhode Island, which Alan Wilson visited with Dan Dimancescu of Boston. There is a fireplace on the upper storey of this structure on the landward side, which is opposite windows on the seaward sides. This arrangement is well known in the ancient world, and these strategically placed windows would permit shafts of light to be seen at night from ships at sea, from known angles. There is also one inscribed stone visible in the upper storey interior wall, which appears to be in Coelbren, and may tentatively be read as 'The Prince's light'.

The Sword of Constantine

There is one remarkable artefact which needs to be detailed before ending this Odyssey along the alphabet trail. In 1993 part of an old house built around 1650 was being demolished in Pennsylvania. Out of the wall being demolished there fell an ancient sword. This sword was clearly much older than 1650, and there was also a Christian cross emblem on the blade and an inscription running down one side of the blade. The sword was sold off at a moderate price to a man from Texas. The story may please all those who love the Arthurian legends and tales of the sword Caliburn or Excalibur.

Jim Michael and Alan Wilson were sitting having breakfast together at La Grange, Kentucky, in 1994, when a letter arrived containing photostats of photographs of this inscribed sword. It was immediately obvious from examination under a magnifying glass that the writing on the sword blade was a Coelbren inscription. Jim Michael sent an urgent request for large, good-quality photographs immediately, which soon arrived. The question was, 'why was an ancient Coelbren-inscribed sword hidden buried inside a wall built around 1650 in Pennsylvania?' Alan Wilson had the answer.

As historians Baram Blackett and Alan Wilson were both aware of the stories of the Sword of Constantine, the great talisman of the British. The story is as follows. When, in 55 BC and 54 BC, Julius Caesar invaded Britain and suffered major humiliating defeats at the hands of the British Caswallon = Viceroy, he suffered also a personal humiliation. In one major battle, Julius Caesar, who often positioned himself in the front three ranks of his army, was targeted by the British Prince Nynniaw-Nennius. The objective may have been to kill Caesar and so demoralise the entire Roman army, but as they clashed together Caesar took a swing at Nennius with his sword and hit him on the helmet. Nennius raised his shield high and when Caesar swung at him again, his sword became stuck tight, embedded in the thick leather shield Nennius was carrying. Caesar could not get his sword out, and in the rush and press around them, and with legionaries trying to save him, they were pushed apart. Metal shields were for ceremonial use, and would split too easily, and shields of seven to ten layers of bull's hide were used in battle throughout history.

So Nennius, who was wounded in the head and died fifteen days later, had captured Julius Caesar's sword, and this became a national trophy for the British, held by the citizens of Caer Troia - London. Later in AD 310, the British Constantine the Great, son of the Queen Empress Helen of the Cross and Constantine Chlorus the Emperor of Rome, sailed from Britain with the army to conquer his rivals and Rome, and to establish Constantinople as the new capital, and he had a sword. Now whether this was Julius Caesar's sword or another is not known. There was however the ancient sword held in London.

Centuries later the Sword of Constantine reappeared when it was gifted to the

Chapter 21 - Conclusions

English King Athelstane of Wessex (AD 894 – 940) by Hugh the Earl of Flanders, whose sister was to marry Athelstane. The embassy to Athelstane was led by Adulf son of Baldwin, Earl of Flanders, who was presumably Hugh's brother, and who was a descendant of King Alfred of Wessex. This is detailed by William of Malmsbury. Later the Sword of Constantine appears, mentioned as such, in a letter from Athelstane to the Bishop of Rome, and coins of Athelstane show him holding the sword. Later it re-emerges in historical records as one of two ceremonial swords listed as owned by King John, and this may explain coins of English kings showing them holding two upright swords.

The Sword of Constantine became an integral part of English coronation regalia, and was in use until Oliver Williams, *alias* Cromwell, defeated and executed Charles I of England in 1649. This victory of the Commonwealth overthrow of the King and the Royal Party was an occasion for looting the Crown Jewels and regalia. Everything went, and so the new Government advertised across Britain and Europe, offering substantial cash rewards, without penalty or question, for the return of these jewels and regalia. Everything came back except one item, and that lost item was the Sword of Constantine.

So, an ancient British national relic in the form of a sword went missing in 1649 and in 1993 an ancient sword inscribed in ancient British Coelbren fell out of a wall in a house built around 1650 in Pennsylvania. This was an area of rapidly expanding colonisation at that time. The British Parliament's advertisements probably never reached America, and if some fleeing royalist, or an acquisitive Parliamentarian, took it and hid it, he either didn't want to return it to Cromwell, or he didn't hear of the offer. This is set out on pages 376 - 384 of *The Holy Kingdom* paperback version.

There were two ancient regalia swords, and Athelstane would have needed two, as he called himself 'Rex Totius Britanniae', or King of the whole of Britain. One would be for Lloegres - England, and the other for the Khumry spread from Cornwall and Wales up through Lancashire and Cumberland to Strathclyde. In 1857 another inscribed sword was dredged up from the mud of the River Thames. This sword is inscribed in what is called 'Anglo-Saxon', and the Sword is dated to the ninth century, which is Athelstane's era.

This is described by Guy Tredaniel in *Energies Sacrées les Runes*, Chapter XI, 1991, page 173, ISBN -2-85707-425-5, (his source, 'Scramasax' cours de runologie, Paris IV). So there are two ancient inscribed swords, and there was another hunt for what was written on the blade of the second sword, and to decipher this.

The clear inscription on the American-owned sword can be deciphered perfectly into Coelbren, and reads:

'The duty of the host (= army) is to him who holds the sword.'

The American owner of the sword is a most reasonable person and is willing to return the sword to Britain for proper conservancy and exhibition, but Wilson and Blackett, in trying to arrange this, are finding that the British museums are frightened of the idea. If this had been a Greek urn or sword, or Roman, Assyrian, or Egyptian artefacts, they would have all been jumping up and down with joy, but the idea of British relics of this magnitude induces paralysis. It seems obvious there is a solid basis for ideas about the great sword Caliburn-Excalibur, but 1857, when Edwin Guest and Bishop Stubbs were in full cry demolishing all ancient British national records and traditions, it was not an appropriate time to find an ancient inscribed sword in the river Thames.

Whether or not the other sword, now in Texas, is the Sword of Constantine or simply an ancient sword, the clear Coelbren inscription running down the blade once again demolishes the accusation that the ancient British Coelbren Alphabet was a creation forged around 1800. It could hardly have been hidden inside the wall of a house built around 1650 if the alphabet was not created until 1800. Any reasonable sane person would think that the sword is highly likely to be that of Constantine, but the constantly negative attitude towards British history and heritage in British colleges overrides sanity.

In 1995, Alan Wilson and Baram Blackett switched over to dealing with the enjoyable task of writing the necessary historical novels as they alone were in possession with facts concerning Arthurian history. They had the pleasant task of dealing with the Trojan War of around 650 BC, following Virgil, Horace, Flavius Josephus, the Frankish histories, the British histories, and other deciphered information, and what is called 'Hittite' history. They also indulged themselves in more personally interesting pursuits in the huge area of directional hidden messages in the ancient sources. Another interesting area is that no one seems to have noticed that the ancestral figure Aballach is invariably named as the son of Alfech-Alpheus in the British records, and as Alpheus is the second husband of Mary the mother of Jesus the Nazarene, this makes Aballach his half-brother. The name Aballach is the equivalent of Valentinian, and one of the major early forms of Christianity is Valentinianism. As a document in the Nag Hammadi Gnostic Christian library contains a description of Valentinianism exhibiting an exact parallel with the British Druidic beliefs, matters become interesting. At the same time, they put into motion the plan to sell up in Wales and to move out of the lunatic area, and then they launched ongoing legal actions against some of their worst tormentors. (The finds of the Holy Family coming to Britain after the Crucifixion and starting Christianity there, rather than Rome, is detailed in the now published *Where Jesus is Buried*.)

Nothing Changes

The present attempts to show British history as Anglo-Saxon imaginary history written large will inevitably fail. British history is not going to go away and vanish no matter how hard the die-hard pro-Roman and pro-Anglo-Saxon academics try to achieve this disappearing trick. Nothing has changed over the twenty-eight years of Alan Wilson and Baram Blackett's co-operative labours. In late 1998 archaeologists discovered the remains of a vast monumental arch buried near Ludgate in London. The British histories assert that King Lludd built a vast monumental arch on this very same spot in celebration of the British victories over Julius Caesar. Common sense demands that this is King Lludd's arch, but having only two labels available to them the archaeologists were unable to call it 'Saxon', and so they obediently designated King Lludd's arch as 'Roman'. In the same way when a huge monumental wall of a citadel was found deep down underneath 'Roman' London this was ignored totally. In 1840-41, during excavations at the junction of Gophir Lane and Bush Lane to build London's sewers, a buried wall twenty-two feet thick was discovered six feet down. The diggers dug down a further sixteen feet without reaching the bottom of the wall. Amazing as it seems the archaeological establishment, which is heavily and almost totally dependent on Government funding, still assures the public that there was no Troia Newydd.

London was known as Caer Troia and Troia Newydd, or New Troy, rather like New York, and traditionally reputed to be founded by Brutus. Just as Rome has its Lapis Niger Foundation Stone (plastered with Etruscan = British Coelbren writing) which is carefully preserved in a museum in Rome, so London has its London Stone. This ancient stone is mentioned in an 1188 reference to Henry son of Elwin de Londonstane. In AD 1450, Jack Cade, who was almost certainly Sion O'Ceint, and John Mortimer, took an oath by ceremonially striking London Stone with his sword. This heritage stone is not carefully kept in any museum, but instead was the subject of official vandalism. After centuries of standing on ground now fronting Cannon Street Station, it was moved in 1742 and set in the wall of St Swithin's church. This was the period when the onslaught on British history was beginning. The top one third was cut off and the bottom two thirds remained buried (under Cannon Street) to allow for road widening. They did not even have the decency to remove it whole. St Swithin's Church was demolished in 1960, and the cut-off fragment of London Stone now lies in its own glazed chamber in the wall of the recently redeveloped 111 Cannon Street.

For centuries, Londoners entered the cellars of the Merlyn's Cave Tavern, and were taken through the entry into the cave systems under Parliament Hill which were known as Merlyn's Cave. This also ceased around 1910 when the caves were sealed up, and no one in modern times has entered these caves. As eternal optimists Alan Wilson and Baram Blackett would like to know if there are any grooves and scratches of ancient lettering anywhere there, or anything else. There is more. It is a great pity that modern scholars are compelled to remain shackled by the chains of mental bondage forged by Edwin Guest, Bishop Stubbs, and their adherents and followers. Their personal loss is only eclipsed by the loss inflicted upon the British nation.

Chapter Twenty-Two

The Reaction in Wales

In 1903, the Records Committee of Cardiff Corporation acted at the behest of the city fathers of the Aldermen and Councillors to publish the Cardiff Records. These were selections from the city archives, records, and memorials, and the local South Wales history. These Cardiff records were edited by John Hobson Matthews.

What they have to say is interesting, and especially so in the light of the wholesale takeover of the Welsh education system by the London Government in the mid- nineteenth century. Typically, silent Welsh fight-backs were taking place in the cathedral and chapels. In Llandaff Cathedral the huge window at the east end behind the altar exhibits named heads of the kings of Israel, starting with David and Solomon and finishing with the coat of arms of King Iestyn ap Gwrgan (Justin, son of Aurelian) who was deposed in 1091. The message sent in this large stained-glass window is very clear and unmistakeable.

In the north wall close to the altar - in the right hand of God position - they erected stained-glass windows which depicted King Tewdrig Uthyrpendragon the grandfather of King Arthur ap Meurig, and King Arthur II himself carrying the Cross on his shoulder, and a window depicting King 'Cadwallader', or Battle Sovereign. Other windows show important sixth-century saints, who were close relatives of these kings. Other similar stained-glass windows were erected in the largest chapel in West Glamorgan. What they were doing was placing records of the banned histories of South East Wales in untouchable places for everyone to see. Ancient British Welsh history was thus silently preserved in the face of the obliteration following forcible annexation in 1536.

The Cardiff Records list and remember the ancient kings, and on page 19 of Volume IV we find:

> 'Now of these Lords before the time of Robert Fitzhammon there was one Chief Lord of Glamorgan whose were the high royalties, and he assembled the other lords every month to his court where all manner of justice were determined and finally settled. These lords sat in judgement on all matters of

law, and twelve free-holders from every lordship to give opinions after what came to their knowledge, and the Bishop of Llandaff sat in the High Court as a Councillor of Conscience according to the Laws of God. This court formed they say by Morgan who was Prince of the country after King Arthur, in the manner of Christ and his twelve Apostles.'

The list of the kings from Morgan Mwynfawr on to Iestyn ap Gwrgan then follows, with notations on their reigns. On page 23 of Volume IV of the Cardiff Records we find:

'Now the county of Glamorgan came to be first a royal lordship from one Morgan a Prince who lived in the time of King Arthur and was his son as some have it, others say he was a cousin of Arthur. Now as to this county it passed in the family from the said Morgan down to Iestyn the son of Gwrgant, which Gwrgant was Prince or Lord of Glamorgan.'

A plethora of impeccably authentic British ancient manuscript and charter records place Morgan Mwynfawr as the successor, either as a nephew or son, of Arthur ap Meurig ap Tewdrig. At this time in 1903, Cardiff was expanding and growing rapidly and it was a time of massive inwards migration from many non-Welsh areas. There was in fact a growing number of immigrant English being elected to serve as councillors and aldermen, and the city council was split into the two factions of the indigenous Welsh and the immigrant English. Squabbles arose, including the crass re-naming of very ancient city streets at the time of Queen Victoria's fiftieth jubilee. The ancient Crockherbtown became the mundane Queen Street, and the Miskin Gate became another boring Kingsway, careless of any Welsh heritage. These street names were ancient as shown by Hunmanby Street, now Womanby Street, the street of Viking traders. Universally towns and cities preserve their ancient street names of eight hundred, one thousand or more years' standing as part of local heritage, but not if immigrants who care nothing for any culture other than their own get to dominate.

The native Welsh faction was acting swiftly to preserve what they could in their native city records. They printed the recorded histories, and they also recorded strange folk remembrances and romantic mentions. On page xi of the introduction to Volume IV, Chapter I, there is:

Chapter 22 - The Reaction in Wales

CARDIFF IN RELATION TO ARTHURIAN ROMANCE, by T.H.Thomas.

'Ancient Welsh literature and the Romances of the Arthurian Cycle furnish so many notices of Glamorgan and Cardiff that it seems fitting that a few, relating definitely to the city should find a place in the "Cardiff Records".

These have no claim whatsoever to be considered historical, yet they indicate the important position assigned to Cardiff in the minds of writers or redactors of the stories as early as the twelfth century to the fifteenth.'

A very quaint MS poem in the Advocates Library in Edinburgh was first published by Henry Weber in *Metrical Romances, etc., Vol. I.*, Edinburgh 1810, and is entitled *Sir Cliges*. In this we find Uther Pendragon, father of King Arthur, established at Cardiff. Of Sir Cliges it is said:

'He dwellyd be Kardyfe syde.'

Having fallen into poverty through boundless hospitality, he is saved by a miraculous growth of cherries at Christmastide, which he takes to the king at the advice of his wife Clarys, who says:

'Ye shill to Cardyffe to the kynge And yeve hym present; And seche a yefte ye may have there, That the better wee may fare all this yere: I tell you weramont.' Sir Cliges graunted sone thereto; 'To moroun to Cardiffe will I goo, After your entent.'

A story in *The Mabinogi* describes local topography accurately around Cardiff. This is the story of Geraint and the Maiden Enid. After the insult given to the lady of Queen Guinevere at the hunt for the white stag, Geraint follows the armed knight through the river Usk at Caerleon westwards, and proceeds

'along a fair, and even, and lofty ridge of ground' arriving at a town 'which is now called Cardiff' where 'at the extremity of the town they saw a fortress and a castle,'

This is a true, general description of the old town of Cardiff. The description of the house of the Earl Ynywl where dwelt Enid is such that it can only be looked for in the neighbourhood of Roath, a British name that implies an ancient fortress. Thus, we may claim Enid as a Cardiff maiden, and the Joust of the Sparrow-Hawk, where Edeyrn ab Nudd was defeated by Geraint ab Erbyn, must have taken place in 'the meadow' which extended around the site of the present City Hall of Cardiff. It may be added that the description of the costume of Geraint (unarmed in the story referred to) coincides with the appearance of a British rider sculpted upon the base of the very ancient cross to be seen in the churchyard of Llandough near Cardiff.

Roath is almost certainly the Welsh 'rhaith' meaning 'law courts', and this fits with other records. The term 'rath' meaning a 'fort' is Irish and not Welsh. The great ridge which was travelled on is almost certainly the old road from Bassalleg through to St Mellon's running past the Druid Stone. The ancient stone at Llandough names a King Erbic - Erbin who ruled around AD 400.

A further story, having its scene in and near Cardiff, occurs in Malory's *Morte D'Arthur*. It tells how

'Kynge Arthur came in to the forest perillous by the meanes of a lady her name was Annowre and this lady came to Kynge Arthur at Cardyf.'

The King rode with her, but repenting, left her. He was set upon by two knights, and the lady attempted to slay him in revenge for the slight. The lady of the lake, Nimue, aware by second sight of his danger, found Sir Tristram, who rescued the King, and Annowre was slain. Nimue rode away with her head tied to her saddle-bow.

Again, Book V, Cap IX. of *Le Morte D'Arthur* recites how King Arthur

'after the grete bataylle acheved ageynste the Romayns' entered into 'hault Almayn',

and so to Italy and besieged a city of Tuscany, which was defended valiantly, so that he 'lacked vytaylle'. He called Sir Florence, a knight, and bade him

'tak with the syr Gawayn my newev, Syre wysshard, syre Clegys, Syre Cleremond, and the Captayn of Cardef with other and brynge with yow alle the beestes that ye there can gete.'

And these knights did doughty deeds and

'token grete plente of bestyal of gold and sylver and grete tresour and rychesse and retorned unto kynge Arthur' (*ibid.*, Chap XI.)

At this moment it might be well to note that Cardiff Castle was first founded in AD 74, and that the King Arthur who made war in Italy in AD 383 was Arthur I son of Magnus Maximus and his first wife Ceindrech. So, there was a great fortress standing here for King Meurig Uthyr Pendragon and his son Arthur II to use.

Also found in Malory is the story of the return of Queen Guinevere with Lancelot to Caerleon and the resulting break-up of the Round Table. Lancelot ('le ancelot' = 'the servant,' naturally mutates to 'l'ancelot'), with a hundred knights sworn never to leave him

> 'for wele nor for wo' departed and 'shypped at Cardyf and sayled unto Benwyk.' (Book XX, VIII)

Then in pursuit King Arthur and Sir Gawaine

> "made a grete boost redy to the nombre of thre score thousand and al thynge was made redy for that shyppyng to passe over the see and so they shypped at Cardyf and there kynge Arthur made sir Mordred ehyef ruler of alle Englond and also he put Guenever under his governance and soo the kynge passed the see." (*ibid.*, XIX.)

The enormous stone port at Cardiff lying on the edge of the Afallach = Orchard Levels is buried in the mud flats. The land almost certainly sank at the same time as several other known areas, at the time of the comet débris impacts of AD 562. Parts of this huge ancient sunken harbour were found when the Alexandra and Roath docks were being built around 1900, and the great sunken port is shown on local city maps drawn in 1859. Naturally this does not appear on Government Ordnance Survey maps.

Another brief note in the *Morte D'Arthur* refers to

> 'sire Lamyel of Cardyf that was a grete lover,'

but we have some of his adventures extant. (Book XIX, Cap. XI.)

In Wharton's *History of English Poetry* are found some extracts from the romance of *Ywain and Gawain*, from which we find that:

> 'King Arthur
> He made a feste, the sothe to say Upon the Witsononday,
> At Kerdyf that es in Wales.'

The episode quoted is *The adventure of the enchanted forest attempted by Sir Colgrevance,* which he relates to the knights of the round table at Cardiff in Wales.

These stories contemplate Cardiff as having been a residence of King Uther Pendragon and Arthur, and as being a port of entry and departure in time of war. It may be suggested that the reason was that, although Caerleon was itself a port, the long course of the River Usk to the sea was not safe in troublesome times, as vessels thereon were within bowshot or slingshot, while to Cardiff there was an open hill-road and a safe passage to the mouth of the Taff River commanded by the fortress at Cardiff.

It will have been noticed that these stories attribute the possession of the castle to Uther Pendragon, King Arthur, the Earl Ynywl the father of Enid, the Knight Edeyrn ab Nudd (by fraud), King Arthur restoring it to Earl Ynywl. *The Fabulliau of Sir Cliges* adds that King Uther made it a gift to that knight. The above notes were collected by Professor Littledale, Mr W. P. James, Rev. R. Butterworth, and the writer.

As Arthur II ap King Meurig ap King Tewdrig, etc., was a reigning Glamorgan king, he would have used Cardiff Castle, no matter who was appointed to maintain and guard the fortress. The main residence, as with the other kings, would have been at Caer Melyn (Norman French Ca' Melot) in north-east Cardiff, about four miles from Cardiff Castle. This is at Lisvane – Llys Faen = 'the stone court', which was also known as Cu Bwrd, 'the mutually together table'. It is also probable that the mountain top Morgraig Castle, now in ruin in a wood, about five miles north of Cardiff Castle was also in use.

When the mass of evidence preserved in the Cathedral and Abbey charters, the Triads, the ancient epic poetry, the Histories, the multitudinous royal and noble genealogies, the inscribed stones, and the place names, ancient forts, grave mounds, and battle fields are also taken into account, what we have is a very well-preserved local history and tradition.

A Booke of Glamorganshire's Antiquities by Rice Merrick, Esq.

This record written by Rice Merrick (Rhys Meurug) and published by Sir T. Phillips in 1578 has been several times reprinted since it was edited and published by James Andrew Corbett in 1887. It contains much historical and topographical information and also several interesting genealogies. On page 7 of Corbett's book there is one of Iestyn ap Gwrgan:

> 'This Justin is said to have had two principall houses or habitacions, wherein bee delighted most to continue, viz, the Castle of Cardiff, being the Cheife Seat of the Signory of Morganwg, And the Castle of (b) Dynaspowys, In honour of his first Wife Denys, Daughter of Blethin ap Cynpin [Bleddyn ap Cynfyn] Prince of Powys, & otherwise comonly called Denys Powys: Witnesse my Genealogicall Manuscript, page 43. The Principall house of the L. of Glamorgan: Where in the first, he kept his Christmas by the space of many yeares; and in the last his

Easters and Whittsontides, - whose Pedigree breefly ensueth.

Justin the Sonne of Gwrgant, Sonne of Ythel (Ithael), Sane of Morgan Moynvawz, Sonne of Owayn, Sonne of Howell, Sonne of Rs, [Rhys], Sonne of Arvaell [Arthfael], Sonne of Gyriad, [Gweirydd-Gwyriad], Sonne of Brichvaell [Brochwael], Sonne of Myrig [Meurig], Sonne of Arthvael, Sonne of Rys [Rhys], Sonne of Hyddhael [Ithael], Sonne of Morgan, Sonne of Adroes [Arthur II], Sonne of Myrig vap Tewdrig [Meurig ap Tewdrig], who was the first founder of the Church of Landaph.' [Llandaff Cathedral].

Such as are disposed to know farther, I remit them to bookes which treat of genealogies, who derive him from Alanys, the 3 Sonne of Camber, Sonne of Brutus. Etc. etc.'

This sums up the entire local tradition; and the genealogies of Arthur son of Maurice (Meurig), son of Theoderic (Tewdrig), are multitudinous. This descent is quoted by hundreds of authors in the eighteenth and nineteenth centuries and it was clearly regarded as a commonplace, and no mystery or argument about it. King Arthur II was simply a Glamorgan-Gwent king, and everyone west of the border knew it as certainly as Alexander the Great was a Macedonian, and Julius Caesar was a Roman. The idea that Arthur ap Meurig ap Tewdrig, etc., would be kidnapped and hauled off to places in England, Scotland, and France, and finally become a Hungarian and a Mongolian in inventions of financially motivated authors would never have occurred to any of them.

The British were not an ancient disparate collection of primitive barbarians, otherwise there would have been not have been centuries of Imperial Roman and royal British noble intermarriages. The British are descendants of two very ancient, highly civilised, cultured, and literate nations. The most priceless relics of the British are their ancient Gutian - Gewissae – 'Wessex' culture and Iceni Language of England, and the Khumric language and the Coelbren alphabet. These are the tools to unlock the imprisoned past. British ancient history is a 'History in Bondage', and the persistent attempts to denigrate and obliterate these marvels have to be rejected and disowned.

Hundreds, even thousands, of educated scholars scattered over hundreds of miles did not collaborate for over a thousand years to fabricate, invent, and forge a completely interlocking, faked, false British history. They did not invent the Cathedral and Abbey Charters, the Triads, the histories, the epic poetry, the multitudinous genealogies, the inscribed stones, the great tomb mounds, the silent ancient battlefields with their war dead cemeteries, and the named ruined fortresses. Nor did they invent countless meaningful field names for the tithe maps, which hold the history written on the land itself. Neither did they invent and fabricate the ancient Coelbren alphabet in circa 1800, for which Julius Caesar and Ammianus Marcellinus can be called as witnesses. The total impossibility of this massive libel and slander is obvious to any person, except those with the outdated nineteenth-century mind-set.

We can have Camelot again in a new Britain, but the price we have to pay is to tell the truth. There is a political expression:

'let him who would tell the truth declare war upon the world.'

Frankly this is a lie, and only a politician could invent it.

William Shakespeare and the letter sent to Gaul

Very rarely do Alan Wilson and Baram Blackett indulge themselves in hypothesis as a means of progress. Their preferred approach is methodically to analyse the records, visit the sites, and see what emerges. As an exercise in light relief, they decided to see what they could do to discover who sent the famous letter from Britain to Afranius Syagrius Flavius Aegidius, King of the Seven Cities in Gaul, in around AD 474, upon which much of Dark Age history depends, and why it might have been sent.

The various British histories all affirm that a letter was sent to Gaul around AD 474, and that this letter sought military assistance. Whom the letter was sent to has long been mistaken, as the recipient named as Agitus by Gildas in his *De Excidio*, and as Aganypus in the *Brut Tysilio* and *Brut Gruffydd ap Arthur*, was misidentified as the Roman Aetius in a deliberate exercise in political correctness. That the British would have written to their Roman enemies for support is a total nonsense. There is therefore a need to find what might link some harassed ruler in Britain with Aegidius. As Agitus/Aganypus is clearly Aegidius the King of the Seven Cities (and for seven years also King of the Franks, whose full name was Afranius Syagrius Flavius Aegidius), there is a possibility of explaining the letter.

As the legendary King Lear-Llyr married his youngest daughter to the King of Gaul it was perhaps a useful exercise to see if there was a British nobleman of around AD 470 who was named Llyr, and who would have had connections of descent or marriage with Gaul. This is no great problem, as the dominant king in

Chapter 22 - The Reaction in Wales

Britain from AD 322 to 367 was King Euddaf son of Plaws Hen-Plautius the Aged, and grandson of Gwrtherin-Victorinus Emperor of Britain and Gaul. In turn, King Euddaf left sons, one of whom was Brychan, who in turn had a son named Llyr. All this is solid history as the sons or nephews of Euddaf-Octavius named as Conan Meriadoc and Brychan accompanied Magnus Maximus and Arthur I in the invasion of Gaul and Western Europe in AD 383.

So, there is a major British prince named Llyr at the correct period for the despatch of a letter to Gaul, and Brychan (sometimes called Fracan) the father of this Llyr would have had territorial claims in Britain and Britanny in Gaul. This Llyr is not recorded as leaving sons, just like the legendary King Lear. He had a brother in St Guenole of Brittany, and a sister St Lleian, who married Gafran. This gives further chronological support to this scenario as Gafran and St Lleian were the parents of the infamous Aeddan Fradog, the traitor who allied himself with the Saxons in this disturbed era around AD 456–470. Aeddan Fradog (Aeddan the Traitor), left a son named Gafran and the descents are well known.

This developing scenario is interesting as the King Llyr of the historical Bruts and the Lear of William Shakespeare had three daughters. One named Ragan married Einion of Cerniw the father of Cuneda, which is again chronologically correct as Cuneda Wledig - Lord of the Restoration the Legate - assumed the military command in AD 434. Another sister named Gonorilla married Maglawn and they had a son named as Morgan. As Cuneda is said to have killed Morgan it become obvious that there was a fight over the lands of Llyr-Lear. This left the third daughter named Cordeilla who was married to the King of Gaul, and at this mid-fifth-century era that has to be King Aegidius of the Seven Cities and of the Franks. As Cordeilla and Aegidius had a son named Syagrius who was killed at the city of Soissons by Clovis and Ragnachar the Franks in AD 486, there is once again a very solid chronological link.

A British kingdom in Lloegres-England survived the holocaust of the comet disaster of AD 562 and the *Bruts of England* record that a British king named as the 'Cadwallader' = Battle Sovereign son of Brecyuales = Brochwael ruled from the Leicester area around AD 700. This is interesting as the legendary King Llyr-Lear is recorded as being buried in this same territory near the banks of the river Stour. It is admitted that the historical Bruts are muddled, largely because in knitting the various ancient records together into a history there was always the same old requirement to match the real and actual history with the nonsensical dating of the Trojan War at around 1200 BC instead of the actual date around 650 BC. *The Trojan*

War of 650BC details the correct Trojan War.

Brut or Chronicles of England Chapter 100.

'And after that this bataile was done, the Britons assemblde ham and went thence, and come unto Liecestre and made Cadwalladre that was Brochwael's son, kyng of Lecestre. and of all the contre.'

Brochwael is a name given to several Welsh kings of the Arthurian dynasty in South East Wales, and to a few in Powys. In the British tradition the Cadwallader, or Battle Sovereign who died around AD 684 was a son of the 'Caswallon' = Ruler of a Division of the State = 'Viceroy'.

So, by simple examination of the British-Welsh genealogies, something which might have a bearing on the King Llyr mystery emerges. King Euddaf-Octavius the son of Plaws Hen-Plautius the Aged, and grandson of Gwrthelin-Victorinus the Emperor of the West in AD 270-272, enters the scenario. King Euddaf expelled the Lieutenants of Constantine the Great in a war from AD 312-322, and dominated much of Britain from AD 322-367, and Euddaf had a grandson named as Llyr-Lear, and the interlocking genealogies of several noble families through marriage alliances, would place this Llyr as being an old man at around AD 474.

The two eldest daughters of Shakespeare's King Lear are said to have married respectively two kings named as Maglawn father of Morgan, and Einion father of Cuneda. This is no problem as Cuneda Wledig replaced Owain Vinddu as military commander in AD 434 and Morgan, son of Maglawn, may be traceable in South Wales. So, Shakespeare's Gonorilla could have married Maglawn, (Maelgwn) and Ragan could have married Einion the father of Cuneda in the early fifth century AD. These two eldest daughters and their husbands then took advantage of their father's wish to retire from kingly responsibility and they totally dispossessed him. Aeddan Fradog ap Gafran joined in the fight for lands with Saxon allies, using his mother's descent as a sister of King Llyr as his right. With no other recourse the aged Llyr then wrote a desperate letter to his daughter in Gaul seeking assistance from his son-in-law Afranius Syagrius Flavius Aegidius.

The ancestry of St Lleian makes her a sister of Llyr, and records her descent as a daughter of Brychan son or nephew of Euddaf, and Brychan was the brother of Conan Meriadauc who became the first King of Britanny in AD 383, when both brothers invaded Gaul with Magnus Maximus. St Lleian married to Gafran the father of Aeddan Fradog, and the grandfather of Gafran ap Aeddan Fradog. As Bradog means traitor, and Aeddan was labelled as Fradog because he allied with the Saxons

Chapter 22 - The Reaction in Wales

this again gives a chronological fix, with Aeddan Fradog playing the traitor in the era around AD 456.

What this all leads to is that King Llyr had a third daughter named Cordeilla or Cordelia, who would be perfectly timed chronologically to have been married to Kjng Aegidius in Gaul, who would have been the recipient of a letter from the beleaguered aged King Llyr-Lear. The Bruts record her as marrying Aganypus, which is Aegidius. This King Aegidius had a son named Syagrius who was later killed by Clovis the Frank, which again serves to tie the chronological pattern into this same correct era. With Ceredig the brother of Binion active in Ireland and being criticised by St Patrick for his mistreatment of the Irish, this gives yet another perfect chronological fix.

All this means that there is a very good case for identifying King Llyr son of Brychan the nephew of Euddaf as the writer of the famous letter to Aegidius in Gaul, and for placing Llyr in the Leicester area in central England.

So, what has all this to do with Arthur II, America, the comet, or anything else?

Why is it so important to identify a British king in the Leicester area after the time of the American adventure of Arthur II and Madoc Morfran?

One of the many supporters of Alan Wilson and Baram Blackett is John Battersby, from Redditch, and he brought it to their notice that there was something strange in Leicestershire.

In the early part of the twentieth century around 1900, workmen were cleaning off the four-hundred-year-old layers of whitewash from the inner walls of the church at Stoke Dry, in Leicestershire. The walls of mediaeval churches were routinely brightly decorated with pictures of holy figures and scenes representing Biblical and saintly events. These murals were in conflict with the views of the puritans of the Oliver Williams, alias Cromwell, period, as they smacked of Romanism, and conflicted with strict Biblical instructions that there should be '*no graven images*', and no representation of human forms. Humans are in god's own image and so representation is not permissible. All over Britain the centuries old wall paintings were plastered over with layers of whitewash, and it became the custom to simply freshen up the fading surfaces with periodic additional coats of whitewash.

In time the very existence of these wall paintings was forgotten, and it is only now in the twentieth century that these hidden paintings are actually sought out.

Mediaeval Stoke Dry painting showing Native Americans?

Detail of headdress

Both photographs taken and kindly supplied by Bob Morgan – 2001

Chapter 22 - The Reaction in Wales

Generally, discoveries are accidental, and so it was at Stoke Dry, where workmen removing the heavy layers of whitewash revealed some remarkable paintings. The central scene shows a crowned king being shot to death with arrows. This is not in itself remarkable as one martyred minor king, St Edmund of East Anglia, was executed by being shot to death by arrows by the Danes. Here at Stoke Dry, however, there are two bowmen who are placed one on either side of the dying king and both are very clearly represented as Native Americans. Both men are brown-/red-skinned and near-naked, wearing only loin-cloths. Both have long black hair, and the figure on the left is painted wearing a Native American feathered war bonnet, whilst the other has feathers upright in his hair.

As this painting has been examined by those regarded as expert in this field of art, and has been identified by them as the work of a painter working around 1300 to 1350, the idea of a representation of two native American warriors killing a king at that time or earlier raises questions. The only recourse available to the historical apologists is to attempt to identify the king being shot to death with arrows as King Edmund of East Anglia, which is nowhere near Leicester and the Midlands. Edmund was murdered by the Danes, and it is astonishing to hear that the men portrayed as near-naked brown skinned men with long black hair, and wearing feather war bonnets, are thought to be Danish Vikings.

The strange name of Stoke Dry appears to be nothing more than the Welsh 'stoc drych' meaning 'the evil blow', which indicates an old British rather than an Anglo-Saxon provenance. Next, as the experts on artistic style and development have firmly nominated a painter who was active around 1300, the depiction of Native Americans in mediaeval Britain some two hundred hears before Columbus raises difficulties. Thirdly, King Edmund was a minor king in the extreme east of Britain and was not anywhere near Leicester and Stoke Dry.

If this painting represents a thirteenth-century artist's idea of the death of King Arthur II, assassinated by native Americans, there is an explanation for it. If it does not represent native Americans and King Arthur, then there appears to be no other possible explanation. If the area remained a British fiefdom until around 700, and perhaps later, then the record of Arthur II's voyage and the naked brown-skinned men with long black hair who wore feathered bonnets, and who killed Arthur II, would have been known in the area. The painting constitutes evidence.

Dating the letter sent to Alfranius Syagrius Flavius Aegidius

Wilson and Blackett found that there are other methods of indicating the probable dating of the famous letter sent to Aegidius-Agitus in Gaul. If the dating formulae recorded in the Welsh histories, including Nennius and the Anglo-Saxon and Norman sources, are used they produce interesting answers. First the reason for sending the letter to Gaul is believed to have been to solicit military aid against a major foreign assault, and the Saxon tribes are the enemy. There is no confirming evidence for this assumption. The letter could well have been sent by one regional British king, who was seeking assistance to ward off other predatory regional British kings. The letter may or may not have had anything whatsoever to do with Saxons. It is reasonable therefore to examine the Nennius dates to see if they give any indication of this event.

They have postulated that the letter was sent to Aegidius around 474, some thirty years after the Roman general Aetius died. Then it is stated that the Saxons were active in Britain five hundred and forty-two years from the time of Edmund Ironside the son of Aethelred. As Edmund Ironside was king for only five month in 1016, this then produces 1016 - 542 = 474, and so AD 474. Another statement is that:

The Saxons were in Britain four hundred and forty-seven years after the Passion, which would be conventionally 33 + 447 = AD 480. Then there is a statement that Vortigern received the Saxons in the four hundred and forty-seventh year of the Lord. This date has to be fixed retrospectively, and in British Apostolic Christian terms it is 33 + 447 = 480 once again. This indicates some major involvement of the Saxons in Britain in AD 474–480.

In Roman Christian terms this dating of Gwrtheyrn-Vortigern and the Saxons would be simply AD 447. This means that an appeal for aid sent to Gaul would be after AD 447 and automatically this eliminates the then dead Roman Aetius from the equation. Only Aegidius the King of the Seven Cities in Northern Gaul remains as a possibility.

The first Saxon arrival in Britain is dated as four hundred and twenty-eight years before the fourth year of Mermanus-Merfyn Frych (the freckled) who dates from 817 to 843, and so his fourth year is AD 821. The dating then is 821 - 428 = AD 393. This must refer to the arrival of Saxon auxiliaries in Britain under Theodosius, and their chief Fraomar, in the brief Roman incursion of AD 393, following the murder of the Emperor Magnus Clemens Maximus in AD 388.

Loth of Londenesia

To illustrate the level of unthinking criticism which has surrounded Khumric records, and which has become commonplace, Alan and Baram are fond of the example of 'Loth of Londenesia'. One critic wrote with scathing sarcasm of the absurdities written in 1135 by Gruffydd ap Arthur (*alias* Geoffrey of Monmouth) and in particular he cited the mention of 'Loth of Londenesia' as an example of alleged blatant invention. So, Alan and Baram decided to take a look at Loth of Londenesia.

It works out in this manner. First, St Samson of Dol was the son of Anna the daughter of King Meurig ap Tewdrig, and of Amwn Ddu the son of Emyr Lydaw. Of this there is no question and the descent appears in the *Lives of the Saints*. Amwn Ddu is simply Amon the Black, or perhaps Eamonn in modern terms. The same cast of characters then appear in the *Brut of England*, and no one is laughing at these English Bruts. Here Amwn has become Aloth, and his father Emyr has been translated into Eleyn, and the whole matter is very simple. In the third stage in Gruffydd ap Arthur, Amwn = Aloth loses the 'A' and becomes Loth, whilst Llydaw changes into Londenesia, and ancient Llydaw is still identifiable in the town of Lisieux in Normandy which name replaced that of the territory of Llydaw around 911-933.

The characters are real and identifiable as close contemporary relatives of King Arthur II ap Meurig, but the style of the names of the father Emyr-Eleyn, the son Amwn-Aloth-Loth, and the place Llydaw-Londenesia-Lisieux changes. It would appear to indicate that fact has to be identified by comparative means, and that there has been an over-hasty rush to judgement. In the same way the much-derided Arthurian Battle of Sassy turns out to be the very well recorded real Battle of Soissons fought by Arthur I son of Magnus in 383, and not a battle of the sixth-century Arthur II.

Gruffydd states that this 'King Arthur' was succeeded in the military leadership by his cousin who was named Constantine. Again, this is perfectly correct in the case of Arthur I son of Magnus Maximus, who was succeeded by Constantine Coronog-the Crowned, who invaded Gaul in AD 406. The genealogy of Constantine Coronog is well known and is available. Again, it is a simple matter of differentiating between Arthur I and Arthur II.

The apparent inventions are many and they disappear like the morning mists when some open-minded clear thinking is applied in place of an approach with a pre-conceived negative mind-set. The fact that Taliesin wrote a marwnad or Grave Elegy to Madoc should have automatically placed Madoc in the sixth century, and not the late twelfth century. The prologue to the dialogue between Arthur son of Uthyr and Lliwlod son of Madoc son of Uthyr, showing Arthur II and Madoc as brothers, should have aroused interest, but it did not do so because of pre-conditioned mind-sets.

As for Uthyr and Uthyr Pendragon, even the briefest excursion into the records shows no fewer than four Uthyr Pendragons and two Dragons. It was not therefore a title that was peculiar to one king. This then brings us to the strange situation where Taliesin, the Chief Court Bard for Arthur II ap Meurig, appears not to have written a Marwnad for his deceased Lord. Taliesin did however write a marwnad to 'Uthyr Pendragon' and again careful examination of the text shows that this grave elegy was intended for Arthur II Uthyr Pendragon. It is of course necessary to ignore the hilarious nonsense translation offered by the Rev. Robert Williams in 1869. As one remarkable example, the Rev. Williams came up with:

'Monks howled like dogs in a kennel,'

and instead what is written is:

'Monks carried the chief/leader to the choir.'

There is a more than subtle difference.

There were three successive sixth-century Uthyr Pendragons in King Tewdrig, King Meurig, and King Arthur, and recognition of this simple fact assists in dispelling many confusions. Equally there is a famous line in a sixth century poem reading:

'For I am Merlyn and men shall call me Taliesin.'

This has been totally overlooked in the imaginative and generally inaccurate blundering about the identity of Merlyn. In gnostic Christian thought the Earth was in the care of Sabaoth-the Little Horse, who was 'enlightened', and Merlyn means 'Little Horse'. The line means;

'For I am enlightened and men shall call me high intellect.'

Ialdabaoth - the Great Horse was 'unenlightened' and he thought he was God, and so the deity threw him down like Satan, and replaced him with his son Sabaoth = Merlyn. It really is all very simple, and if only the academics had not set out over-confidently to write the History of Ancient Britain armed with only 5-10% of the

Chapter 22 - The Reaction in Wales

preserved evidence, we would not be in this mess today.

Visible signs

There are in Cardiff Castle very plainly visible signs of the Coelbren stroke alphabet and of the past migrations of the British people. There is a clear representation of the ancient British Coelbren alphabet carved in the library. This is stated in the records to be Coelbren, but guides escorting tourists around the castle are actually instructed to tell them that this British alphabet representation is instead 'Viking Runes'. As there never were any Vikings in South Wales this needs some explaining. All the more so as the records of the Marquis of Bute, who formerly owned the castle, state clearly that this is the Coelbren alphabet.

There is also a representation in six carved figures of the migrations of the British people. These figures show the countries where the people were and still are. The figures are: l, an Egyptian; 2, a Hebrew; 3, an Assyrian; 4, a Trojan; 5, an Etruscan; and 6, a Welsh Druid. The grotesque misinformation put out about these figures is again a travesty. The Marquess of Bute and his architects knew and specified what they were doing, but political correctness over-rules the facts. The Ten Tribes were in Egypt (1) until Moses led them out, and as Hebrews they entered Canaan and (2) set up Israel and Judea. Then they were deported to Assyria (3) and they left in c. 687BC, and marched west to the Trojan area (4) of western Asia Minor. Then around 650 BC half the people went to Italy (5) as Etruscans, and later the other half sailed for Britain (6) under Brutus in c. 504BC. These six figures outline the historical migrations of the people.

These representations were set up after the attempted destruction of all native Khumric history by the London Parliament in 1846. They convey messages to the future generations of Britain for the good of Britain.

In St Fagan's Castle in Cardiff there is a collection of Coelbren peithynen. These are upright wooden frames in which straight sticks cut in triangular shape were placed horizontally, rather like an old-fashioned scrubbing board. The straight-stroked Coelbren alphabet messages were cut with either a knife, or a small axe, into the flat, smooth sides of these three-sided triangular sticks. So, a row of messages was presented just like the row of printed lines on the pages. There are eleven old peithynen frames in this museum but only two are on show. It is part of a resistance movement.

The journey of the people is startlingly represented in the main windows of

Llandaff Cathedral in Cardiff, which occupies the major part of the east end wall behind the main altar. The window is of several narrow horizontal sections, and it is made up of stained-glass panes containing heads representing kings. These begin with David, then Solomon, the Kings of Israel and Judea; the proceed with Israel kings, and actually finish up with the arms of King Iestyn ap Gwrgan the last Welsh Morganwg king deposed in 1091, and the windows of King Iestyn's ancestors King Tewdrig, King Arthur II, and King 'Cadwallader'. The message is absolutely clear that these Khumry people are descendants of the Ten Tribes of Israel. This is a plain and open statement made in the most ancient cathedral site in Britain, and the intention to somehow inform all the future generations of Britain is stark and clear:

To reiterate, these windows and the other windows depicting King Arthur II ap Meurig ap Tewdrig, King Tewdrig Uthyr Pendragon, and the Cadwallader, and contemporary saints were set up after the Treachery of the Blue Books in the London Parliament was used to destroy the Welsh education system and its history. The 1846 centralisation of education that demolished independent Welsh education only allows for teaching English history in Wales, so little can be done.

The Singer, not the Song -

The Onslaught on the British Cultural Heritage in the Nightmare World of Wales

It was 7am on a mild autumn morning in 2002, and I sat at my breakfast table alongside a large picture window in the sixth-floor restaurant of the opulent Quality Hotel, in Newgate Street, in the centre of Newcastle upon Tyne. I had relaxed into a thoughtful reverie drinking hot tea and looking out at the crimson dawn sky that hung like a velvet blanket over the dark haze below, speckled with a myriad array of lights stretching away into the distance and shining dimly in the lightening dawn. Out there across the city rooftops the dense noisy throngs of starlings that clustered to roost on the ledges of the buildings in the city centre with their bubbly chatters, whistles and mimicry, enhanced the tranquillity.

In this therapeutical dawn atmosphere, I felt a certain euphoria that cleared my mind as I took the summary papers and other documentation from my briefcase and laid them out on my breakfast table. I flicked through my black leather compendium case and selected papers in methodical order.

The night sky had begun to disappear and dawn light was beginning to lift the veils and buildings and spires began to take shape out of the vanishing gloom. What I was about to do was also a form of dawning and bringing light to a situation of impenetrable gloom and a driving away of dark shadows.

The Investigation

The gathering of secret and confidential information is a delicate business. Seldom does one single foray provide the picture, let alone expose the villains or crooks if there are any involved. There is no single factor and no instant wonderful direct solution. The picture appears as if from a jigsaw puzzle that is being carefully assembled piece by piece, and of an unknown picture. The pieces are difficult to fit together and they are often nebulous and misleading, and some pieces do not appear at all. A proficient covert intelligence analyst will discern the picture and cut through any deceit and assemble a picture from a collation of fragments.

Investigations are like this. Often there are pieces that do not belong to the picture being assembled and some belong to other, linked jigsaw pictures, and some are fakes that do not belong anywhere. They never lock together neatly like a real jigsaw with the carefully fretted edges matching with each other, and there are no neat straight edges as guides to the ends of the picture. Lateral thinking is essential as hidden answers rarely emerge in a tidy logical progression.

The questions that are most often asked is: "What happened in over twenty-five years?" and "Why has nothing positive happened?" since Wilson and Blackett attended the House of Lords by invitation to meet with Jack Brooks on 25th February 1981. When Lord Brooks said, "If this is right then there are at least 20,000 jobs in it." Well, with a heavy heart I ask the reader to take my hand and I will lead you into enlightenment.

If patience is a virtue, then Wilson and Blackett are a living testimony to that. Their researches began in 1976, and by 1981 they had published three volumes. Twenty Cardiff businessmen offered - without being asked - to put up £20,000 to fence and protect identified valuable ancient sites. Wilson and Blackett were amazed when told by their lawyer, Mr Paul Mahoney, that the group had been misinformed that Alan Wilson had a long criminal record, and that they had withdrawn their support. Alan Wilson has no criminal record, but now twenty well-known persons had been lied to and without doubt the lies would spread.

Six times between 1982 and 1990 Alan Wilson and his lawyers paid the fee and requested detail of any alleged criminal record against Alan's name. Six times they were assured that there was no criminal record. Meantime the lies were being spread, spread, and spread. Wales has a population of fewer than three million, and those in authority all know each other. They are known as the Taffia, a pun on the

Mafia from the River Taff that runs through Cardiff. Actually, the Mafia are much nicer and more decent people.

It was not until 1990 that Alan Wilson was visited by police from an English force and they informed him of his very extensive criminal record of convictions for burglaries, thefts, frauds, and deceptions, lodged on the Cardiff police computer. In Britain only three persons have access to criminal records: 1, the criminal, 2, his lawyers, 3, the police. But this 'record' had been advertised through Wales as widely as Coca-Cola. It was the old Welsh tactic of attack the singer and not the song. By assassinating the reputation of the singer, no one listens to the song.

In this, my first book about them, it is not possible to list all the disgusting offences and dirty tricks that were committed against Alan Wilson and Baram Blackett in this small space as the full story will fill a large book. A few examples should give the reader some idea of what has been going on.

In the intervening years disgraceful criminal attacks had been launched against Wilson and Blackett. In 1984 late one-night police arrested Blackett and his brother in the street, thinking that they had arrested Alan Wilson. They charged them with committing a burglary of stated listed items fifteen minutes earlier. Next morning newspaper headlines blared out of the arrest and blasting the Arthurian Researches, which no one had mentioned. In the chaos that followed it emerged that the burglary had taken place three months earlier, and the thieves were arrested within hours and all the stolen goods recovered. The thieves had confessed and were sitting in Cardiff Jail. The police had duplicated a phantom crime that never happened, and they had their inevitable Welsh 'eye-witness', who just happened to have a criminal record and who was awaiting trial on very serious charges. They still persisted with a totally bogus prosecution, and the lies told by four police officers were disbelieved by the jury and the case was thrown out.

The police 'eye-witness' was later tried for running a vice ring. It operated out of the BBC bar at Welsh BBC headquarters in Cardiff. Everyone who was anyone in the area got into this bar, all very anxious to get their faces known and to court good publicity. A barman made the contacts for sex, and a taxi driver and an insurance salesman delivered fourteen-year-old and fifteen-year-old boys to clients. The organiser got a surprisingly small jail sentence. The Chief Constable of South Wales resigned with five years still to run on his contract. Significantly none of the clients who paid for these delivered services was ever charged.

The organiser's 'eye-witness' against the Blackett brothers came out of jail after a

Chapter 22 - The Reaction in Wales

short while and went off to Amsterdam with a very substantial sum of money. Presumably this was payment for not naming names. In Amsterdam he set up a male brothel, presumably for his Welsh clients, and he actually got the whole front page and both middle pages of the News of the World, one of Britain's major national Sunday newspapers, on 1st April 1990. He later disappeared.

Copies of widely distributed, disgraceful secretive letters written by a Dr Nancy Edwards of Bangor University, falsely stating that Wilson and Blackett were due for trial in the Crown Courts were passed to Wilson and Blackett. The University of Wales at first denied any responsibility and then when Wilson and Blackett started a legal action against Edwards the University stepped in with all its financial muscle.

The King Arthur Conspiracy - Wilson & Blackett

Letter from:

Adams & Black
Solicitors & Commisioncrs for Oaths,
High Street Arcade Chambers,
Cardiff,
CFI 2QS.

Our Ref: CNW / JMD / 14964

To Dr N. Edwards,
Department of History,
University College of North Wales,
Bangor,
Gwynedd,
LL57 2DG   23 October 1987.

Dear Madam,

<u>Our Clients A. Wilson and B.A.T. Blackett</u>

We have been instructed by the above named, who, as you are undoubtedly aware, are historical researchers.

Following recent legislation our Clients have had access to certain documentation kept by local authorities, which has revealed letters written by yourself that are, to say the least, damaging to our Clients.

We refer specifically to letters written by you in November 1986 to the Ogwr Borough Council on headed University College notepaper, one such letter containing a copy of a report prepared as long ago as 1983 addressed to the Welsh Tourist Board. We are particularly concerned at the contents of your letters, which are prejudicial to our Clients and the effect of your correspondence having proved extremely damaging to their reputation. The letter dated the 3rd November 1986 particularly disturbs us and contains malicious statements, which are, in our opinion, libellous statements. In the third paragraph of the letter you state your belief that our Clients face criminal prosecution. To state such openly without any supporting proof in a letter of this kind is something neither we, nor our Clients, take lightly. Neither Mr Wilson, nor Mr Blackett have for your information, ever been convicted or prosecuted of any criminal offence whatsoever. To publish such an attack on our

Chapter 22 - The Reaction in Wales

Clients' credibility and reputation purportedly relying on a report you had written which was some three years old - and in the same context to admit not even having taken the time to read our Clients latest work, is not only irresponsible but prejudicial and a defamatory statement about our Clients.

Our clients have found it, in recent years, extremely difficult and indeed impossible to obtain backing from local authorities and historical organizations, and had long believed that their reputation had somehow been undermined, although until recently the precise source was unknown to them. Now that they are aware of the source they are extremely distressed and justifiably angered at your writings, which go beyond any form of literary criticism of our Clients' work and we must therefore request on their behalf that you provide our Clients with a written apology and retraction forthwith.

We shall expect to receive such an apology from you within seven days of the date of this letter and such would be without prejudice to our Clients right of legal redress against you for such publications as you have made.

Yours faithfully

Adams & Black with Howell Buchanan & Co.

The University of Wales with all its financial muscle and legal and judicial contacts and political connections then stepped back into the picture to support Dr Edwards and her outrageous libels, and not being millionaires Wilson and Blackett were as disenfranchised as 99.99% of the British population are.

Edwards had co-authored a little book on Welsh churches with a Dr Alan Lane of Cardiff University. Obviously, both knew that if Wilson and Blackett's work was recognised then their obscure little book would be seen as rubbish. Copies of libellous and defamatory letters from academics, civil servants, and others piled up, as Alan Wilson and Baram Blackett now knew where to look. They could have brought several dozen huge legal actions but lacked the funds to do so. Vile libellous and defamatory letters were being written and copies sprayed around everywhere, to central government bodies and local government city and town councils, borough and county councils; to museum staff, tourist boards, the media, etc. In Britain no lawyer acts on a contingency or share basis and 99.99% of folk have no access to the courts.

A series of vandal attacks were made on St Peter's super Montem church, owned by Wilson and Blackett, and in 1986 the Welsh police conspired with a leading Welsh newspaper falsely to accuse them of vandalising their own property, when they provably did not do so. The Swansea and Maesteg vandals who were seen at the site were used as the accusers. The object of the exercise was to smear Wilson and Blackett with more bad publicity. The vandals were unaware that Wilson and Blackett owned the ancient church, but they knew that if they were convicted of desecrating an ancient monument the penalties are up to ten years' imprisonment and unlimited fines. This was no small conspiracy.

Examining a plethora of newspaper cuttings regarding plans to set up open cast coal mining projects brought the involvement of local politicians into the spotlight. Julian Hodge had set up the Bank of Wales and he involved George Thomas and James Callaghan in his enterprises as Directors of his bank. The near defunct Ryan company set up by Hodge to remove old coal tips and recover waste coal was converted into Ryan International Open Cast Coal Co Ltd and sold to South African business interests who were desperate to get their money out of South Africa before Nelson Mandela got out of jail. Land acquisition was organised to buy up land where later the politicians would build the huge new Royal Mint. Nicholas Edwards, a senior minister in Margaret Thatcher's administration, was also recruited as a director of Ryan.

Wilson and Blackett were busy identifying a plethora of immensely valuable ancient sites most of which were right on top of huge coalfields that were perfect for open cast mining. The fact that Arthur II and his father and many others were buried on top of these targeted coalfields, along with numerous other associated ancient sites, was clearly unwelcome news for certain business and political interests.

If Alan Wilson and Baram Blackett were seen to be correct then the open cast coal-mining plan was finished. There are over 7,000,000,000 tons of good coal right under St Peter's and other major Arthurian sites in the Rhondda Drift alone. So, the financial size of the problem is enormous.

In the event, the demand for coal in Britain fell drastically as alternative fuels was used and the steel industry shrank. The coal that was required by the surviving major Welsh steelworks was brought in very cheaply from China and Australia and elsewhere in huge bulk carriers. The plans for vast open cast coal mining enterprises never materialised, and the opportunity to create a huge tourist

Chapter 22 - The Reaction in Wales

industry was spurned and lost. The loss of the cultural and heritage advantages could have been circumvented by frank and open discussion if directness had prevailed. The fifty-four deep coal pits in Wales - most of which were profitable - closed down, but academic reputations were salvaged.

However, Wilson and Blackett continued with their remarkable researches and undertook lecture tours, which included Oxford (twice), Cambridge, and tours in America including the prestigious Bemis Lecture in Boston. They believed that their open approach might compel recognition.

Most of the persistent attacks were traced back to the offices of the Glamorgan-Gwent Archaeological Trust Company Ltd based in Swansea, and to an employee of the Welsh Development Agency. Others who were active in spreading lies were traced. This private company was set up by ten persons, three of whom were employees of Cardiff University, and three of whom were employees of the Welsh National Museum. It was a massive gravy train and by 1985 it was pulling in over £521,000 in public funds, and in 1986 £567,000, and charging for its services, and including Manpower Services Commission perks and property development deals. Similar companies were set up by academics and others in West Wales, in North West Wales, and North East Wales. With over £10,000 a week in grants falling through the letter-box, and if it cost £1,000 a week to pay the few staff and rent the cheap offices, there has to be creative accountancy involved somewhere. How can this Limited Company do the aforesaid and then also register itself and pose as a charity?

Finally a widely circulated e-mail was received:

> DATE: Saturday 13 Sept 2003. 12:53 : 02 + 0100
> SENDER: British Archaeology discussion
>
> SUBJECT : gareth dowdell is history
>
> Fans and admirers of Gareth Dowdell will be interested to know that he has been sacked as Director of the Glamorgan-Gwent Archaeological Trust for gross misconduct. etc

Numerous telephone calls from several people to the office confirmed that this e-mail was genuine. Unfortunately, they woke up to him after twenty years as the King of the Cultural Vampires, attacking those whom he perceived as a threat to the hugely lucrative grant-farming enterprise. Sadly, the rest of the destructive pack has so far escaped. Very large and very deep pork barrels as they would say in the USA.

From Bangor University in North Wales a Dr Nancy Edwards had written foul libels in widely and distributed secretive letters where they made false allegations that alleged that Wilson and Blackett were to be on trial in the Crown Courts on criminal offences. All a pack of lies and totally untrue. The Chancellor and Vice Chancellor of the University of Wales denied any responsibility, as did the Principals of Colleges. Then when Wilson and Blackett commenced legal action against Dr Nancy Edwards the University of Wales sprang to her defence with all its financial muscle.

Astonishing as it may seem, when in 1986 Wilson and Blackett asked local civil authorities to fence and protect two extremely valuable and important ancient sites, the secretary of the moneymaking machine of the Glamorgan-Gwent Archaeological Trust Company Limited, one Gareth Dowdell (with no qualifications in archaeology or history) wrote and campaigned against protecting these historic sites. In support of the unqualified Dowdell, vicious attacks were made on Wilson and Blackett by Professor W. H. Manning, a Ph.D. and B.Sc. chemist who wrote on Cardiff University Archaeology Department headed paper, but never mentioned the fact that he was a director of this money-spinning Archaeological Trust Company Limited. Manning was supported by Alan Lane, a Scottish archaeologist with no real knowledge of Welsh history, specialising in the ancient megaliths in Brittany. Nancy Edwards of Bangor and Alan Lane of Cardiff co-authored a little book on Welsh churches and if Wilson and Blackett are right and the British-Welsh histories are correct, then their book is wrong. The links and motives are everywhere.

W. H. Manning played semantics with Lane and they concocted this private and confidential clandestine letter allegedly written up by Lane and signed by Manning, which was nothing more than a fabrication of distortions and an apocryphal sabotage of genuine research. This calumniation of falsehoods was copied and widely distributed throughout authorities in Wales. Jealousy and avarice *inter alia* ruined prodigious opportunities like insects in a harvest crop.

Manning the chemist and Lane the Scottish specialist in the archaeology of ancient Brittany hatched this conspiracy with the confidence that their cloak-and-dagger plot would remain undetected. For the University to tolerate the aforesaid is to accommodate them, and to accommodate them is to facilitate them. The University has decided to close ranks against the best interests of the British and

Chapter 22 - The Reaction in Wales

Welsh people, and there is little point in attempting to reason with them any further.

Large-scale conspiracy and theft

In 1988 the Welsh public were regaled with banner headlines of a major battle between Mrs Margaret Thatcher, the then Prime Minister, and Cardiff University. The Prime Minister demanded that the principal and the entire Senate, the entire governing body of Cardiff University must resign forthwith. If they did not resign then the Prime Minister would use her powers to close down the University leaving twelve thousand five hundred students in the streets. Not even the Taffia-Mafia could keep this out of the Press, TV, and Radio media, but they managed to stop the news from reaching across the border into England. The row erupted when well over £20,000,000 in funds was found to be missing. In the end after negotiating the customary amnesty for White Collar crimes, the principal, the entire University Senate, and some two hundred and forty employees resigned. Thatcher solved the problem very well by drafting in the principal and governors of the tiny Cardiff Technical College of twelve hundred students, and they now ran the combined University and Technical College of thirteen-and-a-half thousand students.

It is a sick joke that all the burglars and thieves who have ever been sentenced to serve time in Cardiff and Swansea jails have never managed to steal anything like twenty-eight million pounds in all their crimes collectively.

Cardiff University still stands firmly in the way, and blocks all progress in the research of ancient British-Welsh history. Their latest excuse in 2004 is that Wilson and Blackett had 'a falling out' with unnamed staff at the University. Just how they had a 'falling out' with persons whom they never met, wrote to, telephoned, e-mailed, and or communicated with in any way, is not explained. Wilson and Blackett admit to having defended themselves and their characters and their researches against academic attacks. This now prevents other decent academics from co-operating with Wilson and Blackett, and Alan Wilson again offered 'to open their books' in 2004, and to lead University academics to immensely valuable sites of national importance.

The worst features of all in the massive catalogue of offences committed against two decent researchers are those committed by barristers and the courts. In 1990 a freak occurrence brought the clear evidence that there was an extensive and totally bogus criminal record on the Cardiff police computers against the name and address of Alan Wilson. This allowed Alan Wilson finally to begin attempts to get the police into court, and with great difficulty he finally got legal aid. With matters set to roll into court a barrister was consulted in London. This barrister, Simon Carr, stated to a shocked Alan Wilson and his lawyer, Patrick Henry, that:

'Within the last two weeks there has been a change in the law, this means that the law is against you and you cannot win against the Police. It will take a new Act of Parliament before anyone can now proceed in the courts against the Police.'

Carr insisted on informing the legal aid authorities immediately. Wilson's lawyer, Patrick Henry, objected that there had been no change in the law and asked that the matter be delayed until this was verified. Carr was unable to substantiate his statement and he insisted that it was his duty to report to the legal aid authority immediately. Carr did this and Alan Wilson lost his legal aid and could not proceed. It then turned out that there had been no change in the law and that Alan Wilson was free to proceed against the police with the unchanged law in his favour. He had no funds to do this.

An outstanding example of Dowdell's misconduct came in 1994 when Alan Wilson's and Baram Blackett's homes were raided, once again, by twelve South Wales police officers. They had a bogus warrant that alleged that Alan Wilson had entered and burgled St Peter's super Montem church, and that he had removed a large oak casket, and that he possessed 'archalogikal artifax' [sic]. Alan Wilson is co-owner of St Peter's and it has to be a first even for the bent corrupt Welsh police to accuse a man of entering his own property. The oak casket inside the church belongs to the church that Wilson and Blackett own, and it was never removed by anyone. The bizarre situation was that a man was being accused of entering his own property and stealing an item that belongs to him, and which was not moved. The matter of owning unspecified archaeological artefacts is absurd, as anyone can own anything, Greek, Roman, Egyptian, British, anything.

Det.-Sgt. Allinson admitted that this illegal raid had been mainly instigated by Gareth Dowdell, Secretary of the Glamorgan-Gwent Archaeological Trust Company Limited. The Det.-Sgt. said that the police had to act on information lodged by Dowdell, which was ludicrous, as the accusation was that Alan Wilson had burgled his own property and stolen from himself. The search warrant was shown to be defective and most likely a forgery.

This 'Mickey Mouse' warrant was invalid because it spelled artefacts as *'artifax'*, and it was clearly a subterfuge for more sinister intentions. The police caused chaos to the research projects office files and data, and an entire manuscript was stolen

Chapter 22 - The Reaction in Wales

along with a thousand pounds that Alan Wilson had in cash. So, for several hours twelve officers tore Baram's and Alan's flats apart looking under carpets and in coffee jars for a three-foot-by-three-foot-by-eighteen-inch oak box that they themselves owned, and which was still at St Peter's church which they also owned.

Once again after a huge struggle legal aid was obtained to proceed against the police for this hideous charade, and for six years the police messed about delaying and prevaricating. The same ominous warnings were received 'they will never allow this into court' and so on, and to put it succinctly this again turned into a disgusting wild goose chase. There is evidence that the South Wales police several times tried to scupper the legal aid when it was twice wrongly terminated in attempts to de-rail the case, and battles were fought to reinstate it.

Then with two weeks to go before the trial in the High Court the legal aid granted to Alan Wilson and Baram Blackett was illegally terminated. There was the usual chaos and with matters getting out of hand legal aid was restored. In early 2000 Wilson and Blackett again put their case before the Legal Services Commission Committee, and legal aid was again reinstated with the proviso that after five years of police prevarication the case had to go to court as soon as possible.

Another lawyer was appointed and a London barrister, David Holland, was consulted on case strategy to be used in court after five years of nonsense and prevarication by the police defendant. To Wilson and Blackett's amazement, Holland announced "You will never get this into court." With a trial date set this was an amazing statement. Holland then stated that it was wrong to take the Chief Constable to court and individual officers should be taken. This was insultingly absurd, as a chief superintendent and a chief inspector of police had instructed three detective- sergeants who in turn instructed nine constables. Having got past this idiocy, Wilson and Blackett listened in amazement as Holland stated

> 'Within the last two weeks there has been a change in the law in a decision made by the Law Lords, and where as the law was previously been in your favour it is now against you. It is not possible for you to proceed against the police.'

He claimed that this notice had been published in The Times newspaper between 1st and 14th December, which is totally untrue.

It was an exact rerun of the Simon Carr allegation in 1993. Angela Nunn, the lawyer, protested that she had not seen or known of any such important change in the law, but Holland was adamant, and he insisted that he must inform the legal aid authorities immediately. He did this and Wilson and Blackett lost their legal aid.

The conference concluded around 5pm and Holland had already written and posted his 'opinion' before the 5pm post deadline. Immediate checks showed that no notice of any change in the Law of Misfeasance in Public Office had been published by *The Times* newspaper between 1st and 14th December, as Holland had alleged, and the Law Lords had not changed the law with a new ruling. There is evidence that Holland had been 'paid a visit', to give fraudulent advice.

Alan Wilson finally gave up after decades of trying to get Holland or the South Wales Police into court. Baram Blackett persisted and after seven preliminary hearings he was cheated when he arrived at Clerkenwell County Court to find that the case was not listed to be heard in either court and no judge was named to hear the matter. Instead, he was shown into a private side room where no public or press could be present, and here a 'deputy assistant judge' named Glasner ruled that an appeal in the matter of Misfeasance in Public Office that was turned down by the Law Lords, was in fact now the law. This 'deputy assistant judge' Glasner, who admitted not having read the case papers, has now overruled the decision of the Law Lords and stated that what is not the law is the law.

A full and comprehensive four-page letter listing the catalogue of illegal and criminal offences committed against them was sent to the Lord Chancellor's Office, to the Head of the Judicial Correspondence Unit, to the judges who had several times reinstated the case under the heading of 'Conspiracy to Pervert the Course of Justice'. Unfortunately, Wilson and Blackett had not foreseen that they would again become the victims of the human imbecility factor. These are but a few of the offences perpetrated against Wilson and Blackett. The total catalogue of crimes committed against Wilson and Blackett over the twenty-five year period is extraordinary and although fully documented and listed it is still difficult to believe. This is what happened to Baram Blackett in the bent courts.

Chapter 22 - The Reaction in Wales

Letter of 23 April 2004
To Mrs Turrell,
The Secretary,
Head of the Judicial Correspondence Unit,
4th Floor,
30 Millbank.
London,
SW1P 4XB.

CONSPIRACY TO PERVERT THE COURSE OF JUSTICE. CASE No. BNIO00 183.

Dear Mrs Turrell,

This is a relatively small case that has been deliberately caused to fall into a farce by devious means including obfuscation, legal chicanery, and obreption.

To save your honour's time, I will be as succinct and as concise as possible in chronological form.

1. In 1995 Legal Aid was granted to take the Chief Constable of South Wales Police to court because the South Wales Police made an illegal raid on my home with a false and defective Search Warrant, D/S Allinson who led the raid on the word of a known crook (now sacked from his employment) blamed myself, and my colleague, for the burglary and robbery of our OWN PROPERTY. An absolute nonsense. The search left my home in total turmoil and disorder and the items that belong to me and that were alleged to have been removed from my own property elsewhere were in fact still at the other property. There were more sinister intentions.

2. After several years of struggle and obtaining three meritorious barristers' opinions to confirm that I had a just case which merited legal aid that aid was granted. Over the years legal aid totalling £30,000 was utilized by solicitors and barristers and the files were extensive. I have eleven witness statements in my favour. I have been sucked into a vortex of mendacious legal trickery and obfuscation. With only two weeks to go before the trial in the High Court in November 2000, this legal aid was wrongly terminated.

3. Legal aid was regranted upon appeal and my solicitor managed to get the trial postponed. It was decided to seek advice from a London barrister on the plan of the

case strategy to be employed in the forthcoming case. After five years of time wasting by the defendant this was necessary.

4. A meeting was arranged with one David Holland, barrister, of 29 Bedford Row, London, WC 1, for 14 February 2000, and Holland suddenly changed the date to 15 December 12 2000. He had been visited by 'representatives' of the corrupt South Wales police, who were seen and heard at his chambers.

5. At the delayed conference or ambush, Holland had clearly been 'serviced' and he conducted a total charade with myself and my co-plaintiff Mr Alan Wilson, and our solicitor. Holland had the barefaced mendacity to fabricate pathetic lies in his calculated sabotage of our case. He was obviously involved with and favouring the Defendant the Chief Constable of South Wales Police, and was doing everything he could to prevent the case from proceeding on to trial in open court. His lies included-

A You will never get them (the police) into court. Ludicrous as the case had been listed for Trial.

B. You should be taking the Det/Sgt Allinson to court and not the Chief Constable. Idiotic as there were three Det/Sgts involved and nine Constables from the armed response squad, and they were all acting on orders from a Superintendent of Police and a Chief Inspector.

C. *'Within the last two weeks there has been a change in the law. Previously the law was in your favour, but now there has been a change which is adverse to you.'* This alleged change was challenged by our solicitor, but Holland was adamant that this sudden change in the Law of Misfeasance in Public Office had been reported in The Times newspaper. He refused to wait until this could be checked or until the Law Lords alleged decision had been published properly and in full. Holland claimed that it was *'my duty'* to report the matter instantly to the Legal Aid Services Authority.

D. Holland had not been hired to write an opinion on the merits of the case but he now claimed that the unnoticed change in the law required that he must do so. He had actually already written this opinion before the strategy conference took place as it was posted immediately after the sham conference which ended on Friday after 5.00 pm.

E. I and my colleague, Mr Alan Wilson, went immediately to *The Times* newspaper office and we also wrote a letter to *The Times* Legal Department & Correspondent.

Chapter 22 - The Reaction in Wales

There had been NO change in the law whatsoever, and Holland was a complete liar. The opinion sent to the Legal Aid Services by Holland resulted in the loss of legal aid to both myself, and my colleague Mr Alan Wilson. The situation had been manipulated to remove the safety net and umbrella of legal aid and costs in a very difficult and important case.

F. When we arrived at Holland's chambers, we saw a scruffy little man sitting near the door of the room adjacent to the conference room. Twice, myself, and Mr.Wilson left the room to discuss how to try to deal with Holland's lies. On the first occasion we found this unkempt individual bending down outside the door obviously trying to listen at the keyhole and he immediately went into the adjacent room. On the second occasion we found him actually kneeling down and trying to peep through the key hole, and this time we asked him who he was and he ran off down the stairs. There was conspiracy.

G. The situation created by Holland's lies was a disaster for myself and Mr Wilson as neither of us had the means to take an action in the High Court against the public funded police who had £ millions at their disposal, and we could not afford a lawyer. There was absolutely no need of an opinion of any sort from Holland, let alone a pack of lies. I would never ever have brought the action over events of six years earlier in 1994 if we had not been given legal aid. Both myself, and Mr Wilson, had expended months of effort and had spent several thousand pounds in addition to the legal aid. We were left stranded.

H. I have the correspondence from the Legal Department of *The Times* of London, who confirmed that no such changes in the law were made and certainly *The Times* never ever published any such report. I have reports from the House of Lords that confirm that there was an appeal made of 25 May 2000, and the outcome added strength to my case and was to my advantage, and not to my disadvantage. Nothing whatsoever had happened in the two weeks of 1st to 14th December 2000 as alleged by Holland.

I. I made enquiries and approached the AIRE Centre and explained what had happened and their reference is NN/4101 HR of 05 June 2002. Their advice was that I should take a legal action and sue the barrister for fraudulent advice. The court service is reference GMO.228.02 and a letter from their administration DMD.OM ALC CM2168 that states that the barrister is liable if his unrequired imposition of an opinion is incorrect in law.

J. I then took advice from three solicitors of repute and integrity, and I decided to bring a County Court action against Holland for his nefarious imposition and the despicable legal sabotage. This action was met with all manner of skulduggery by the Defendant and the insurance company's solicitors, and this began a second wild goose chase.

K. Six times this case has been subjected to attempted derailment by Deputy District Judges, and each time it has been reinstated by honourable judges. 1. District Judge Gamba reinstated the case, 2. District Judge Lay reinstated the case, 3. District Judge Stary reinstated the case, and the aforesaid were in Brighton and Newcastle, as I moved from Brighton & Hove to Stockport to plan my move to Newcastle. This move and the stream of delays meant that the case should have been transferred to Newcastle or to London, and I wish to respectfully point out that under Court Rules CPR 26r 26.2 and Civil Procedures Rules 1/ CPR/ 30.2, as no amount of damages sought is specified then the case should remain in the Claimants area, and it cannot be transferred without the knowledge or consent of the Claimant. In this event the case was correctly transferred to Newcastle by District Judge DP Jenkins on 2 October 2002.

L. The next thing that I heard was that the case had been transferred to Clerkenwell. The County Court, 33 Duncan Street. N1 8AN, in London, without knowledge or consent. I do not know how this happened but I was soon made aware of it.

M. I was in hospital and unable to attend in London where the case had been wrongly transferred without my knowledge. Therefore, I faxed a message to the court and I also telephoned the court and wrote to the court. The case was then struck off again by another Deputy District Judge. I appealed against this decision and the case was reinstated by Judge Armon Jones. Then something else crawled out of the woodwork and a niche in the law allowed the Defendant of the appeal, and once again the case was heard in my absence and yet again it was struck off, and farcical is not a strong enough word.

N. I appealed against this decision most rigorously and the case was set for hearing in the Clerkenwell County Court, London, NJ 8AN on 17 June 2003. This time District Judge Hasselgrove heard the case and listened intently to both sides, and Judge Hasselgrove refused to allow the case to be struck off. He ruled that the case should be kept at Clerkenwell, which is in Holland's backyard.

O. I was assured by a phone call from the court that everything was in hand and I would hear in due course and all would be done properly. Eventually I received a dubious notice of a hearing that did not specify the judge's name, and the date was set for 27 October at 2 pm at Clerkenwell. I was not informed who the Judge was and I went along to the court with a colleague as a witness. There was no notice of the number of the court where the hearing was to take place and no judge named on the court lists. We were directed into a small side room, which was not a courtroom. No press or other awkward interested parties could be present. There we were met by Holland's latest Agent Provocateur who was yet another Deputy District Judge named Glasner. The first thing that Glasner said was that he had not read the case file. Against my better judgement I remained in this non-court private little room throughout the theatrical ordeal. Glasner insisted that the case against the South Wales Police was held in the Bristol County Court and not in the Bristol High Court, and as he had admitted that he had not read the file it is impossible to know how he could say that. The case was held in the Bristol High Court and it was not a trivial matter at all. This alleged hearing in near secrecy on 27 October 2003 was a total sham. It was the latest pre-arranged fix by one of Holland's cronies. Glasner struck the case out and he also ruled that there was no right of appeal. I said that "This is third world level, and the legal fabric has turned to pus - this is a sick joke." This should be on tape if everything was recorded.

P. I have been in contact with the Lord Chancellor's office, and with the House of Lords, and I have been advised that I should ask for the case to be reinstated and rightfully transferred to Newcastle where it should have been all along, in compliance with CP Rules and Court Rules. Every time a Deputy District Judge interferes then Holland gets the case struck off and every time a proper Judge hears the matter in open court the matter is reinstated.

I ask that this Case be reinstated and that it be transferred to Newcastle upon Tyne where it should have been before, and that any and all hearings are before a fully appointed judge.

Yours faithfully.

This is what happened to Baram Blackett and Alan Wilson in their joint and separate attempts to get the police into court beginning in 1990, and in mid-2004 they are still not there.

Britain is not a country where the rights of the native-born ethnic British individual are well protected. Britain is the only country in the world that does not have a written constitution. All that exists is a hotchpotch of laws passed eight hundred or six hundred years ago, five hundred years ago, three hundred years ago and so on. This lack of a written constitution is because a written constitution is a corporate national act where the people have all rights and they agree to surrender some part of their rights into a written form of law for the mutual benefit of all. The written constitution serves to limit and restrict extremist politicians and bureaucrats, and to control their excesses by compelling them to act within the Constitution. British politicians in Parliament reject the control of their excesses, and no longer see themselves as the servants of the people. The 'rights' of Parliament are set above the rights of the people. There can be no clearer demonstration of this evil than in the mistreatment of Alan Wilson and Baram Blackett.

Alan Wilson and Baram Blackett have placed copies of all the documentation of this mayhem and wrongdoing with a number of supporters in Britain and in the U.S.A. They have also distributed copies of their major researches in the event of either or both of them having an 'accident.'

Time and again Alan Wilson and Baram Blackett have asked Prime Ministers and Ministers of Government to set up a Public Inquiry into this disgusting and scandalous state of affairs. The Government does nothing because unlike American Governments, which act right out in the open, they prefer not to investigate scandals. This is only the tip of the iceberg in this scandalous and disgusting campaign of organised criminality. It is intended to publish the whole matter in detail. The cultural heritage of Britain is at stake and nothing less than the truth, the whole truth, and nothing but the truth, will suffice. The very birthright of the British nation is at stake.

The 'experts' are clearly in turmoil and they do not seem to know what to think or do. We have a Professor of *Astrophysics*, a Professor of Dendrochronology, and a respected University astronomer, all publishing that comet débris struck Britain, in the mid-sixth century. Headlines such as *'Comet Caused Global Nuclear Winter,* say experts' (*Western Mail*, 4 February 2004); *'900 Years Before Columbus Madoc Discovered America'* (*Western Mail*, 9 March); *'Comet Disaster Throws New Light on Dark Age'* (*Daily Telegraph*, 4 February 2004), and there have been international conferences on the dangers, yet Alan Wilson and Baram Blackett began publishing this in 1986 and are considered to be historically incorrect.

In conclusion to this, suffice it to say that ordinary citizens and those in office may one day wake up from their sleep and apathy, and only then can the veil fall from the United Kingdom's eyes, exposing the overall betrayal of its history and cultural heritage, and the loss of other opportunities including tourism. The matter is one of restoring the birthright of the British Nation.

Appendix No 1 – Arthur's northern journeys and colonisations

To illustrate what is happening and to show how information keeps flowing in and making this a never completed process, we have chosen a late Message from Bob MacCann in Sydney, Australia, which arrived too late to be included in the general texts as this book went to print. We quote Bob MacCann's E-mail sent to Baram Blackett & Alan Wilson.

[This process continues in 2022 through the BritainsHiddenHistory group that brings together researchers and fans from around the world via social media and video sharing such as YouTube.]

Subject - Mercator's letter to John Dee.

11 March 2004

Dear Alan & Baram,

I have managed to get a photocopy of "A letter dated 1577 from Mercator to John Dee" by E G.R Taylor in Imago Mundi. Although the original transcript has been badly damaged by fire resulting in many missing bits, it contains fascinating information. The parts referring to Arthur apparently came from a now lost manuscript called "Gestae Arthur".

Statements concerning Arthur

Arthur is said to have conquered the Northern Islands and made them subject to him. On one of his journeys he is said to have lost nearly 4000 people when they entered the "indrawing seas" in which the current flows strongly north.

A description of a journey dated 530 is then given. Arthur gathered a great army and stayed in the northern islands of Scotland through winter. In May 3, a part of it crossed over into Iceland and explored the north. Then 4 ships returned from Iceland and warned Arthur of the indrawing sea. Arthur therefore did not proceed to the indrawing sea but peopled all the islands between Scotland and Iceland and also settled people in Greenland. (Taylor therefore infers that the indrawing sea begins

Appendix 1 - Arthur's Northern Journeys

beyond the south eastern shores of Greenland).

The following year (531) Arthur repeated this strategy. This time details of the numbers are given. He took a fleet of 12 ships containing 1800 men and 400 women. Of these 12 ships, 5 were driven onto the rocks in a storm, but the rest made their way between the high rocks on June 18 (44 days after they had Set out). This ends the description of his journeys.

Another piece of information concerning Arthur is that in 1364 a group of 8 people visited the King's Court in Norway. They claimed to be descendants of the settlers from Arthur's expeditions.

Some Implications. *Arthur's Motivation*

The presence of 400 women on one of his voyages indicates that his intention was to resettle his people, not conquest. It would have taken a major disaster for him to resettle his people in this way. This provides indirect evidence of the catastrophe that hit Britain and rendered it uninhabitable.

How far did he go?

At the time of Mercator, it was thought that there were various indrawing seas with strong currents leading to the North Pole. If a ship were caught in one of these, it would not be able to escape. It is likely that the Davis Strait on the western coast of Greenland was the indrawing sea that most explorers in this region would have experienced. When Frobisher was at its mouth in the 16th century his lieutenant George Best reported.

"This pace seemeth to have a marvellous great indrafte and draweth in to it most of the drift ice and other things which doe flote in the sea." (Taylor, p.68)

It is likely that Arthur settled Greenland and explored around its southern tip to get to the Davis Strait. On one of his expeditions he may have lost his 4000 people in this indrawing sea in the Davis Strait. So it is likely that he got at least to Western Greenland. Given that his motivation was to find good land to settle in, it is plausible that he would have crossed over to Markland (Labrador) in Canada which had an abundance of 'brazil wood.'

The Advanced state of his shipbuilding.

On the second journey mentioned. Arthur had 2200 persons and 12 ships, averaging about 183 persons per ship. If he lost 4000 persons, this is the equivalent of 22 ships! This was clearly a massive undertaking in large ships. In contrast, the expedition of Columbus comprised the Santa Maria, with a crew of 36, the Nina with a crew of 24, and the Pinta with a crew of 28. In Magellan's voyage in 1519 he took 5 ships and 260 sailors, averaging 52 sailors per ship. Arthur's ships seem to have been comparatively large compared to those mentioned above, nearly a thousand years later.

Land Hopping makes the journey to America plausible.

This point is very important to me and others similar to myself who may have an unrealistic view on how a trip to America might have first occurred. I typically visualise a map projection that has the meridians of longitude as parallel lines and imagine the expedition setting out over vast expanses of ocean. Although all map projections distort, this map projection, which many people would use in their visualizations of such a journey greatly distorts things in this northern region.

It was not until I looked at a polar map with the North Pole at its centre and the meridians converging to a point that I realized how close Iceland was to North Scotland and how close south eastern Greenland was to Iceland. By tracking around the southern tip of Greenland and establishing progressive settlements, it would only be a matter of time before the Davis Strait was crossed and good country found in Labrador. It would then be natural to continue down the east coast of America.

Although this may seem of little consequence to you, I believe that the inclusion of such a map in your book (with parallels of latitude as circles and the meridians converging at the North Pole would greatly strengthen your case in the eyes of the average reader. It would show people just how close together these stepping stones are. It makes the discovery of America almost inevitable and such a map shows that no one was better placed geographically to do this than the British. As a Word attachment to this E-mail I enclose an example of this sort of map. You can probably find better examples.

Integrating this Information with your Research.

If your argument of a 33 year dislocation in historical dates can be applied here,

Appendix 1 - Arthur's Northern Journeys

then presumably these journeys took place around 563 and 564. Your other sources show Madoc's expedition in 562. It's possible that these are the same expedition and that while Arthur was the overall commander, that Madoc scouted ahead and set out down the American coast. Anyway, regardless of how you interpret it, it adds weight to your arguments.

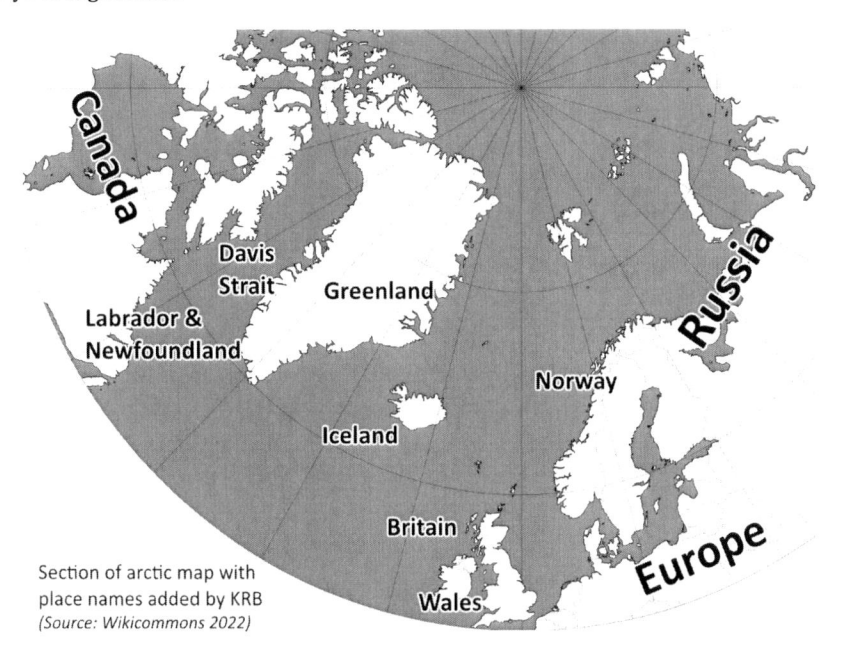

Section of arctic map with place names added by KRB
(Source: Wikicommons 2022)

Thank you Bob MacCann for the map suggestion – you are right and eighteen years later here it is! (KRB)

Further related material.

The Mercator letter to John Dee involves several persons who provided information. One was a priest who claimed to be descended from Arthur's original expeditions. He was at the King of Norway's Court in 1364. The priest related a story that in the year 1360 a Minorite, an English friar from Oxford, who had mathematical skills, explored the Northern lands and possibly America and wrote an account of his travels called "Inventio Fortunate." This work is now lost but it did exist and several people refer to it.

I searched the Internet and found that this theme was the subject of some books by an author named Gunnar Thompson. His first book was "The Friars Map of Ancient America 1360 AD" (1996) and his second book was "Lions in the New Land" (2003). Thompson claims that King Edward III sent out people to map as much as was possible of the world, following an original proposal by Roger Bacon in 1266. The Friar's assignment was to sur- vey the isles in the North Atlantic to find the lost overseas colony of King Arthur. These books might be worth looking at to see what he says about Arthur's colonies.

Good luck in your future research. If you are unable to easily get a copy of the Imago Mundi paper, I could send you a photocopy.

Best wishes Bob MacCann

Wilson & Blackett Notes

The points that are raised by Bob MacCann on ship sizes and numbers is of interest. Between c AD 275 and 293 Britain and all Northern Gaul was ruled by King Carawn, who was also known as the Admiral and Emperor Carausius. He was recognized as joint equal tripartite Emperor with Diocletian and Maximinian, who ruled Constantinople and Rome respectively. This King Carawn, or Carausius the Admiral, had large and powerful fleets and it is known that in the "Roman era" the Romans themselves had ships that could carry as many as 700 passengers on Mediterranean journeys. Therefore, the size of King Arthur II's ships should surprise no one. The British King Carawn -the Emperor Carausius, was claimed to have left no trace in Britain on a *BBC Timewatch* programme, yet his tombstone was found at Penmachno and is still in a Welsh Museum, and his vast marble decorated place lies with its great walls protruding up through the ground at Caer Mead. To excavate this great palace would mean admitting that the British Kings ruled right through the alleged "Roman Period" and that this Arthurian Dynasty existed. Public attention is diverted away to 'exotic' eastern places in Greece, Italy, Egypt, and elsewhere, and to excavate the great palace of the British Kings would inevitably mean the slaughter of huge herds of diseased sacred cows of academic theories.

During the excavation of St Peter's super Montem Church in1990 seven stages of successive re-buildings and enlargements were traced and the first building was

Appendix 1 - Arthur's Northern Journeys

established as being First Century AD. This means that the historical records are accurate and the Church is not 12th Century Norman as CADW - Welsh Heritage asserted.

Whilst the excavations were taking place the stone found by Blackett and Wilson was on display at St Mary hill Golf Club [*near to St Peter's Church/Caer Caradoc.*] Mr Gwyn Jones, the owner, states that an academic from Aherystwyth University took crystaline scrapings from the grooves of the inscriptions. He went off and had these tested and analysed and found that these samples showed that the stone had been carved in antiquity. Then the metal cross from the church was analysed and the abominable No-Men suffered a third defeat when their assertions that it was made of lead were disproved and a 79% + silver content, and a 14 % copper content, etc was established during analysis. There is a host of other sites with physical evidence as s evident in this volume.

The King Arthur Conspiracy - Wilson & Blackett

Sources.

The principal documents used in this Research are well known and available, but they are very rarely read by anyone.

1. The Myvyrian Archaiology of Wales, A vast collection of Ancient Manuscripts was published by Dr Owen Jones, Edward Williams, and Dr William Owen Pughe in 1801 - 1804 - 1806, in an enormous tome. All the ancient Epic Poems discussed are in this volume.

2. A complete version of the Myvyrian Archaiology of Wales was published by the Welsh Manuscript Society in 1820. This publication is the one used by Alan Wilson and Baram Blackett. It contains several hundred of the most ancient Welsh Poems from around AD 450 onwards.

    It also contains all Three Series of the Historical Triads, and also the Philosophical, Ethical, and Legislative Triads.

    Also included are all the major national Histories -The Brut Tyssilio, (St Tyssilio died c AD 684), the Brut Gruffydd ap Arthur, (misnamed Geoffrey of Monmouth), the Brut y Tywysogion (History of the Princes, the Brut y Saeson (History of the Saxons). The Brut y Tywysogion vel y bu Ryfeloedd, the Brut Icaun Brechfa, the Hanes (King) Gruffydd ap Cynan, and items like Parthau Cymru, and Henwan Plwyfan Cymru.

    It includes some of the Lives of the Saint, the Welsh Laws, historical music, etc.

3. The Liber Landevensis or The Book of Llandaff published by the Welsh Manuscript Society in 1840. It contains all the surviving Cathedral Charters and those Charters of Llancarfan Abbey from around AD 400 up to around AD 1130, as long with complete versions of the Lives of several important Saints, and a number of important historical notices.

4. The Iolo Manuscripts, published by the Welsh Manuscript Society in1848, that contain some of the important texts preserved by Edward Williams. These include the Genealogies of the Kings from Brutus around 500 BC down to Iestyn ap Gwrgan AD1091. There are a number of important early mediaeval noble genealogies and records and a vast array of Lives of the Saints genealogies, and ancient Epic Poetry.

5. The Bruts of England published by the English Manuscript Society in AD 1908. These

Sources

commence with the arrival of Albyne in circa 1600 BC, and the later arrival of Brutus around 500 BC. They deal with pre-Anglo-Saxon Britain and include the combined Arthur I and Arthur II and important notices like the coronation of Arthur II as King of Glamorgan. These histories then run on down the ages into mediaeval times.

6. Standard Greek and Roman Histories were consulted. Julius Caesar 'De Bello Gallico', Tacitus, Strabo, Martial, and others.

7. The Christian Holy Bible and the Apocrypha published by Oxford University Press in 1896 was consulted, as was Barddas pub 1852, and various works by named modern researchers like D.Delta Evans, E.O.Gordon.

8. Readers and researchers should have no difficulty in accessing any of the sources mentioned throughout the text of this volume.

Index

A

Agitus/Aegidius 400, 656-62

Allegro, John   620

Ammianus Marcellinius 499, 616, 656

Ammwn 380

Andragathius - Arthur I

Arcady 390

Arthrwys - see Arthur II

Arthun - Arthur I

Arthur I, King   393, 397, 399, 414, 436, 444, 580-1, 623, 624, 626, 649-59, 686-93

Arthur II ap Meurig, King   354, 355, 356, 359, 363, 364, 365, 366, 367-73, 373-8, 378-9, 383, 386-8, 394, 396-7, 401-3, 406-22, 423-9, 436-52 452-7, 477-87, 501-2, 509, 525, 532-9, 541-4, 581, 588, 601, 640-5, 651-6

Atherston 530, 580-1

B

Baedan, Battle of 401, 414, 428

Baillie, Prof. Michael 357, 374, 628, 635

Becket, Thomas 388

Bent, John   588

Bent, Thomas W.   587

Berkley, Sir William   460

Bible, Holy 389, 463, 467, 469

Brendan, St. 355-6, 373, 453, 517, 525, 592

Brochwael - Brocagnus 363-4, 655-8

Brock   557

Brown-skinned man 366-7, 378, 661

C

Ca' Melot   654

Cade, Jack   647

Cadfan 396

Cadoc, St   403, 499

CADW   430, 691

Cadwallader   396, 649, 657-8, 666

Caer Caradoc   366, 416, 422, 427-9 , 691

Caer Effrawg   394, 428

Caer Mead   690

Caer Melyn   352, 353, 369, 654

Caer Septon   387

Caer Troia - London 644, 647

Caerleon   353, 380, 394, 651-3

Caerleon Film College   406

Camlann   357, 366, 379, 414, 428, 628-9

Canterbury, Archbishop of 355, 377, 389, 394,

Caradoc I ap Arch   428

Caradoc of Llancarfan 351, 392, 414, 464

Carolina, South 460, 463

Catherine, Queen of France 641

Cerniw 369, 393-4, 407, 657

Chiles, John   465

Coed Cad Einion   380

Coelbren alphabet 355, 359, 360, 375-6, 398, 406-7, Ch. 15, 470-1, 477-87, 495-501, 502-8, 509, 511, 512-14, Ch.17, 566-8, 572-77, 592-607, 618-19, 639-55, 665

Columbus, Christopher 374, 381-2, 451, 458, 529, 688

Comet, the   356-60, 361, 367-88, 389-98, 401, 410-1, 416-7, 422, 427-9, Ch 14, 459, 469, 487

Coyners, Sir John 555

Cu-Bwrd 352, 369, 654

D

Davey, John   463

Denise of Powys 352-3

Dighton Rock   514-5, 521-5,

Dragon 383-7, 396-8, 407, 418, Ch 14, 555-64, 589-92, 589, 664

Dyfrig/Tyfrig, St. 437-8

E

Ealde Cyrcenas 6378

Edison, Thomas 447

Edward III, King 690,

Edward IV, King 382

Edwards, Morgan   462

694

Index

Edwards, Nancy 669-71, 674

Edwards, Nicholas 672

Elizabeth I, Queen 485

Em-Rhys 365-6, 393

Emyr -Eleyn 663

Emyr Lydaw 441, 663

Erigena, John 499

Er-of 374-5

Er-yr 367-75

Evans, Dr William 456, 483

Evans, J. Gwenogfran 408-9

F

Farquarson, Robert 533

Fitzhammon, Robert 353

Fleming, Sir John 352

Fleming, William 352-3, 464

G

Galbraith, John 522

Gallman, Robert E. 519

Gawayn 652, 653

Genovesius 444

Glamorgan 352-4, 363, 380, 387, 393, 421, 427, 441, 443, 457, 485, 556, 576, 580, 588, 649-55

Glamorgan Gwent Archaeological Trust 673-6

Gratian, Emperor 393, 580

Gruffydd ap Arthur ("Geoffrey") 352, 380, 389, 396-400, 429, 436-7, 455, 563, 650, 663, 692

Guttyn Owen 382

Guy of Warwick 580

Gwalchmai 365, 379

Gwenon, Admiral 356-9, 392, 452-4, 626

H

Hakluyt, Richard 351, 355, 377,

Henry II 352-3, 388

Henry II 388

Henry son of Elwyn 647

Henry V 641

Henry VI 641

Henry VII Tudor 641

Henry, Patrick 676

Hinds, Thomas 466

Huail 441

I

Iestyn ap Gwrgan 352-4, 577, 649-50, 654, 666, 692

Illtyd 402, 403, 406, 408, 416, 421-6, 441, 444, 588, 630

Iron Bear see Arthur II

Ithael I & II 387, 396-8, 588, 655

J

Jefferson, Thomas 464

John of Asia 629-35

John the Baptist 506, 11

John, King 388, 645

Jones, Dr Owen 692

Jones, Edward 381-2

Jones, John (Bassaleg) 462

K

Kentucke / Kentucky 355, 374, 413, 450, 451-2, 457-9, 564-5, 468-83, 494--501, 505-8, 516-9, 528, 530-1, 545, 564, 574-5, 577-8, 592, 606-7, 636, 644

L

L'ancelot 444

Lear-Llyr 656-9

Leicester 569, 657, 659, 661

Leo - Lion - Regulus 387-8, 469

Leoline, Sir 374

Leonard, St 556

Llan Athbodu 262

Llan Conuur 363

Llan Cyngualon 363

Llan Pencreig 363

Llan-Badarn-Fawr 441

Llan-bad-fawr 430

Llancarfan 351-3, 356, 363-4, 403, 414, 441, 464, 692

Llandaff (and Cathedral) 352, 356, 361, 363-4, 395, 429, 438, 440-1, 569, 572, 649-55, 666, 692

695

Index

Llan-Illtyd-Fawr ("Llantwit Major") 441, 444-5

Llewellyn Sion 355, 641

Lliwlod 364, 366-72, 378-9, 418, 664

Lloegres-English 371, 394-5, 506, 550, 624, 645, 657

Lluyd, Humphrey 351

Llwyd, Edward 375, 580

Llywarch ap Iestyn 353

Lubbock, John 584

M

Madoc ap Meurig, Prince Ch12, 401, 403, 409, 410, 411, 420, 422, 427, 450-7, 462-4, 477-8, 484, 501-9, 511-2, 524-5, 529-30, 549, 560, 593, 626, 637, 664, 689

Map, Walter 352-3, 464, 570

Mary Cleophas 571

Mascen Wledig 393, 399, 426, 454, 528, 597,

Maxen Maximus see Mascen Wledig

Mayer, Robert 447

Mellungians 467, 636-8

Menevensis, John 499

Meredudd 381-2,

Merlyn 366, 373, 389-97, 409, 417, 437, 482, 489, 664

Meurig ap Tewdrig, King 351, 363, 364, 365, 375, 379, 395, 396, 403,

427, 429, 437, 438, 440, 541-2, 652, 655, 664

Michael, James B. (Jim) 354-5, 450-66, 468-501, 517-9, 528, 543, 565-77, 598, 617-20, 644

Morfran 354-6, 365, 377, 380-1, 387, 403, 450, 452-3, 478, 501

Morris, Sir John 605

N

Napoleon 539

Natanleod 364

Newton, Isaac 357, 358, 389-90, 601

O

Oldbury 528, 530

Onbrawst, Queen 351, 436, 440

Owen ap Howell Dda or Dyfed 380

Owen ap Owen Fawr 380

Owen Gwynedd 351-3, 376-80, 450, 464

Owen Wan 380

Owen, Robert 382, 439,

P

Pawl, St 408

Pennington, Prof Lee 374, 519, 528-31, 577,

Phene, Sir John S. 558

Pig-Pen 470-83

Powell, Dr 351, 377

Pratt, William 537-8

Prophecies - Eryr 383-6

Prophecies - Merlyn 389-97

Prophecy of Caer Septon 387

Pugh, Dr William Owen 692

R

Ragan 657-8

Raleigh, Sir Walter 636

Regulus see Leo

Rhys ap Tewdwr 352,

Rhys Cain 485-6

Rhys Meurug 654

Rice, Merrick 654

Robert, Duke of Normandy 388

Roberts, Lieut. Joseph 464-5

Robertson 377

Romain, William F. 553

Ross, Dr John 469

S

Schoolcraft, Henry 460

Shakespeare, William 656-7

Slade, Colonel John 571

Spratt's Farm 528-31, 564

Stephens, Thomas 408

Sunman, Peter 468

T

Tacitus 693

Index

Taliesin 364-79, 423-8, 435-7, 482, 485, 664

Tathall 393

Teithfallt 393, 428, 485, 587

Teithrin 393, 587

Tewdrig 351, 364-5, 393, 402, 427, 437, 438, 444, 485, 509, 587, 649, 655, 666

Theodorus 587

Thomas MP, George 672

Thomas, T. H. 651

Trevithick, Thomas 447

Tudor Kings 641

Tudor, Edmund 641

Tudor, Owen 641

Twyn Caradoc 428

Tyssilio, St. 437, 455, 692

U

Uthyr & Uthyrpendragon 356, 364-5, 366, 368, 375, 378, 396-8, 407, 429, 436-7, 485, 633

V

Vandals 394, 399, 406, 454-5, 528, 623-5

Ventris, Michael 627

W

Walter de Treyes, Sir 555

Warwichshire 528, 530, 580-1

Webb, William Dr. 575

Weber, Henry 651

Wiggins Point Stone 540-9

William II Rufus 388

William of Malmsbury 645

William The Conqueror 352, 387-8,

Williams, Edward (Iolo) 435, 467, 486, 558, 595, 607, 692

Williams, John 463

Williams, Rev. John 463

Williams, Rev. Robert 408, 414-5, 423

Wilson, Mrs. Elizabeth 456

Worm - German 393

Worm - Lambton 554-6

Worm-Laidley 554-6

Worm-Meister Stoor 556

Worm-Sockburn 555